EQUALITY

EQUALITY

AN AMERICAN DILEMMA,

1866–1896

■

CHARLES POSTEL

FARRAR, STRAUS AND GIROUX | NEW YORK

Farrar, Straus and Giroux
120 Broadway, New York 10271

Library of Congress Cataloging-in-Publication Data
Names: Postel, Charles, author.
Title: Equality : an American dilemma, 1866–1896 / Charles Postel.
Description: First edition. | New York : Farrar, Straus and Giroux, [2019] |
    Includes bibliographical references and index.
Identifiers: LCCN 2019000171 | ISBN 9780809079636 (hardcover)
Subjects: LCSH: Equality—United States—History—19th century. | Social
    movements—United States—History—19th century. | United States—
    Social conditions—19th century. | United States—History—1865–1898.
Classification: LCC HN90.S6 P67 2019 | DDC 305.50973—dc23
LC record available at https://lccn.loc.gov/2019000171

Designed by Richard Oriolo

Our books may be purchased in bulk for promotional, educational, or
business use. Please contact your local bookseller or the Macmillan Corporate
and Premium Sales Department at 1-800-221-7945, extension 5442,
or by e-mail at MacmillanSpecialMarkets@macmillan.com.

www.fsgbooks.com
www.twitter.com/fsgbooks · www.facebook.com/fsgbooks

1   3   5   7   9   10   8   6   4   2

To the memory of Sableu—an egalitarian

CONTENTS

EQUALITY

INTRODUCTION: EQUALITY

THE CIVIL WAR, fought over racial slavery, unleashed a torrent of claims to equal rights. Former slaves and women's rights activists, miners and domestic servants, farmers and factory hands, pressed their demands. This contest resulted in extraordinary experiments in collective action as, in their pursuit of equality, millions of men and women joined leagues, unions, Granges, assemblies, and lodges. Taking stock of these experiments forces us to rethink some of what passes for conventional wisdom about the United States and its history.

In the conventional telling, as the French and other continentals raised the banners of "Liberty, Equality, and Fraternity," Americans embraced the first at the expense of the other two. They spurned egalitarian and collective ideals, we have been told, because of their exceptional commitment to individual liberty. But the decades that followed the Civil War place this wisdom in a different light. The great social movements of the time reflected an understanding that without equality there could be no freedom, and without solidarity there could be no equality.

Equality and solidarity, however, were fractured and contradictory. Too often, divergent notions of equality clashed with one another; too often, fraternity and solidarity rested on division and exclusion. These dynamics get to the heart of an inescapable dilemma: mighty farmer, labor, and women's rights movements undertaken in the name of equality were accompanied by the destruction of political, economic, and civil rights for African Americans and other racial minorities. Decades that brought forth herculean efforts to overcome the economic inequality of corporate capitalism and the sexual inequality of the late Victorian social order also witnessed the extreme inequities of Indian dispossession, Chinese exclusion, Jim Crow, disenfranchisement, and lynch law.

This book is an exploration of equality and its contested meanings in the wake of the Civil War. It focuses on developments from the late 1860s to the 1890s—that is to say, from Reconstruction through what is known as the Gilded Age. The point of departure for this exploration involves the killing fields at Gettysburg. The design for a soldiers' national cemetery at that fateful battlefield has provided the thematic lines of inquiry that this book explores.

■

THE CIVIL WAR'S MOST DEADLY BATTLE, fought over the first three days of July 1863, left some eight thousand bodies decaying in the fields outside the small Pennsylvania village of Gettysburg. Teams of Union soldiers, Confederate prisoners, and local residents had buried some of the fallen in shallow graves. The layer of soil was spread too thin for protection from predators and could not disguise the shape or smell of decomposing corpses. The rotting dead at Gettysburg demanded attention. They posed a health risk to the local citizens, who already had enough grievances about the war. The political requirement of showing respect to the dead necessitated swift action to identify the bodies and make arrangements for their proper interment. As land sharks circled hoping to cash in on high prices for a future burial ground, an interstate commission formed to finance and direct the reburial in a suitable cemetery. Six weeks after the battle, the commission hired William Saunders, a landscape architect and an administrator in the Department of Agriculture, to draw the cemetery's layout.[1]

Saunders had to work quickly. The hot weather sped decomposition, making it ever more difficult to recover and identify the bodies. The desire of farmers to get back into their fields posed an even greater threat. "Everything was hurried to get at work and remove the bodies," Saunders noted, as the local farmers, "anxious to plow for crops" and "seemingly careless about the dead," tilled over the shallow graves, putting the corpses "in danger of obliteration."[2]

On November 17, Abraham Lincoln called Saunders to the White House to discuss the architect's plans for the Soldiers' National Cemetery at Gettysburg. The president "took much interest in it" and was "much pleased with the method of the graves." He also noted that the design "differed from the ordinary cemetery." Lincoln said it was "an admirable and befitting arrangement" and signed off on the plans, at least according to Saunders's record of the meeting in his journal.[3]

The design answered three major problems of how to inter the Gettysburg dead. The first problem was how to bury so many with equal respect to each. The Civil War was one of the first industrial wars. It applied the technologies and organizational methods of the railroad, the telegraph, and mass production to the slaughter of human beings. The killing at Gettysburg was the crowning achievement of these new methods. In such a war, massed troops facing sheets of artillery and rifle fire blurred the hierarchical distinctions of military command. The new ways of war had left thousands of indiscernible corpses of officers and soldiers rotting on the field, rendering old categories meaningless.[4]

Military cemeteries traditionally reinforced in death distinctions in life; commanding tombstones for commanding officers towered over humble markers for humble soldiers. By contrast, Saunders wanted a plan that would take account of the equality of condition of the dead and "allow of no distinction." He wanted to "secure regularity" and to ensure that "the headstones are precisely alike." He devised a starkly rationalist system forming a "continuous line of granite blocks," each exactly nine inches high with a ten-inch face. The inscriptions on every marker were to record the identical information: name, company, and regiment. In later years, first Saunders and then other administrators obliged the demands from various constituencies for special monuments and markers at the cemetery. But the power of the original design lay in what Saunders described as "uniformity and simplicity." Just as the new means of warfare made no distinctions in mass death, Saunders designed an egalitarian system of mass burial.[5]

The second problem was how to avoid any "unjust discrimination" between the states. The cemetery was to hold Union corpses (with the Confederate dead left to separate mass graves). But among the Union dead, Saunders thought it was essential that the soldiers of each state be given equal treatment. This posed a challenge given that more bodies came from some states than from others and given the sloping and uneven terrain of the grounds. His solution was to divide the state lots into pie-shaped slices arranged in a semicircle, with each state sharing an equal proportion of high and low ground. With this formation, "the position of each lot would be relatively of equal importance," and thereby Saunders paid tribute to another type of equality regarding the relationships between states.[6]

The third problem was how to bind the lots into a single whole so that "each state would be part of a common center." Saunders's solution was to place at the top, rising above the rest, an imposing national monument. Equality demanded that each state receive its proper due, but that did not imply a loose or decentralized confederation. Saunders believed quite the opposite. He placed a national monument—"at the central point on the highest reach of the ground"—to honor the birth of new centralized national power rising from the ashes of war. The cemetery "must ever be a national institution," observed a newspaper reporter who reviewed

Saunders's scheme, noting that "all the sections tend towards a common monument and bear the same relation to it." At the same time, "no State will be permitted to embellish its own lot, but what is done for one will be done for all."[7]

Finally, it is noteworthy that there was one problem that did not confront Saunders in his design. In other Civil War cemeteries—especially with the growing number of African American enlistments and casualties in the later phases of the war—the bodies of soldiers were segregated by race with separate burial plots for "Colored Troops." But this was not the case at Gettysburg. The record indicated that there were no black soldiers among the Union dead, or at least Saunders assumed this was the case in making his design for the cemetery.

African American residents of Gettysburg and surrounding villages bore their share of suffering and death. Invading Confederate soldiers destroyed the farms of African Americans, murdered free black men, and kidnapped free black women and children into slavery. Confederate troops confirmed their dedication to destroying black freedom with the terror they unleashed against the African Americans in that corner of Pennsylvania. But the men to be interred in the Gettysburg cemetery were white men. The neat rationality and egalitarianism of Saunders's plan could thereby avoid the troubled ground of race and racial equality.[8]

Two days after the White House meeting, the landscape architect sat on the podium at the Gettysburg cemetery as President Lincoln announced "a new birth of freedom." The nation would be rewarded for the sacrifices of war with the preservation and expansion of freedom on the bedrock of equality. "Four score and seven years ago," Lincoln said, "our fathers" had built a new nation "dedicated to the proposition that all men are created equal." His words involved a tortured reading of the nation's founding. Lincoln avoided explicit reference to the dilemmas of race and racial equality, even though the enslavement of African Americans had led to national division and to the slaughter at Gettysburg. Lincoln spoke of equality in abstract and universal terms.[9]

Saunders might have been struck by the symmetry between his

design and Lincoln's address. As the historian Garry Wills writes in *Lincoln at Gettysburg*, "In all this, [Lincoln's] speech and Saunders's artifact are in aesthetic harmony. Each expressed the values of the other."[10] The ten sentences of Lincoln's oration were as economical and unadorned as Saunders's nine-inch curbs. The president put into spare and simple words the same notions of equality and national purpose that Saunders had put into his spare and simple cemetery design. The war and the destruction of slavery provided a new context for these ideas and gave them new force. In that sense, as Wills puts it, Lincoln's address at the Soldiers' National Cemetery at Gettysburg signaled a "revolution in thought."[11] And, as we shall see, Saunders's design fit within the structures of the egalitarian and nationalist ideals of the post–Civil War decades.

■

EQUALITY, OF COURSE, HAD BEEN a potent idea in American affairs since the country's founding. The Declaration of Independence advanced the proposition that "all men are created equal," a proposition that would soon be bolstered by the egalitarian ideals of the French Revolution. Nonetheless, for the next eighty-five years equality had a troubled place in the constellation of political ideas animating the new nation. Slavery, Indian removal, and the other requisites of the existing structures of hierarchy and power made equality a flash point of conflict and danger. With slave owners—who defended the right to own black people as chattel and to work them like beasts—holding the trump cards in political affairs, the most dedicated antebellum champions of equality were often marginalized and abused abolitionists, women's rights activists, and labor radicals.[12]

The Civil War destroyed the institution of slavery and thereby changed the context. Emancipation was followed by intense and violent conflict over the status of African Americans in a postbellum America. The four million former slaves emerging from bondage understood that freedom without equality was meaningless. They organized Equal Rights Leagues and political conventions to press the issues. Would they enjoy equal protections under the law? Would they be assured of the same rights of speech, association, and movement that other Americans took for granted? Would they have equal rights to landownership and to public lands? Would they have equal access to public education and public accommodations? Would they exercise the same rights to sit on juries, to vote, and to hold elected office that white Americans, or at least white men, exercised?[13]

The logic of emancipation and the strivings of the freed people pushed these questions of equality on the national agenda. The Radical Republicans who led the postwar Congress pursued what the historian Eric Foner describes as "the utopian vision of a nation whose citizens enjoyed equality of civil and political rights, secured by a powerful and beneficent national state."[14] The ratification of the Fourteenth Amendment in 1868, ensuring "equal protection of the laws," codified this vision in the federal constitution. Two years later, the Fifteenth Amendment extended voting rights to black men in a critical step toward political equality. Meanwhile, most Democrats, North and South, rejected racial equality but pursued other ideas of equal rights drawn from their own party's traditions. Meanings of equality fractured across partisan, regional, economic, gender, and racial divides.

As the guns of war fell silent, notions of equality became increasingly untethered from the struggle against slavery and racial oppression. The status of the former slaves was referred to at the time as the "Negro question," yet for many white Americans the "Negro question" had little to do with their own thinking about equality. They assumed that the question was put to rest with emancipation and, if not then, it was surely settled with the constitutional amendments of 1868 and 1870. In reality, nothing was settled. Resurgent forces of white supremacy trampled on the promise of these amendments. The "Negro question" burned on.

At the same time, the war and emancipation spurred the egalitarian strivings among the nation's farmers, workers, women, and other constituencies. Millions of citizens engaged in the contest over exactly how the principle of equality would shape postbellum America. The contest proved to be a fractious, messy, and hard-fought conflict about power. It was about political power in the nation's capital and in state and local governments. It was about the economic power of corporations and other business interests. It was about power relationships in daily encounters between employers and employees, skilled and unskilled, whites and nonwhites, and men and women. It was a struggle waged in electoral campaigns, courtroom deliberations, legislative negotiations, and newspaper and pamphlet wars, as well as in recurring debates in meeting halls, workshops, plantations, farms, and homes across America.

Within these debates, the meanings of equality were open to a wide range of interpretations. Social theorists, then as today, worked toward tidy definitions: equality of opportunity was one thing, the sociologist William Graham Sumner explained, equality of condition was something else again. But such clear lines failed to hold in practical life and politics. "Equality" became a catchall for a variety of sentiments and principles. The starting point or common denominator was often Lincoln's free-labor ideal of an "open field and a fair chance" with "equal privileges in the race of life." This notion of equality of opportunity, however, confronted the reality of unequal political, economic, and social power that fueled the fires of post–Civil War protest and social mobilization.[15]

To gain an open field and a fair chance required, as many participants understood, efforts to equalize economic and political life and overcome the inequities of power, wealth, and condition. Added to this, the spread of religious and secular beliefs about the equal moral value of human beings leaned toward egalitarian ideas of human solidarity. In short, the pursuit of equality pulled millions of American men and women toward what the historian James Kloppenberg calls "progressive social and economic equalization" and into the broad egalitarian current of a transatlantic social democracy.[16]

■

DURING HIS ANTEBELLUM TRAVELS TO the United States, the French sociologist Alexis de Tocqueville famously noted the "power of association" among its citizens. This power gained strength in the post–Civil War years. Merchants, doctors, and lawyers formed and expanded business and professional societies. Manufacturers, bankers, and railroad executives combined into trusts and corporations. The most striking feature of this age, however, was the extent to which farmers and laborers, domestics and housewives, and other ordinary men and women also joined organizations. This wave of combined action runs counter to the Horatio Alger myth of the lone go-getter rising from rags to riches through individual pluck and luck. In reality, the postbellum decades were collective decades, when a farm association or labor cooperative or similar collective undertaking was widely understood as a means to pursue one's individual social, economic, and political interests, as well as the social good.[17]

In the wake of the Civil War, the historians Charles and Mary Beard observed that "fraternalism was a 'general mania.'" A dense web of unions, fraternities, cooperatives, leagues, clubs, and other voluntary associations spread from coast to coast. Nominally nonpartisan, these organizations were profoundly political. The historian Anne Firor Scott placed these associations "at the very heart of American social and political development." They mobilized key constituencies of class and interest; they expanded the scope of democratic participation; they served as the building blocks of reform politics; and they constituted the "people's lobbies" that forged the modern state. In so doing, they also shaped and reshaped the meanings of equality in the United States.[18]

This is a book about how the millions of men and women who joined voluntary associations understood the problem of equality in their historical moment. Associations reflected shared moral commitments and common responses to the intellectual and political world in which they were formed.[19] The people who made up these postbellum collective efforts mainly believed in the idea of freedom and opposed the idea of slavery. They often harked back to an idealized republican past and looked forward to an idealized republican future. They tended to embrace visions of progress, modernity, and the advance of civilization. And they understood that the pursuit of equality served as a lever for the realization of freedom, good government, and progress.

Given the profusion of movements that emerged in the aftermath of the Civil War, this work takes a selective approach, focusing on the farmers' Grange, the Woman's Christian Temperance Union, and the Knights of Labor. These movements had much in common. Though formally nonpartisan, they were national in scope and ambition and would have outsized impact on the politics and thinking of their day as well as on later generations of reform. And all three served as key sites of the post–Civil War contest over the meaning of equality.

The book begins with the farmers' Grange, the largest, strongest, and most impactful social movement of its time. William Saunders hosted the founding meeting of the Grange in his office in a federal building in Washington, D.C. Not only did the landscape architect help plan the design for the Grange; he also served as its national president for its first six years of existence as it emerged as a vast organization of the nation's farmers. The Grange provided other constituencies with "repertoires" for national collective mobilization, and in their own ways the Woman's Christian Temperance Union and the Knights of Labor made use of those repertoires.[20] The following pages explore how, for better and for worse, the same egalitarian and nationalist ideas that guided the design for the cemetery at Gettysburg shaped and reshaped the meanings of equality and solidarity during Reconstruction, the Gilded Age, and beyond.

■

THE FIRST DECADES OF THE twenty-first century have ushered in a second Gilded Age of savage inequalities. Unequal power and wealth have begotten more unequal power and wealth. The political class has bent the regulatory, taxing, and legal structures to favor its corporate and well-heeled sponsors at the expense of everyone else. The expansion of corporate power has stripped workers of unions, livable wages, health care, and pensions. The parallel growth of wealth and poverty has resulted in economic inequality unseen in nearly a century.

The politics of racial, ethnic, and sexual intolerance and inequality has experienced a similar escalation. Political candidates have been riding campaigns of exclusion, disenfranchisement, unequal justice, and scapegoating to offices in statehouses, the U.S. Congress, and the White House itself. Inequality is our gaping social and political wound.

This is a work of history that seeks to understand the men and women who appear in its pages on their own terms. Writing history, however, does not take place in a vacuum, and this book is a product of the demands of our times and the urgent need to imagine expansive and inclusive notions of equality and solidarity to meet our contemporary crisis.

PART I

·

FARMERS' GRANGE

1.

FEDERAL ORIGINS

O N DECEMBER 4, 1867, the new organization was founded in William Saunders's office located in a modest stone building at the intersection of Fourth Street and Missouri Avenue in the nation's capital. The organization announced itself to the world and elected its first officers. A popular magazine later reported that the seven celebrated "founders" of the new order included "one fruit-grower and six government clerks, equally distributed among the Post-Office, Treasury, and Agricultural Departments." The "fruit-grower" was in fact a retired Wall Street financier who owned a vineyard in upstate New York. Yet, in a leap of faith, this unlikely group invented a new kind of association for America's farmers.

They called it the National Grange of the Patrons of Husbandry. For the first year or two, it hardly grew beyond the confines of a small circle of federal employees, with the Potomac Grange in the nation's capital the first and most promising of its local Granges. But the Grange soon caught fire. Thousands of local Granges spread across farm country, initiation fees from new Granges piled up in the Washington office, and the Grange set in motion powerful forces of change in post–Civil War America.[1]

I.

AT THE HEIGHT OF ITS POWER, the Grange's center of gravity lay in the fertile and sunbaked agricultural districts of the Midwest, the West, and the South. But its origins in the federal bureaucracy and its early years in the nation's capital were fundamental to the Grange's history, a history that disrupts the usual narratives we have been told about the post–Civil War decades. These narratives might be called tales of declension, because they suggest a fall from grace and a loss of freedom and possibility.

In one such tale, Gilded Age farmers represented local and decentralized resistance to the centralized and hierarchical institutions of business and government, only to be later co-opted by these centralizing forces. This is the story told in Grant McConnell's influential work *The Decline of Agrarian Democracy*, in which the Grange stood for "equality and freedom" against centralizing power but whose twentieth-century heirs reinforced such power. The sociologist Elisabeth Clemens tells a similar story of transition from the "agrarian democracy" of the Grange and kindred organizations to the "economic corporatism" of later organizations that "emerged as central components of a project of bureaucratic state-building."[2]

The problems with this narrative begin with the fact that from its very inception the Grange was part of the bureaucratic project. The original blueprints for organizing the Grange called for placing the "grand head" within the Department of Agriculture, from which it would direct and discipline the state and local organizations. Although the Grange never succeeded in its plans to merge with the Department of Agriculture, and although it never achieved the same level of bureaucratic state building that was made possible in the twentieth century, it was not for a lack of effort. The Grange was indeed a movement of rural democracy, but it was a movement that in theory and practice pursued egalitarian goals through bureaucratic and centralized means.[3]

Much of the Grange's social vision was formed during its gestation, birth, and first years in the nation's capital. The founding Grangers had witnessed firsthand what appeared as the enormous capacity and promise of federal power to reshape the national landscape. This is what provided the confidence and imagination for the launching of a national organization of farmers—an organization that they figured would soon fuse with that energized federal power and serve as a pillar of the new national order.

To realize its vision, the Grange developed a new template for associational life that fused two types of organizational functions. The Grange served as a fraternal society, a benevolent association where farmers and their families could socialize and provide each other with mutual assistance. At the same time, the Grange fought for what it defined as the "agriculture interest" or the "class interest of farmers" within the national political economy.[4] This combination of functions allowed the Grange to build a movement with a wide membership base, a uniform and centralized organizational system, and a national scope.

The Grange served as a vehicle of farmers' advocacy and an instrument of the farming class that provided a counterweight to the rising power of corporations. The rules of Grange meetings prohibited discussion of partisan politics, yet the Grange was profoundly political. By combining the strength of numbers, a disciplined organization, a network of influential farm journals and other media, and strong connections both in state capitals and in Washington, the Grange emerged as a political force. It realized a host of legislative victories at the state level, from regulating grain elevators and railroads to improving agricultural research and education. In doing so, the Grange pioneered a new politics of the mass interest group.

The Grange also gave new meanings and new life to the idea of equal rights. The reconfiguration of the ideas involved with the notion of equality is one of the Grange's most significant contributions to the next generations of reform. Franklin Roosevelt pointed to this contribution in a letter he sent to the Grange in October 1941. Roosevelt had joined the Grange early in his political career with an understanding of its political value among rural voters. On the eve of U.S. entry into World War II, FDR stressed the importance of its ideas. He wrote,

> In the course of my membership in the Grange for more than twenty-five years, I have often thought of the creed and purposes which members of the Order adopted and announced at their national organization meeting in 1873 at Georgetown, D.C. "We desire," said the founders, "*a proper equality, equity and fairness; protection for the weak, restraint upon the strong. . . . These are American ideas, the very essence of American independence.*"
>
> All of us subscribe to these ideals and principles. Our supreme task is to make them prevail.[5]

In his letter, FDR referred to a meeting of the National Grange held in a Georgetown living room that pledged the organization to "a proper equality, equity and fairness." The same words would become the most cited passage of the celebrated "Declaration of Purposes" that the Grange adopted the following year.[6] FDR reached for these words in the context of mobilizing the country to confront tyranny and war in Europe and Asia. The Grangers, of course, had declared in favor of "a proper equality" in the aftermath of a different war against a different tyranny.

Along with much of official Washington, the early Grangers focused their attention on stitching the nation back together. The Grange pledged to serve as a bridge for national unification. As the Grange's "Declaration of Purposes" put it, "We cherish the belief that sectionalism is, and of right should be dead and buried in the past. Our work is for the present and the future. . . . We shall recognize no North, no South, no East, no West."[7] The Grange promised to move the country beyond sectional conflict over the status and rights of the former slaves. In practice, this meant white solidarity between the northern farmer and the southern planter, and silence on the question of equality for African Americans. But the premise was clear enough: forging equality and solidarity among the nation's farmers would restore equality and harmony between the states and between the sections.

Meanwhile, freed slaves and free people of color made their way to Washington seeking refuge, opportunity, and equality. The stream of new arrivals meant that from 1860 to 1870 the African American population grew from 19 percent to 33 percent of the District. In January 1867, black delegates from across the country gathered in Washington for the second annual meeting of the National Equal Rights League. The nation's capital was the logical meeting place as black Washingtonians pressed their own equal rights claims and as the Republicans in Congress saw the city as a trial ground and example for black political and civil rights. In these years, the nation's capital was, as the historian Kate Masur so aptly puts it, a "crucible of equality." It was a place where it was impossible to escape the heat of the black struggle for equal citizenship, although the Grangers tried their best to do so.[8]

The Grangers studiously avoided the questions of racial equality, at least in public. Rather, they promised a vision of national reconciliation that would move the country beyond the old sectional quarrels and restore equality and harmony between the states. No one in Washington or beyond misunderstood the double meaning of such a promise: on the one hand, the Grange wanted no part of the black struggle for equal rights; and on the other hand, it was sending an offer of solidarity to the white planter class of the South. The advocates of white supremacy quickly recognized a potent ally. By the early 1870s, the Grange had become a refuge for rural white power across the former Confederacy.

Civil War–era Washington was also a congenial environment for the Grange's commitments to sexual equality. Thousands of white women from across the country worked in federal agencies during and after the war, attracted by employment as clerks and other professions from which women had traditionally been barred. The Universal Franchise Association, organized in Washington just months before the Grange, petitioned Congress to "equalize the laws respecting women" in the nation's capital and demanded that the salaries of women working as federal clerks be made equal to those of male clerks. Women's work within the federal bureaucracy was part of the wider experience of women's mobilization in the Sanitary Commission, the Freedmen's Bureau, and other agencies during the war and its aftermath, an experience that helped propel a new wave of demands for women's rights.[9]

Prior to the Civil War, the women's movement joined with the abolitionist movement in an interconnected struggle for racial and sexual equality. At the conclusion of the war, many women's rights advocates hoped that the abolition of slavery would open the way for equality between men and women. Their logic was impeccable: Just as the former slaves received equal rights protections, why should they not also be extended to women who faced systematic discrimination in terms of economic, legal, and personal rights, not to mention the denial of the right to vote? The Grange played a crucial role in that struggle.

The Grange also provided an organizational field for working out the meanings of sexual equality. When the fires of war were still smoldering, and when the Grange was still in its planning stage, its organizers insisted that women have equal rights, including voting rights, within the organization. Exactly what that meant was often sharply argued. Although the National Grange held back from endorsing women's suffrage at the national level, it attracted to its ranks women's rights activists across a wide spectrum, including the likes of Marie Howland, a communitarian socialist and an advocate of social and political equality for women. The Grange's role as a vehicle for sexual equality was widely recognized. The 1874 Woman's Suffrage Convention resolved to regard the Grange as one of the "practical auxiliaries of the woman suffrage movement."[10]

The meanings of equality articulated by the early Grangers in Washington would remain bedrock commitments of the Grange movement. The interrelated and overlapping issues of *political equality* between the nation's regions and states and *social equality* among farmers and between men and women proved essential to its impact and legacy. But as it expanded beyond its Washington roots, the Grange increasingly focused on *economic equality* between economic classes and business interests. For the Grange, economic equality meant fair and equitable relationships within the country's systems of trade, transport, and finance. Agricultural clubs and societies had protested unfair treatment in the past. But the Grange went further than any previous effort to establish a broad-based organization dedicated to the business interests of farmers.

The Grange ideal of economic equity and fairness was often framed as a struggle against the inequity of monopoly. Grangers protested, boycotted, and lobbied against a wide variety of "monopolists," from local grain millers and mule traders to farm equipment and sewing machine manufacturers. To cut out middlemen and gain more equitable access to markets and trade, they built extensive networks of cooperative stores, cotton gins, grain elevators, and purchasing, insurance, and marketing agencies. And the Grange undertook extensive political lobbying and legislative action to reshape the terrain of rural commerce.[11]

Most famously, the Grange confronted a formidable opponent: the railroad corporation. With a transportation network that now spanned the continent, a handful of such corporations exerted unprecedented economic leverage over the rural economy. The Grange charged that the railroad corporations violated basic principles of equity and fairness. They functioned as monopolists when they rigged the freight rates for hauling farmers' products, colluded with grain elevator operators and merchant houses, and purchased preferential treatment from courts and legislators by means of bribery and corruption. Granger blocs within the state legislatures in Wisconsin, Illinois, and other states across the Midwest and the West set up commissions and passed laws to regulate the railroads, grain elevators, and warehouses. Such state laws proved of limited value in regulating national commerce. But the Grange's great success was that it had placed notions of economic equality and fairness at the top of the agenda of post–Civil War reform.[12]

These Grange ideas about equality made sense to the membership as interconnected parts. Because they recognized women as farmers and part of the farming class, Grangers argued that women's rights and economic rights were inseparable. Conversely, because they did not recognize the former slaves as belonging to either the economic class of farmers or the sexual category of women, they embraced a notion of equality that justified a profoundly unequal white power. The Grange's vast numbers and relatively disciplined national structure gave such meanings of postbellum equality organizational force.

Although by the late 1870s the Grange was already falling into disrepair, its anti-monopoly critique of railroad and other corporations would remain a hallmark of powerful reform movements for the next half a century. The other legs of its equal rights agenda made a similarly large imprint. Realization of the post–Civil War promise of women's equality, in one form or another, would be a preoccupation of the next generations of reform. And so too would the effort to transcend a racialized sectionalism. Even where reform movements accepted nonwhites into their ranks, nationalist notions of equality across state and region rarely admitted discussion of the equal rights demands of African Americans and other racial minorities. When it came to ideas about equality, the Grange would cast a long shadow over the post–Civil War landscape.

II.

AMONG THE FIRST GRANGERS WHO met in William Saunders's federal office, Oliver Kelley was the one who provided much of the inspiration and energy for launching a national organization of farmers. Kelley had arrived in Washington as a refugee from failure. The son of a tailor, he was born in 1826 in Boston, where he attended the public schools before heading west. He briefly worked in Chicago as a reporter for the *Chicago Tribune* and then in Burlington, Iowa, as a clerk in a telegraph office. In 1849, he arrived in the Minnesota Territory, where he would later claim that he "commenced as a farmer." But "farmer" for Kelley, as with many of his fellow settlers, was only one of his many hats. He also described himself as a real estate dealer, notary public, justice of the peace, lawyer, newspaper reporter, and land agent.[13]

Whatever hat he wore, Kelley was always a booster and an enthusiast, devoting much of his abundant energy to high-risk real estate ventures. On his arrival in Minnesota, he joined the speculative frenzy that gripped the new territory. Acting on information that the legislature might move the capital from St. Paul to Itasca, farther up the Mississippi River, Kelley purchased a riverbank lot near Itasca and then plunged into politics in an unsuccessful effort to persuade the legislature to relocate the capital. The next big project involved a land scheme in the proposed river town of Northwood. To stimulate land sales, Kelley set up a bridge company, a mortgage firm, even a factory that produced O. H. Kelley and Company's Excelsior Metal Polish. But Kelley's plans for Northwood were swept away in the financial panic of 1857, sending him back to farm his lot near Itasca.[14]

Fascinated by technology and invention, Kelley turned his property into an experimental farm. He tinkered with the latest in irrigation techniques and corn-shelling machinery. He collaborated with the U.S. Patent Office in Washington, which provided him with seeds for his experiments with sugar millet, Hungarian wheat, and other exotic crops. With the coming of the Civil War, Kelley shifted to growing vegetables for an expanding produce market. However, his farming operations, already deep in debt, withered in the drought of 1863. Meanwhile, Kelley wrote copy for rural newspapers and traveled the state taking statistical surveys and compiling reports about farm conditions. These reports caught the attention of the Minnesota senator Alexander Ramsey, who offered Kelley a clerkship in Washington in the new Department of Agriculture. With all of his other ventures in ruins, Kelley jumped at the chance.[15]

Party differences made Kelley's appointment by Ramsey somewhat unusual. Kelley was a lifelong Democrat. He was skeptical about Republicans and had little interest in the Union war effort. By contrast, Ramsey had been the Republican governor at the outbreak of the Civil War and the first governor to call up troops for the Union cause. But the two men also had much in common. Ramsey and Kelley had worked the same political side of the Itasca land deal, and like other land speculators they shared a deep antipathy toward the Indians of Minnesota.[16]

In the early 1850s, Indian tribes still made up the majority of the territorial population. Ramsey, the territorial governor at the time, was responsible for making treaties with the tribes. His deal making helped him amass a fortune in real estate, although it also resulted in a congressional investigation into accusations of bad faith and fraud. During the same years, Kelley traded with the Winnebago Indians across the river from his Itasca property. But that did not stop him from supporting the territorial project of Indian removal, a project that expelled the Winnebago from their homes and put an end to Kelley's venture in the Indian trade.[17]

The insatiable appetite of white farmers and land speculators for Indian lands pushed the tribes to the edge of starvation and despair. On August 17, 1862, the Dakota Sioux pushed back, the Minnesota militia and the federal army mobilized, and the result was months of brutal warfare known by the settlers as the Dakota War. This was part of a wave of violence. While waging war on the Confederate army to the South, the Union army also waged war to the West—raids, massacres, forced relocations—against the Dakotas, the Cheyenne, the Comanche, the Navajo, the Shoshones, and other Native peoples.[18] Governor Ramsey seized on the Dakota crisis to pursue his long-held ambition of driving Indians out of the state. In the aftermath of the conflict, the Dakotas faced expulsion and retribution. A military tribunal originally sentenced 303 Indians to death by hanging. President Lincoln reduced the number of the condemned to 38, and on December 16, 1862, on Lincoln's order, the 38 Dakota men were hanged in a mass execution.[19]

These were murderous times. On a single day, September 17, 1862, at Maryland's Antietam Creek, Union and Confederate soldiers suffered twenty-three thousand casualties. Before the week was out, President Lincoln issued his Emancipation Proclamation, an executive order freeing the slaves held in the rebel states. Willy-nilly, the horrors of Civil War battlefields increasingly meshed with the destruction of African American slavery.[20] But for many Minnesotans, the Dakota War presented horrors much closer to home. And these horrors were linked not with emancipation but with ethnic cleansing, land grabbing, and speculation.

Oliver Kelley remained aloof from the dramas of the Civil War and the emancipation of the slaves. Like the farmers at Gettysburg who simply wanted to get in their crops, Kelley spent the war years sowing seeds on his experimental farm. He arrived in Washington in August 1864 only weeks after Jubal Early's invading Confederate troops had approached to within five miles of the White House.[21] But as Kelley settled in to his desk job at the Department of Agriculture, he was already thinking past the war to his next ventures.

A window of opportunity opened at the war's end. President Andrew Johnson and the Department of Agriculture sent Kelley to the South to conduct a survey of agricultural conditions. The old plantation economy lay in ruins, and his superiors wanted Kelley to report on what might be done. He spent several months in the winter and spring of 1866 among a group of plantation owners near Charleston, South Carolina, and it was during that time that he came up with the first plans for a fraternal order uniting the agricultural population of the country.[22]

Kelley needed collaborators to realize his plans for a national organization of farmers. He found them among the clerks and functionaries toiling within the bowels of a federal bureaucracy that had been energized by the demands of war and its aftermath. During those days of national crisis, a clerkship in Washington provided a haven for talented and restless souls in need of a salary. Kelley himself had started as a clerk in the Department of Agriculture, followed by a position in the Post Office Department. His collaborators in founding the Grange included John R. Thompson, who had served with the Vermont Volunteers at Gettysburg before taking a post in the Treasury Department, and Aaron B. Grosh, who had worked as a country schoolteacher and Universalist minister before seeking a less strenuous life as the librarian for the Department of Agriculture. William M. Ireland, the chief clerk in the finance office of the Post Office Department, was a long-term resident of the capital and would preside over the city's local Potomac Grange. John Trimble started his career as an Episcopal minister in New Jersey and served as a school principal in Kentucky. But with the outbreak of war, he sought refuge in Washington, where he filed war claims as a clerk in the Treasury Department.[23]

Kelley also recruited William Saunders into his group of collaborators, but unlike the others Saunders held a prominent place in Washington. Born in 1822 in St. Andrews, Scotland, Saunders studied horticulture at Edinburgh and apprenticed with noted Scottish and English landscape architects. He arrived in New York at the age of twenty-five and soon made his mark with his designs for urban parks in Philadelphia and Baltimore. In 1860, he designed the Oak Ridge Cemetery in Springfield, Illinois (and five years later he would design the grounds for Lincoln's Tomb at the same cemetery). As one of the nation's foremost landscape architects, Saunders was an obvious choice to design the cemetery at Gettysburg. In 1862, the new Department of Agriculture had appointed Saunders supervisor of gardens and grounds in Washington, D.C., and until his death in 1900 he was in charge of designing and maintaining the city's parks and landscapes. He also played an important role as a federal administrator and scientist, directing plant propagation projects across the country.[24]

Saunders's position gave him connections. The Supreme Court justice Salmon Chase, the Illinois senator Lyman Trumbull, and General Ulysses S. Grant sought out his advice on questions from flower ornaments to farming. Saunders befriended Walt Whitman, who, despite his fame (and infamy) as a poet, had found refuge clerking in Washington. Whitman was eventually dismissed by a "rigidly righteous" and "squeamish functionary," as Saunders described him, who found "some expressions in [Whitman's] poems which were considered heathenish or irreligious." Years later, Saunders also made the acquaintance of Frederick Douglass, the former slave and abolitionist and civil rights advocate, whom he met frequently at the home of a common friend and neighbor, Hiram Pitts. Like many white observers, Saunders was impressed by Douglass's "noble" looks and "appropriate language." And like some of Douglass's other white acquaintances and neighbors, Hiram Pitts ended the visits after he "tabooed" Douglass for marrying his white niece Helen Pitts, a clerk in the federal pension agency and a women's rights advocate.[25]

Saunders was a committed scientist, and it was that commitment that first drew him into Oliver Kelley's circle and the scheme to build a national organization for farmers. With his botanical training, Saunders spent many of his waking hours cataloging plant varieties or examining the mildew that afflicted the nation's vineyards. He also developed a design for fixed glass roofs for greenhouses, making use of innovations in plate glass manufacturing and piped heating technology. Saunders introduced the navel or seedless orange to California after importing two trees from Bahia, Brazil, budding new plants, and sending them to fruit growers in Riverside County. Along with the navel orange, he propagated hundreds of varieties of trees, vines, shrubs, and other plants across the American landscape. Saunders saw the potential in Kelley's plan for a farmers' organization as a vehicle for disseminating agricultural knowledge. Moreover, he quickly recognized its latent power as a means to engage in nation building on the basis of rational and egalitarian principles.[26]

Saunders in turn recruited the only Grange founder who was not on the federal payroll. Francis M. McDowell had made his money as a partner in a New York brokerage firm. His working years involved traveling to European capitals and selling his company's bonds for building the Kansas Pacific Railway. Afflicted by illness in the early days of the Civil War, McDowell retired to the small town of Wayne in western New York, where he invested in the burgeoning grape-growing industry. A shared interest in grapevines brought him into contact with Saunders. McDowell would serve as the treasurer of the Grange and play a major role in building its financial system.[27]

III.

DURING THE SUMMER AND FALL OF 1867, Kelley, Saunders, and their collaborators negotiated the details of their plan for a national organization of farmers. At times the negotiators failed to see eye to eye. But along with their interest in agriculture, they had common ideas about remaking

the country along rational and equitable lines. They believed that harmony had to be restored among the states, not on the old confederated
terms, but with a centralized authority unleashing the nation's latent
power. The organization they looked to build would be strictly egalitarian in structure and membership, thoroughly national in scope, and united
with a "National Head" to "supervise and direct the interests and affairs
of the entire unity." In other words, the values that guided Saunders's
plan for the cemetery at Gettysburg corresponded in striking ways to the
founding values of the Grange.[28]

The new organization would erase distinctions among farmers, uni-
fying the farming interest as a class. Unlike the farmers' clubs and horticultural societies of the past that often focused on the farming elite, this
new order would promise a strict equality among all persons with an interest in agriculture. Most strikingly, at a time when women's exclusion
and subordination were prominent and explicit features of American political, social, and religious life, the plan promised equality between the
sexes. In practice, the promise of sexual equality gave way to a reality of
often limited participation for women and unequal gender roles within the
Grange that became a source of friction between men and women members. A group of women in the Kansas Grange, for example, protested
that even though women did "all kinds of work" on the farm, they were
not given the chance to speak in meetings. "As to talking," they noted,
"the men have so much to say that there is no time for us."[29]

Moreover, when it came to matters of race and class, the notion of
equality of all people was a delusion. It was a plan that in practice ignored
the humanity of African American, Chinese, Mexican, and other farm laborers and often exalted white plantation owners, ranchers, and speculators. Yet in stated principles, there were no exclusion clauses and no
exceptions. "Any person interested in Agricultural pursuits" was eligible
as long as women were over the age of sixteen and men over the age of
eighteen. The organizational structure stressed simplicity and regularity.
It made no distinctions between each local unit or "Subordinate Grange."
Each such Grange had a minimum of nine men and four women as

members, and a maximum of twenty men and ten women. Each such subordinate Grange had exactly equal rights within the state Grange. And each state Grange had equal rights within the National Grange. It turned out that the original plan was *too* simple. Because intermediate bodies between local and state Granges were not allowed for, organizational cohesion proved difficult in states with hundreds and even thousands of local units. By 1874 in Iowa, for example, farmers had set up 1,999 separate and fully equal Grange organizations.[30]

The focus on local units and state organizations might suggest a preference for local and state autonomy. But the plan also envisioned that a unified center—variously referred to as "the central division," "the grand head," "the National Temple," "the United States Lodge," the "National Head," and ultimately "the National Grange"—would regulate any such autonomy. The center would formulate and enforce procedures, guide the organization, and provide a check on local variation. Francis McDowell, the retired financier, wrote the rules that gave members of the National Grange extended terms in office and other enhanced powers. Saunders and the other members of the National Grange embraced the same vision of centralized authority.[31]

The extraordinary authority that the Grange reserved for national and state officers would provoke intense debates within the organization. Dissenters demanded "more equality" in the face of the "despotism" of the leadership and the lack of representative means of decision making. Grange officers pushed back against the "unthinking crie[s] for '*Equality!*'" with lectures about the necessity of "order versus chaos," "rulers and ruled," and "lawful obedience." These debates would never be resolved. Still there were adjustments, with state Granges gaining more autonomy, as county and other intermediate bodies formed within the states. But in the main, at least as long as the Grange was on the upswing, the supporters of the centralized, top-down system had the upper hand.[32]

In the early stages, the plan for the "central division" placed it inside the federal bureaucracy. "The grand head of the organizations will be an auxiliary to the department of agriculture," Kelley explained to Saunders.

He also projected that "Congress will appropriate a million of dollars annually" for federal projects undertaken by the Grange. And if all went well, the Department of Agriculture would be elevated to a cabinet-level department, William Saunders would be elevated to secretary of the department, and the National Grange would sit at the pinnacle of national power.[33]

The idea of locating the National Grange within the Department of Agriculture never materialized. For some time, it appeared that the plans for the Grange were, as Kelley feared, nothing more than "large 'air castles' on a foundation of inspiration."[34] Indeed, the plan was wildly ambitious. But these were speculative times, and the seven collaborators meeting in Saunders's Washington office had one thing going for their big gamble: their "air castles" were inspired by the rationalist, nationalist, and egalitarian ethos of the post–Civil War moment.

IV.

CREATING FROM SCRATCH A NATIONAL organization of farmers represented an enormous undertaking. Nothing in Kelley's past suggested expertise in organization building, yet on his return from the South, Kelley threw himself into the task. "I was starting out in a new business," Kelley explained, but being "totally inexperienced," he opined that "one less fitted for such work could scarcely be found."[35] This was only half-true. In fact, Kelley's experience with the newspaper business and with high-risk ventures proved invaluable for his new undertaking. As Kelley fully realized, to make his plan work would require a combination of bold publicity and speculative nerve.

But first he had to figure out what this organization might look like. To brainstorm the possibilities, Kelley undertook an extensive correspondence with Saunders and McDowell. He also discussed his plans with his niece Caroline Arabella Hall, who proved to be Kelley's closest and most dedicated collaborator. Much of the process of invention took place under a cloud of pipe tobacco smoke in room 48 of Washington's United States Hotel, where Kelley met after work with Trimble, Ireland, and other colleagues in the federal service.[36]

Kelley and his colleagues understood that education would be the main function of the new organization. They lived in a world of rapid innovation, with steam power and telecommunications being applied to industry, transport, and trade. Agriculture, they believed, must not be left behind in a progressive era of science and technology. If only farmers would "discard their old almanacs and signs of the moon," Kelley told his friends, "imagine what a volcanic eruption we can produce in this age. Everything is progressing. Why not the farmers?" The new farmers' organization would be a means to circulate scientific literature, to compile agricultural statistics, and to "have the best talent in the country lecture to the people."[37]

Education, however, might only accomplish so much. Since the early days of the Republic, farmers had set up a variety of agricultural and horticultural societies to promote education and scientific methods. But too often such efforts proved fleeting, with only the most prosperous farmers having the wherewithal to participate and the membership being too narrow to be effective. Kelley and his friends wanted to invent something new. "The old style of Farmers' Clubs, like the sickle flail, were very good in their day," as one of Kelley's compatriots explained. "But they are of the past, and are too far behind all other enterprises in the progress of civilization." The present and the future demanded a new type of "systematic organization": more powerful, more dynamic, with a membership counted in the millions. As Kelley put it, "Give us an association that will aid and protect the farmers as a class."[38]

According to Saunders, the time had passed for political mobilizations based on states' rights, abolition, and other "political theories." The conclusion of the Civil War and "the calm and prosperity of peace, called for new organizations, based upon the industrial arts." Farmers needed to organize themselves in the same manner as the other industries. Only then might farmers protect their interests in relation to the other industrial classes within the national political economy.[39]

Kelley and his colleagues defined the "true interests" of the farmers with broad strokes. They resisted the notion that they were simply building "a commercial or monied institution" and emphasized the higher

interests of spreading science, cultivating civilization, and purifying politics. But questions of "interests" most often hinged on economic matters.
They discussed how the organization would serve as a rural "board of
trade," understanding that farmers would only join if they believed it
would bring them financial gain. As one of Kelley's correspondents explained, "The great majority of our countrymen are ruled by pecuniary
considerations." Therefore, "taking society as we find it," he explained,
"we shall be compelled to so frame our work as to increase the chances
of pecuniary success." The Grange would serve the collective needs of
the farming class through economic combination, cooperation, and
mutual aid.[40]

From the outset, the Grange grappled with the tensions between its
collective and its entrepreneurial ambitions. These tensions intensified as
the organization grew and members questioned the salaries of officers and
the amount of dues money that went into the Grange's state and national
coffers. It should be kept in mind, however, that in the post–Civil War years
it was widely understood that reform movements had an entrepreneurial
side much as religious movements of the time did. A successful cooperative or mutual aid society might have financial rewards for its lecturers
and agents, much as an evangelical enterprise might reward its successful preachers.

In making their plans, the founders of the Grange calculated the financial possibilities of a successful dues-paying society. The accountants
among them tallied the money even before the Grange had a single member. By one calculation, they figured that if the national office charged
each member ten-cents-a-month dues, a membership of a million farmers
would yield over a hundred thousand dollars a year to the national office.[41] Saunders and some of the other founders might have been less keen
about the moneymaking side of the operation because they had either a
secure government position or independent wealth. But for Kelley it was a
make-or-break venture. The mortgage debt on his Minnesota farm "kept
[his] spirits in perpetual eclipse." The financial success of the Grange
would finally release him from his personal financial nightmares.[42]

The Grange founders set a target of a million members because they understood that only a broad, national membership would sustain their plans for a class-based organization. Big numbers were the key. Kelley and his associates looked for a formula that would combine the "interest" function of the organization with an "expressive" or social function of a fraternal society. By providing farmers with opportunities to socialize, recreate, and enjoy themselves, the organization would attract a wide and stable base of support.

The Freemasons provided a model for much of the early planning about the structure and social functions of the new organization. By the end of the 1850s, Freemasonry had recovered from the anti-Masonic hysteria of a generation before. More than two hundred thousand American white men, many of them clerks, editors, lawyers, teachers, merchants, and other professionals, enrolled in Masonic lodges as places to socialize. Membership was especially high in Mississippi and several other slave states, where over 10 percent of white male adults enrolled as Masons. African American Masons built their own "Prince Hall Lodges," which were started by a black abolitionist and Freemason named Prince Hall and which white Masons viewed as "clandestine" and illegitimate. By that measure, Masonic fraternity was a white brotherhood, a brotherhood that survived the divisions of the Civil War and its aftermath.[43]

According to Masonic legend, when the Confederate general Lewis Armistead was mortally wounded at Gettysburg, he gave the Masonic hand signal calling for assistance and, recognizing the signal, the staff of his fellow Mason the Union general Winfield Scott Hancock came to his aid. Although there was little truth to this tale, it evoked the power of fraternity even as Masons murdered each other on Civil War battlefields.[44] Kelley had his own story of fraternity across the Mason-Dixon Line. During his trip to the South, he relied on his membership in the Masons to open the doors and hearts of plantation owners who might otherwise have shunned a northern agent of the federal government. For Kelley, Freemasonry provided proof of his contention that white fraternity was the key to sectional reconciliation.[45]

Freemasonry provided other lessons. It showed that white brotherhood required transcending differences in religious creed. "Religion is the bond of man to his God," as Kelley would have learned from the Minnesota Masons, "Masonry is the bond of man to man." Freemasonry also provided an example of an organizational system. Its secret and ritualized rules and regulations and its hierarchical ladder of ascending degrees of membership provided a centralized and stable structure. Compliance with that structure was at the heart of the Masonic system. "Obedience to authority," the Masons emphasized, was "the very essence of the institution."[46]

Kelley and his associates incorporated much of this system into the rules of their organization. They adopted a scale of seven degrees of membership, each with its designated level of authority. A local chapter, known as a subordinate Grange, included members of the first four degrees: Faith (laborers and maids), Hope (cultivators and shepherdesses), Charity (harvesters and gleaners), and Fidelity (husbandmen and matrons). The top three degrees, Pomona, Flora, and Ceres, were held by county, state, and national leaders. The hierarchical and closed nature of this system trumped more egalitarian notions and would later emerge as a flash point of controversy within the organization. But Saunders, Kelley, McDowell, and the others believed that it was essential to provide a stable leadership and to safeguard the central authority of the national office with the elevated powers of the "seventh degree."[47]

Also borrowing from Freemasonry, Kelley and his co-workers developed a secret system of handshakes and ceremonies, which again they believed would stabilize the organization. But they also hoped that mysterious and exotic rituals would fascinate the curious and attract potential members. The Freemasons had derived their "traditional rituals" from bits and pieces of the historical record about the ancient worlds of Egyptian craftsmen and Christian crusaders. Kelley and his colleagues engaged in a similar act of invention. They spent months rummaging through the literature on the ancient world, inventing rituals drawn mainly from the pagan myths of classical Greece and Rome.[48]

The key to successful rituals, the founders believed, was their ability to satisfy the farmer's desires for knowledge, social life, and entertainment. Literary readings, poetry, and picnics would be essential. Kelley thought that feasts or festivals with alluring food and drink could also play a role. Hungry and thirsty after a long day in the office, he came up with the plan for holding harvest festivals featuring pies and oysters.[49] Then there was the problem of what to drink. Hard liquor would not be suitable for family entertainment, and banning alcoholic beverages would be grim. Wine, however, would be just right. Kelley and Saunders discussed holding festivals to honor Bacchus and considered the planting of grapevines as a requirement of membership. They dropped that particular proposal but looked for other ways to deliver revelry and merriment. Thinking that filling meetings and picnics with cheerful song might be attractive to members, Kelley traveled to music stores in New York City in search of "music with snap in it."[50]

Such was the process of ritual invention, a process that posed something of a paradox. As self-professed partisans of modernity and science, Kelley and Saunders celebrated the arrival of what they understood as a progressive age. They viewed the spread of scientific ideas and methods as the mission of the new organization. Yet they also recognized the disintegrative force of the speculative commercial tide unleashed in the Civil War's aftermath. Indeed, Kelley and several of his collaborators had abundant experience with high-risk real estate gambles and other smash-and-grab enthusiasms. To protect the organization from such dangers and provide a degree of stability, they sought to moor the organization to a newly invented "ancient ritual."

Inventing an ancient past to serve a modern present was not the work of the founders alone. During the same years, wealthy Americans cluttered their homes with ornamental symbols of a premodern past. Corporate executives, who made their fortunes in steamships, railroads, and the most up-to-date dynamos, bought up European and Oriental relics by the cargo load. The historian Jackson Lears writes that upper-class collectors of antiquities were unaware of their social function as "premodern emblems of authority."[51] This could not be said of Kelley and his colleagues, who were fully aware of this social function. Although they lacked the resources to purchase classical statuary, they recognized the need to give their invented organization the gravitas of the ancients. Along these lines, they devised fancifully elaborate rituals that invoked the names of Greek and Roman deities.

V.

FROM THE OUTSET, THE ARCHITECTS of the organization understood that success depended on the participation of women. With an eye to recruiting women, they gave Demeter, Ceres, Pomona, and other pagan goddesses a prominent part in the "ancient ritual." This was also a gesture toward equality between men and women, an issue that the founders addressed from the early stages of planning. Kelley's niece Caroline Hall was the first to suggest that women have an equal place in the organization. The other founders, with only mild resistance, accepted her proposal. They did so in part because of their practical understanding that the presence of women, who made up half of the farmers' ranks, was essential for a broad-based agricultural association. And they did so in part because of a shared understanding, at least at the ideological level, that equality between the sexes would be a natural result of post–Civil War evolution.

The new organization must either accept equality between the sexes or be "run over and buried out of sight by the advancing tide of progress." This is how Anson Bartlett explained the matter in a letter to Oliver Kelley. A leader of the Ohio Dairymen's Association, Bartlett owned a large-scale cheese factory that he believed contributed to women's freedom by liberating them from the drudgery of making butter and cheese at home.[52] He wrote to Kelley that the proposal to make the new organization "common to both sexes was to me one of its best features and strongest recommendations." Bartlett was a friend and collaborator, and Kelley replied to him in full agreement. Although he claimed to not be a "Woman's Rights man," he recognized that just as the farming interest would obtain equal rights with other interests, women would be recognized as the equal of men. He reassured Bartlett that equal rights was his "guiding star."[53]

At the time, most political, social, and religious organizations either relegated women to explicitly unequal and separate status or barred the doors to women altogether. Whereas the Freemasons excluded women, the Odd Fellows and other fraternal orders admitted women to separate and lower degrees. Kelley had toyed with a similar structure, but as Anson Bartlett explained to him, "earnest, active energetic women" would reject such a structure as a mere "bauble" and a "wheedling attempt" to win their favor "without placing them in a position where they can wield such influence as they otherwise might." "Let us then," Bartlett suggested, "so frame the work of this Order that there shall be at least the appearance of equality; varied of course, to suit the conditions of the sexes."[54]

In this spirit, Kelley redrafted the rules to provide for separate but equal degrees for women and men. In practice, this turned into a jerry-rigged system of nominal equality. In recognition that women's income was often only a fraction of their male counterparts', the founders reduced women's dues to a fraction of what men paid and in the process undermined women's equal position. Similarly, to ensure that women would have a voice at the upper levels of leadership, the wives of male officers were given voting rights at the same leadership level as their husbands. Making their position contingent on their husbands', however, tended to diminish the power of their voice. The question of whether the organization would endorse women's political equality proved too controversial, and the founders nimbly stepped around the issue. Meanwhile, the separate system of degrees, with their separate rituals, reinforced prevailing social conventions whereby women were relegated to a "separate sphere" of nurturing, child rearing, and domestic obligations. Despite such limits, as the founders predicted, the organization's novel promise of sexual equality stirred public interest and attracted women to its ranks.

To attract members, Kelley and his colleagues agreed that the name of the organization had to be original. They rejected "The Lodge" and "The Temple" as too ordinary and too close to Freemasonry. They toyed with such possibilities as "The Field," "The Bee-Hive," "The Garden," and "The Vineyard." Other suggestions included "Knights of the Plow," "Patrons of Industry," and "League of Husbandry." "The Independent Order of Progressive Farmers" might have been the most fitting of the proposed names, but it lacked the allure of mystery. After considering some fifty different names, Kelley came across the word "grange" in the title of a novel. "Grange" was an archaic term for barn or granary, and Kelley discovered its meaning in *Webster's Unabridged*. This was just the type of name that the founders had been seeking, with the right mix of the exotic and the ancient.[55]

At the December 4, 1867, meeting in Saunders's office, the founders ratified the organizational system and elected each other national officers. Saunders was given the top post of worthy master, and Kelley was appointed national secretary. After months of feverish planning, the existence of the National Grange of the Patrons of Husbandry was announced to the world. Now all that was needed was to sell what the founders had created to America's farmers.

VI.

KELLEY RESIGNED FROM HIS FEDERAL JOB in the Post Office Department to devote his full attention to the launching of the Grange. His first instinct was to turn it into a moneymaker by recruiting people with money. To raise cash, he proposed selling the top degrees in the Grange at twenty-five dollars and fifty dollars each to "men and women of means." The rules of the new organization required that members have an interest in agriculture, and a considerable number of prosperous urbanites at the time drew their wealth from the farm economy. Kelley's first organizing efforts focused on such men and women in Harrisburg, Pennsylvania, Columbus, Ohio, and Madison, Wisconsin. He helped grain dealers and commission agents form Granges in New York City and Boston. In Chicago, Kelley recruited Thomas B. Bryan, who made his millions in real estate and who agreed to cover some of the Grange publishing expenses. In Minneapolis, Kelley recruited John S. Pillsbury, a timber and real estate magnate who would soon thereafter put his fortune into flour mills of what would become the famous Pillsbury Company. But Kelley grew tired of begging for money from millionaires, whose level of commitment never failed to disappoint.[56]

In Fredonia, New York, Kelley helped organize the first functioning Grange outside Washington, D.C.[57] Then, in the fall of 1868, he made a breakthrough by organizing the North Star Grange in St. Paul, Minnesota. From the start, divisions between "city citizens" and "tillers of the soil" afflicted the North Star Grange's mainly middle-class and professional membership. The farmer members of this fledgling Grange eventually gained the upper hand—more precisely, the members aspiring to be farmers, because most of these first rural Grangers had little or no experience farming in what was to them a promising new land. They described themselves as "energetic pioneers in Agriculture, Horticulture and Pomology" who would "bring to light science and truth to the great benefit of the state." They had dreams of conquering the rich prairie soil to grow wheat for the world market; of shipping fruits, vegetables, and dairy products to feed the burgeoning industrial centers of Milwaukee and Chicago; and of boosting land values with the mutual advance of railroad and plow.[58]

Much of the discussion in the early days revealed how little these first Minnesota Grangers knew about farming in their new environment. Some members recommended planting apple trees, while other members feared the trees would not survive the state's cold winters. One member had purchased eight hundred acres of prairie but asked at a Grange meeting how to go about breaking the stubborn prairie sod. Some of his colleagues suggested plowing with oxen and then sowing turnips, others countered that it would be better to use horses, at which point they all came to agreement that the best course of action was simply to hire a good man to do the job.[59]

During the early years, much of the discussion within the North Star Grange focused on the damage wrought by the potato beetle. The Milwaukee market for potatoes beckoned, but "destruction from those constant gormandizers" ruined the crop. Some members suggested that fresh horse manure would kill them, others suggested lime, while still others had heard that lime only "fatted" the bugs. Some members thought nothing could be done "because they migrated in the air." Oliver Kelley intervened by stating the obvious, "that the habits of the potato bug were not yet fully understood."[60]

The North Star Grange marked an inauspicious beginning. Yet it served Kelley's purposes as a testing ground for the plans and rituals drawn up back in Washington. Soon several other Granges took hold nearby, giving Kelley the platform he needed for nationwide publicity. By "securing the aid of the press," Kelley predicted, the Grange "will be an organization that will, in a few years' time, rule in this country." Caroline Hall shouldered much of the responsibility for getting the word out. Her first big undertaking was to contact the nation's extensive network of rural newspapers. She compiled hundreds of addresses of editors of farm journals and rural publications and wrote more than a dozen letters a day requesting support.[61]

Caroline Hall would prove to be the National Grange's most able manager and organizer, at least in its early years. Like her uncle Oliver Kelley, Hall was born in Boston and attended the public schools there, before moving with her family to Minnesota, where she taught school. She eventually quit her teaching job to work for the Grange full-time, taking on much of the correspondence, distribution of literature, and other responsibilities. She also compiled materials for the organization, including the Grange songbook. She accompanied Kelley when he returned to Washington to work for the National Grange, and she drew a six-hundred-dollar annual salary as his invaluable assistant. However, it could be argued that Kelley, who received all of the acclaim, actually assisted Hall, who did so much of the work. In later years, Hall would gain recognition as "equal to a 'Founder of the Order'" for her contributions to the early Grange.[62]

Kelley and Hall knew more about cultivating the press than they did about potatoes, and they understood the value of the carefully seeded newspaper item to promote a sale. Every week, they sent editors batches of glowing news stories about the nation's farmers flocking to the Grange.

When a Catholic newspaper attacked the Grange, Kelley welcomed the attention as "the richest thing out there," because "it will help advertise us all over the country." He similarly welcomed attacks from the religious press in Chicago: "The more they 'cuss' the better we shall be advertised, and at no expense to us." All publicity was good publicity. "Give me printer's ink," Kelley wrote to the Grange treasurer, Francis McDowell, "and I can control public sentiment on this continent. That's the power the Patrons want, which, with female influence, is to make the Order a success."[63]

VII.

AFTER SEVERAL YEARS of being an organization with a national head in Washington and a handful of functioning local Granges, in the early 1870s the Grange grew exponentially into a truly national organization. By 1875, 860,000 men and women—corn farmers, cotton growers, and wheat ranchers—paid dues and packed into farm buildings, schoolrooms, and other spaces where the Grange held its meetings.[64] They were sustained by more than twenty-one thousand local Granges organized in every state in the Union, with nearly eight thousand Granges in the states of the former Confederacy. Granges crowded the Deep South, the Pacific coast, and the midwestern prairie. Most of the farmers in Nebraska joined the organization, setting up a local Grange for every eighty-four persons engaged in agriculture. But it was not just Nebraska. In agricultural districts across the country, it was not uncommon for the majority of the farmers, or at least the majority of the white farmers, to enroll as dues-paying members of the Grange.[65]

These numbers suggest that the uniform structure of the Grange aligned with the rough uniformity of American farming. Individual farmsteads in Nebraska, for example, were spread across a perfect grid of quarter sections drawn by the Public Land Survey System. Each farmstead, relying mainly on the labor of the family unit, and equipped from a common arsenal of plows, harvesters, and other mainly horse-driven machinery, produced a given number of bushels of the same wheat, corn, or oats.

There was variation. Property lines took different shapes in the Southwest, on the East Coast, and elsewhere. In the Northeast, urban demands for dairy, fruits, and other products made for greater diversity in farming. In parts of the South, farmsteads produced cotton or tobacco by the bale and the pound, and in plantation districts the family farm was the exception rather than the rule. Nonetheless, across much of the country patterns of farming had a symmetry and regularity. The historian James Huston argues that these patterns formed the "basis of the American claims of equality." And it was within these patterns that the Grange flourished.[66]

The thoroughness with which the Grange organized farm districts, however, often masked the divisions of wealth and power within the agricultural population. The Grange movement emphasized the commonness of the American farmstead. Yet even within the relative uniformity of farming in the Great Plains states, for example, hired hands working for wages made up 20 to 30 percent of the farm population. These laborers usually had ambitions of becoming farm owners themselves. They often enjoyed the status of "social equal" in that they ate meals with the family for whom they worked, and some of them were relatives of the family or had a chance at marrying into the family. And a good number of them also attended Grange meetings, even though such meetings had little to say about the needs and interests of wage-earning farm labor.[67]

Membership numbers alone fail to give a picture of the potential power of the Grange. The organization represented by far the largest profession in what was still an agricultural country. For the 1870 census, almost half of all Americans named farming as their primary profession. There were more than twice as many farmers in the United States as there were factory workers, miners, and mechanics combined.[68] And in the 1870s, the eventual collapse of the farm population was still far into the future; over the next fifty years, the farm population would continue to grow, although at a slower rate than in other industries.

The Grange wielded influence within the farm population well beyond its ranks. Many farmers who sympathized and cooperated with the

Grange did not sign up as members. A Catholic farmer, for example, might have been reluctant to defy his church's prohibition against accepting the secrecy required in the Grange's membership rituals but might have joined with Grange neighbors for public picnics and supported its economic and political agenda. Other sympathetic farmers lived in remote places that might not have been able to sustain the minimum membership of a Grange. Many other farmers belonged to a variety of other agricultural clubs and societies that often made common cause with the Grange, amplifying the Grange's political leverage.

The newspapers, meanwhile, turned the Grange into a national power. The networks of rural editors, journalists, advertisers, and correspondents served as the instruments of Grange organizing. The well-known editors of the big agricultural journals played an outsized role in what was a top-down system of organization building. The pages of *The Prairie Farmer* (Chicago), *The Iowa Homestead and Western Farm Journal* (Des Moines), *The Ohio Farmer* (Cleveland), the *Rural World* (St. Louis), the *Pacific Rural Press* (San Francisco), *The Rural Carolinian* (Charleston), and similar papers built the Grange into a colossus—at least in the minds of their readers. It was not just the specialized rural press, however; hundreds of newspapers in towns and villages across much of the country carried extensive news of the Grange, often reserving a full page to report on Grange events, speakers, enterprises, and political campaigns.

The newspapers sold the Grange to the nation's farmers. But why did the farmers respond? What did the Grange offer to so many men and women that they found it worthwhile to attend meetings and pay monthly dues? The simplest explanation is that, just as Kelley and the founders had guessed, American farmers were keenly interested in the social benefits of fraternity. Much like urban members of fraternal societies, Grangers enjoyed the dinners, picnics, and cultural events. This was especially the case for farm families living on isolated and desolate farmsteads. At the same time, the focus on agricultural science attracted men and women like those in Minnesota's North Star Grange who faced unfamiliar pests and challenges of farming in unfamiliar terrain. And the fraternal benevolence of such a large-scale national organization offered a degree of security in the face of grasshopper plagues, floods, and drought.

Women played a key role in the Grange boom. Numerous observers attributed the success of the organization to their participation. As Kelley put it, women "are our main stay."[69] Other fraternal societies either excluded women altogether, as with the Freemasons, or allowed them a subordinate role in women's auxiliaries. Women sustained the work of the churches but rarely enjoyed the rights to a voice or a vote within religious institutions. The Grange, by contrast, welcomed women on at least nominally equal terms. In practice, men were in charge of much of Grange life, and women were often relegated to the task of decorating meeting halls or preparing picnics. Yet women Grangers were appointed or elected to serve as lecturers, secretaries, and other responsible positions within the organization.

As Kelley had hoped, "female influence" helped to secure the success of the Grange. But the meanings of this influence were understood in different ways. Some Grangers, especially in the South, emphasized female difference and the moral influence within the organization of wives and mothers on husbands and sons. William Simmons of Charleston, South Carolina, reassured his fellow plantation owners that "there is no more danger of [their wives] becoming a woman's rights woman at the Grange than there is of her becoming one at the fireside, for at each place [she] is in company with her husband."[70]

Other Grangers focused on equal rights and the influence of the Grange's position in favor of sexual equality. Marie Howland, a personal friend of William Saunders's, pushed the Grange to take steps to realize equal rights in practice. Born to a family of poor New Hampshire farmers, a teenage Howland went to work in the textile mills before she made her way to New York City, where she taught in a mission school in the Five Points district and became involved in Fourierist socialism. She and her husband, a fellow disciple of Charles Fourier from Charleston, South Carolina, spent the Civil War in England and afterward spent the next twenty years on their farm in Hammonton, New Jersey. A number of egalitarian activists visited her farm, and Howland counted among her friends Victoria Woodhull, the 1872 presidential candidate of the Equal Rights Party and outspoken advocate of women's political and sexual equality.[71]

Howland pressed her case that the Grange should accept that women's equality involved more than formal status or position; women needed a practical equality in familial relations and society. From this perspective, Howland urged Saunders to make the social functions of the Grange more equitable and therefore more attractive to women. She recommended, for instance, that meetings and festivities have less "tea, coffee, [and] oysters" that involved cooking and washing. Women, she noted, already "have too much of that at home heaven knows."[72]

Moreover, in a letter to Saunders, Howland cautioned that the Grange's business ventures tended to attract new members with little understanding of the "soul" of the organization. "Women will not attend the Grange," she wrote, "when it has become a business caucus." She penned this warning in the winter of 1876, but by this late date the Grange had for some time devoted its energies to the male-dominated spheres of business and politics. The more it functioned as a business caucus, and the more it took the shape of an anti-monopoly political party, the less emphasis the Grange gave to the social and educational activities that attracted women to the movement. As Howland had suggested, this shift in focus would eventually prove part of the Grange's undoing. But it was equally the case that without its business function, without its focus on "equal and exact justice" in the realms of economics and anti-monopoly politics, there would have been no Grange boom in the first place.[73]

2.

ANTI-MONOPOLY

CAMPAIGNS AGAINST MONOPOLY roiled the political waters in the months before the military campaigns concluded at Appomattox. Newspaper editors, business leaders, politicians, and labor and farm reformers pledged themselves to the fight. Anti-monopoly meetings and rallies were held from coast to coast. In February 1865, James Scovel, who had recently served as Lincoln's commissioner to London, addressed the national "Anti-Monopoly Convention" in Trenton, New Jersey. "Monopoly," Scovel told the convention, "creates a mental servitude worse than bodily slavery." He predicted that the impending victory of the Union soldiers would open the way to the defeat of "the two great political falsehoods of the nineteenth century." "Slavery and Monopoly," he said, "will go down together unwept into a common grave."[1]

The war had ushered in a new economy. It left southern towns and farmsteads in ruins. But in much of the rest of the country, the war spurred growth of new industries in new terrain. The railroad provided the driving force. Feeding the railroad required exponential growth in the output of iron, coal, and timber, not to mention opening tens of millions of new acres to farming staple crops to provide a market for the new rail lines. Railroads were accompanied by the telegraph, with transatlantic and transcontinental cables completing a telecommunications revolution. A new type of industrial corporation also rode in with the railroads, pooling unheard-of quantities of capital and organizing thousands, and even tens of thousands, of employees.[2]

Anti-monopolists fastened their attention on the railroad corporations and the financiers who controlled them. In the planning stages and the first years of the Grange, however, Oliver Kelley, William Saunders, and the other Granger leaders kept their distance from the anti-monopoly movement and showed no particular interest in railroad corporations. This distance and lack of interest are surprising because four years later the Grange *was* the anti-monopoly movement. Across the Midwest and the West, the Grange effectively lobbied statehouses to demand the regulation of railroad rates and practices. By 1873, these efforts produced a wave of "Granger laws," the first major success of the postwar struggle against corporate power. And beyond lobbying, the Grange dove into political campaigns behind anti-monopoly candidates, factions, and third parties.[3]

Kelley and the other early Grangers were won over to the fight against monopoly by reading the mood of the membership. They came to the recognition that for the Grange to succeed it would have to tap into the surging anti-monopoly sentiment sweeping rural America. As a result, the anti-monopoly cause captured the Grange, while the Grange became the vehicle of popular anti-monopoly politics. The two were a good fit. The anti-monopoly ideal corresponded closely to the vision articulated by the Grange founders: nationalist, centralizing, rationalist, and egalitarian.

Anti-monopolists, Grangers included, understood that the baneful effects of monopoly could be felt throughout the national economy. Railroad corporations might have been the worst offenders. But monopolies lurked in every corner of the nation's commercial affairs, trampling on the principles of fair and equitable exchange. Because monopoly was so ubiquitous, the meanings of the term tended to be very broad, multilayered, and subject to change. To make sense of post–Civil War anti-monopoly agitation, it is essential to clear away a number of misconceptions.

To begin, the critique of monopoly was not about small economies fighting big economies; in given circumstances, an offending monopoly might be as small as the village blacksmith, and rarely was bigness itself the source of complaint. Although anti-monopoly campaigns often focused on railroad corporations, anti-monopolists also tended to support railroad development; corporate failures to build new trunk lines or expand rail networks were an integral part of the anti-monopoly critique. Anti-monopolists disliked "special privileges" provided by the government to private entities, but this did not mean rejecting a governmental role in the economy; anti-monopoly reform often demanded expanding governmental combinations with private businesses and corporations. The fight against monopoly did not reflect resistance to commercial prerogatives and the money economy; anti-monopolists waged a many-sided struggle to gain equal access to the channels of commerce. Finally, the fight against monopoly did not grow out of a protest against impersonal rationalization of the economy; more often than not, anti-monopolists sought to bring rational system and bureaucratic order out of the real and perceived turmoil of the increasingly corporate economy.

The ways in which order and system took hold in the economy point to another tale of declension about post–Civil War society. In the usual narrative, the growth of capitalist power, and especially the managerial revolution of the corporation, imposed an iron cage of rational systems on the natural patterns of economic life, while the movements of working people arose in resistance to the juggernaut of these large-scale systems. This telling, however, underestimates the speculative disorder and mayhem that the corporate owners of railroads, banks, coal mines, and other industries imposed on the post–Civil War economy.[4]

More than that, this narrative fails to account for the role played by social movements of farmers and workers in the development of the new structural order. Under the egalitarian banner of "anti-monopoly," Grangers and their allies fought to regulate markets, straighten and widen the channels of trade, and gain equitable access to and uniform management of transportation, banking, and other essential services. Anti-monopoly was about taming the prevailing corporate chaos.[5]

I.

IN THE SPRING OF 1870, Kelley wrote to Saunders reporting that "discussions upon how to raise crops" had become "stale." All Grangers, he explained, "want some plan of work to oppose the infernal monopolies. This seems to be uppermost in the mind of every member I have conversed with. The 'how to do it,' is the rub."[6] Kelley suggested mutual insurance companies as a good place to start. But when it came to opposing monopoly, there were no simple answers. Part of what made it so challenging was that monopoly proved to be a moving target.

When James Scovel addressed the Trenton Anti-Monopoly Convention in 1865, the term "monopoly" tended to have a specific meaning. It frequently referred to a government grant of a charter or franchise providing a private company "exclusive privileges" within a given market. That was how it was discussed at the Trenton convention. "The Railroad Kings of New Jersey"—the Amboy and Delaware and Raritan Transportation Companies—held such charters, which, according to the anti-monopolists, kept rates high and fed political corruption. In granting such charters, the government was artificially creating monopoly that impeded free competition and economic growth. Breaking the monopoly system, Scovel argued, would allow the construction of competing lines, with the result "that new railroads may cover, like a net-work, the face of the State wherever the necessities of the people may require them."[7]

The critique of monopoly, however, extended beyond the exclusive government franchise. Anti-monopolists soon focused less on state charters and more on the public functions of railroad and telegraph corporations.

They argued that they were public entities because they required an array of governmental subsidies and protections, starting with land grants and rights-of-way. Moreover, they argued that they were public highways comparable to post roads, navigable rivers, and canals, and therefore should be under public control. If railroads were public highways, then the monopoly problem was less about governmental intervention in the private economy and more about the private abuses of what were public economies. Removing these abuses meant placing the "semi-public" railways under fully public state regulations.[8]

The control of the railroads by a small group of financiers provoked particular alarm. Anti-monopolists attributed the helter-skelter boom and bust of railroad development to the speculative risk taking of the financial houses of New York and London. The decisions of railway management, anti-monopolists argued, were based more on the profitability of overpriced "watered stock" and other investment schemes than on the effective transport of passengers and freight. Spikes in fares to pay investors drove off customers and left new railroads nearly deserted. Demand for short-term gain led to long-term failure. Shoddy work and lack of investment in sound roadbeds resulted in accidents and destroyed track. To satisfy investors and privileged customers, railway managers ordered trains to run faster than the track could bear, leading to yet more havoc. "The public is not only taxed to pay a dividend on the diluted capital stock," argued the anti-monopolists, "but to repair the damage done while they incur useless and wicked risks of what the western people call 'everlasting smash.'"[9]

In the summer and fall of 1867, to bring order to the chaos of the nation's railroads, anti-monopolists held conventions in dozens of cities from Belfast, Maine, to Houston, Texas. The conventions demanded a rationalized national system. The names for their system included "The Cheap-Freight Equal-Speed System," "The National Equal-Right Cheap-Freight Policy," or just "The Equal Rights Railway Plan." The conventions enjoyed support among farmers and laborers, merchants and manufacturers, and were endorsed by dozens of members of Congress from the western and southern states, as well as from New York and Pennsylvania. They were held under the auspices of a new organization headquartered in New York City.[10]

Its program was summed up in the name: "The National Anti-Monopoly Cheap-Freight Railway League, for Promoting Reform in Railway Management, by Securing EQUAL RIGHTS and Cheap Transportation, with Consequent Increased Development of Our Industrial Energies and National Resources."[11]

As the name suggests, the anti-monopolists stressed a nationalist vision focused on the growth of the national economy. The Civil War, provoked by the challenge that secession posed to national power, unleashed powerful nationalist impulses. Even in the midst of a war to restore the Union, part of this energy turned toward the conquest and development of new terrain in the trans-Mississippi West. The 1862 Dakota War in Minnesota marked one of the initial outbursts in a systematic campaign of violence and destruction that over the next quarter of a century expropriated much of the land of the western Indians. That same year, Congress passed the Homestead Act, opening up millions of western acres to white settlement. The prospects offered by the combination of the Homestead Act and the conquest of Indian land seized the popular imagination. Miners, farmers, ranchers, and speculators of every sort poured into the new territories.

All of their hopes—and with them the broader nationalist enterprise—ran along the iron bands of the railroad. But the railroad corporations offered little evidence that they were up to the task of building a rail network capable of sustaining the nationalist project. For political and ideological reasons as much as economic ones, new lines were needed to link California and the West Coast with the older states. Similarly, not only did the heavily damaged tracks of the former Confederacy need rebuilding, but new roads were needed to heal sectional divisions. Moreover, everywhere that new track might bring new farmlands, new mines, and new industries into contact with profitable markets, farmers, investors, and boosters clamored for railroad expansion. This was true not only in the new territories of the West but also in much of the Midwest and the South.[12]

The Anti-Monopoly Cheap-Freight League sought to construct such a national system. By building seven new trunk lines crossing the country, east and west, north and south, it would bring "hitherto inaccessible parts of our vast territory" into "the circle of the world's activities." It was called the Equal Rights Railway Plan because it put in place a grid of lines that would give the Texas cotton farmer and the Pennsylvania iron manufacturer equal access to national (and global) commerce. In the process, it would heal the wounds of war. As the *San Antonio Express* explained, "Reconstruction now absorbs the attention of the nation . . . but next to this great political work, comes the grand plan of *cheap-freight Railways*, which must follow reconstruction, *and bind the Nation with double bands of iron.*"[13]

The anti-monopoly plan would build trunk lines durable enough to carry the load of multiple competing carriers. It would impose rules limiting the speed of trains and requiring the construction of separate tracks for passengers and freight. It would guarantee equal freight rates per mile, without regard to the nature of the product, the size of the shipment, or the distance of transport. And all of this would be made possible by squeezing out the controlling role of the financiers and bringing a rational system to railway management. A mix of public and private investment, combined with strict limits on interest rates on the bonds issued for construction and on the profits of the roads, would put an end to the high-risk "smash" of financial speculation in the railroad business.

Railroad managers introduced new bureaucratic techniques and uniform structures of management to run their vast operations. And by such means, they brought a new rational order to the American economy. At least this is what is stressed in the usual narrative of business history. Railroad corporations, however, were also deeply implicated in crises and upheaval. In his study of the transcontinental railroads, Richard White documents the personal egoism and speculative mayhem that afflicted corporate decision making and the resulting industrial fevers and financial panics of the late nineteenth century. In so doing, White provides a valuable corrective to the usual narrative about railroad corporations bringing system and order to the economy. The other side of this corrective requires taking into account the role of reform. From the closing days of the Civil War, anti-monopolists protested the anarchy of the speculative corporate imperative. Anti-monopolists unleashed their campaigns against corporate power with the fighting words "system" and "plan." [14]

The National Cheap-Freight Railway System initially enjoyed support within the political class, especially among triumphant Republicans. The plan would splinter into competing parts as it made its way through the legislative process. Yet the fact that a proposal for a "national system" was on the political agenda reflected the postwar zeitgeist. In that regard, it is striking that Oliver Kelley, William Saunders, and the founders of the Grange initially stood aloof from the anti-monopoly agitation; supporting railroad legislation involved political entanglements that Grange leaders hoped to avoid. But when the Grange finally did take up the cause of anti-monopolism, it did so precisely in the rationalist, egalitarian, and nationalist spirit of the Equal Rights Railway Plan. [15]

II.

RAILROAD CORPORATIONS BORE THE BRUNT of the anti-monopoly critique. But for many Grangers, the term "monopolist" applied to a range of economic actors. Exactly who belonged in the ranks of "infernal monopolies" shifted according to time and place, but the usual suspects included bankers, lawyers, grain elevator and cotton gin operators, insurance agents, grain and cotton purchasers, farm machinery dealers, and local merchants. All of these were monopolists, according to the Grangers, because they disrupted harmonious business relationships and clogged the rational flow of commerce. Ultimately, Grangers viewed monopoly as an expression of class inequality, with monopolies tipping the balance between classes and interests to the detriment of the farmer.

Grangers often referred to their order in class terms, "a class organization" with the purpose of equalizing class relations. Aaron Grosh, one of the Grange founders, explained that the purpose of the organization was to make the "farming classes" the "equals of other classes in social standing and influence." The Grange lecturer Ignatius Donnelly, talking to members of the North Star Grange in St. Paul, explained that the "great object" of the organization was to "uplift your class" by "secur[ing] justice from other classes, not to oppress others but to prevent others from oppressing you." In his dramatic fashion, Donnelly told the North Star Grangers, "Society is but a struggle of . . . class against class." But despite the similarity of language, Donnelly and other Grangers mainly did not use the word "class" as a sociological concept as Marx or Weber used it. Rather, "class" was another way of saying business interest, and a business that preyed on another was a monopolist.[16]

Grangers understood that the power of monopoly rested on organization, and if farmers were to avoid being eaten alive, they needed to take up the same weapon. As the South Carolina Grange observed, "all other classes"—merchants, editors, doctors, insurance men, lawyers—engaged in "class combination and association," but when the farming class did so with "an eye to its own interests," the "merciless monopolists, shoddy sharpers and predacious predators" attacked the Grange as a criminal combination.[17] Dudley Adams, a leader of the Iowa Grange, explained much the same thing. Railroads, telegraphs, and "all business relations of civilized life," Adams noted, rested on the principle of united effort. Every other economic interest made use of this principle except the farmers:

> Merchants have their Board of Trade, Shoemakers have Knights of St. Crispin. Lawyers have their conventions, and Physicians their conclaves, where prices are fixed, and no one dare disobey the edicts of these unions. But how is it with the Agriculturalist? Alas! We have nothing of the kind. Each one is working away against all the world and against each other, unaided and alone. Immense in numbers . . . yet we are powerless. . . . The little squads of well drilled lawyers and doctors charge through and through our poor disordered mass, and freely plunder our pockets. Railroads, telegraphs, commission men, mechanics, join in the pursuit with no fear of successful resistance. Like rabbits, we are the prey of hawks by day, and owls and foxes by night.[18]

The struggle against monopoly, in the Granger worldview, involved a multifaceted resistance to economic predators of all types. Because monopoly was such a complex foe, Grangers pursued the struggle against it along multiple yet interrelated lines of attack. They looked for ways to "dispense with a surplus of middlemen" and to squeeze them out of the economy.[19] They sought to use their numbers to strengthen the negotiating power of the farming class. They built insurance companies, farm implement factories, and other cooperative businesses as alternatives to privately held firms. They explored means to rationalize national and international patterns of trade. Most famously, they demanded governmental regulation of railroads, grain elevators, and other industries.

The pursuit of economic benefits for Grange members undergirded all of these efforts. "We have got to study up some pecuniary advantages to be gained by members of the Order," Kelley wrote to McDowell in the winter of 1868. "Set your wits at work." That spring, Kelley proposed that Minnesota Grangers organize a state business agency to lease flour mills and then hire agents in St. Paul and New York City to facilitate the shipping and sale of grain and the purchase of supplies. The state's business agent system started with a far more limited arrangement involving the wholesale purchase of jackasses. But over the next several years, agents for the Minnesota Grange were negotiating with farm implement manufacturers and other industries as Grangers across the country unleashed a wave of business innovation to uproot monopoly and improve the farmers' place in the commercial system.[20]

Although the national and state organizations did what they could to guide and coordinate the process, much of the innovative energy came from the members of the local Granges. The activities of the Kendaia Grange in Seneca County, New York, reveal the far-ranging scope of the business experiments of local Grangers. In January 1874, farmers met in the Kendaia schoolhouse to charter their Grange, and over the next year business questions dominated the work of their weekly meetings. They organized a boycott of the local threshers who refused to thresh oats for less than two cents a bushel. They sent a delegate to Syracuse to arrange bulk purchases of salt and groceries. They negotiated terms with local blacksmiths. They agreed to boycott the agent of the Wiard Plow Company in favor of direct negotiations with plow manufacturers. They investigated the insurance business and drew up a policy statement for county and state cooperative insurance systems. They also debated whether to establish a Grange store to bring down the price of supplies, or if they could do the same thing by pooling monthly purchases.[21]

The Kendaia Grangers were also acutely interested in what farmers were doing elsewhere in the country. They corresponded with Grangers in Michigan, Arkansas, and other states. They organized a lecture on the business of seal farming in Alaska. When Nebraska Grangers struggled with swarming grasshoppers, the Kendaia Grangers sent fifteen dollars in aid. They took part in the National Grange's surveys of farm profitability and deliberated on national reports on "the productions of the country." The National Grange circulated lists of manufacturers and wholesale houses that agreed to sell to Grangers at reduced prices. To be effective, these price lists were "strictly confidential." But as with many other local Granges, the Kendaia Grange struggled to persuade its members to protect the "business secrecy" of these national lists.[22]

The Iowa Grange, at the center of the Grange boom with nearly a hundred thousand members, built a dense complex of cooperative businesses. They set up dozens of local cooperative stores, fifty-three grain elevators and warehouses, and a state agency trading in hundreds of thousands of dollars a year in farm machinery, wagons, sewing machines, lumber, and dry goods. The Iowa Grange also purchased the patent on Werner harvesters with the hope of manufacturing farm machinery that would cut out the cost of transportation from Chicago and East Coast factories. Financed by members' dues, the Werner harvester factory was both expensive and high risk, yet for Iowa farmers weighed down by debts on their farm machinery, it seemed worthwhile.[23]

In Illinois, the Winnebago County Grange set up a cooperative store in Rockford as a central depot for machinery and supplies. Their members embraced plans for a statewide mutual insurance company, cooperative warehouses, butter and cheese factories, and direct negotiations of shipping rates with the railroad corporations.[24] Grangers undertook similar enterprises across much of the Midwest and the West. In the South, the Virginia Grange experimented with a wide variety of enterprises, including the Patrons Bank, and Texas Grangers built some of the most successful cooperative businesses, including cotton gins and supply stores.[25]

But most Grange enterprises proved unstable. Short-term success often sowed the seeds of long-term failure. Local merchants fought the cooperative stores by undercutting their prices. National mail-order houses matched the discounts offered on the National Grange's price lists, because farmers publicly boasted of the savings they realized on these "strictly confidential" lists.[26] Lack of access to capital and business networks added to the pressure of price competition. Even many of the strongest Grange businesses could not survive the long years of economic depression in the wake of the 1873 financial panic. A series of bank failures in the Austrian capital of Vienna proved to be the start of a transatlantic financial crisis and economic depression that lasted for the rest of the decade. The collapse of the Northern Pacific Railway, which was part of Jay Cooke's banking and railroad empire, signaled a financial and industrial collapse that also wreaked havoc on the nation's farmers. In the midst of the depression, Grangers looked to Europe for an economic lifeline.

III.

GRANGERS HAD ALWAYS RECOGNIZED THE international dimensions of their project. But their interest in transatlantic possibilities grew in the depression years of the mid-1870s until they absorbed much of the organization's attention. This was the case with the national leadership, as well as among farmers in local Grange halls who "hail[ed] with joy" the prospect of international cooperative trade. Grangers turned to Britain and the Continent to bring a rational system to their cooperative enterprises, to expand the scope of the Grange's work, and to realize "direct trade"—the reconfiguration of the patterns of international trade to break monopolies and strengthen the commercial position of farmers.[27]

Edward R. Shankland, a prominent fruit grower from Dubuque, Iowa, and a member of the Grange National Executive, observed that the several hundred Grange stores in the United States were failing in their mission of bringing order to the rural market. Most such enterprises were simply joint-stock companies "pretending to be co-operative stores." This left the stores directionless, isolated, and without coordination from one store to the next. Shankland discovered the solution in the cooperative systems of England and Europe. That was where the Grange would find models for "complete organization" and "symmetrical" business systems.[28]

Shankland and his fellow Grangers were especially enthusiastic about the cooperative system built by the English weavers of Manchester. It was known as the Rochdale system, and its principles restricted shareholder earnings and devolved profits to the customers of the cooperative enterprises. The National Grange adopted these principles in the hopes that they would be widely applied to Grange enterprises. At the same time, efforts to expand the Grange itself and its organizational system did not stop at the water's edge. Transatlantic expansion would bring new energy and resources to a movement that was languishing under conditions of a long depression. American Grangers made bold plans to set up Granges to "benefit all farmers of every civilized race." As it turned out, the Rochdale model was more difficult to replicate than its American admirers had hoped. And, despite the success of Granges in Canada, the plans to build Granges among British, French, and German farmers went nowhere. Nonetheless, the transatlantic connections, at least briefly, stoked the fires of Grange enthusiasm.[29]

What's more, the Grange viewed these transatlantic connections as part of an effort to reroute the channels of international trade. In the post–Civil War years, American farmers sold into a market driven by the British and European appetite for grain for their bakeries and fibers for their textile mills. The violence of Indian removal, the Homestead Act of 1862, and the expansion of the railways combined to open millions of new acres of land to Euro-American men and women seeking to grow grains and cotton for the transatlantic market. But to sell their grains and fibers, western and southern farmers were at the mercy of railroads, ware-houses, purchasing agencies, and other businesses, many of which were based in the port cities of the Northeast.

Such patterns of trade often lay at the center of the Grange critique of monopoly. In a letter to Kelley, William Corbett, Grange supporter and editor of the Chicago *Prairie Farmer,* warned of the "monstrous monopo-lies" that were "crushing the life out of the producing classes." And none were more monstrous than the railroad corporations cornering the trans-portation routes to the European market. "You, wheat growers of Min-nesota, who pay three times as much to get your crops to New York as it costs to send it from there to Liverpool," he wrote, "feel and know that the hand of the giant oppressor is upon you." The only way out was to redi-rect the grain trade to New Orleans. "You know," Corbett wrote to Kelley, "how the monopolies scoff at and ridicule all efforts . . . to send your grain by way of the Mississippi river."[30]

For many Grangers, slipping the grip of monopoly meant using more water transport, and fewer rail lines to the northeastern seaboard, and less financing, warehousing, purchasing, and other services located in New York, Philadelphia, and Boston. They called such a reconfiguration "direct trade" because it would make international commerce more equi-table, economical, and rational. In the Midwest, "direct trade" meant cam-paigning for a water system connecting the Great Lakes with Gulf Coast ports at New Orleans or Mobile. The Alabama Grange also endorsed this system. In Georgia and South Carolina, Grangers lobbied state legislators to improve port facilities and other "direct trade" infrastructure. Califor-nia wheat growers signed on to Grange plans for "direct trade" sales and shipping, with a fleet of fifty chartered ships sailing out of San Francisco under Grange control. The Texas Grange, with strong support from the Na-tional Grange, pushed for federal subsidies for constructing the Texas & Pacific Railroad running from Midland to San Diego. "Justice to the South-ern States" demanded such a link to the Pacific, which would provide better access to the Asian market.[31]

But it was mainly the European market that seized the Grangers' attention. By bringing farmers into closer contact with manufacturers on the other side of the Atlantic, "direct trade" promised to reduce the cost of clothes, tools, and other supplies. The British Cooperative Union also saw an opportunity in such an arrangement. In 1875, the Grange and the British cooperatives came to an agreement and founded the Mississippi Valley Trading Company, soon thereafter renamed the Anglo-American Co-operative Company. The idea was that the American Grange would adopt a national cooperative system based on the Rochdale model. British and European farmers would also form their own Granges, and this transatlantic company would establish "direct trade" with British co-operatives (and other European manufacturers) and thereby reorganize transatlantic commerce.[32]

In the spring of 1876, James W. A. Wright, the founder of the California Grange, traveled to London and Berlin to work out the details. While in Europe, he met with Otto von Bismarck's ministers of education and agriculture and explained to German farmers the advantages of the Grange. He did the same with British farmers. Wright also held discussions with the leaders of the British cooperatives. He was most impressed with the numbers that they showed him. With more than four hundred thousand members, they did over sixty million dollars of business a year. As Wright put it, "What an army of consumers for our farm producers! What a host of manufacturers to help supply our farm wants!" With those numbers on their side, the Grange leadership forged ahead with their plans for reorganizing the patterns of transatlantic trade. Of course, not everyone agreed. Some Grangers feared that the Anglo-American Co-operative Company was merely a snare of British capitalists. But for the moment, the transatlantic connection looked like the answer to breaking the grip of monopoly and to realizing the Grange vision of more rational and equitable commercial relations.[33]

IV.

FOR "DIRECT TRADE" TO BECOME A REALITY, laws needed to be passed and federal funds allocated to build canals, harbors, and other shipping infrastructure. The same was true of the publicly owned trunk lines of "equal rights railways." Even cooperative enterprise needed favorable legislation to flourish. In short, the Grange's plans for restructuring the economy required political action. Moreover, political action was essential to block the growing political and economic power of the corporations. Railroad, banking, and other corporations, with their vast resources and monopoly positions, posed an extraordinary menace to popular governance. They were the source of "class legislation," a term employed by anti-monopolists to describe laws and policies that favored powerful corporate interests at the expense of equity and fairness in commercial arrangements.[34]

Oliver Kelley and his colleagues had understood from the outset the political potential of their organizational innovation. From its earliest planning stages, the Grange was to be a farmers' political lobby, focusing on Washington and with the immediate goal of enhancing the power of the Department of Agriculture. By the early 1870s, with the success of farmer candidates in the state legislatures, the Grangers had turned much of their attention to the politics of the statehouses. Yet Kelley recognized that the Grange must be political without being partisan. In some places, it would function as a party faction or a third party while denying it was either. The Grange would challenge the domination of Republicans and Democrats while making political alliances with one or the other or both. In short, the Grange engaged in an impressive array of political activism while maintaining a formal rule prohibiting the discussion of politics inside the organization. Much of this political activism sought to reorder the political economy along the lines of what they perceived as a rational and egalitarian nationalism.[35]

The Grangers kept up their efforts to make the Department of Agriculture a cabinet-level federal agency. They lobbied for "a bureau of commerce in one of the Executive Departments of the government" to gather economic statistics and regulate trade and transportation. Grangers were divided over reducing the tariff on imported goods, but they proposed a series of other tax reforms, including taxing railroad property and removing the tax exemption on church property. Many Grangers supported a federal income tax. Grangers campaigned for federal and state action to improve public education, and some of them wanted a constitutional amendment for federal funding of the public schools. They championed state college programs for agricultural research and study. They pushed for transportation and infrastructure programs, including canal and other water projects, as well as railroad expansion. They also lobbied the U.S. Patent Office, fighting the patent claims made by the manufacturers of fence gate latches, sewing machines, and other products.[36]

In September 1873, the economist Amasa Walker explained to a meeting of the Boston Grange that the solution to the nation's transport problem could be found in political action to pass laws fixing railroad rates and "building new and competent lines, at the expense of the national government."[37] However, the learned economist was behind the times, because across the Midwest and the West the Grange had already unleashed a political army in pursuit of these goals. American farmers had been demanding railroad regulation since before the Civil War, and in the early 1870s with the Grange functioning as a powerful political bloc such state regulations came in batches. The striking feature of what were known as Granger laws was their focus on the problem of uniform and equal treatment. Farmers, anti-monopolists, and Grangers welcomed the expansion of the railroad networks. From Minnesota, to Oregon, to Texas, farmers understood that their success as farmers depended on their proximity to a viable rail depot. That is why they campaigned hard to bring railroads to their districts and to make them more efficient. In doing so, they accepted the logic that railroad systems by their nature were big, powerful, and centralized. But farmers also had specific grievances against discriminatory and capricious management of the lines. And the Granger laws were regulatory steps to address such inequities.[38]

Unequal rate schedules and arbitrary treatment by railway managers caused bitter resentments among farmers, both as shippers and as passengers. Railroads offered discounted rates to the potentially most profitable customers, which tended to be big companies making big shipments. In a related pattern, shippers with large orders over long hauls often paid less per mile for each ton shipped than a farmer who sent his grain on a short trip to a port or depot. Rates on routes where two or more railroads competed for traffic were often deeply discounted compared with noncompetitive routes. When it came to passenger service, farmers resented the practice whereby railroad managers gave free passes and other preferential treatment to curry favor with lucrative customers and pliable legislators, judges, and newspaper editors.[39]

Across the Midwest and the West, the Grange campaigned for state laws to prohibit discriminatory and unequal railway rates. But as these demands translated into legislation, railway managers countered by raising all rates, which led farmers to press for stronger laws to enforce both uniform and fair rates. The Grange realized its most important victory with the Illinois railway law of 1873. The grounds for success were laid with changes in the Illinois Constitution three years earlier, which recognized railroads as "public highways." This addressed one of the key legal grievances confronting the anti-monopoly movement: railroad corporations had foiled every effort at public regulation with their claims to private rights. As the Illinois farm leader William Corbett explained to Oliver Kelley, "on the plea of public interest" state governments provided railroad corporations with charters, rights-of-way, land grants, and other favors, and "to do this, they are public corporations, acting for the public good." But once they are up and running, "this public character ceases, and railroad companies are private institutions and not amenable to Legislatures or Courts."[40]

In April 1873, a coalition of the Illinois Grange and farmers' clubs held a convention in Springfield to press the legislature for a new railway law. By July, they achieved victory with the most comprehensive railroad regulations in the country. What became known as the Illinois Granger law banned free passes and expanded regulations on grain elevators and warehouses. It gave the railroad commission the power to set a table of maximum rates for passenger and freight service and made railroad corporations that charged unfair rates subject to the charge of extortion.

But the heart of the legislation was enforcing uniform rates: charging different rates for the same service was penalized as criminal discrimination. This was the first of the so-called strong commission systems, where violations of uniform and equitable rate structures carried criminal penalties. The following year, at the high tide of the Grange's power, Wisconsin, Minnesota, California, and other states also adopted laws that barred free passes, established commissions to set rate tables, and made discriminatory rates a form of criminal extortion.[41]

Even strong commission systems, however, were only as strong as the regulators that directed them. Ignatius Donnelly belonged in the camp of the Grange minority that was skeptical of regulatory commissions because they believed that railroad corporations would bend the commissions to do their bidding. Donnelly's role in the passage of the Minnesota law was instructive. Earlier in his career, first as a member of Congress and then as a corporate attorney in Washington and New York, Donnelly put himself at the service of the railroad corporations, including the Dakota & Western, the Lake Superior & Mississippi, and Jay Cooke's Northern Pacific. The citizens of Minnesota wanted more railroad access, and Donnelly did what he could to arrange federal land grants and other government favors to make that happen. If he also profited from the process, such was the business of politics.[42]

Yet on his return to Minnesota, Donnelly was soon pulled into the anti-monopoly activism sweeping the state. Demands for railroad regulation filled the lecture halls. In 1871, Horace Greeley addressed such an event in Minneapolis. Greeley was the editor of the *New-York Tribune* and a leader of the reform faction of the Republican Party that was soon to emerge as the Liberal Republicans. He spoke "as a friend not only of the railroads in general but of the land-grant railroads in particular," which he argued now required a "reconstruction" of policy. The monopoly problem, Greeley explained, lay with the ability of "a dozen or so of railroad magnates" to consult in secret to raise freight rates. By these means, a "bevy of railroad kings have arbitrarily reduced the value of every farm, every quarter-section, every bushel of grain, in the Great West." The solution was for the state of Minnesota, "and every State, to affirm and exercise its right of fixing proper and reasonable rates of fare and freight."[43] The following year, Donnelly campaigned for Greeley's Liberal Republican ticket. By this time, he had shifted his political interest from Reconstruction and race relations to "reconstructing" railway freight structures.[44]

When Donnelly emerged as a leader of the Minnesota Grange, his critics reminded voters of his time spent as a corporate attorney and lobbyist for the railroad corporations. But Donnelly rejected charges of hypocrisy. Like Greeley and many other anti-monopolists, he viewed railroad promotion and railroad regulation as compatible undertakings. At the same time, with an insider's knowledge, Donnelly had insights into how difficult it would be to tame the railroads. He was particularly concerned about the influence of corporate lobbyists on the workings of regulatory commissions. He therefore favored regulating railroad rates by state law rather than leaving the matter to commissioners who could easily be bought. But in this Donnelly held the minority view, because most of his fellow Grangers expressed confidence in the commission system and the ability of the Grange to hold the commissioners accountable. Ultimately, Donnelly conceded to this political reality and supported the commission system.[45]

The railroad corporations dispatched an army of lawyers to slay the Granger laws. But the laws not only survived; they were vindicated when the Supreme Court handed down its decision in the celebrated case *Munn v. Illinois*. Argued in 1876 and decided in February 1877, the case involved warehouses that stored grain heading for the port of Chicago. The owners of the warehouses challenged the power of the legislature to regulate how much they charged and how they weighed and inspected the grain. The Supreme Court majority affirmed the public interest in regulating grain warehouses that performed such an important public function. Warehouses represented a new technology in the farm economy, but as the Court argued, there was nothing new in regulating a business that had such a public function. As the decision of the Supreme Court majority explained,

It has been customary in England from time immemorial, and in this country from its first colonization, to regulate ferries, common carriers, hackmen, bakers, millers, wharfingers, innkeepers, &c., and in so doing to fix a maximum of charge to be made for services rendered, accommodations furnished, and articles sold.[46]

For the Supreme Court majority, adding grain elevators and railroads to this list was in line with a long tradition. In so doing, the Court backed one of the anti-monopolists' central claims, affirming the public interest in regulating railroads and other businesses that controlled the farm economy. Farmers across the country had looked to the Grange to press for this very issue. The Granger laws had their weaknesses, not the least of which was the fact that they only regulated railroads within state lines and were ineffective when it came to interstate traffic. Nonetheless, the Granger laws marked a stunning success for the principle of equality and uniform treatment in commercial affairs.[47]

Corporate executives and their lawyers took due notice of the Grangers' egalitarian claims and introduced a novel innovation in legal argument: that state regulations violated the equal rights protections of railroad corporations. Farmers in Illinois demanded regulations to compel grain elevator companies to weigh their grain fairly and to not use their monopoly position to impose discriminatory rates. But as the corporate attorneys argued before the Supreme Court in *Munn v. Illinois*, it was the state of Illinois that was violating the equal protection clause of the Fourteenth Amendment by singling out grain elevator companies for state control. This was how Justice Stephen J. Field argued in his dissent. Most observers at the time, and the Supreme Court majority, thought that the Fourteenth Amendment left in place the right of governments to regulate properties that served a public function. But Field countered that the protections of the Fourteenth Amendment extended to protecting the private property of railroad corporations from public regulation. Field believed that the equal protection clause had "a much more extended operation than either court, State, or Federal has given it." The logic of Field's dissent was steadily gaining traction among business, political, and academic elites.[48]

The post–Civil War conflict over equality had taken on yet a new dimension. Adopted in 1868, the Fourteenth Amendment had the explicit purpose of checking the efforts of white southerners to re-subjugate the former slaves as a racial caste without equal rights or protections under the law. By 1876, when it came to protecting racial equality, the resurgent forces of white power were on the verge of rendering the Fourteenth Amendment close to worthless. Meanwhile, slowly but surely, corporate power was fashioning the same amendment into a legal cudgel to strike down regulations requiring railroad and other corporations to treat farmers fairly and equitably. This was made possible in a post–Civil War context when the question of equality had become unmoored from the problems of emancipation and racial justice. The deepest irony here is that it was the farmers' Grange that bore much of the responsibility for that unmooring.

3.

RACE AND REUNION

I N JANUARY 1866, the Department of Agriculture sent Oliver Kelley on a tour of the former Confederate states to make a survey of agricultural conditions. Shortly before Kelley's departure, President Andrew Johnson invited him to the White House for an interview. The two men had a meeting of the minds when it came to the key problem at hand. Marching armies had shattered fences, burned and pillaged farmsteads, and devastated stocks of horses, mules, and oxen. The war had also smashed chattel slavery, the labor system that had served as the engine of the southern economy over the previous two centuries.

With the end of slavery, many white observers believed that the freed people would not be productive workers without the compulsion of whips and chains. The resulting "labor problem" thereby posed the greatest obstacle to rebuilding the economies of the former Confederate states. Kelley's solution, explained during his White House visit, was to subsidize immigration by white farmers and laborers from the North and from Europe to replace the labor performed by African Americans. Johnson apparently liked what he heard. Kelley noted that regarding the "relative advantage of immigration," the president "coincided in my views."[1]

Kelley's assignment was part of a wider policy of the Johnson administration for postwar Reconstruction. Johnson had been a Democratic senator from Tennessee who owned slaves and had defended slavery against Yankees and Republicans but who also resented the power of the planter elite. He was a unionist who opposed secession and was the vice president at the time of Lincoln's assassination. As the new president, Johnson pursued a policy of national unification aimed at consolidating white power and restoring the full and equal rights of the former Confederate states.[2]

Only weeks after Johnson's meeting with Kelley, Frederick Douglass and a delegation of African American leaders arrived at the White House to press their demand for equal voting rights without regard to color. Johnson replied to Douglass and his colleagues with a self-righteous lecture about how it was the poor white farmers of the South who had been "kept in slavery" by "the colored man and his master." Justice now demanded, according to Johnson, that the state governments be in the hands of the white farmers who had been so oppressed. If white voters elected state governments that denied blacks the ballot, such were the rights of the states. In any event, Johnson told his visitors, the better option was colonization—for African Americans to emigrate "elsewhere." Douglass viewed Johnson's colonization proposal as an attempt to revive a slave owners' scheme of inequality and degradation.[3]

In his mission to the South, Oliver Kelley proved a reliable instrument of Johnson's postwar policy. Kelley visited Atlanta, Memphis, New Orleans, Mobile, and Chattanooga. To the extent he consulted with actual farmers, he reported that his attention "was devoted principally to the planters and plantations." He spent six weeks in Charleston, South Carolina, where the local rice and cotton planters welcomed him on their plantations. Cordial discussions revealed not only a common interest in Masonic brotherhood but also a common perspective about the challenges of Reconstruction.[4]

In Kelley's view, northern capitalists pursued a policy to "depreciate property in the South." The destruction of slavery had, indeed, depreciated a great deal of southern property. But Kelley showed no recognition that this had been property in human beings. Nor did he reveal any sign of interest in the humanitarian crisis facing the four million freed people, who just months before had emerged from slavery often with no property beyond the clothes on their backs. Rather, Kelley was attuned to the needs of the white farm owners. And he understood that satisfying those needs required sectional reconciliation, with "the people of the North and South [knowing] each other as members of the same great family."[5]

"The politicians would never restore peace in the country," Kelley concluded. "If it came at all it must be through fraternity." More specifically, the best hope of reunion—mending the sectional wounds of the Civil War—would be through a national fraternal organization of farmers. He proposed this idea during his stay in Charleston. He wrote to his niece Caroline Hall that such a society would help "restore kindly feelings among the people." She responded with "sympathy for the women of the South" and with support for her uncle's plan. Caroline Hall would soon become Kelley's reliable lieutenant, putting his ideas of national reconciliation in motion.[6]

Kelley went to the South to do a survey for President Johnson. He returned to Washington with a vision of race and reunion and a plan for turning this vision into a reality. Kelley avoided the white supremacist language employed by his southern president. He preferred the sentimental language of "family," "brotherhood," and "kind feelings." Yet, as with Johnson's Reconstruction policy, Kelley's idea for a national organization of farmers focused on the equality of states. And, again as with Johnson's policy, this equality rested on white solidarity and disregard for the equal rights claims of the former slaves.

As the Grange expanded as a national movement, Johnson and Kelley's views about race and reunion would be bitterly contested among black and white farmers. In the South, black farmers and their white allies joined the Union Leagues and other Republican-aligned efforts that to one degree or another defended black freedom and equal rights, but these farmers did not join the southern Grange.[7] In the North and the West, there were farmers inside and outside the Grange who continued to believe in notions of racial equality, but their views became increasingly marginalized within the movement. As a result, the most powerful farmers' organization in U.S. history to that point turned its back on the equal rights demands of African Americans and leveraged its power to defeat Radical Reconstruction and post–Civil War experiments in racial democracy.[8]

Exploring the role of the Grange in the contest over racial equality opens the door to new understandings of the forces aligned against Reconstruction. Here, too, there is a tale of declension that goes something like this. The northern upper classes supported abolition and the first steps toward racial fair play. But elite opinion makers such as Edwin Godkin, Horace Greeley, and Charles Francis Adams Jr., reflecting wider racial and class prejudices, soon had a change of heart. The power of the Grange, the militancy of the labor movement, and the political mobilization of the freed people forced a new calculation. Northern elites stepped back from Reconstruction and federal efforts to defend the political and civil rights of the former slaves in the South as they looked anxiously over their shoulders at the post–Civil War democratic and egalitarian surge among farmers and workers.[9]

Under the title "Equality," Charles Dudley Warner gave a precise expression of this view in an 1880 essay in *The Atlantic Monthly*. As a journalist, Warner first gained fame writing about his garden and his cat and would entertain a generation of readers with tales of his global travels. Today, he is best known as the co-author with Mark Twain of a satirical novel lampooning the fortune hunting and corruption that had overtaken postbellum Washington. The title of that 1873 novel, *The Gilded Age*, would later become synonymous with the inequities of late nineteenth-century capitalism. Inequality, however, was not Warner's concern.

Warner, as a person of position, raised in a prosperous New England household and educated at the University of Pennsylvania, could poke fun at the careerist, the speculator, and the money-grubber. He did so, however, for the same reason that he came to oppose equality for African Americans, women, farmers, and wage earners, because they all disrupted the natural hierarchies of the social order. In his essay "Equality," Warner argued that the "equalizing, not to say leveling, tendency of the age" was pushing society toward a dangerous uniformity as the "dogma of equality" threatened to "obliterate" necessary differences between classes, sexes, and races. This was a sentiment widely felt among northern elites who turned their backs on the Reconstruction experiments in racial equality.[10]

But this was only half of the story. The other half was that this same egalitarian surge among the working classes arose in opposition to federal Reconstruction. Most notably, the Grange played a key role in realizing a nationalist vision of sectional reconciliation. It called for fraternal goodwill across the Mason-Dixon Line and a new understanding that "recognized no North, no South, no East, no West."[11] In practice, this was an exclusive and white nationalist understanding. In the name of equality for the southern planter, the Grange demanded the former slave owners be restored to their place of power and privilege. And in the name of equality between states and sections, the Grange called for lifting the federal occupation of the former Confederacy and putting an end to federal efforts to protect the civil and political rights of the former slaves. The southern Grange organized the white planter class and assisted the Ku Klux Klan and other paramilitary organizations dedicated to the overthrow of the biracial Reconstruction governments. Meanwhile, Grangers from California to Ohio mobilized as a political bloc in solidarity with their southern counterparts.

I.

WHEN IT CAME TO POLITICS, nothing weighed on Oliver Kelley more than the post–Civil War sectional strife. The Grange, he believed, had a historic political role to play in facilitating national reunion. "In my humble opinion," Kelley wrote to his friend Francis McDowell in the spring of 1868, "this Order, with its influence, will inaugurate a party that will sweep the country of the present race of politicians. There is nothing else that can restore peace and quiet between North and South."[12] Restoring fraternity across the Mason-Dixon Line, as Kelley saw it, meant first and foremost ending the dispute about the status of the former slaves. He accused "the present race of politicians" of perpetuating the sectional divide by focusing the political debate on the terms of Reconstruction. What Kelley never mentioned, because it was so well known that it did not have to be said, is that this struggle hinged on the questions of freedom and equal rights for black Americans.

Daniel Harrison Jacques, the editor of the Charlotte, South Carolina, newspaper *The Rural Carolinian*, provided Oliver Kelley with his first opportunity to organize the Grange in the South. Like Kelley, Jacques was a displaced Bostonian. In the 1840s, he had been attracted to a Fourierist and cooperativist socialism. When he started his career as a newspaper editor in Athens, Georgia, he thought of himself as the only socialist in the state. At the time, he attributed his intellectual isolation to the fact that the "wealthy slave-holding class live in luxurious ease" and therefore "are well satisfied with things as they are." Whereas in Jacques's mind "the white industrials—(mechanics &c) are too poor, too ignorant and too stupid to be reached at all." He found the only hope in "the small class of highly educated men with some of the colleges."[13]

After the war, Jacques edited one of the rural South's most influential periodicals. *The Rural Carolinian* was the region's messenger of progressive farming. Launched in 1869, the paper campaigned for crop diversification, improved use of fertilizers, soil drainage, cooperative marketing, and replacement of black labor by way of white immigration. In the winter of 1870, *The Rural Carolinian* published a Grange circular, sparking excitement across the lower South. "I am sowing the good seed throughout this State and the South," Jacques wrote to Kelley. "I think I have set the ball in motion in Alabama, as well as Mississippi." Jacques thought that winning the South might be easier if the National Grange moved its headquarters. As he explained to Kelley, white southerners might "suspect ulterior objects in movements originating at the North, or in Washington." As it turned out, Kelley had already started plans to move the national office to Louisville to increase the Grange's appeal to the white farmers of the former slave states. No doubt, Jacques and Kelley had a point.[14]

Despite these concerns, it should be noted that the location of the national office never proved a major obstacle to the success of the Grange in the South. It might, in fact, have been an advantage, augmenting the Grange's nationalist message that struck a chord among white southern farmers. William Simmons, a South Carolina planter, was an early convert. At first he questioned the authority of "a head centre or 'National Grange,' located at Washington, to which all other Granges were subservient, and from which emanated all authority, information, and plans of work of any importance." But after taking into account the power of national organization, Simmons concluded that "being subject to the will of the National Grange . . . began now to look like an advantage, certainly like a necessity."[15]

Daniel Jacques's most important contribution to the Grange was to introduce Oliver Kelley to David Wyatt Aiken. A partial owner of *The Rural Carolinian*, Aiken was both secretary and treasurer of the Agricultural Society of South Carolina and a leading figure in the region's "progressive new school of agriculturalists." As Jacques wrote to Kelley, "No man among us exercises a greater influence." Aiken spoke Jacques's language of progress and improvement. The son of a wealthy slaveholding family, Aiken graduated from South Carolina College before taking a tour of Europe. In London, he entertained audiences of "inquisitive English males & females, whose curiosities were unlimited on any subject pertaining to the land of Slavery." On his return, Aiken devoted himself to his twin passions: scientific agriculture and pro-slavery politics. In 1858, he took part in the Southern Commercial Convention in Montgomery, Alabama, that threatened secession if Congress refused to reopen the African slave trade. In

January 1861, he joined South Carolina's Secession Guards. And when the war came, he fought at the First Battle of Bull Run, was elected colonel of his regiment in the Army of Northern Virginia, suffered a severe wound at Antietam, and recovered enough to serve at Gettysburg.[16]

Aiken received a medical discharge in July 1864, after which he began a career in Democratic Party politics. From 1864 to 1866, he served as a representative from the Abbeville district in the South Carolina legislature. Republican election victories in the spring of 1868 ushered in South Carolina's great radical experiment in racial democracy. In response, Aiken threw himself into the efforts to overthrow "Africanism and tyranny" and restore white power. "If this is to be a white man's government," Aiken demanded, "have we not the power, and should we not exercise it?" It was time to pay back the "Radical day jabbers" of the Union Leagues and to "drive them off." "Fellow planters, harvest time is here at hand," Aiken urged in an April letter to the press, a time of season when everyone knew that the only "harvest" he was referring to was in Republican and African American blood. "Threaten no one, denounce no one," Aiken advised, while issuing threats and denunciations left and right. Even compared with other Democratic Party leaders, the violence of Aiken's invective and his thinly veiled appeals for assassinations and violence stood out as "injudicious" and "extreme."[17]

The assassination of Benjamin Franklin Randolph would fix Aiken's place in South Carolina politics. Randolph, a free black man from Kentucky with a degree from Oberlin College, had arrived in South Carolina during the war as a chaplain with the Twenty-Sixth U.S. Colored Troops Regiment. He stayed on to become a leader of the Republican Party, and as the assistant superintendent of education he worked to open schools across the state. The mainly black citizens of Orangeburg elected Randolph as their state senator, and it was widely expected that he would win a seat in the U.S. Congress in the November election of 1868.[18]

On October 16, Randolph traveled to Abbeville County, where his campaign message of racial equality resonated with the freed people who made up the majority of the county's population. That afternoon, when the train he was traveling on stopped at a depot, three gunmen dismounted their horses, walked up to Randolph as he stood on the platform, shot him multiple times, and rode off unmolested. Assassins murdered several other Republican leaders in the county over the following three days. But the Randolph case drew the most attention because of his standing in state politics and because Aiken, one of the county's most prominent citizens, was charged as an accomplice in his murder.[19]

Aiken had promised that if "the hyena Randolph" set foot in Abbeville County he would end up with "a piece of land *six feet by two*.'" Aiken's murderous intent was confirmed in a deposition given by William Tolbert, one of the confessed gunmen in the Randolph killing. Tolbert testified in a separate court case involving the suppression of the black vote. He recounted how a meeting of the local Democratic Club had come to the "general understanding" that any Republican speakers in the county "were to be shot, killed, stopped." They also discussed that Randolph posed a special threat to Aiken and that as the leader of the Union Leagues in the state he must be killed. The Democrats only disagreed about the means of disposal of Randolph's corpse.[20]

Newspapers across the state published Tolbert's deposition. Democrats responded with mocking derision, while Aiken boasted of the "universal sympathy" for his cause. Arrested on murder charges, he even boasted of enjoying the sympathy of the constable and the jailer, who did their best to make sure their prisoner had "comfortable quarters" and "very excellent meals." Meanwhile, Aiken's political allies unleashed a campaign of intimidation against his accusers. The charges against Aiken went nowhere, although he never denied his part in Randolph's assassination.[21]

Even as the front pages of South Carolina's newspapers focused public attention on Aiken's role in racial mayhem and murder, Aiken calmly pursued his other passion: "agricultural progress." Toward this end, he organized the Abbeville Agricultural Society, which soon became the South Carolina Agricultural and Mechanical Society. Aiken's original plan was to build an organization from Virginia to Texas to address issues facing the planter class in the postbellum South. The planters needed more than white power; they also needed to understand such matters as the properties of guano and to acquire "chemical and scientific knowledge." Planters needed to manage their soil better, to diversify their crops, and to bring the light of science to agricultural practice.[22]

Aiken did not hesitate when in the summer of 1872 he received Oliver Kelley's invitation to join the Grange. He readily recognized the Grange's potential both for reasserting white power and for spurring agricultural improvement. Aiken responded to the "Southern Bourbons" who accused the Grange of being an "'ism' from Yankeeland" by pointing out that hats, shirts, and shoes came from the North, too, and like these practical necessities the Grange would serve a practical purpose for the southern planter. He also reassured doubters that the Grange would protect the equal rights of the southern states. Within the organization, Aiken explained, South Carolina would be "equally powerful there with the great State of New York."[23]

Aiken served as Kelley's special deputy and organized the South Carolina state Grange in 1872. The following year, he joined the national executive committee of the National Grange, and by 1875 he was the chairman of the National Grange. This was no small matter. It reflected Aiken's success in organizing the southern wing of the Grange, and with every such success Kelley's vision of sectional reconciliation on the basis of white power came that much closer to realization.

II.

IN THE FIRST YEARS OF THE 1870S, the Grange took hold and then grew quickly across the former Confederacy. South Carolina and Mississippi had two of the strongest state Granges in the country. William Saunders explained that the reason why "there is not a colored member of a Southern grange" was that the Granges "represent the wealthy planters, the owners of the farms and plantations."[24] The southern Granges also attracted less wealthy and poor white owners of middle-sized and small farms. However, they showed little interest in recruiting tenant farmers, sharecroppers, or farm laborers. Nor did the Grange organize black farmers, although nothing in the rules mentioned race or prohibited Granges from accepting black members. Some northern farm reformers even expressed hope that by enrolling southern blacks, the Grange would be able to tutor the former slaves for "duties as a man and a citizen."[25] However, despite reports of African Americans joining the movement, including a Grange in Louisiana that accepted black members, in reality the Grange, in the South as well as the North, was a white organization. The white Grange reportedly set up a so-called Council of Laborers for the black field hands who worked the farms of white southerners, but it never had a viable existence.[26]

Though white southern farmers looked to the Grange as a place for neighbors to socialize and provide one another with mutual aid, it was more than a fraternal society. They viewed the Grange as a means to build up "an intelligent, educated, and scientific class of farmers and farmers' wives." David Wyatt Aiken described education as "one of the grand objects" of the organization: "to banish ignorance from our doors, to elevate the farmer intellectually, and to teach him he has mind as well as muscle." The Grange itself served as an adult school in rural communities. Local Granges organized schoolhouse lectures on "The Best Method of Killing Cotton Worms" and "The Best Method of Hiring Freemen" and on other practical needs of "progressive farming."[27]

The Grange also served as a powerful lobby in southern state capitals for building up agricultural and mechanical colleges and departments of agriculture. Grange members viewed tax money as well spent if it went toward scientific research and higher education. But tax money for public elementary schools was different. Despite high illiteracy rates across the rural South, many white Grangers viewed public spending on education for African American children as wasteful and oppressive. Because the freed slaves had so little property, Grangers proposed taxes on dogs as a way to make African Americans pay their share of school taxes. But it was more than just money. Public schools set up by the "black Republicans," Grangers feared, were teaching black children dangerous ideas about equal rights.[28]

Like their northern and western counterparts, farmers in the South looked to the Grange to circumvent merchants and other middlemen. They set up cooperative stores and cotton gins. Texas Grangers proved especially successful in running efficient cooperative businesses. Grangers designed plans for textile mills and other industries that would put Alabama and South Carolina "in the very fore front of the manufacturing states." The National Grange's negotiations with European manufacturers also drew enthusiastic support from southern farmers. Since before the Civil War, cotton planters had been agitating for "direct trade" between southern and European ports. The National Grange reinforced that agitation with similar demands from midwestern and western grain farmers.[29] At the same time, the white farmers of the South hoped that the Grange would resolve a set of specifically southern problems. As one historian put it, the success of the Grange in the South "must be attributed largely to the sectional character of its demands."[30]

Most immediately, white farmers looked to the Grange as a means to resolve what they perceived as a labor crisis. "What we want is more labor, better labor, more reliable labor," explained a South Carolina editor, and "this can be properly regulated through the Grange order." The emancipation of the slaves, Aiken explained, and the transition of the planter from "master to employer" had exacted "radical changes . . . in [the] theory and practice of plantation economy." The planter could no longer rely on the forms of control and discipline that slavery offered. The worst of it, in Aiken's estimation, was that "the freedwomen were but idle spectators," because they sought to withdraw their labor from the cotton fields. He blamed the Radicals and their notions of equal rights for convincing black women, "these imps of feticism," that they might entertain the ideal of protection from heavy field work in the same way that many white women did.[31]

For Aiken, the labor problem required first and foremost the destruction of the Radical experiment in racial equality. Grangers usually described this in class rather than racial terms: by upsetting the racial hierarchy, Radical Reconstruction had toppled the natural order of class relationships. Dr. James Blanton, a tobacco planter and the master of the Virginia state Grange, explained that the "agricultural class" needed to act on "the just and wise principles of political economy" to restore the proper relationship between capital and labor. Radical Reconstruction had allowed labor to "control capital," "reversing entirely the general law which everywhere else obtains, that capital should control labor."[32]

Southern Grangers campaigned for tough new state laws and local ordinances to control black labor. Nightmares of their former slaves pillaging their crops, burning their barns and woodlots, and refusing to work tormented the minds of white planters. When the so-called Farmer or Grange legislatures came to power in the mid-1870s, they pushed through draconian laws directed at controlling African American farmers and laborers. The Alabama Grange, representing the planters of the Black Belt, underwrote escalating retribution against trespassing, burning woodlands, stealing crops and livestock, selling produce after dark, and violating labor contracts.[33] The Virginia Grange demanded a "comprehensive vagrant law . . . that *all* must work." Violators were to be subject to forced labor, with the state mandating "a chain gang for every county." Virginia Grangers also demanded a revision of the criminal code to make "misdemeanors and cases of petty larceny punishable by being put in the chaingang."[34] Under pressure from the Grange, legislatures from Arkansas to Georgia made stealing a chicken or pig, or small quantities of corn or cotton, grand larceny punishable by years of involuntary labor and the loss of the franchise. Severe punishment for petty crimes fed a convict lease system that provided railroad, mining, and lumber capitalists with a steady supply of involuntary and unpaid labor.[35]

Grangers accepted that slavery was dead. But white farm owners remained dedicated to close and direct supervision of the black laborers who picked their cotton and plowed their fields. That is why Grangers preferred a wage system of farm labor. The alternative was mainly sharecropping, an arrangement whereby the sharecropper worked a section of the landowners' property and received a share of the proceeds of the crop at harvest. The freed people tended to favor such an arrangement because it provided a degree of autonomy in setting the rhythms of work. It also meant white men had less direct supervision over black women, a step that the freed people valued in light of the pervasive sexual cruelty and exploitation in the time of slavery.[36]

Sharecropping, at least initially, allowed families to make their own decisions about women and children working in the fields, a point of friction that, as noted above, Aiken found a particular irritant. Aiken spoke for many white farm owners when he criticized sharecropping for establishing an unacceptable equality between the white farm owner and the black sharecropper. "When the negro becomes a copartner in the plantation," he noted, "the employer sacrifices intelligence to ignorance, judgment to vanity, and self-respect to race and color."[37] Meanwhile, Granges in Georgia and elsewhere did what they could to push wages of farmworkers "to the condition of servitude." The farmers of Alabama's Black's Bend Grange made a pact to cut the pay of their African American field hands to twenty-five cents for every hundred pounds of cotton picked.[38]

Immigration, Grangers argued, would provide the answer to the South's "labor problem." Back in the winter of 1866, Oliver Kelley discussed with President Johnson how encouraging immigration to the South would restore the region's prosperity.[39] Agricultural clubs and societies had been making the same argument. But it took Kelley's movement to make immigration a political issue across the former Confederacy. State Granges lobbied state capitols for tax and land schemes to attract northern and European immigrants to the cotton fields and tobacco patches of the South. The Mississippi Grange posted offers in Ohio newspapers of free leaseholds of forty acres of land "to every white family that will come and live there." Such immigration agitation, no doubt, served the ideological purpose of reinforcing notions of white solidarity and supremacist arguments about African American inferiority. Immigration also entered the political calculus as a possible means of diluting black votes.[40]

Usually, however, Grangers discussed immigration as a labor question. The Virginia state Grange set up the "Special Committee on Immigration" as a solution to the "unreliability and unfaithfulness of our new system of labor."[41] The wealth of the South, the Alabama Grange concluded, "will never be unearthed by African bone and muscle. . . . [A] substitute must be had; and this can only be furnished by the new fields" of the North and Europe. Aiken's Agricultural Society called on the farmers of the South, "in respect to the all-important subject of labor," to attract "foreign white labor as rapidly as possible."[42]

Aiken, however, had his doubts about white immigrants who expected to be treated as equals. He rejected the idea of "equity" between "capital and intelligence on the one hand, and labor and brute force on the other," even if the laborer in question was a German immigrant. In 1870, Aiken penned an open letter criticizing the idea of a "promiscuous social equality with strangers from any quarter." His letter drew an angry response from the German immigrant community. A decade later, he was still cautioning against equality between landowners and farm laborers, including immigrant laborers. "If any man occupies my land as my equal," Aiken warned, "he must do it after my death."[43]

A writer at *The New York Times* dubbed Aiken's views "graveyard equality" and suggested that such attitudes might deter European immigrants from making South Carolina their destination of choice. Aiken's "graveyard equality" also helps explain why he led the Committee on Chinese Immigration, "a question occupying the attention of Southern planters." By 1870, Chinese immigrant workers had completed the epic labor of the transcontinental railroad, and on the West Coast they formed a significant part of the labor force in mining, agriculture, cigar making, and other industries. A much smaller number of Chinese workers made their way to eastern shoe factories and southern sugar and cotton plantations, provoking speculation that immigration from China would soon have the same impact on the workforce of Massachusetts and Mississippi that it had on California. At least, that is what Aiken hoped. In the Chinese immigrant he looked to find the obedient laborer who would reinforce the South's racial and class hierarchies. As it turned out, it was easier said than done to replace black labor with labor from Europe or China. Immigration proved to be one of the southern Grangers' most advertised and least successful campaigns.[44]

The Grange in the southern states, as in the northern states, focused its public activity on agricultural affairs and farm life. Newspapers, especially Democratic newspapers, devoted regular columns to Patrons of Husbandry picnic schedules and the business activities of its purchasing agents, along with advice from neighborly Grangers about livestock, gardens, and homes. The Grange, after all, was an agricultural fraternal society. Yet it came to prominence at a time of extraordinary political violence. The white South refused to countenance the former slaves' aspirations for freedom and equality. The Ku Klux Klan, the White Leaguers, the Red Shirts, and other paramilitary auxiliaries of the Democratic Party waged asymmetrical warfare against African Americans and Republicans across the former Confederacy.[45]

Black observers had no doubts as to where the Grange stood in this conflict. This new secretive organization of white farmers, they believed, was part of the Democratic-KKK nexus of beatings, whippings, hangings, and shootings. African Americans would explain to those who would listen that the southern Granges "have become Ku Klux organizations" dedicated to reducing the freed people "to the conditions of servitude." When the African American citizens of Georgia petitioned Congress for arms and a militia for self-protection, they pointed to the "secret society known as the 'Patrons of Husbandry'" as a threat that "they fear intends to bear oppressively on them." As a means to justify such violence in South Carolina, Democrats spread rumors that the Republicans were encouraging black farmers to kill Grangers with "sword or club and torch."[46]

In this murderous partisan and racial context, the Grange provided a platform for the Democrats and a haven for the likes of David Wyatt Aiken and other determined (and murderous) white supremacists. In those ways, it played a key part in the struggle to restore white power. As the Alabama state Grange put it, the organization promised deliverance to its "long oppressed" members, who under the regime of Radical Reconstruction suffered "frauds, extortions and exactions, unparalleled in the history of civilized people."[47] Or, to put it in plain language, the Grange offered the "oppressed" white planters and farmers a vehicle for toppling the biracial Reconstruction governments and stripping the black people of the South of their newly won freedoms. And in doing so, it also provided the white South with a bridge to potential allies in the North and the West.

III.

IN MUCH THE WAY OLIVER KELLEY had hoped, the Grange represented a national fraternity of farmers dedicated to sectional reconciliation. The "Declaration of Purposes of the National Grange" expressed this vision in emphatic terms. "We cherish the belief that sectionalism is, and of right should be, dead and buried with the past. . . . We shall recognize no North, no South, no East, no West." This passage, along with the document's equally emphatic words about "equality, equity and fairness," expressed the post–Civil War commitments to nationalism and equal rights. These were the passages that gave the declaration its celebrated reputation as a "mighty Bible of the rights of man," passages that would be pasted into charters of farmers' organizations and other reform movements over the next half a century.[48]

For the Grange, this pairing of equality and sectional reconciliation pointed to regional realignments in the political economy. Grange leaders promised to "unite in one body the largest class engaged in any vocation" and, in so doing, "bind again the North and South in one nation, as one people."[49] In the first place, it meant removing obstacles to an understanding across the Mason-Dixon Line. The protective tariff, for example, tended to benefit the more industrial North at the expense of the more agricultural South and to set northern and southern farmers against each other depending on the products of their farms. The Grange in Michigan, where many farmers owned sheep, helped to restore tariff rates on wool in 1874. The following year, the Grange in Texas, where cotton farmers bore the burden of the tariff on industrial goods and viewed it as an obstacle to cotton exports, asked the National Grange to lobby Congress to abolish all protective tariffs.[50]

Many Grangers understood that fighting over tariff rates was harmful for sectional reconciliation and for establishing a national organization of farmers. Accordingly, the National Grange did its best to skirt the sectional minefield of tariff policy. The one tax question that the Grange did take on directly, however, was the repayment of the cotton tax. Between 1865 and 1868, Congress had imposed a tax on raw cotton. Six years after the tax lapsed, the Grange pressed Congress for sixty million dollars to repay the tax that had been collected from southern cotton growers. Grangers argued that the cotton tax was discriminatory against the former Confederate states and that repayment would help bury the sectional divisions of the past.[51]

At the same time, the Grange sought to unify the South, the Midwest, and the West against the unequal financial and economic power of the Northeast. This meant breaking the grip of the railroad corporations, and the Wall Street financiers that controlled them, over the nation's transportation infrastructure. This meant liberating midwestern and western grain producers and southern cotton growers from their dependency on dealers, agents, shippers, and manufacturers in Boston, Philadelphia, and New York. This meant challenging the power of the financial houses of the Northeast over the nation's banking and monetary policies. Equality and national reconciliation meant, paradoxically, a new sectional realignment to overcome real and perceived inequities in the post–Civil War political economy.

Significantly, this was an exclusively white vision of equality and national unity. African Americans constituted about a third of the agricultural population of the lower South and majorities in South Carolina and Mississippi. Yet African Americans were not included in the "South" for which the Grange demanded equal rights. To be exact, the Grange privileged the interests of a white South that sought to run roughshod over the rights of the men and women who had just emerged from slavery. The author of the "Declaration of Purposes" was one of the most articulate champions of this vision.

James W. A. Wright, the leader of the California Grange, was known as the "eighth founder" of the Grange because of his prominence in the organization and his authorship of the declaration. The son of a Boston missionary, he grew up in the cotton districts of Mississippi and Alabama. He was the valedictorian of the Princeton class of 1857. Serving in the Confederate army, he was hit by a minié ball at Missionary Ridge and recovered from his wounds in a Union prison camp in Nashville. He escaped from prison to Canada, ran the blockade from Bermuda, and rejoined the Confederate war effort.[52]

By 1868, Wright had made his way to California's San Joaquin valley, where he tried his hand in the insurance business. He also purchased 740 acres on which to plant cotton. Wright soon emerged as an authority on cotton growing, which was still an experimental crop in California. He was also considered an expert in the management of the Chinese laborers who picked his cotton for a penny a pound. Although this was about four times the pay of their African American counterparts back in Wright's home state of Alabama, the steep racial divide that separated "farmer" and "laborer" provided him with a familiar environment.[53]

When the Grange arrived in California, Wright quickly established himself as its leading light. As a popular speaker, he lectured his fellow Grangers on topics as diverse as the May Day customs of the Druids and the prospects for organizing Granges among the Jews of Palestine. He was viewed as an expert in national and international trade and traveled to Britain and Germany as the deputy of the National Grange to pursue negotiations for "direct trade." Wright spoke about the need to end federal Reconstruction to achieve sectional reconciliation and educated his fellow Californians on the nature of the struggle then taking place in the southern states.[54]

In drafting the "Declaration of Purposes," Wright worked closely with David Wyatt Aiken, the Grange leadership's most militant white supremacist. He also had the help of Ezra S. Carr, a professor of agriculture at the University of California. Although he was from upstate New York, Carr shared with his southern collaborators a glowing view of the model slave plantations of the antebellum past and praised the "glorious work" of the Grange to restore the South to its former brilliance. In short, the declaration might have announced the end of sectionalism, but its authorship reflected the reality that this was to be pursued on terms acceptable to the likes of Aiken and the white planter class of the South.[55]

In the reconciliatory spirit of the "Declaration of Purposes," Granges throughout the North and the West extended solidarity to the white Granges of the South. But when they did so, they mainly avoided direct discussions of race. The treatment of the sectional problem focused on equal rights for the southern planter, with little or no public mention of African American farmers and laborers. Oliver Kelley told President Johnson that the only solution to the southern labor crisis was to encourage immigration but in the public record refrained from spelling out the racial underpinnings of such a policy. In his personal correspondence, William Saunders wrote disparagingly of the "darkey" but avoided such matters when discussing Grange affairs.[56] Even Aiken, who as a Democratic politician likened African Americans to "imps" and "hyenas," skirted all race talk in his capacity as an officer of the National Grange. This silence was strategic. The Grange leadership knew that for their movement to succeed, it had to navigate potentially sharp divisions among the nation's farmers. In this regard, the so-called Negro question posed a special danger for the success of the Grange.

From Ohio to California, many Grangers were Democrats and shared their party's antipathy toward the former slaves and toward federal Reconstruction. This led Republicans to paint the Grange as merely the "offspring of Copperheadism." They made this charge against those who had been part of the Democratic opposition to the Union war effort, as well as against Democrats who expressed a variety of objections to Republicans and their interventions in the South in defense of the rights of the former slaves.[57] Democrats, meanwhile, recognized in the Grange a potential ally in the common struggle. As Manton Marble's New York *World*, the national voice of the Democratic Party, put it, "The Farmers' Granges and the Democratic Party have . . . a similar tone of sentiment, common objects, and substantially the same missions, and they must ultimately be found fighting side by side against the same enemy."[58]

The *New-York Tribune* had the same estimate of the Grange as "the new and rising political power." The Grange was laying the foundation for "a political revolution, based on the farming, planting and laboring interests." Under the Democratic Party standard, according to the *Tribune*, the Grange had the potential to "sweep the West and the South, with New York to back them." And such a Grange-Democratic sweep would validate Democratic principles of white supremacy. "A government that could emancipate four millions of slaves and elevate them suddenly, with all their ignorance, to the full privileges of citizens," the *Tribune* predicted, "can hardly resist the pressure of the many millions of farmers and working people of the white race."[59]

The Grange also enrolled many farmers who were part of the rural constituency that had supported Radical Reconstruction and equal rights protections for African Americans. This included Republicans who had been drawn to the party by abolitionism, antislavery, and the Union war effort. However, by the early 1870s a section of these Republican Grangers grew disaffected with federal Reconstruction. The national government had already done enough—too much—in defense of the equal rights of the former slaves, and now it was time to fight for the equal rights of the nation's farmers.

The Grange encouraged such disaffection. Again, as the New York *World* explained, "The new agricultural, anti-monopoly politics" of the Grange had "abruptly broken" the "line of continuity of Republican politics." The old politics based on antislavery and equal rights for the former slaves were now "defunct." In this context, the New York *World* predicted, the Grange had the power "to control the country" if it "sufficiently shatters and disorganizes the Republican party in the West." Republican editors accused *The World* of misreading the farmers. But by this time, the Liberal Republican revolt had opened fissures within Republican ranks, and the Grange threatened deeper disorganization, playing its part in the shifting Republican policy toward the South and racial equality.[60]

IV.

NO ONE BETTER REFLECTED THIS Republican evolution, and the way that it intersected with the trajectory of the Grange, than Ignatius Donnelly.

He was born and raised in Philadelphia and headed west as a young man. When he arrived in Minnesota in 1856, much like Oliver Kelley, he threw himself into land speculation, scientific farming, and politics. Donnelly and John Nininger, the brother-in-law of the territorial governor Alexander Ramsey, drew investors to establish Nininger City on the Mississippi River south of St. Paul. Despite good political connections, the Nininger City project suffered fatal wounds from the panic of 1857.

Donnelly turned to politics and made a promising start. He opened doors by switching his allegiance from the Democratic to the Republican Party, and in 1859 he successfully ran for lieutenant governor on the same Republican ticket that put Ramsey in the governor's office. When the Civil War began, Ramsey was back in Washington, leaving Donnelly in St. Paul to issue the proclamation of April 16, 1861, mobilizing Minnesota's volunteers for the Union war effort. Donnelly stayed safely away from conflict except in August of the following year, when he rode with the troops to put down the Dakota Sioux. Donnelly parlayed his brief role in this other front of the Civil War into a run for a seat in the U.S. Congress.[61]

Donnelly campaigned as a free-labor, antislavery Lincoln Republican. On the eve of the November 1862 election, he told the voters of his faith in a "free government" of "absolute equality . . . without regard to all accidents of birth, education, wealth or intelligence."[62] Voters sent him to Washington for the next six years, where Donnelly would emerge as an outspoken champion of the nationalist ideals of freedom and equality that Lincoln articulated at Gettysburg. In an 1864 address to Congress, Donnelly explained that the Civil War had produced a new framework in which the nation was "absolute, supreme, [and] irresistible" in relation to the power of the states. "We have found that State lines, State names, State organizations," as he put it, "are in most cases, the veriest creatures of accident." At the same time, Donnelly demanded the use of that national power to protect the freedom of the four million Americans emerging from slavery. "A great nation," he said, must protect the former slaves from their "late masters" and "a prejudice bitterer than death."[63]

In a January 1867 speech in the House of Representatives, Donnelly renewed his call for federal action to defend "equal justice and equal rights" for the nation's African American citizens. Anything short of that meant "four million human beings consigned to the uncontrolled brutality of seven other million human beings! The very idea is monstrous."[64] Later that year, Donnelly supported a Minnesota referendum to extend the suffrage and political equality to the state's black citizens. It was narrowly defeated. Larger majorities of white male citizens in Ohio, Kansas, and Connecticut also rejected black voting rights at this time. In 1868, voters in Michigan and New York did the same. These northern ballots in favor of political inequality signaled the type of racial contradictions that would soon take their toll on the Radical project.[65]

Donnelly's Republican career, meanwhile, was rudely interrupted. Alexander Ramsey, now a U.S. senator, fearing that Donnelly might emerge as a competitor, supported a rival Republican against Donnelly in his 1868 reelection campaign. The seat went to the Democrat, and Donnelly began a search for a new political home. He briefly dabbled in a third-party coalition with the Democrats. He also moved away from his previous views about federal Reconstruction. Donnelly came to the conclusion that the question of black rights in the South had been resolved; the pressing question of equality now turned on the restoration of political rights to the former leaders of the Confederacy. Donnelly noted in his diary, "Not a single issue of the many which agitated us in the past remains alive today—slavery—reconstruction—rebellion—impartial suffrage—have all perished." In their place, he believed, was a new struggle of economic interests pitting western farmers against eastern bankers and industrialists. With "the struggle between the North and the South having ended," Donnelly predicted that "the struggle between the East and West commences."[66]

Donnelly wrote these notes at a moment when the "old" questions burned hot enough. The freedom and equal rights of the former slaves hung in the balance across the former Confederacy. The former slave owners and other white southerners engaged in a remorseless struggle to again subjugate the African American population. Only three years earlier, Donnelly had denounced the prospect of black southerners "being consigned to the uncontrolled brutality" of white southerners as a "monstrous" idea. Now the Ku Klux Klan—with their targeted assassinations and other means of terror—knocked on the door to deliver such a consignment. Yet Donnelly was not listening, or he did not want to hear.

The contradictions of racial politics in northern places such as Minnesota had caught up with Donnelly. In the process, his ideas about equal rights became untethered from his earlier commitments to racial equality. Donnelly moved in the same direction as other Republican exiles and dissenters. He shared the views of his friends Carl Schurz and Lyman Trumbull, senators from Missouri and Illinois, and other leaders of the Liberal Republican movement in opposition to the economic and Reconstruction policies of the Grant administration. When the Liberal Republicans nominated the *New-York Tribune* editor, Horace Greeley, for president in 1872, Donnelly had his doubts, because he disliked Greeley's support of the protective tariff. But Schurz, Trumbull, and Greeley all spoke Donnelly's language when it came to Reconstruction.[67]

As far as the Liberal Republicans were concerned, the passage of the post–Civil War constitutional amendments made federal Reconstruction both unnecessary and unconstitutional. The Fourteenth Amendment equipped African Americans with citizenship and "equal protection of the law." The Fifteenth Amendment gave black men equal suffrage. The nation had already done enough. With "perfect equality" realized, Lyman Trumbull reasoned, if black citizens had a complaint, they could appeal to the courts. Carl Schurz argued that it was Reconstruction that violated equal rights because it disenfranchised leaders of the former Confederacy. In a campaign speech in Ohio, Horace Greeley put these two claims together to argue that "there is no longer reason for contention concerning the rights of black men," because now the positions had been reversed, and it was time to demand that "the white men of this country shall have equal rights with the black men."[68]

At the same time, the Liberal Republicans and other critics of the Grant administration attacked the sincerity of the Republican Party's commitments to racial equality. The Republicans, they argued, were masters of corruption who saw federal Reconstruction as an opportunity for lucrative railway contracts and monopoly dealings and who manipulated the black vote for their own fraudulent aims. These charges had a self-serving purpose. To be politically successful, the Liberal Republicans needed a bloc with the Democrats, the avowed party of white supremacy. To make such a bloc more palatable to disenchanted Republicans, it was important to emphasize Republican fecklessness when it came to black rights.

The reality, however, was more complicated. Some Republican constituencies did, indeed, show little concern for the fate of the former slaves. But during the 1870s and beyond, many Republicans, for a variety of reasons, and often in vacillating and conciliatory ways, held to their commitments to equal rights for African Americans and to the need for federal action to protect those rights.[69]

Most important, the Republican Party remained the political home for many African Americans who understood the lack of viable political alternatives. In 1864, Frederick Douglass described the Democratic Party as "our bitterest enemy" and as "positively and actively reactionary." He also noted that "the Republican party is negatively and passively so in its tendency." Nonetheless, as the crisis of Reconstruction unfolded, African Americans, from political leaders such as Douglass to local activists in rural districts of the South, had reasons to stick with the Republican Party. As for the Liberal Republicans, the implications for the cause of racial justice were clear enough. Douglass viewed such movements as "impudent frauds, devised by demagogues for corrupt purposes."[70]

V.

WITH THE LIBERAL REPUBLICAN COLLAPSE after the 1872 election, Donnelly found new opportunities in the Grange tide sweeping Minnesota. A dynamic and entertaining speaker, he was soon the main attraction on the Grange lecture circuit. Oliver Kelley thought that it was money well spent to pay Donnelly the handsome sum of forty dollars plus expenses for each lecture.[71] Donnelly's fame as the author of popular (and mainly fantastical) books on a wide range of subjects—from the ancient civilization of "Atlantis," to proof that Francis Bacon was the true author of Shakespeare's plays, to the futuristic dystopia of a global oligarchy—was still in the future. But on the lecture circuit, he had already earned a reputation for his intellectual scope and his ability to light the imaginative fires of his audience. He transported his listeners to the big possibilities awaiting them.[72]

In one of his stump speeches, for example, Donnelly spelled out the advantages of a plan for a vast canal project linking Ontario's Georgian Bay with the Gulf of St. Lawrence. Shortening the distance between Duluth and the Atlantic by way of such a canal would only cost twenty-four million dollars, a bargain as Donnelly explained, given that it would "put the Atlantic at our very door," make "practically an air-line" to New York and Liverpool, and provide "FREE WATER COMMUNICATION WITH THE EXTERNAL WORLD." The first result of the Georgian Bay canal, he assured listeners, would be a 50 percent boost in the price of a bushel of wheat. Donnelly was not the only Granger to make big promises about big canals. But perhaps no one could do so with such élan. In one such lecture, a newspaper reported, Donnelly "took his seat amid a perfect storm of shouts" of approval.[73]

Grange activity in Minnesota crested in the summer of 1873. Rural picnics pulled together thousands of Grangers to hear Donnelly and other lecturers speak on the needed reforms of the day. In his diary, Donnelly described a procession in Northfield that stretched for one and a half miles—an "immense gathering" of "twenty-two granges with banners and regalia." They gathered under the Grange motto: "Equal and exact justice for all, special privileges to none!" For Donnelly, this slogan had now been set free from the problems of racial equality and justice that had been at the center of his congressional career. The other banners and flags lofted by the Grangers made it clear that "equal and exact justice" was about regulating railroads and pursuing anti-monopoly politics. Only ten years out from Gettysburg, the equal rights revolution had taken a sharp turn.[74]

Donnelly explained the historical meaning of this turn in a lecture he gave to a thousand farmers gathered in a cool glen on a hot July day. The local Granges in Mower County, Minnesota, had invited Donnelly to speak on the need for a new political party. His speech drew a parallel between antislavery and anti-monopoly. Just as "anti-slavery sentiment gave birth to a new party, the anti-monopoly sentiment would likewise give birth to a new party." Slavery involved robbing the labor of "a people living a thousand miles away," Donnelly noted, but corporations were now robbing "*our own industry.*" "In the great war we fought for our brethren now we must fight for OURSELVES." "The old issues concerned black men," Donnelly told the gathered farmers, "the new issues concern white men."[75]

The push for a new anti-monopoly party opened a rift within the membership. The two sides were ably represented at the 1873 meeting of the Minnesota Grange. The grand master of the state Grange, George Parsons, was a loyal Republican who insisted that the organization stick to its constitutional obligation to steer clear of politics and focus on crop statistics, road improvements, and other needs of the farmer. Donnelly countered that for the farmers to get the government measures they needed, they had to harness the "irresistible power of the ballot box." He reassured his audience that where the Grange constitution banned the discussion of political questions, the purpose was only to prevent a certain type of discussion. "It was meant to prevent E. F. from calling G. H. an 'Abolitionist,' and G. H. from calling E. F. a 'Copperhead.'" In other words, the constitution banned political discussion of race and section. At the same time, discussing politics in the "broad sense"—that is, relating to "political economy" and "the science of government"—was not only allowed, according to Donnelly, but obligatory.[76]

Parsons and his allies attacked Donnelly for dragging the Grange into partisan political schemes. Donnelly fired back that it was the Republican Parsons who was the narrow and petty slave to his political party. The big political promise of the Grange, Donnelly insisted, was not to "convert men into Republicans or Democrats" but to "*swallow all the political parties.*" The Grange would bring about a "universal party," which Donnelly defined as "the party of the people of the West, the planters of the South, and the poor men of the whole nation."[77] Exactly why the "planters of the

South" deserved special designation within this "universal party" he left unexplained, but this was another way of advocating for a "universal party" that included only the white South.

Donnelly and his supporters won the argument. They took effective leadership of the Minnesota Grange, and their new Anti-Monopoly Party made its first electoral campaign in the fall of 1873. In practice, the campaign amounted to negotiating fusion agreements with the Democratic Party to run joint tickets to defeat Republican candidates. The agreements produced mixed results at the polls. The election sent Donnelly to the state senate at the head of a bloc of Granger legislators. But the governor's office remained in Republican hands, because a popular Republican candidate won over much of the farm vote with his support for regulating railroad corporations.[78]

The Anti-Monopoly Party was essentially the Grange by another name. But it also drew the support of political factions of disaffected Republicans, including supporters of the short-lived Democratic-Liberal Party. Republicans reportedly made up four-fifths of the party's founding convention. The Democratic-Liberals showed little interest in railway regulation, trade, or monopoly and focused their attention on the Grant administration's southern policy and defeating federal Reconstruction. Making use of the equal rights language of the Republican Party from which they had recently decamped, the Democratic-Liberals called for "perfect equality before the law for all persons, without regard to race, color or political opinion." At the same time, they demanded an end to the "plunder" of the "corrupt rule of carpet-bag politicians" and the need to restore "home rule" to the South.[79]

Donnelly led the Grange into the Anti-Monopoly fusion with the Democratic-Liberals and soon thereafter enmeshed the Grange with the Democratic Party itself. This last step brought accusations of betrayal, egoism, and unprincipled ambition from some of his Grange allies. The accusations, however, were inspired more by electoral setbacks than by principles. Donnelly had a restless mind and an outsized ego. But from the outset, he made no secret about the logic of his political strategy. The political turn of the Minnesota Grange was premised on a vision that the political power of the farmers would topple the doubly corrupt Republican rule of monopoly and federal Reconstruction. And in one form or another this meant a Grange-Democratic bloc. Minnesota Grangers understood this. So did political observers across the country as the Grange emerged as a rising political force.

VI.

IN 1873, JAMES DABNEY MCCABE, an author who ten years before had won acclaim in the South for his play *The Guerrillas*, extolling slavery and the Confederate war, wrote a history of the Grange with the stirring subtitle "The Farmer's War Against Monopolies." Within a year, McCabe predicted, this war would give the Grange sufficient political power "to decide the majority of the popular elections throughout the Union."[80] It would be difficult to measure the accuracy of McCabe's prediction. But there is no question that the Grange had struck on a powerful political formula: the Grange-Democratic bloc that Donnelly had put together in Minnesota was replicated in a variety of forms from California to Tennessee. Political observers predicted that a Grange-Democratic combination would "revolutionize" Kansas. In Indiana, too, Grangers threatened to "throw Indiana to the Democrats." Such assumptions were based on simple calculations. The Grange counted among its members a sizable bloc, and in places a majority, of rural constituents. As the chair of the Georgia state Grange, Leonidas Livingston, put it, Grange members would "vote en masse" to advance their collective interests. And when they did so, they would constitute a "fearful power in politics."[81]

The direction in which Grangers would cast their votes seemed clear enough. The Grange vote would be a vote for railroad regulation, soft money, direct trade, and other economic measures in the interest of farmers. The farmers' movement, observed the New York *World*, "brings our politics to the class of ante-war questions—questions connected with the business, finances, and industrial interests of the country, a class of questions" that *The World* claimed favored the Democrats. At the same time, it was widely assumed that white Grangers would cast their votes for white supremacy.[82]

The editors of *The New York Herald* predicted that the Grange would "carry off the balance of power" in favor of the Democrats. But rather than emphasizing economic questions, the *Herald* editors focused on the Enforcement Act, or Ku Klux Klan Act, of 1871, which gave President Grant the power to employ federal troops and to suspend the right of habeas corpus to suppress the paramilitary groups that used murder and intimidation to deprive African Americans of their equal rights protections. The *Herald* described the Ku Klux Klan Act as a "pernicious measure of sentimental equality" that hung "like the sword of Damocles over the heads of the white race." The Grange opposition to the "odious" bill, the *Herald* predicted, would swing the elections in the direction of the Democrats.[83]

The Democrats did, indeed, sweep the 1874 congressional elections and take control of the House for the first time since before the Civil War. The reasons for their sweep are multiple and complex. The terrible economic suffering as a result of the panic of 1873 meant this was an uphill election for incumbent Republicans.[84] Racial politics also played a role, and prior to the vote observers predicted that the Grange's hostility to federal Reconstruction would influence the outcome. As expected, Republicans did poorly in Granger strongholds such as Indiana, Illinois, and Ohio. In Iowa, much as in Minnesota, the Republicans resisted the Grange-Democratic coalition, but they did so with their candidates joining the Grange and adopting Grange principles.[85]

The Democrats picked up ninety-four seats in twenty-eight states, and nowhere did they gain as many seats as in Pennsylvania. The industrial crisis had weakened working-class loyalties to the GOP. At the same time, the Grange tapped into farmers' discontent with the Republican administration, including its Reconstruction policy. Victor E. Piollet served as the Pennsylvania state lecturer of the Grange and led the efforts at Grange-Democratic fusion. A rural entrepreneur with holdings in railroads, lumber, and other industries, Piollet had served as Polk's paymaster of the army during the Mexican War and had worked in James Buchanan's presidential office. After the Civil War, he rose to prominence in the state Democratic Party as it campaigned against ratification of the Fifteenth Amendment. Democrats argued that giving African Americans the vote meant that white people were being subjected to "hellish iniquities of their oppressors." "This Is a White Man's Country!" was the fighting slogan of the Pennsylvania Democrats.[86]

Piollet, however, grew tired of the Democrats' political weakness in the state and looked to the Grange as a way to gain political traction. Republican editors warned Pennsylvania farmers during the 1874 election campaign that the Grange had fallen prey to "the Democratic manipulators" and to the political ambitions of Piollet. Using the Grange as his base of support, Piollet gained the Democratic nomination for state treasurer and mobilized the Grange behind the Democratic ticket. Some members of the Grange protested Piollet's use of the organization for such partisan purposes. The protest only went so far, however, because Piollet would soon be elected master of the state Grange.[87]

For Piollet and his supporters, Grange-Democratic fusion demonstrated broadness of mind, not partisanship. It signaled a rejection of sectional division under Republican policies of Radical Reconstruction, because only with the Democrats could the Grange realize its vision of fraternal solidarity across the Mason-Dixon Line. "The Grange movement was an aftermath of the Civil War," as the official history of the Pennsylvania Grange explained. "As war had alienated from each other people of the North and South, this Order magnified fraternity. The god of hate was to give way to a great National Brotherhood." The official history failed to mention that this "National Brotherhood" rested on the bitter alienation of the races, while the "god of hate" unleashed the furies of white supremacy.[88]

Grange-Democratic fusion proved more complicated in Ohio because of the strength of Republican opposition among the seventy-five thousand members of the Ohio state Grange. Yet in Ohio, too, the Grange would align with the Democrats to support national reunion on terms favorable to the white planters of the South. In February 1874, inspired by the "Declaration of Purposes," the delegates to the Ohio state Grange sent telegrams to all the state Granges of the southern states. "Seven hundred brothers and sisters send you their greetings," the Ohio delegates wrote, "and clasp your hands in faith, friendship, and justice." "Greetings of ten thousand patrons," the white planters of the South Carolina Grange responded, "may our Order bind us together more firmly than the ties of blood." The Tennessee, North Carolina, and other Granges responded similarly. The Ohio Grange recorded this event in its official history, underscoring that the Grange "was the first organization after the Civil War that brought the North and South together in fraternal good will."[89]

In pursuing these political goals, the officers of the Ohio Grange had to proceed with tact and care to avoid partisan warfare within their own ranks. A September picnic of the Knox County Grangers revealed how the nonpartisan and nonpolitical Grange moved into the center of the political storm. The master of the Ohio state Grange, Seth Ellis, repeated the usual homilies about keeping partisan politics out of the organization. At the same time, he told the picnic audience that it was the duty of Grangers to fight against political corruption all the way to the top of the Grant administration. He was then joined on the speaker's platform by Governor William "Old Bill" Allen, a former Peace Democrat, fierce opponent of federal Reconstruction, and self-styled Jeffersonian. Answering the governor, Columbus Delano, Grant's secretary of the interior, brought up the recent history of slavery, reminding the assembled Grangers that Jefferson worked his farm with slave labor. There were some among the Knox County Grangers who supported Delano, but "Old Bill" Allen proved to be the crowd favorite.[90]

What happened at the Knox County picnic was repeated in Grange meetings, rallies, and picnics across Ohio in the lead-up to the 1874 elections. The party that controlled the Grange would gain the farm vote, or so partisans believed. In this contest, the Democrats, with their attacks on the Grant administration and federal Reconstruction, usually gained the upper hand. Republican newspaper editors grew discouraged and started to dismiss Grange picnics as "Democratic pow-wows." They were not far from wrong. The rural vote moved toward Ohio's Democratic Party, which gained seven congressional seats in the November election.[91]

VII.

IN THE SAME ELECTIONS OF 1874, the Democrats in Tennessee swept the state, and in doing so, they also sent the former president Andrew Johnson back to his old seat in the U.S. Senate. The Grange played a special role in the remarkable revival of Johnson's political career. The Civil War divisions between secessionists and unionists had fractured the political landscape, leaving the former president subject to charges of "treason to the Democratic Party" and "hostility to the South." The Grange would provide Johnson with a new political home.[92]

Other politicians of the day used the Grange to advance the aims of their party, but Johnson's party was the Grange. Johnson remained both a nationalist and an egalitarian in the narrow sense that he resented the privileges and place of the planter elite. He also clung to his belief that it was a mistake to give black men the vote, and continued to advocate that African Americans should be separated from white Americans "by voluntary colonization or otherwise."[93] In Tennessee, the owners of the big estates were less interested in the Grange than they were in South Carolina and the lower South, with middling white farmers making up the core membership of the Tennessee Grange. This was Johnson's natural constituency, and the Grange made for a good ideological fit. He lectured widely across the state extolling the virtues of the Grange, defending its class-based organization, lauding its policy of nonpartisanship, and ascribing to it principles of "equal and exact justice."[94]

During the election campaign of 1874, Johnson built a common front against federal Reconstruction. From his Grange platform, he worked to bring together factionalized Democrats and disaffected Republicans. The unification of the white vote allowed the Democrats to win nine of ten congressional districts. Afterward, Johnson appealed to the legislature to reward his services by returning him to the U.S. Senate. He promised to go to Washington as an independent, representing "Union sentiment" and "ante-bellum Democracy." Back in the Senate, Johnson gave but one speech. It was in March 1875 during a special session to debate the crisis in Louisiana, where white supremacist militias battled the Reconstruction government. Johnson denounced the "Caesarism" of President Grant for employing federal troops to New Orleans to stem the violence. That July, a stroke killed the sixty-six-year-old Andrew Johnson. Within months, intimidation and violence by white citizens killed Louisiana's brief Reconstruction experiment in multiracial democracy.[95]

VIII.

IN LOUISIANA AND ACROSS THE LOWER SOUTH, the Grange played its part in the mobilization that toppled the Reconstruction governments. On January 16, 1875, the Louisiana state Grange met in a joint session with its Mississippi counterparts and issued a statement on the political crisis gripping their states. The statement took the form of an appeal to the "trusty, hardy and worthy sons of toil in the West and the North," that their Grange brothers and sisters might come to their aid in the struggle to restore white power.[96]

The authors carefully worded their appeal for a Grange audience by framing it in terms of anti-monopoly. But in this case, the "huge monopol[ies]" they sought to overthrow were the multiracial governments of Radical Reconstruction. As for proof of their tyranny, the appeal repeated the regular litany of charges used to discredit the Radical administrations: that they were governments of "satraps" and "speculation" whose taxes were "eating up what little property the late unhappy war left us" and which had brought federal troops into "our houses, homes, and legislative halls." "Give us peace," read the appeal of the southern Grangers, "and rule of the people."[97]

At the time when the Louisiana and Mississippi Granges issued this appeal, the forces of white supremacy were unfolding what turned out to be their final push for power. There was nothing peaceful about it. Nor was it about "rule of the people," but about white rule and racial subjugation.

In Mississippi, white power groups escalated their war of terror. The Democrats had decided to carry the election that fall "peacefully if they could, forcibly if they must." In September, they killed more than thirty Republicans at a political rally in the "Clinton riot." With state troops and local militias no match for the White League paramilitary forces, the Republican governor, Adelbert Ames, asked President Grant for U.S. troops to restore the peace. But Grant refused the request.[98]

The Republican president and his advisers calculated that the use of federal troops to protect black rights would come with a political cost. They had their eyes on Ohio and feared that federal action in Mississippi might tip the tightly contested gubernatorial election in that vital swing state. In Ohio's elections of that October, the Republican candidate Rutherford B. Hayes squeaked out a narrow victory. A year later, as he sat in the White House, Hayes remarked that "had troops been sent to Mississippi in 1875," his Democratic opponent "would have been Governor of Ohio and probably now President of [the] US." In the Mississippi election the following month, the Democrats swept to power with a massive show of rifles and even cannons to drive Republicans and African Americans from the polls.[99]

The Democrats in Louisiana and South Carolina followed the same "Mississippi Plan" of capturing the ballot through the use of the bullet. White League violence paralyzed the Republican Party and its elected officials. In both states, the elections of 1876 resulted in the Democrats setting up rival administrations intent on dislodging Republican governments, governments that then appealed to the new Hayes administration for federal protection. But Hayes was not about to listen. Well before his election, he had doubts about federal protections of black rights and favored a "let-alone policy" toward southern affairs.[100] Once in the White House, Hayes argued that removing U.S. troops and allowing "home rule" in the South would promote peace and reconciliation. In terms of practical results, however, under the president's new "Southern Policy" the Democratic paramilitaries drove the Republican Party in the South to the edge of extinction, terror overwhelmed the last of the multiracial democratic governments, and national unification would take place on the basis of white power.[101]

There is no single explanation for why the Republican leadership adopted such a "Southern Policy." A number of developments ultimately compelled Hayes and the other Republican leaders in Washington to abandon their earlier commitments to protect the freedoms and equal rights claims of the former slaves. Imposing a settlement on an irreconcilable white South beset the national government with constitutional, political, and military quandaries. Solutions grew more difficult as the financial corruption surrounding the Republican politicos eroded the political legitimacy that the Republican Party had gained from its victory in the Civil War. And to compound the Republican political crisis, the terrible depression of the 1870s turned public attention to economic and financial matters. Meanwhile, northern business and political elites looked to renew alliances with their white counterparts in the South. These same elites grew cautious about the democratic franchise. They came to distrust the black vote in the South in much the same way as they were alarmed by rising farm and labor movements making use of the ballot box to push for Granger laws and other "class legislation" to check corporate power.[102]

All of these developments came together to unravel the political agreements that had sustained the earlier national efforts to defend the hard-won freedoms of the people emerging from slavery. The Grange leveraged its power toward such an unraveling. It adopted a vision of national unification based on subordinating the equal rights of the former slaves to the principle of equal rights among the states. In key states, it formed a nonpartisan voting bloc dedicated to such a vision, and in doing so, the Grange provided an ideological way station for Republicans moving to the Democratic position. Moreover, unlike the Liberal Republicans, who shared a similar critique of federal Reconstruction but whose appeal focused on urban professionals and businesspeople, the Grange organized large swaths of the rural majorities across the North and the West.[103] In short, the collapse of federal Reconstruction cannot be told without taking into account the Grange and how the most powerful mass organization in the country's history to that point weighed in on the pivotal issues of black rights, states' rights, and national reunion.

IX.

THE NATIONAL CONFLICT OVER RECONSTRUCTION came to a resolution of sorts with the contested elections of 1876. Across much of the former Confederacy, Red Shirts, White Leagues, the Ku Klux Klan, and other paramilitary auxiliaries of the Democratic Party employed violence and terror to drive African Americans and Republicans from the polls. Ballot rigging, vote buying, and fraud also marred the voting. When the votes were counted, the Democratic candidate for president, Samuel Tilden of New York, claimed victory. But the Republicans disputed the results in South Carolina, Louisiana, and Florida. At an impasse, Congress appointed a commission that gave Rutherford B. Hayes a majority of Electoral College votes. To calm the political waters, Hayes suggested a new policy of noninterference in southern affairs and of retreat from federal support for Reconstruction—a new policy that is often referred to as the Compromise of 1877.

When Hayes took office, South Carolina was in the throes of political crisis. An event known as the Hamburg Massacre had set the tone of political combat. In July 1876 in the small town of Hamburg, several hundred armed white men had confronted a small group of African Americans who made up a company of the National Guard. The attack on the National Guard unit left seven dead and initiated an exceptionally brutal election campaign. Supporters of the Democratic candidate for governor, Wade Hampton, employed the "Shotgun Plan" of intimidation and bribery to defeat the Republican incumbent, Daniel Chamberlain. After the polling, the two camps contested the outcome. Chamberlain held on to the governor's office, but only with the protection of federal troops. Hampton refused to recognize the Republican administration and set up a separate government. On orders from President Hayes, the federal troops were removed on April 10, and the next day Wade Hampton was the undisputed governor of South Carolina.[104]

Hampton's rise to power marked a turning point. He had been one of the South's richest planters, owning three thousand slaves. During the war, he financed his own "Hampton's Legion." He fought at Seven Pines, Fredericksburg, and Gettysburg and ended the war as a celebrated general of the Confederate cavalry. Because of his prominence as a Confederate hero, Hampton's entry into the 1876 governor's race signaled a bold message of white southern defiance. Hampton carried with him the hopes of redemption of white power. Across the former Confederacy, redeemers raised the slogan "Hampton or Hell!"[105]

The huzzahs for Hampton echoed beyond the South. Three weeks after Hampton's victory, some fourteen hundred Grangers met for a May Day picnic in Colusa, California. The speaker was the master of the state Grange, James Wright, who praised the new Southern Policy of President Hayes that allowed Wade Hampton to redeem South Carolina for white power. "We, my fellow-Patrons," Wright told the assembled Grangers, have "a special reason to rejoice" at the success of Wade Hampton, "a brother in our cause." He explained that Hampton himself was "a prominent Patron of Husbandry" whom he had met two years earlier at a Grange meeting in Charleston.[106]

On December 2, 1878, President Hayes invited a delegation of the National Grange to the White House. During his term as Ohio's governor, Hayes had felt the strong political pressure of seventy-five thousand Grangers in the state, including the prospect that Grangers would vote as a bloc in opposition to Radical Reconstruction. As president, Hayes understood that Grangers represented a constituency that must not be ignored. Hence the invitation to the White House, where William W. Lang of the Texas Grange thanked Hayes for his part in bringing "law, order and good government" to the South: "As farmers, coming from all sections of this vast country, we tender hearty approval of your efforts to restore peace and self government to every portion of the country." At which point the Texas Granger proceeded to warn the president that the Grange would "exceedingly regret any departure from what is termed your 'Southern Policy.'" The meaning was clear enough. Any renewed federal effort to protect the civil and political rights of African Americans in the southern states would be met by a renewed challenge from the white farmers of all states.[107]

The election of 1876 and the advent of Hayes's Southern Policy marked a triumph for the Grange vision of sectional reconciliation. It also brought Grange leaders to prominent places within southern politics. In that same election of Ku Klux Klan terror, David Wyatt Aiken leveraged his position as the master of the South Carolina state Grange to win a seat in the U.S. Congress, where he served until his death in 1887. During his tenure in Washington, Aiken fought legendary battles to extend the rural postal service and other measures to expand federal power for the benefit of the farmer. He put at the top of his legislative agenda the Grange demand to elevate the Department of Agriculture to full cabinet rank.

At the same time, Aiken doggedly resisted any federal measures to protect the equal rights of African Americans. He proved a fierce opponent of federal power when it involved voting rights, education, public works, or any other measure that might undercut white power. Aiken also pressed the sectional demands of the South. He lamented the weakness of the "'Copperhead' branch of Northern Democracy" in Washington, where too many Democrats supported pensions for Union soldiers (but not for southern veterans of the Florida and Mexican wars), failed to promote former Confederate officers in the U.S. Army, and rejected candidates from the South for president.[108] Significantly, Aiken's militancy for southern rights and his passion for white supremacy proved no obstacle to maintaining his celebrated status within the Grange. In 1885, the National Grange nominated Aiken to serve as the U.S. commissioner of agriculture. And on his death in 1887, the Massachusetts Grange memorialized Aiken as a close friend who over the years as a member of Congress "never relaxed his vigilance or devotion . . . to the interest of the farmers of the land."[109]

The Grange had propelled Aiken, Hampton, and other white planters to electoral success. Once in office, many of them found a comfortable home in the refurbished and reinvigorated Democratic Party of white supremacy. As they consolidated their political base, some southern

Grangers saw less need to reach out to northern and western allies. Talk of sectional healing lost some of its appeal, because in the redeemed South of white supremacy Grange leaders often no longer felt the same compulsion to temper their language or avoid a full-throated defense of the Lost Cause.

During the week before the visit to the White House, the National Grange held its twelfth annual meeting in Richmond, Virginia. It met in the House of Delegates—the same building that not so long before had served as the capitol of the Confederacy. Dr. James Blanton, a tobacco planter and the leader of the Virginia state Grange, welcomed the delegates with a militant speech about the noble and majestic cause for which Virginia had fought in the Civil War. Secession came, he explained, because "love for the Union" had given way to the "deeper, stronger, and more fervent love for equity, justice, liberty."[110]

Blanton proceeded to lecture the assembled Grangers on the "crimes of the deepest dye" that "fanatical zealots" had unleashed against Virginia and the South. They had waged a "cruel and desperate war," "stripped [the South] of her property," and subjected the South "to all the horrors of a most wicked despotism." Just in case any of the delegates missed the point, all the enemies of "equity, justice, [and] liberty" happened to be northern and western critics of slavery and southern race relations. Blanton concluded his speech with a "battle cry" against any future such enemies: "Eternal enmity to all who would pollute with hostile touch the sacred ark of our liberties."[111]

Seth Ellis of the Ohio Grange was assigned the pitiable task of responding to Blanton's welcome. He did his best to flatter his host while gently reminding the delegates, "We come on an errand of peace. We have no animosities to heal. We have only love in our hearts." But such "love" talk had lost much of the power it once had. The Grange's vision of sectional reconciliation had won a stunning victory with the elections of 1876 and the toppling of the last Reconstruction governments. In turn, at least for many white planters and farmers of the South, victory had robbed the Grange of its essential appeal.[112]

Oliver Kelley was in Richmond at the time of the convention but refused to attend the proceedings. By this time, his restless energy could no longer be contained within the organizational restraints of the Grange, and he had moved on to new ventures in Florida. Back in Minnesota, his daughters did what they could to keep up the Itasca farmstead as a family summer home. Kelley, meanwhile, set up the northern Florida town of Carrabelle, which he named for his niece Caroline Arabella Hall, and devoted his talents to an unsuccessful career in Florida real estate speculation. He moved permanently to Carrabelle in the fall of 1877, only months after the defeat of Reconstruction in Florida and the redemption of white power.[113]

PART II

WOMEN'S TEMPERANCE

4.

SEX EQUALITY

IN THE EARLY WINTER OF 1875, the U.S. Congress grappled with the vexing question of what should be done about the racial mayhem in Louisiana. In the lead-up to statewide elections, the White League and other Democratic paramilitary groups had unleashed a torrent of violence against black voters and Republican leaders. When federal troops intervened in the ensuing political crisis, Democrats in Congress cried foul. The Democrats had just regained a congressional majority, and in this instance their protests were joined by a growing number of Republicans. In January, Carl Schurz, a Republican senator from Missouri, submitted a resolution condemning the use of federal soldiers in New Orleans as "repugnant to the principles of constitutional government."[1]

The Senate resumed debate about Schurz's resolution on Monday morning, the first day of February. Thomas Norwood, a Democrat from Georgia, read a protest from the Georgia state legislature against the federal action in New Orleans for subjecting the "oppressed people of Louisiana" to a "galling military despotism" and violating the equal rights of the states. The former Confederate states, the Georgians argued, were entitled to self-government and "perfect equality," because "each State is the equal of, and is entitled to all the rights and powers to, each and every other State."[2]

The Louisiana Republican senator Joseph Rodman West responded to such claims with an exposition of the political "violence, murder, and killing [that] prevailed throughout the State." West recounted the history of the Colfax massacre, where, two years before, "one hundred men were slaughtered, and slaughtered simply because they were maintaining their right to their own political opinions";[3] the Coushatta massacre of August 1874, in which the White League "hacked to pieces" six Republican officeholders; and the attacks of the following September, "where some fifty or sixty lives were sacrificed" to intimidate African American voters. Senator West promised the Democrats of his state "fair and equal justice" if only they would accept the laws of the land rather than being "a party of murderers."[4]

While the senators debated the deadly business in Louisiana, their eyes turned to a Senate page as he dragged onto the floor of the chamber a large roll of papers tied with blue ribbons. The papers were thousands of petitions collected by the newly formed Woman's Christian Temperance Union (WCTU) asking Congress to outlaw alcoholic beverages in Washington, D.C., and the U.S. territories. Annie Wittenmyer, the president of the WCTU, had collected the petitions to bring the women's campaign against alcohol into the halls of the national legislature. Senator Oliver Morton of Indiana agreed to give her a hand, and during a break in the action he presented the petitions signed by Wittenmyer and her co-worker Frances E. Willard, along with what Morton claimed were "100,000 other persons."[5]

In truth, about half that number of people had signed Wittenmyer's petitions. And hers was not the only temperance memorial presented to the Senate that day. Wittenmyer's petitions, nonetheless, had their significance. Women had inserted this memorial into the men-only world of congressional politicking, and the massive roll of petitions attested to its backing by a broad social mobilization. This was a sign of things to come. Less than three months earlier, the WCTU had held its founding convention in Cleveland, Ohio. But it would soon emerge as the most extensive and powerful women's organization in U.S. history. It would couple the political demand for prohibition of alcohol with the demand for women's right to vote. It would not stop there but press an array of issues pertaining to sexual equality within the family, community, workplace, and broader society. It also took up questions of national power and equal rights among regions and states. Unlike the Grange, the WCTU organized among racial minorities, had African American members, and actively engaged the problems of racial equality. But it did so within a white nationalist framework of sectional reconciliation that, like the Grange, recognized "no North, no South, no East, and no West."

I.

THE WCTU EMERGED OUT OF THE Woman's Crusade against the evils of the liquor trade. In December 1873, Dr. Diocletian Lewis, a Harvard-educated homeopathic doctor, gave a lecture in the western New York town of Fredonia calling on women to take action to protect themselves and their children from the dangers posed by alcohol. Dr. Lewis had given much the same lecture hundreds of times during the previous twenty years with minimal results. But in Fredonia, it provoked action, with two hundred women descending on the local saloons. Through song and prayer, they hoped to convince drinkers and saloon keepers of the sinful nature of their ways. The women of Fredonia then proceeded to organize the first Woman's Christian Temperance Union. Dr. Lewis then traveled to Hillsboro, Ohio, where he gave the same lecture, and the women of Hillsboro responded with an even more determined effort to close down the local liquor dealers. In the next weeks and months, the Woman's Crusade spread across Ohio and beyond.[6]

The crusade protested hotels, saloons, restaurants, drugstores, and other businesses involved in selling alcohol. The immediate goal was to compel proprietors to sign a pledge to forswear the sale of alcoholic beverages. The crusaders organized elaborate street theater of marches and prayer vigils, often gathering on the curbside in front of the offending business to sing psalms and recite Bible verse. In Hillsboro and a number of other small and medium-sized towns, they scored well-publicized victories and claimed that 281 saloon keepers had agreed to sign their pledge. The crusaders also set up vigilance committees to make sure the pledges were kept. In one case, women took axes to the barrels of an Ohio liquor dealer, filling the gutter with whiskey and gin. But it should be noted that—unlike Carry Nation, who some thirty years later wreaked havoc on saloon property with her famous hatchet—the crusaders wielded their axes with the owner's blessing. As news of the crusade spread, women took to the streets in more than nine hundred communities in over thirty states and territories.[7]

The Woman's Crusade drew wide popular support. *The Ohio Farmer*, the Cleveland newspaper of the Ohio Grange, reported that "the war against whisky is extending all over the land," with "thousands of homes" already "made brighter by the great warfare" against the liquor trade. Although the initial burst of activism eventually ran its course, the crusade had demonstrated women's potential power in the nation's political life. Frances Willard, who at the time served as the dean of women at Northwestern University, had never before cared about temperance, noting that it was "a question with which I had nothing to do." But the Woman's Crusade convinced her that the struggle against the liquor trade was the vital challenge that the women of the country faced. "There is a war [over the saloon] in America, a war of mothers and daughters, sisters and wives," Willard observed. She predicted "an irrepressible conflict" over the liquor trade that would be waged across the nation's political battlefields. Prayers and emotional appeals might play their part, but the conflict would be decided in the trenches of election campaigns and legislative action, "a war," as Willard put it, "to the knight and the knife to the hilt."[8]

Activists gathered at Chautauqua in upstate New York in August 1874 to lay plans for channeling the energy of the Woman's Crusade into a national organization. The following November, several hundred delegates and observers from sixteen states gathered in Cleveland for the first national convention of the Woman's Christian Temperance Union. The convention endorsed the methods of the crusade: employing prayer and emotional suasion to win both drinkers and providers of drink away from their ways. But from the outset, it was clear that the WCTU would be going into politics. Its founders drew up its organizational scheme on the basis of congressional districts in the hope of optimizing its political impact, reflecting the expectation that the war on the liquor trade would ultimately focus on the national legislature. The convention's political demands included a congressional investigation of the liquor trade, bans on intoxicating beverages at governmental functions, and temperance education in the schools. Soon thereafter, the WCTU collected the great roll of petitions demanding prohibition in the nation's capital and the territories that would be delivered to the floor of the U.S. Senate.[9]

In the ensuing years, the WCTU's legislative agenda would cover a wide field of reforms, from women's suffrage to the eight-hour workday. But prohibition—governmental action to suppress the manufacture, distribution, and sale of alcoholic beverages—always remained its "ultimate goal."[10] The women of the WCTU did not come up with this idea, but they built on a history of temperance politics that stretched back into the early years of the Republic. Not all temperance organizations endorsed prohibition. In the 1830s, thousands of local temperance societies committed members to signing a personal pledge to abstain from drink. In the 1840s, hundreds of thousands of artisans and laborers, men and women, joined the Washingtonian organizations, most of which were similarly dedicated to individual abstinence. Prohibition, nonetheless, was always an undercurrent of the temperance movement.

Maine adopted the first statewide prohibition in 1851, and over the next four years twelve other states across the Northeast and the Midwest followed suit. The porous enforcement of these so-called Maine Laws meant that they failed to put the liquor trade out of business. The poor results led many voters and state legislators to reconsider prohibition laws.[11] But with the close of the Civil War, the temperance movement gave prohibition a new life. In 1869, the Independent Order of Good Templars (IOGT), whose ranks had boomed to several hundred thousand members, provided the base for the founding of the Prohibition Party dedicated to government action against the liquor trade.[12] During the late 1870s, the IOGT and the WCTU would forge a functioning alliance behind prohibition. But by this time, the IOGT had lost much of its momentum as the WCTU arose as the country's most powerful temperance organization.

The WCTU, however, was unlike any previous temperance organization because it was also the nation's largest organization of women. The Washingtonians had their female Martha Washingtonian auxiliaries. The IOGT accepted women on at least a nominally equal footing, permitting women to speak in meetings and hold office, although one IOGT member would recall that women's role was "to be seen, not heard." In the WCTU, by contrast, women were the only voting members and officeholders. By 1890, with some 150,000 dues-paying members, the WCTU had more than ten times the membership of the largest women's suffrage organization of the day, the National American Woman Suffrage Association, and more than seven times the membership of the General Federation of Women's Clubs.[13]

The WCTU was by far the biggest and most influential women's organization of the post–Civil War decades. Here it needs to be noted that the Protestant churches had more women members, and their female foreign mission societies might have been larger than the WCTU. But the WCTU was an autonomous, ecumenical, and political association in a way that the Methodist Home Missionary Society, for example, was not.[14] At the same time, the WCTU took on a missionary role and had ties with the churches. Most members of the WCTU also belonged to one or another of the Protestant denominations, and they used their church connections and networks to build their organization. Yet the autonomy of the WCTU was one of its most significant features: it guarded its independence from the churches and brought women together across denominational boundaries. With an eye to ecumenical equality, every WCTU organization from the top down had vice presidents from each of the denominations of their members. A small union in Londonderry, Pennsylvania, for example, appointed a Presbyterian, a Quaker, and a Methodist as vice presidents.[15] Among their responsibilities, the vice presidents cultivated ties with their churches, which was not always a simple proposition given that some church leaders disagreed with prohibition and still others disapproved of an organization of women taking part in politics.[16]

Evangelical work to save souls for Christ was one mission of the complex and multidimensional undertakings of the WCTU—wielding scripture in "a direct attack against the *sin*" of intemperance. They called this "Gospel Temperance" because drinking could only be cured with "the same basis of treatment as any other sin."[17] But it turned out that was just one of many cures. Much of the work of the WCTU focused on public health and was done in the name of "hygiene," "scientific temperance instruction," and a variety of other scientific, medical, and educational rubrics. These ideas about sin and health often fit comfortably together within the temperance movement. Dr. Lewis, in the speeches that had launched the Woman's Crusade, combined Gospel teachings and medical expertise. The WCTU did the same. Moreover, the WCTU steadily moved toward the position that Christian work meant treating alcoholism as a social problem and a medical disease. True, "intemperance, or the predisposition to intemperance, may be a disease, very likely it is," the WCTU would argue, but it was also "a malady of the mind," which only Christ could cure.[18]

This public health orientation placed the WCTU within the broad currents of late nineteenth-century reform. In historical memory, especially in light of the disastrous results of national prohibition during the 1920s and early 1930s, temperance and prohibition are linked with nativist bigots, religious cranks, and oppressive law enforcement. In 1956, Upton Sinclair, the author who half a century before had brought to national attention the poisons in the nation's meat, wrote *The Cup of Fury*, exposing the alcoholic poisoning of the American mind. Sinclair's fiery temperance tract seemed out of place by the mid-twentieth century, when the ties between prohibition and most other social reform movements had been strained or severed.[19] But in the heyday of the WCTU, the idea of unleashing the power of government to combat the liquor trade was widely understood as being of a piece with other reforms to make society better. Indeed, the WCTU would take up causes such as banning child labor, enacting an eight-hour workday, removing toxic chemicals from medicines, abolishing convict labor, and funding public education—all for the public good.

Members of the WCTU had other motives, too. Many of them were the wives of ministers, lawyers, doctors, and managers, and as part of the professional and business classes they looked to prohibition to control and supervise employees, servants, and other members of the lower classes. Moreover, the WCTU was composed of churchgoing Protestant women, and its struggle against beer and whiskey often fused with anti-Catholic and nativist agendas. And by its very nature, the campaign for prohibition fed the spirit and methods of vigilantism and police repression. This was apparent even with the Woman's Crusade, which employed vigilante committees and the Pinkerton National Detective Agency to enforce anti-liquor agreements. And it was not just alcohol and narcotics. The WCTU's Department for the Suppression of Impure Literature, for example, served as a citizens' auxiliary to local, state, and federal censors. In a number of ways, the WCTU was, from the outset, class-bound, sectarian, and repressive, but that was not the sum total, because it was also expansive, open-minded, and even emancipatory. Such was the conflicted nature of post–Civil War social reform.[20]

II.

ANNIE WITTENMYER, THE FIRST PRESIDENT of the WCTU, exemplified this conflicted nature. A committed Methodist, she tended to be rigid in her religious and moral judgments, and she had little use for women's suffrage or some of the more expansive reforms that Frances Willard and other WCTU leaders would come to embrace. Two groupings emerged within the leadership, with the "conservatives" aligning with Wittenmyer and the "liberals" with Willard, or at least this is how Willard and her supporters characterized the division. A WCTU member from a "lonely little farm house" in Jonesville, New York, wrote to Willard to criticize Wittenmyer's "very conservative views."[21] But Wittenmyer was also deeply committed to public service and to women's active and courageous engagement with the problems of the world. Her experience during the Civil War made her particularly well suited to organize a national voluntary association of women dedicated to prohibition and public health.

When the first wounded arrived in camps near her home in Keokuk, Iowa, in the spring of 1861, Wittenmyer threw herself into the work of collecting and distributing supplies for sick and wounded soldiers. The Iowa state legislature appointed her the state agent of the Sanitary Commission. She wrote letters to women across the state urging them to organize local aid societies and gather supplies that she delivered to the field hospitals at the front. Wittenmyer later moved from the Sanitary Commission to its partner the Christian Commission, which together represented the largest and most highly organized philanthropic effort in U.S. history, undertaken "in a purely Federal and national spirit." Bringing a system to the kitchens of the military hospitals is where Wittenmyer made her main contribution to the war effort. Patients in military hospitals faced hunger and death as a result of the prevailing chaos of food delivery and preparation. Wittenmyer attacked the disorganization and imposed a system called "Special-Diet Kitchen Work" that provided for detailed record keeping and a division of labor to meet the specific dietary needs of individual disabled and convalescent soldiers.[22]

Wittenmyer set up over a hundred hospital kitchens in all theaters of the war. She organized a corps of women to direct the distribution of supplies and preparation of meals with military efficiency, which in the large hospitals provided more than a thousand special meals three times a day. These women "were *not cooks*," she insisted, because "they only superintended the work." Wittenmyer served close to the front lines from Vicksburg to Petersburg, followed Sherman to Atlanta, and won the support of General Grant and other military officials. She navigated the political bureaucracy and gained allies in Washington. By the closing months of the war, her system for feeding sick and wounded soldiers was adopted by the Sanitary and Christian Commissions and by the officers and surgeons of the U.S. Army.[23]

After the war, Wittenmyer put her organizing skills to work as a founder of the Methodist Home Missionary Society. Her role in the Methodist home missions gave her another leading role in a sprawling and complex organizational system. She also edited the Methodist newspaper *The Christian Woman*. Wittenmyer's accomplishments provided her with perfect credentials to serve as the first president of the WCTU. Many other women activists in the temperance movement had also volunteered in the Sanitary and Christian Commissions, as well as in the home missions and other work of their churches. These experiences helped to shape a WCTU cadre of women trained in efficiency and organization, committed to public service, and energized by the post–Civil War nationalist ethos.[24]

The WCTU's highly complex organizational system resembled bureaucratic structures of railroad and other business corporations. But it is not clear how much was copied from the corporate model, because in the post–Civil War decades the industrial corporation was itself still taking shape and readily borrowing from organizational systems devised elsewhere, including within reform movements.[25] The WCTU's system had several guiding principles. The first of these was the importance of a national center that could forge the movement into a national political movement. At the same time, the WCTU emphasized equality of rights of the state WCTUs, with each state union sending a vice president to the national organization. And in the name of states' rights, the state unions were allowed to go their own way on a number of key issues.

This structure of the WCTU resembled that of the Grange with its focus on a national head and equal rights for the states. But in practice, the Grange's national office was never as strong or effective as its founders had hoped it would be, whereas the WCTU's national officers exercised extraordinary power. This difference was reflected in the press of each organization. The Grange relied on a network of state and regional rural newspapers, most of which were edited by allies and friends of the Grange. The WCTU had state and local newspapers, too, but they paled in significance compared with *The Union Signal*, the WCTU's newspaper that was edited by the national office and that had a hundred thousand subscribers. Willard described the weekly *Union Signal* as the national organization's "field piece that is fired 52 times a year." The national officers also directed the Woman's Temperance Publishing Association, which produced twenty-four books and two million leaflets annually, as well as periodicals for children and for German readers. The WCTU planned and eventually built a national headquarters in Chicago to serve as "the temperance mecca of the continent."[26]

III.

THE DYNAMISM, CHARISMA, AND TALENTS of Frances Willard gave the WCTU a unique dimension compared with the Grange and other voluntary associations of the time. The founding convention of the WCTU in 1874 elected Willard to the position of corresponding secretary, and she quickly gained recognition for her magnetic oratory, breadth of vision, organizational skill, political talent, and unlimited energy. She succeeded Annie Wittenmyer as president in 1879 and would remain the WCTU's guiding force until her death nineteen years later. A Japanese woman from Tokyo addressed Frances Willard as "the Queen of Love, and President of Reformers."[27] Many American women expressed much the same. They called her "Saint Frances," hung her picture in their homes, and had streets, schools, and buildings named after her. In the broad orbit of public opinion, Frances Willard would emerge as the most celebrated woman of her generation.[28]

Born in 1839 near Rochester, New York, and raised in Oberlin, Ohio, and then on a farm in Janesville, Wisconsin, Willard came of age in the same middle-class, Protestant, and Republican milieu as many other WCTU members. But in other ways, she was an odd fit. From the time of her youth, she went by the name Frank and bridled against doing the girls' chores on the farm. Her sister warned the sixteen-year-old Willard that she must not appear "strong-minded" when she was saddened that her brother went off to vote and she could not. This was the moment she first realized the constraints on her own political ambitions.[29] Willard joined the Methodist Church of her family. But she wore her Methodism lightly, learned from the Buddhists, Quakers, and Catholics, and embraced expansive and liberal notions of spirituality. Willard read fiction, political economy, and natural science and graduated from a small women's college in Evanston, Illinois, where her parents and siblings had also made a home.[30] When the Civil War came, her instinct was to volunteer as a nurse with the Sanitary Commission. She shared the strongly pro-Union and Republican sentiments of her father, who, nonetheless, persuaded her to stay home and pursue her teaching career, a career that brought her to eleven different institutions in six cities and towns.[31]

In 1868, Willard and a companion set out for a two-year tour of Europe. They made extended stays in Rome and several German cities and took trips as far as Moscow and Cairo. Willard visited sights associated with her literary and political heroes and threw herself into the study of language and art and everything the Europeans could teach her about social reform and the "woman question." These two years abroad shaped her cosmopolitan outlook. And she would later make frequent references to her transatlantic experiences to take the nativist sting out of the temperance message. In the face of charges that the WCTU's campaign against the saloon was anti-German, for example, Willard recounted in an address to the Illinois Senate that she had "lived in Berlin, Dresden, and Leipzig," where she had "enjoyed many a beer garden," and only later did the force of argument convince her of the dangers of drink. Even then she had her doubts about legal proscription. As a friend from Paris reminded her, enforcing total abstinence appeared "inconsistent with the charity and the liberality of the Gospel."[32]

Willard returned to Evanston with worldly knowledge that was much in demand in the field of women's education. She was offered the presidency of Evanston College for Ladies, where she learned about organization and put in practice her ideas about women's empowerment. When her college was absorbed by Northwestern University, she became a professor and the university dean of women. Despite her accomplishments and reputation, Willard soon concluded that the male-dominated world of academia offered her narrow choices and possibilities. She resigned from Northwestern and months later threw in her lot with the newly formed WCTU.[33] Nothing in her life would have pointed to temperance work. But temperance work and the WCTU unleashed her enormous talents and allowed her to pursue her long-standing interests in women's rights and politics. Willard adopted a blistering schedule on the lecture circuit. In a given year, she would travel tens of thousands of miles to give hundreds of lectures in every corner of the country. And she did so while writing, editing, politicking, and directing the national office of the WCTU.

Willard held the reins of power within the organization. In 1883, she submitted a proposal to make this power nearly absolute: a system of "bureaus" covering organization, lecturing, the press, and the other essential work of the WCTU, with "all of these under the special control of the National President."[34] No leader could have asked for more authority. The bureau proposal was tabled, but Willard did just as well without it, effectively setting the agenda and calling the shots within the organization. She defined the WCTU's political vision and strategy, made key organizational decisions and appointments, packed conferences and other decision-making bodies with her loyalists, and showed little tolerance for critics who challenged her leadership.[35] But Willard also knew when to hold the reins loosely. She crafted an organizational structure that allowed enough autonomy to satisfy a membership with an array of priorities and concerns. At the same time, her own political agenda continued to expand as she pushed the WCTU to plunge into the great political conundrums of post–Civil War equal rights.

Frances Willard's "Do Everything" policy was perhaps the clearest expression of her organizational ideas. "Do Everything" meant that each local union made its own decisions about what type of work it wanted to do. It might focus its energies on educating children or prisoners about the dangers of alcohol, or on fighting tobacco or prostitution. This allowed flexibility for a small union with minimal resources to focus its energies, whereas a big and active union might engage in a variety of undertakings. According to Willard, "Do Everything" represented a combination of "*laissez-faire* principles" and "state rights," as opposed to the "uniformity of organization and method" and the strong "central power" that Annie Wittenmyer's presidency supposedly demanded.[36] But "Do Everything" did not mean *do anything*. Rather, it meant working within a highly centralized structure of choices. By analogy, it was like the menu of individual choices offered by Wittenmyer's centralized system of hospital kitchens; "Do Everything" meant picking and choosing among the WCTU's departments of work.

By the early 1880s, the national WCTU had thirty or so departments that organized each front of its activities. A growing number of these departments focused on issues other than temperance: women's suffrage, child labor, factory conditions for women, narcotics, tobacco, prostitution, prison conditions, and other social questions. Each state WCTU had corresponding lists of similar departments, with the local unions then choosing from among that list of options. The departments, meanwhile, were directed by a system of superintendents. Originally, the WCTU, like most voluntary associations, conducted its work through committees, but in the name of efficiency and accountability Willard replaced committees with individual superintendents. Appointed and empowered, a WCTU superintendent directed the work of the entire department. The "Do Everything" policy, then, functioned within this top-down system of departments and superintendents.[37]

IV.

DESPITE ITS RANGE OF ACTIVITIES, the WCTU focused its attention on the danger of alcohol. Why the danger appeared so threatening at that moment in history is not readily obvious. People had been drinking alcoholic beverages for millennia. In the early years of the nineteenth century, the consumption of countless barrels of hard cider and spirits made for a level of intoxication that would never be matched; the United States was what historians have described as an "alcoholic republic."[38] By the 1830s and 1840s, alcohol intake fell steadily as temperance movements grew in strength. Consumption rose again during the post–Civil War prosperity, but with significant changes in what people drank and where they drank it. The biggest shift was the rise in the popularity of beer. The other shift was from drinking at home or on the job to drinking at the neighborhood saloon, a saloon that was supplied by large-scale liquor dealers and big consolidated breweries.[39]

These changes in drinking habits and the rise of a "liquor interest" spurred the temperance cause and at least in part explain why prohibition would capture the attention of the country's most powerful women's organization. The agitation against the big breweries and liquor associations fused with the broader equal rights demands against monopoly. The WCTU framed its struggle against the liquor trade in the same terms employed by Grangers and other anti-monopolists in their critiques of railroad, banking, and other "interests" plundering the citizens and corrupting the political process. The president of the Minnesota WCTU, Mrs. S. H. Barteau, attacked the liquor traffic as a "money monopoly" that made three times as much as the nation's bakers and "five times as much as would clothe the whole population of the United States."[40]

"The immense amount of capital invested in the liquor traffic," and its relation to "our agricultural and general business interests," explained the editors of *The Signal*, the WCTU newspaper, was a problem facing "all classes in our communities." John McDonald's *Secrets of the Whiskey Ring* compared "illicit whiskey frauds" to the Crédit Mobilier railroad-financing scandal and provided a "chain of evidence" of liquor corruption through the halls of power and right up to President Grant. Inside her copy of this exposé, Willard made a note of the wine served in Grant's White House.[41]

At the same time, the WCTU viewed intemperance as an industrial problem requiring industrial organization. Workers who drank were undisciplined and dangerous employees who posed a threat to public safety. The WCTU set up an array of committees targeting workers in transportation, timber, mining, and other industries. Under the Committee of Work

Among Railroad Employees, for example, the women of the RRWCTU No. 9 met with workers in the roundhouses of the Baltimore and Ohio Railroad. They also met with the president of the railroad, the banker John W. Garrett, who was "hearty in his endorsement" of the WCTU's efforts and who banned liquor sales at the stations on his railroad. The organizational system put in place for this regulatory effort mirrored a corporate structure, with the women of the WCTU, and their amazingly titled Committee on Inducing Corporations and Employers to Require Total Abstinence of Their Employees, bringing their own bureaucratic sensibility to the task at hand.[42]

The WCTU's industrial temperance work aimed at improving discipline, morale, and safety. And its campaign for enforced abstinence was a potentially draconian weapon in the hands of corporate managers over their employees. But this was not only about labor control from above. The WCTU also recognized the "inherent antagonism between labor and liquor" and increasingly looked to labor organizations that, for their own reasons, promoted discipline, order, and temperance among their members. By the mid-1880s, the WCTU combined with the Knights of Labor to promote temperance as a labor reform, just as the WCTU supported the eight-hour day, child labor laws, and other regulatory measures of the labor movement.[43]

The popularity of the saloon as the site for drinking, rather than the home or workplace, turned the light on another threat. The liquor trade menaced the home and the women and children inside it. Unlike railroads, steel producers, or other interests, the liquor interest sold a poison that not only ruined the minds and bodies of drinkers but also wreaked a special vengeance on their wives and children. This was the WCTU's core argument: the most vulnerable victims of the liquor trade lived in the homes of intemperate men. The saloon exacerbated the inequalities between wives and husbands. Mothers and their children suffered the beatings of men returning from the saloon in an intoxicated rage. The saloon took food out of the mouths of mothers and daughters and sons when husbands spent their wages on beer and spirits. And these familiar inequities served as a point of departure for the WCTU venture into the wider field of women's equality with men.

V.

TO SPEAK OUT IN FAVOR of sexual equality was a bold and, for many people in post–Civil War America, unwomanly and unpopular thing to do. To avoid the stigma attached to women's rights advocacy, the WCTU wrapped itself in the language of human equality. In 1879, Frances Willard wrote that the concern of temperance women was "not the 'woman,' but the 'human' question." She later explained that the human question was "deeper, higher, and far more sacred." Zerelda Wallace, the president of the Indiana WCTU, would similarly tell a national temperance convention in 1881 that the proper term was "Human Rights" for what was "ignobly called 'Woman's Rights.'" By the end of the 1880s, Willard would speak more directly about women's equal rights, but she continued to emphasize human rights "as our deepest motive." Over a hundred years later, Hillary Rodham Clinton would use similar words at a world conference on women in Beijing, stating, "Women's rights are human rights." For Willard and Clinton, the interconnectedness of women's rights and human rights was the same. But whereas Clinton looked to unabashedly affirm women's equal rights claims, Willard asserted them obliquely. Or as she put it, "A reform often advances most rapidly by indirection."[44]

For Willard and the WCTU leadership, women were too dutiful, noble, and self-denying to merely work for their own rights rather than to prioritize the rights of children, the next generations, and a wider humanity. The women of the WCTU, they argued, were only entering the political fray and claiming rights to do battle with a liquor business that was poisoning their families. This oblique argument for women's rights played a key part in the WCTU's organizational and political strategy. Frances Willard, like many other leaders and members of the WCTU, was a supporter of "woman's rights." But Willard and the WCTU leaders had political ambitions, and they looked to mobilize on a broader political footing, in contrast with what was understood as the narrow appeal and political weakness of women's suffrage or equal rights movements. Formulations about children and humanity, they believed, allowed the WCTU to cast a wide net and to mobilize women who were reluctant to join a movement too closely identified with "the woman question."

These formulations provided the WCTU with a rhetorical suit of armor to fend off blows from husbands, fathers, preachers, politicians, and other potential critics. To join the WCTU meant supporting the idea of women speaking in public. Willard and other WCTU leaders made their names on the lecture circuit, and the WCTU opened the field for less well-known women, especially in the West, where a woman could earn a hundred dollars a month lecturing on temperance. This was at a time when it was still rare and often controversial for women to speak before public audiences, even in venues such as the Chautauqua Assembly that were otherwise friendly to reform causes.[45] Similarly, the WCTU developed a cadre of editors, publishers, printers, business managers, and superintendents. This was at a time when such professional and skilled employment was regarded as the territory of men. The WCTU engaged in the work of politics: lobbying, petitioning, and canvassing. This, too, was at a time when women were mainly excluded from such work. Nor could women vote.

VI.

FOR FRANCES WILLARD, voting rights got to the heart of the problem, because political victory over the saloon required arming women with the ballot. By the early 1880s, most of the leadership and much of the membership of the WCTU moved to this position; women's suffrage, along with prohibition, climbed to the top of the WCTU's political agenda. But it did so amid dissent and opposition. Annie Wittenmyer was the most prominent opponent of women voting. An anti-suffrage faction broke from the WCTU. It did so with the support of the church leaders who viewed women voting as threatening "greater dangers to our family life than Mormonism and unlimited divorce."[46]

The state unions were often divided. At the annual gathering of the Minnesota WCTU in 1878, the president pledged that the members were not demanding rights, nor "are we clamoring for the ballot." The next day, the delegate from Duluth clamored for the ballot, and the union endorsed a suffrage amendment to the federal constitution. In California, the WCTU was so badly divided on the issue that it was unable to even debate the question of women's suffrage until 1886. And the WCTU in the southern states never came around to endorsing women's right to vote. The "Do Everything" policy accommodated this divergence of views. If the members of a local or state union did not want to take part in the work of the Franchise Department, that was their right.[47]

Meanwhile, the WCTU leadership ushered the movement toward women's political equality. It did so, however, by the indirect route that Frances Willard called the "Home Protection Ballot." At the time, the phrase "home protection" was used for tariffs to protect domestic industries. In a play on words, Willard used the phrase to advocate for the right of women to cast votes to protect their homes.[48] Initially, the WCTU focused on the right to vote on issues pertaining to mothers and their children, allowing women to participate in "local option" referendums to restrict liquor sales in their communities, or in school board elections. But the WCTU soon expanded its demands for women's suffrage. "The temperance question," an editorial in *The Signal* explained, "is one of power-ballots" for women. Yet the "Home Protection Ballot" still implied a qualified suffrage, granting the vote only to literate, temperate, and morally fit women.[49]

Even when Frances Willard spoke expansively about political equality, she accepted the principle of excluding the wrong types of women from the vote. A woman signing her name E. R. wrote to *The Signal* with a defiant protest against Willard's position. As an "advocate of equal rights," she asked, "Is an ignorant woman *worse* than an ignorant man? Would you deny the franchise to a woman like Sojourner Truth, for instance, and she can neither read nor write?" Qualifying the women's vote, she argued, imposed "two standards of morality" on men and women and obscured the role of "*bad men*" and "*starvation wages*" in the making of immoral women. Ballots for women, E. R. insisted, could not be separated from deeper questions of equality and social justice: "Liberty and equal rights for *all*—for the oppressed and down-trodden of earth; for the black woman as well as for the white; for the poor outcast as well as for the favored few." The editor of *The Signal*, Mary B. Willard (Frances's sister-in-law), gave a terse reply. "Let there be one standard of morality, and let women conform to it, no matter what men may do," she wrote. "In our opinion," she concluded, women's ballots must not "increase the number of vicious votes."[50] E. R. lost this debate, and most of the leaders of the WCTU continued to support a qualified women's ballot.

More often than not, the argument for limiting the women's ballot hinged on the question of the moral double standard. The WCTU waged a focused campaign for "equal rights in morals": a man who was intemperate, committed adultery, or hired a prostitute should suffer the same opprobrium as a woman who was intemperate, committed adultery, or engaged in prostitution. For husband and wife to be equals, they had to share the moral high ground in what the WCTU called "the white life for two."[51] A moral test for the women's vote was a logical step toward sexual equality on the basis of a single and higher moral standard.[52]

Meanwhile, Elizabeth Cady Stanton and other leaders of the women's movement who had been involved with the temperance movement prior to the Civil War had grown skeptical that a focus on the liquor trade could advance the cause of women's equality. Stanton criticized the Woman's Crusade as failing to demand equal rights and to attack male power. "All kinds of slaves," she wrote, "seem to have a blind instinct, compounded of ignorance and hypocrisy, that teaches them just how to please their masters."[53] Nonetheless, by the early 1880s, Stanton and the equal suffrage organizations widely recognized the power of the WCTU and looked to forge a political alliance of "Temperance & Suffrage voters." Suffrage activists tended to identify with both causes. Officers of the women's suffrage associations were frequently also members of the WCTU.[54] Here it should be noted that such officers were among those within the WCTU who first discarded the rhetorical shield of "home protection" to advocate directly for women's equality. Lide Meriwether, for example, the president of the WCTU in Tennessee and a founder of the Equal Rights Association in Memphis, spoke forthrightly about women as an "unrepresented class" demanding equal suffrage and "equality before the law."[55]

VII.

ALONG WITH PROHIBITION AND VOTING RIGHTS, the WCTU waged a multisided campaign to break down the legal inequities between the sexes. This included reforming prostitution statutes so that they would apply equally to men and women and equipping wives with the same rights as their husbands when it came to property, guardianship of children, and the right to sue. One of the WCTU's more successful legal campaigns involved the age of consent. In the mid-1880s, twenty states set the age of female consent in sexual matters at ten years old. For reformers, such children needed the protection of the law in the face of the unequal power of adult men. There was also a racial dimension, because white WCTU members in the South often employed black girls in their homes, girls who suffered sexual violence and abuse at the hands of the members' husbands and sons. The WCTU women complained of the "untidy and ignorant" habits of their help. But they viewed the sexual exploitation of black girls in white homes as a danger to the status of white women and looked to laws raising the age of consent as a check on this danger. The WCTU blanketed state legislatures with petitions to raise the age to eighteen, campaigns that slowly but surely raised the age of consent across much of the country.[56]

The WCTU's work on prison reform involved a similarly perilous mix of sex and race. Prison reform and the humane treatment of prisoners were one front of the WCTU's efforts to promote temperance and clean living. It was especially concerned with the fate of girls and women condemned to the convict labor system that prevailed in much of the South and beyond. In the labor camps, female prisoners, who were mainly African American, were subject to rape and sexual violence by white bosses and overseers. The WCTU led efforts to ban convict labor for women and girl prisoners. Rebecca Latimer Felton, a former slave owner and prominent

WCTU leader from Georgia, was an outspoken opponent of putting women and girls on convict labor gangs, arguing that the interracial sexual violence perpetrated by white men posed a danger to black and white women and to the racial order.[57]

Along with its many-sided legal campaigns, the WCTU addressed the sexual inequities within the household economy. The problem of economic equality, an editorial in *The Signal* noted, had to address the fact that women's domestic chores amounted to "half the manual work of the world," a burden that needed to be lightened by training schools in household management and "cooperative kitchens in every village." For her part, Lide Meriwether called for "cooperative housekeeping" and other measures to alleviate the household chores that blocked women's professional and personal development. Along these lines, the WCTU's most ambitious undertakings were kindergartens and coffee shops. The Department of Kindergartens described its work as a service to poor children, but kindergartens served mothers and the women who worked in them, too. In Chicago, the WCTU hoped to "dot the city over with free kindergartens." By the early 1890s, San Francisco had more than sixty kindergartens, while the WCTU-supported kindergartens in Oakland and San Jose were absorbed by the public boards of education.[58]

The WCTU's coffeehouses provided business opportunities for WCTU members and attempted to break the gender barrier of the saloon. In Chicago, Charleston, San Francisco, and other cities, the coffeehouses served lunch and refreshments for "gentlemen and ladies," as well as for the "working man with his dinner pail" outside "the malarial influence of the bar-room." Like other cooperative businesses of this era, the very success of the WCTU coffeehouses meant that they soon faced stiff competition from private restaurateurs. The coffeehouse business might have been hurt, too, by the debates within the WCTU over whether caffeine was a dangerous stimulant.[59]

Meanwhile, the WCTU's Department of Hygiene focused on the unequal burdens on women's bodies. It undertook temperance education about the poisonous effects of alcohol, tobacco, and narcotics, as well as "bad air, bad food, bad raiment." Women's corsets, lack of exercise, poor diets, and lack of knowledge about how their bodies worked were debilitating, too. Dress reform, bicycle riding, and whole grain bread all had a place in the WCTU's hygiene work.[60] So too did lectures, seminars, and meetings about "the physiology of woman." The WCTU in Glade Run, Pennsylvania, for example, held a special meeting where a female doctor discussed "the proper care and keeping" of the body and the importance of education about "the great mysteries of life." The meeting brought some of the women to tears, and apparently such topics came with a sanction of secrecy and a penalty of one dollar for divulging what was discussed.[61]

Frances Willard, with her "Do Everything" philosophy, embraced the full range of the WCTU's agenda. She wrote a book about learning to ride a bicycle and the potential role of cycling in women's autonomy and empowerment. She urged the WCTU to make cooperative kindergartens a national priority. And she was concerned about the unequal burdens of household work, promoting schemes for "a public laundry system, so complete as to drive the washtub out of every kitchen," and "a caterer's system so complete as to send the cooking stove into perpetual exile." Her ideas about bicycles and cooking stoves were at once whimsical and speculative. But Willard was also a hard-charging, ambitious politician. And she would never lose sight of her political goals as she poured her energy and talent into making the WCTU a political force that would reshape the country's partisan and sectional political map.[62]

5.

WOMEN'S PARTY

FRANCES WILLARD UNDERSTOOD that for the WCTU to emerge as a political power, it needed to forge a national presence. In 1879, when she was elected president of the organization, most of the WCTU's support came from Republican districts in the Northeast and the Midwest, with no organization below the Mason-Dixon Line. Willard recognized that the WCTU would never emerge as a force on the national political stage as long as it remained within these Republican and northern spaces. In her boldest and most celebrated political move, she traveled to the South and organized the WCTU across the former Confederacy. Her southern venture would become the story of the WCTU's national emergence, a story told and retold over the years in ever more triumphal terms.

I.

PRESIDENT JAMES GARFIELD INVITED Frances Willard to the White House in March 1881 to discuss her upcoming trip to the South. The stated purpose of her trip was to gain "knowledge of the moral treasures of the land," and Willard assured the president that her motives in visiting the South were "harmony" and "fraternity," "not less than" temperance. Garfield expressed that this was "identical" to his own policy in southern affairs and hoped that her goodwill tour would serve "to unite the two sections with sweet ties of sympathy." With the official blessings of the White House, Willard and her secretary and ever-present companion, Anna Gordon, set out for Charleston, South Carolina, the first stop in a three-month tour of the former Confederacy.[1]

Willard worried about a possibly cool reception from her hosts. She was, after all, a Yankee, a Republican, and a woman who spoke before public audiences in favor of women's suffrage and other controversial causes. But when she arrived in Charleston, she received the best of "Southern hospitality." Her hosts, ex-Confederates who had been "schooled in slavery" and who were now loyal to the Democratic Party of white supremacy, embraced her like a lost sister. As Anna Gordon wrote to Willard's mother, "Frank's meetings are most successful and her audiences larger than any other lecturer ever had in Charleston. She is winning all hearts . . . and the very best people are among her hearers." A high point of the visit came when the officer who "fired the first shot on the flag at Fort Sumter" gave Willard a personal tour of the fort in Charleston harbor. Gordon concluded her report on these exciting events with "How strange is life!"[2]

Willard's southern hosts expressed gratitude for her temperance work. But most of all, they welcomed her message of sectional reconciliation. She promised to bridge the "bloody chasm" of distrust by forging a national sisterhood against the liquor traffic. Old hatreds would be overcome by the WCTU's nationalist vision of unity for "God and Home and Native Land." In Charleston, Willard stayed in the home of Sallie Chapin, who responded in kind by telling her guest that North and South had "no time for mutual recrimination." It was time for "re-united hearts" and plans for "the defense of homes equally endangered on both sides of the Mason and Dixon's line." Willard's unity message was similarly embraced by a minister who introduced her at a public meeting by rendering the initials of the WCTU as "We Come To Unite," a rendering that "the audience universally approved." In Alabama, a woman explained the significance of Willard's nationalist message. "While you were being taught to spell nation with a big N," she told Willard, "I was being taught to spell Alabama with a big A. But those days and their terrible fruits are past." Ellen Hebron of Hinds County, Mississippi, met Willard and saw in her "*a woman* [who] has welded all sections into one grand nationality" and "a live Queen reigning in the hearts of her subjects."[3]

On her return from her southern tour, Willard let it be known that she was no longer a Republican woman with northern sensibilities but a woman who would claim the ground of "nationalism against sectionalism," free from partisan or regional prejudice. The reception she received from her southern sisters had put to rest old concerns about the resistance of the white South to the Reconstruction amendments. As she put it, the trip "'reconstructed' me." Moreover, the tour proved an organizational success, launching the WCTU across the former Confederacy. This, Willard understood, meant that the WCTU would emerge as a truly national force in American politics. Respecting the equal rights of states and knowing "no North, no South, no East, no West," the WCTU would be the driving force of a new "home protection" political party. She spelled out her political vision at the WCTU convention the following October. "Politics," she explained, was "the mightiest force on earth except Christianity." And conditions were now ripe "for a new political party along the lines of longitude; a party that shall wipe Mason and Dixon's line out of the heart as well as off the map, weld the Anglo-Saxons of the New World into one royal family, and give a really re-United States."[4]

Frances Willard's trip to the South gave the WCTU a new beginning as a national political movement. At least, this was how she told the story, which bore a striking resemblance to another origins story: Oliver Kelley's trip to the South fifteen years earlier and the birth of the Grange. Kelley was commissioned by President Johnson to do a survey of agricultural resources; Willard was commissioned by President Garfield to survey moral resources. To his surprise, the planter elite in Charleston welcomed Kelley with open arms; to Willard's surprise, the elite in Charleston did the same for her. Kelley's Masonic connections opened doors for him across the South; Willard's Methodist connections did the same for her.[5] Kelley went to the South with a message of equal rights for the states and sectional reconciliation; Willard went to the South with the same message. Kelley returned from the South with a plan for a new nationalist political force based on protecting farmers and planters; Willard returned from the South with a plan for a new nationalist political force based on "home protection."

The similarities between these two stories suggest that the Grange played a role in shaping Frances Willard's political imagination. Raised on a Wisconsin farm, Willard came of age in the world of rural reform. Her father, Josiah Willard, pursued scientific farming and rural politics. In the days when Oliver Kelley was conducting agricultural surveys of Minnesota and corresponding with the Smithsonian in Washington about plants and soils, Josiah was doing much the same in nearby Wisconsin. Originally a Democrat, he was elected to the state legislature as a Free-Soil Party candidate in 1848 and later joined the Republican Party. As a leader of the Wisconsin Agricultural Society, he introduced Abraham Lincoln when he addressed the society in 1859. By that time, Frances Willard had published a number of articles in local newspapers and farm periodicals, including *The Prairie Farmer*, a newspaper published in Chicago that would later become the voice of the Grange across the upper Midwest. When she returned to Evanston in the early 1870s, the Grange was at the height of its power in Illinois, and as a person with a keen interest in politics Willard must have taken note.[6]

Moreover, the Grange and the WCTU had a common milieu. Women activists often wore multiple hats as suffragists, prohibitionists, and farm reformers. The famed Civil War nurse Clara Barton, for example, sympathized with all three of these causes and worked with both William

Saunders and Frances Willard.[7] Eliza Gifford, a champion of "equality of the two sexes" and "equal condition of citizenship," was a leading figure in the New York state Grange, the New York State Woman Suffrage Association, and the WCTU. Whereas the Grange mainly organized men and women on farms, the WCTU focused on middle-class women mainly in cities, towns, and villages. But the boundaries between town and farm and the WCTU and the Grange were often porous. It is only partly a coincidence that in 1874 the first WCTU was organized in the small town of Fredonia, New York, the very town where the first rural Grange was formed six years before.[8] By this time, the Grangers of upstate New York had embraced the temperance cause, and many Grangers would soon join the WCTU. A woman from Poplar Ridge, New York, claimed of her Grange that "nearly all the ladies were also W.C.T.U.s."[9]

Such overlapping memberships between the WCTU and the Grange were more common in the towns and villages of rural New York than elsewhere. This was especially so in the wake of the crisis of the 1870s. The New York state Grange came through the depression years in better shape than the Granges in much of the Midwest and the West, where the WCTU gained strength just as the Grange fell into steep decline. This meant that by the late 1870s for most members of the WCTU the Grange was more of a memory than an active presence, providing familiar tropes and cultural and intellectual resources. In its pursuit of sectional reconciliation, the WCTU also drew from the Methodist and other Protestant churches and from the Liberal Republicans and the wider political zeitgeist. With the Grange, however, the WCTU shared a national founding story and a vision that their voluntary associations would serve as "longitudinal" bridges across the Mason-Dixon Line to reunify the country.[10]

II.

DESPITE A COMMON NARRATIVE, Frances Willard's trip to the South deviated from Oliver Kelley's in one key way. The story of Kelley's reception in Charleston focused on the hospitality of the white elite; Willard's story had the same focus but included addressing an "immense audience" of Charleston's African American citizens. "Everywhere the Southern white people desired me to speak to the colored," Willard wrote. She also attended a temperance convention in North Carolina where "black and white sat down together" and "ex-masters cheered to the echo of the utterances of the ex-slaves" in favor of prohibition. In interviews with northern newspapers, Willard reported that "there is much drinking among the negroes, but the whites discourage it." The former slave owners, she explained, understood that "a tame Negro is better company than a wild one" and therefore welcomed his education in temperance. "Of course, they do not accept him as a social equal," she added, "nor does he ask this equality." Yet Willard saw the inclusion of African Americans in temperance work as a sign of a rising South that was accepting equality between the races and that would soon "efface all phases of the politico-commercial color line."[11]

Frances Willard could and did speak fluently about racial equality. She was raised in an abolitionist home and proudly claimed the traditions of William Lloyd Garrison and Frederick Douglass. She was not alone; many WCTU women claimed this same emancipationist and egalitarian tradition. This included a small but influential number of African American women in the northern states who took part in the organization on at least nominal terms of inclusion and equal status. In practice, the WCTU could be inconsistent and halfhearted about its commitments to racial equality, both in terms of the internal workings of the organization and especially in terms of its political agenda. Yet to the extent that racial equality was part of the WCTU's organizational culture, its southern venture and the brutal realities of the newly redeemed South put this culture under pressure.[12]

The WCTU leadership employed several coping strategies. The first was to proclaim victory. Despite overwhelming evidence that the white South sustained a reign of terror and brutality to strip African Americans of property, education, and legal and civil rights, the WCTU baldly announced that racial equality had arrived, or nearly so, across the former Confederacy. Frances Willard returned from her southern tour to report that in regard to the white and black people of the region she had "found that the era of good feeling had indeed set in" and that there was a "marked decline in conflicts over the [color] line." Not only did the black man have the ballot, but "he has received acceptance" and was treated with "kindness as a rule," and black schoolchildren had "distanced the poor white in education." Quoting Frederick Douglass to the effect that prejudice about the color of one's skin was the result of differences in one's conditions of life, Willard reported happily that "this difference narrows into nothing" as the South was quickly moving toward an equality of conditions. As for political violence and terror, Willard bore the good news that "the ku-klux and bulldozer have retreated" to the extent that "if the bulldozer still lives, it is only in exceptionally bad spots" where the black man is "swathed in whiskey."[13]

The second coping strategy was to focus on intemperance as the new slavery. White temperance leaders in the South held that freedom for the "four millions of Southern negroes" had led to their ruin in the "clanking chains of this liquor bondage."[14] The WCTU leadership accepted this argument and pointed to their efforts to free the former slaves from "this more universal slavery" as proof that the organization remained on the righteous path of freedom and equality.[15]

In October 1881, Sallie Chapin, who had months before hosted Frances Willard in Charleston, addressed the national meeting of the WCTU held in Washington, D.C. She reassured her northern sisters that they had nothing to fear from the former slave-owning class, who only looked to unite in the common struggle against the liquor trade. "Slavery is dead, forever dead," she explained, because the former slave owners did not want to resume the onerous responsibility of caring for their human property. Meanwhile, according to Chapin, "the negro is more of a slave to the whisky seller than he ever was to an owner"; intemperance was imposing a worse slavery on the black people of the South than the slavery that had recently ended. "Before the war," Chapin recounted, "it was an offense punishable by law to sell liquor to a slave," and now the former slaves "say they want whiskey and more of it." As a result, she concluded, the freed people had fallen under a "far more abject slavery than we ever held them in."[16]

Mary Torrance Lathrop, the president of the Michigan WCTU, greeted Chapin's address with sympathy. She lamented that "the Southern people"—that is, white southerners such as Chapin—"have been alienated from us by years of sectional strife." Not just the South, she explained, but American civilization as a whole faced the alcohol-fueled threats of immigrants from Europe and Asia and of "the freedmen coming up into a liberty they know little how to use." The solution to this "problem of civilization," according to Lathrop, was for the North and the South to unite against the liquor trade, "this last great slavery and this last great National curse." Frances Willard concurred; prohibition of alcoholic beverages was "our new antislavery war." Prior to the Fourteenth Amendment, she told the same national meeting of the WCTU, ending slavery "was the determining factor in American politics." But now that the former slaves had equal rights protections and black men had the franchise, freedom from the tyranny of the liquor traffic was "the greatest issue now pending on this or any continent."[17]

Emancipation from the liquor trade could only be accomplished by way of what Willard described as "the union of the best elements of the North and South." Somewhat ironically, however, the measure of who counted among "the best elements" was not exactly equal. Whereas in the North "the best" tended to refer to middle-class reformers, in the South the WCTU tended to designate "the best" to be those in the highest social rank of the former slaveholding elite. Frances Willard pursued a friendship, for example, with Varina Davis, the wife of Jefferson Davis. During her southern tours, she met Davis in New Orleans and again in Memphis and established a long-term bond of sisterhood. "The ties of our two faiths—in God, and in our own sex," Davis wrote to Willard, "bring us near to each other."[18] In Memphis, Varina Davis was a close associate of Elizabeth Fisher Johnson, the first president of the Tennessee WCTU.

Willard also befriended Jane Johnson, the wife of Bradley T. Johnson of Baltimore. A former brigadier general in the Confederate infantry and an unreconstructed defender of the Lost Cause, Johnson demanded that the heroes of the Confederacy be given "equality in every respect" and "equal recognition." Willard did so, and Jane Johnson and the other elite women of Baltimore rewarded her accordingly, making her an honorary member of Maryland's Ladies' Memorial and Beneficial Association of the Confederate States.[19] Meanwhile, for president of the Georgia WCTU, Willard recruited Jane Eliza Sibley, the wife of William Sibley, scion of the family that owned Sibley Cotton Mills and who ranked among the wealthiest and best-known merchants and industrialists of the Confederacy and the postwar South.[20]

By the early 1880s, as the superintendent of southern work, Sallie Chapin would emerge as the WCTU's most prominent leader after Willard, and their close partnership would play a major role in the WCTU's politics of national reunification. Chapin was almost as busy on the lecture circuit as Willard, spreading the message of sectional unity in the war on the liquor trade. In 1882, the WCTU held its national convention in Louisville as a gesture to the women of the South. In his welcoming address, the former Confederate officer and temperance lecturer Colonel George Bain emphasized the role that the two women played bridging the sectional divide. "Miss Willard in the South and Mrs. Chapin in the North," he said, "have done more to bring together the divided sections, than all the politicians who have ever gone to Washington."[21]

In terms of political messaging, Willard understood the value of Chapin's reputation as a prominent member of the former slaveholding elite and her sterling pro-Confederate credentials. One of Chapin's brothers had been a leader of the South Carolina secession convention, and another brother died in the war. Her husband also fought, while she served as the president of the Charleston Soldiers' Relief Society. After the war, Chapin's family fell on hard times. Her husband succumbed to alcoholism as his cotton crops were lost to caterpillars and his carriage business failed. Meanwhile, Chapin did what she could to keep the faith. She took part in the Ladies' Memorial Association to raise funds to decorate the graves of the Confederate dead and cultivated a public image of the prewar southern lady. As a Florida newspaper put it, Chapin's "manner, accent, gesticulation and general appearance carried the listener back to the old ante-bellum days and pictures of high-toned, refined southern homes."[22]

In 1872, Chapin wrote a Civil War novel dedicated "to the children of the Confederacy." Her book, *Fitz-Hugh St. Clair, the South Carolina Rebel Boy*, defended racial slavery, secession, and the southern war effort and did so without apology or regret. The book fixed Chapin's name as an unbent supporter of the Lost Cause. But the book was also a defense of women in the face of ruin as a result of whiskey-soaked husbands, the moral double standard, and other inequities. The last paragraph of the book declared, "We are not pleading for 'women's rights,' but for the redress of women's wrongs."[23] Chapin's support for temperance and for women's protection made for a good fit with her northern sisters in the WCTU. Lost Cause loyalties did not prevent Chapin from joining hands with her northern sisters in the common struggle. Moreover, such loyalties proved invaluable for Willard's plans to transform the "sisterhood of the women's party"—that is, the WCTU—into a new political force for national reunification.[24]

III.

FRANCES WILLARD BELIEVED THAT THE WCTU'S political goals could only be realized through a political party. The Grange and other voluntary associations maintained at least the pretense of nonpartisanship. Willard, by contrast, made no secret of the fact that she was a party person who sought to make the WCTU a party vehicle. In 1881, she joined the Prohibition Party, took a position on its central committee, and soon emerged as its most celebrated leader. For Willard, the Prohibition Party—or, as she preferred to call it, the Home Protection Party—offered a means "to disturb the balance of parties" and thereby force prohibition on the national political agenda. In this regard, she might have been inspired by the example of her father's Free-Soil Party, which helped push antislavery into the political mainstream. The Prohibition Party was also the only party that welcomed women's full participation, and Willard thrived in the political atmosphere of its conventions and campaigns. But, perhaps most important, the Prohibition Party aligned with Willard's vision of sectional reconciliation.[25]

The Prohibition Party formed in 1869 with the support of the Independent Order of Good Templars and made slow but steady headway in local and state political contests. By the 1880s, a party whose name announced its commitment to outlawing alcoholic beverages successfully situated itself in the middle of the post–Civil War debates about equality. At its 1882 national convention, the Prohibition Party demanded the "abolition of all monopolies . . . injurious to the equal rights of citizens." It called for government regulation of railroad corporations "to protect the interest of labor and commerce." The convention's approval of a resolution demanding the "civil and political equality and enfranchisement of woman" was "greeted with loud shouting and the waving of handkerchiefs." Meanwhile, a delegate from Tennessee introduced a resolution "against proscription and persecution on account of color," and to "demand full and exact political equality for all Americans." The Prohibition Party had black members and recruited among former slaves. Nonetheless, in response to this demand for racial equality, another delegate shouted, "Sumner did that long ago." And the convention proceeded to bury the resolution for equal rights and protections for African Americans.[26]

In practical terms, the scuttling of equal rights demands for black southerners opened the door for white southerners, who rejected such demands, to enter the Prohibition Party. This included Sallie Chapin, who joined Frances Willard as one of the three women on its central committee. But to put an elite southern woman like Chapin in the leadership required a compromise on women's equality, too, given that Chapin and other southern prohibitionists did not support women's suffrage. Willard proposed that the Prohibition Party make the "woman's vote subsidiary," and leave the decision to support suffrage to each state party. At the 1882 Prohibition Party convention, Willard defeated efforts by delegates who wanted a national demand for women's voting rights. She insisted that "civil and political equality for women" was a matter for the states, to be "remitted to the party in those States." As with the WCTU, the Prohibition Party made equal political rights for women a matter for the state parties to decide. This allowed Chapin to declare a victory for southern principles and states' rights. And it allowed Willard to promote the Prohibition Party as the party of sectional reconciliation.[27]

Willard and Chapin presented their "states' rights" policy as a matter of allowing the traditional and conservative South, what Chapin called "the slowest foot in the last battalion," to go its own way in relation to the more advanced North and West. Resistance to the women's vote did vary by region, although northern women such as Annie Wittenmyer opposed women's suffrage much as Sallie Chapin did. And there were southern women who held views about women's political equality that matched those of the most determined northern suffragists. Belle Kearney of Mississippi, one of the WCTU's most prominent lecturers, was both a fiery advocate of women's suffrage and an unabashed defender of white supremacy. Kearney saw the WCTU as the vehicle of her political ambitions, "the generous liberator, the joyous iconoclast, the discoverer, the developer of Southern women."[28]

In her memoir, *A Slaveholder's Daughter*, Kearney recounted stories of her father and brothers trying—and failing—to plow a field after the slaves on their cotton plantation gained their freedom. Her memoir also told of the virtues of slavery, secession, Redemption, and the rule of "Anglo-Saxon blood" over "the inferior race." At the same time, her father belonged to an "Equal Rights club" supporting women's equality before the law, and Kearney herself was the president of the Woman Suffrage Association in Mississippi. "The enfranchisement of women," Kearney believed, "would insure immediate and durable white supremacy."[29]

The Tennessee WCTU president, Lide Meriwether, even more consistently than Kearney, argued for women's political, economic, and social equality. She belonged to a circle of Memphis women, including her sister-in-law Elizabeth Meriwether, who argued forcefully for women's political equality while with similar force opposing political equality for African Americans. Historians have described such southern women as "redemption feminists," because they embraced a potent mix of women's rights and white supremacy.[30] In this regard, Willard's "states' rights" policy was as much about resistance to racial equality as it was about women's equality.

Moreover, the temperance movement in the South attracted people who were too unconventional to fit easily into Willard's categories. Ebenezer Dohoney of Paris, Texas, was one of the Lone Star State's least traditional politicians. On the eve of the Civil War, Dohoney's first stint in politics was to campaign against Texas seceding, and although he would serve in the Confederate army, he maintained an independent streak in politics and life. He favored equal rights for women and in 1871, when he served in the state legislature, proposed that Texas adopt women's suffrage. He joined the Greenback Party to campaign against monopolies and for labor rights and in 1882 unsuccessfully ran for Congress on the Greenback ticket. In 1885, he published a book that covered the spectrum of the eclectic and conflicting ideas of a post–Civil War iconoclast. He dedicated the work, *Man: His Origin, Nature and Destiny*, to "independent thinkers" who have "no respect for orthodoxy in Church or State." Although he argued for a type of Christianity, he did so in the name of scientific discoveries in the realms of phrenology, animal magnetism, and spiritualism. Although he accepted the scientific racism of Louis Agassiz's division of humanity into racial hierarchies, he argued forcefully that "every human being" had "equal rights under the laws of nature" and therefore must have equality under the laws of government. Applying this egalitarian view to both race and sex, Dohoney argued that "the State has neither right nor power to make any distinctions on account of sex, race, color, or previous condition, as to who shall vote or have a voice in the government."[31]

When Frances Willard made a whirlwind tour of Texas in 1882, Dohoney opened doors for her and defended her from conservative critics who objected to a woman speaking in public. This was the beginning of a close alliance between the two. Intellectually, they shared unorthodox interests ranging from phrenology to cooperative socialism.

The main thing they shared, though, was political heterodoxy. Soon after they first met, Dohoney left the Greenbackers to join Willard in the leadership of the Prohibition Party. For her part, Willard had closely watched the Greenback Party and incorporated its lessons into her vision for third-party action. The Home Protection or Prohibition Party, Willard believed, needed to pick its battles carefully. Power for a third party lay not with winning elections but in punishing one or the other of the two major parties for rejecting the demands of prohibition, sectional reconciliation, and in certain situations women's political equality. In this way, "very soon this new 'party of great moral ideas' will hold the balance of power," Willard predicted, first at the local and state levels and then "in the nation itself."[32]

With the WCTU giving the Prohibition Party new energy, it scored small victories across the Midwest, punishing the dominant Republicans in a number of local contests. The third party's biggest triumph was its apparent contribution to the defeat of the Republican candidate James Blaine in the 1884 presidential election. The Prohibition Party had focused its energies on the swing state of New York, where by a margin of a little over a thousand ballots the GOP lost the states' Electoral College votes and thereby the presidency. The Prohibition Party's twenty-five thousand votes represented only 2 percent of New York's voters, but more than enough to hand the Republicans their first loss of the White House since Frémont's defeat in 1856. The Republican campaign was beset by a number of troubles, but the party leaders blamed the WCTU and the prohibitionists for their loss, while Willard and the WCTU leadership claimed credit for the success of their strategy.[33]

IV.

THE WCTU AND THE PROHIBITION PARTY had made their mark "in the nation itself," encouraging Willard to press forward with her third-party strategy of sectional reconciliation. In May 1888, she gave a Decoration Day address before a group of five hundred Union and Confederate veterans who had gathered in Indianapolis for the Prohibition Party convention.

A big banner across the hall read, "No North, No South, No Distinction in Politics, No Sex in Citizenship." Willard told the veterans that "no other than the Prohibition Party ever dared to be so great as to ordain a scene like this" that brought together the Blue and the Gray. This was the "greatest party [which] stands for nationalism as against sectionalism" and that "spells 'nation' with the tallest kind of a capital 'N.'" According to Willard, the Republicans made use of the issue of black voting rights and "that timeworn utterance about a 'free ballot and fair count,'" only to divide the sections against each other. The Prohibition Party would transcend such divisions. "One Anglo-Saxon race, having one queenly language and a heroic history," she told the assembled veterans, would unite for "the protection of our homes."[34]

Willard assured her listeners that her third-party strategy was aimed at punishing Republicans and Democrats alike. But this was something of a deceit. Temperance voters in the South, at least the white voters, were mainly Democrats, and across the former Confederacy the Democratic grip was strong enough that the Prohibition Party had few chances to influence competitive elections. This is why Sallie Chapin could embrace the Prohibition Party without fear of undermining the Democratic Party and the racial structure of the South, and do so while "looking on quietly amused at our Republican sisters" as the WCTU's political strategy undercut Republican strength in the North.[35]

Belle Kearney similarly supported the Prohibition Party, but her brothers warned her that eventually the third-party agitation would threaten Democratic Party hegemony. Most white southern members of the WCTU agreed with Kearney's brothers and remained loyal Democrats. When southern state WCTUs petitioned the 1888 Democratic convention to act against the liquor trade, they did so on the grounds that this was the best way to protect Democratic and white power. "Through the saloon," the southern WCTUs warned, "the old Republican carpet-bag and scalawag bosses can control the ignorant negro vote, and endanger both our homes and Democratic supremacy."[36]

Temperance voters in the North, meanwhile, tended to be Republicans or former Republicans, and the Prohibition Party focused on competitive races with the clear aim of subtracting from Republican votes. This arithmetic underscored the need to field candidates who could attract Republican voters to the third party. One potentially attractive candidate was the U.S. Army general Oliver O. Howard, or at least Willard thought so and tried to recruit him to lead the third-party campaign. Howard was a professional soldier, a celebrated commander in the Civil War who later directed campaigns against the Nez Perce and other Indians in the West. He was also a self-styled "humanitarian general" who founded Howard University and was the commissioner of the Freedmen's Bureau during Reconstruction. Howard sympathized with prohibition, women's rights, and other reform causes. He was also a Republican who believed that the GOP's commitments to the former slaves were not "yet completed." Howard understood the arithmetic of a third party and replied to Willard, "I must not be instrumental . . . in depleting the ranks of the Republican Party" when it still had its work to do for racial equality.[37]

Meanwhile, Willard's political vision met resistance within the WCTU. It is difficult to judge the strength of this resistance given Willard's authority and the dissenters' lack of organizational leverage. This left those disparaged as "malcontents" with the choice of either swallowing their disagreements or going elsewhere. But dissent there was, including among women who were not willing to jettison their partisan and sectional loyalties. Annie Wittenmyer had little interest in women's suffrage, third parties, or sectional reconciliation. Her politics were shaped by her Civil War experience and by memories of places such as wartime Nashville. The Confederate women she met seeking refuge in Nashville's hotels, she would recall, were "more intense in war spirit" than the men and, "in their blind partisan fury, prolonged the contest to the last extreme of desperation." For a Republican stalwart such as Wittenmyer, sectional reconciliation was a difficult sell. It was especially difficult on Willard's terms, which meant buying into her notion that sectional conflict was a mere misunderstanding in which the women of the two sections found it "hard for us to hate each other."[38]

Brewing discontent led to open revolt. In 1888, Judith Ellen Foster, the president of the Iowa state WCTU, led a breakaway group called the Non-Partisan WCTU that rejected Willard's political strategy. An Iowa lawyer, Foster had worked with the Republican legislature to pass a pro-hibition referendum in 1882 that made Iowa one of the driest states in the country. For Foster and her allies, the Republican Party remained the best option for realizing the WCTU's goals. Blaine's defeat in the 1884 presidential election reinforced Foster's opposition to a third-party strategy and her commitment to the GOP, which put her on the party's payroll as an organizer and speaker. Other supporters of the Non-Partisan WCTU came from Ohio and other midwestern swing states and might have shared the concerns of Howard, Wittenmyer, or Foster about race, section, and party. In any event, despite the name, the Non-Partisan WCTU drew its support from "staunch Republicans" and for a time posed an alternative to Willard's third-party strategy.[39]

As it turned out, Frances Willard's political ambitions could not be contained within the Prohibition Party, and by the late 1880s her attention turned to building a broader reform coalition. She looked for alliances with the Knights of Labor and other labor and farmer organizations. Under the roof of the National Council of Women she also looked to form an alliance of women's groups to mobilize "organized womanhood" as a political force. Initiated by Susan B. Anthony and Elizabeth Cady Stanton, the National Council of Women held its first meeting in Washington, D.C., in April 1888, and Frances Willard was elected its first president. Her inaugural address was notable for how little attention she paid to prohibition or sectional reconciliation. Rather, she called for a general sisterhood—from temperance woman to Knights of Labor woman—to engage the struggle for women's interests and sexual equality. This included equal access to education and the professions; equal wages for equal work; an equal moral standard and access to the courts; and equal rights to property and to the guardianship of children. Willard then proposed a system of councils of women to bring "the combined influence of us all" to bear on legislation at every level of government. Her indirect route to women's equal rights was becoming a more direct one. Her role in the National Council of Women suggested how close she had come to Anthony and Stanton in her advocacy of sexual equality.[40]

The National Council of Women also provided a platform for Frances Ellen Watkins Harper, a WCTU leader whose conflicted relationship with Anthony and Stanton reflected the tortured nature of post–Civil War equality. Harper knew Anthony, Stanton, and Frederick Douglass from the time they worked together in the abolitionist movement of the 1850s. Harper, like many abolitionists, embraced a humanist ideal of equality without regard to race or sex. But after the Civil War, this ideal was put to the test when the Fifteenth Amendment provided equal suffrage without regard to race but failed to extend suffrage to women. The Fifteenth Amendment, according to Stanton and Anthony, had established an "aristocracy of sex," and together they broke with the Republican Party and supported the Democratic campaigns for the restoration of white power in the former Confederacy. Harper and Frederick Douglass, on the other hand, welcomed the Fifteenth Amendment while continuing to agitate for women's political equality and defending the Republican project of federal Reconstruction.[41]

Demands for equal political rights for women and African Americans provoked a tragic schism, a deep wound that never healed. At the 1891 meeting of the National Council of Women, Harper reminded her sisters that black lives mattered. In a country "where men are still lynched, murdered, and even burned for real or supposed crimes," she explained, no right was more precious than "the claim for protection to human life."[42] Harper made her address as charges and countercharges would soon fly back and forth across the Atlantic Ocean over Frances Willard's failure to speak out against lynch law, and even to apologize for lynching in the name of protecting white women. The charges and countercharges struck a nerve within the WCTU. In her policy of sectional healing, Willard performed a balancing act, forging an alliance with the white "unreconstructed" South while maintaining the WCTU's influence and work among African Americans. The lynching controversy, and especially Harper's role in it, suggested the failure of the balancing act.

V.

FRANCES ELLEN WATKINS HARPER had been the WCTU's "superintendent for work among the colored people of the North," but her title failed to reflect her reputation and influence as a literary figure, advocate of women's equality, and champion of African American rights. When she was twenty years old, Harper published her first book of poetry, marking the beginning of a writing career that would make her a popular poet and novelist with both black and white readers. Her fame on the lecture circuit was akin to that of Sojourner Truth, and she was also known as "the Fred Douglass among colored women." Harper had worked with Truth and Douglass in the abolitionist movement, and she lived a long life in that movement's traditions of racial and sexual egalitarianism.[43]

Frances Watkins was the daughter of a former slave, born free in Baltimore in 1825. Her mother died when she was a small child, leaving her to be raised and educated by an uncle who directed an academy for black youth. The slave state of Maryland was an increasingly perilous place for free blacks, and in 1851 Watkins headed north, first to teach in Ohio and then to Philadelphia, where she became involved with the Underground Railroad. Her reading of Solomon Northup's *Twelve Years a Slave* inspired her abolitionist resolve against a system that "fattens and feasts on human blood." As a paid lecturer for the Maine State Anti-Slavery Society, Watkins shared the platform with Susan B. Anthony, Frederick Douglass, William Lloyd Garrison, Sojourner Truth, and other abolitionists working for equal rights without regard to race or sex. Her literary eloquence and polished manner facilitated her success on the New England lecture circuit, as did her appreciation for her adopted New England. Like other New England abolitionists, Watkins viewed John Brown as "the hero of the nineteenth century," and she spent two weeks with Brown's wife in the days before his execution.[44]

In 1860, Frances Watkins used the money that she had saved up from her books and lectures to purchase a farm outside Columbus, Ohio. This would be the home she shared with her new husband, Fenton Harper, and their infant daughter. Four years later, Fenton died. Court officers took hold of the farm and all of Harper's personal possessions to pay off her husband's debts. This was a harsh lesson in the consequences of women's lack of economic rights. In 1864, Harper returned to the lecture circuit and joined with Frederick Douglass in the founding of the National Equal Rights League to work for full citizenship, including political equality and equal access to education for African Americans in the North and the South.[45]

At the same time, Harper's lack of rights as a new widow heightened her commitment to gain women's equality before the law. But she did so recognizing that women's equality was no panacea and would not solve the problem of racial caste. "I do not believe that giving the woman the ballot is immediately going to cure all the ills of life," she told the Woman's Rights Convention in 1866. She reminded the delegates of the daily humiliations of racial caste and noted, "You white women speak here of rights, I speak of wrongs."[46]

The same convention agreed to form the American Equal Rights Association (AERA), dedicated to political equality for both African Americans and women. In part, the AERA was the response of Susan B. Anthony and Elizabeth Cady Stanton to signs that the equal rights revolution unleashed by the Civil War would bypass women. The year before, the abolitionist Wendell Phillips had said that it was the "Negro's Hour" for voting rights. Meanwhile, the Fourteenth Amendment had for the first time introduced the category "male" into the Constitution. The AERA was also a response by Frederick Douglass to the failure of the Fourteenth Amendment to provide equal voting rights for African Americans.

But the unity on which the AERA was founded broke against the reality of the Fifteenth Amendment extending suffrage to men without regard to race. Anthony and Stanton viewed the amendment as betrayal. More, they warned that giving the vote to black men would result in rape and violence against white women. This was not the first time they had given voice to such fears or to ideas about white women being superior to black men. But by 1868, these ideas led to political rupture when Anthony and Stanton lined up with the Democratic opposition to racial equality and Reconstruction. This included endorsing Frank Blair as the Democratic candidate for vice president, whose campaign motto was "This Is a White Man's Country; Let White Men Rule." Blair returned the favor by voicing support for women's suffrage as a means of protection from the "brutal negro." The Democratic editor Manton Marble of the New York *World* exploited the issue for partisan gain, publishing Stanton's endorsement of Blair to show that the Republican plan to equip black men with the vote meant subjecting white women to a "despotism of bestial passions."[47]

Frances Harper, for her part, joined Frederick Douglass, Sojourner Truth, and other former abolitionists to support the Fifteenth Amendment and the extension of political equality to black men. At the same time, Harper endorsed a proposed Sixteenth Amendment for women's suffrage and continued in her belief in equal rights grounded "on our common humanity." Harper's 1869 novel, *Minnie's Sacrifice*, explored this "common humanity" in the context of slavery, the Civil War, and Reconstruction. Serialized in *The Christian Recorder*, the novel provided a rebuttal to the Lost Cause narrative, featuring the horrors of New Orleans slave pens, the heroism of African American Union soldiers, the hopes of love transcending racial inequality and division, and the brutality of the Ku Klux Klan. By 1869, "men advocating equal rights did so at the peril of their lives, for violence and murder were rampant in the land." Minnie, the novel's heroine, explained that given this context "I would not throw a straw in the way of the colored man" and his voting rights. But "reconstructing the government," she insisted, required "bring[ing] into our politics a deeper and broader humanity" and providing women with "equal laws as if she were a man." Minnie pointedly asked, "Is it not the woman's hour also? Has she not as many rights and claims as the negro man?"[48]

Meanwhile, Harper traveled to the South to learn about the women and men coming out of slavery and to campaign for their equal rights. Between 1865 and 1876, she lectured extensively across the former

Confederacy, often at great personal risk. In Charleston, she spoke in Freedmen's Bureau schools and black churches and visited the state legislature at the invitation of Francis Cardozo, the African American secretary of state. She visited plantations where newly free men and women welcomed her to supper in "the old cabins of slavery." She also met with former slaveholders and encouraged both "white people and the colored" to find a "community of interests" but added that "community of interests" suggests equality, not "increasing the privileges of one class and curtailing the rights of the other." This was, however, exactly what she feared was under way as "some of the old rebel element" favored "taking away the colored man's vote."[49]

In April 1875, Frances Harper gave a lecture in Philadelphia on the violence consuming the former Confederacy. She reported on the White Leagues with their "covenant of death and agreement with hell." She told of the "cowardly murderers of Vicksburg and Louisiana." It was not just the "mangled corpses," "the scent of blood," and "our bones scattered," but the impunity surrounding the murderers. "And who cares?" Harper asked, as much of the country remained silent in the face of the violence. This she contrasted to the protests about the "invasion of Southern rights by our soldiers," and "how our great commercial emporium will rally its forces" to protest "military interference" to defend black lives and "common justice and simple mercy." For Harper, this inequity was the country's "great problem" to be solved: the "white race," she told her Philadelphia audience, "has yet work to do in making practical the political axiom of equal rights."[50]

VI.

HARPER GAVE THIS SPEECH IN PHILADELPHIA just weeks after the U.S. Senate debates over these same murders in Vicksburg and Louisiana, debates interrupted by the delivery on the Senate floor of the WCTU's prohibition petitions. At the time, the white leadership of the WCTU was a part of what Harper viewed as a problem to be solved. The problem within the WCTU would only grow more intractable in the 1880s with Frances

Willard's tour of the South and her policy of sectional reconciliation. Yet these were the same years during which Harper joined the WCTU leadership. How was it possible that Harper could find a home in an organization that was so compromised on the issue that she viewed as so central to "the political axiom of equal rights"? Answering that question provides a window into the broader questions of why African American women joined the WCTU and how they negotiated their place within the movement.

Temperance had long been part of Frances Harper's repertoire of reform. As a lecturer for the Maine Anti-Slavery Society, she had experience with the prohibition politics of the Maine Law. The heroine in her 1869 novel, *Minnie's Sacrifice*, "long[ed] for the hour when woman's vote will be leveled against [grog shops]; and have . . . the power to close them throughout the length and breadth of the land." Harper viewed "slavery and intemperance" as the "twin evils" of her time. In that sense, she joined the WCTU for the same reason other women joined. This included a dedicated contingent of mainly educated and middle-class African American women.[51]

Lucy Thurman, who would become the WCTU's superintendent of work among colored people in the 1890s, had taken part in the original Woman's Crusade when it came through her hometown of Toledo, Ohio. The previous superintendent was Sarah Jane Woodson Early, who taught at Wilberforce College in Ohio, before moving to Nashville and emerging as the WCTU's most prominent African American leader in the South. The WCTU offered these African American women unique opportunities as lecturers and organizers. They might not have been equal opportunities; Lucy Thurman protested bad treatment by the national WCTU and lack of financial support for her organizing. But at a time when the nation's institutions closed their doors to women's political activism, especially African American women's political activism, the WCTU provided political space.[52]

But a racial line formed across this political space. In the North, individual black women crossed the line to join local WCTUs, and several unions in New Jersey and Connecticut integrated their memberships, although in New York and elsewhere blacks and whites formed separate unions. During its first years, because the WCTU's messaging was ambiguous, it left some black activists wondering if they were welcome in the organization. Frances Harper was aware of the WCTU but did not join until 1883, because she "was not sure that colored comradeship was very desirable." When the WCTU went to the South, its mainly white organizers recruited thousands of women from Texas to North Carolina into black unions. Many of these women had experience with the Good Templars, who mandated segregated lodges. The black WCTU unions often met in Methodist, Baptist, and AME churches and, like the churches, were organized separately from their white counterparts. But here, too, in places the lines were crossed. Black and white WCTU members worked together canvassing to restrict alcohol sales by way of local option ordinances. White and African American women also met within the state WCTUs, or at least they did until the 1890s, when they formed separate state unions. African American women in North Carolina avoided the designation of "colored" unions because they wanted to leave the door open to any white women who wanted to join them and because, as they put it, "we believe all men are created equal." The African American state unions took the name "State WCTU No. 2."[53]

The white WCTUs in the South drew a line between cooperating for the common good and any type of interaction that suggested social equality. What they called "interracial cooperation" to get out the vote for a temperance ordinance was one thing. But they deemed unacceptable anything that suggested social equality between black and white WCTU members. The white South might acquiesce in the political equality required by the post–Civil War amendments, but this did not mean recognizing African Americans as being equals in the social hierarchy. Notions of white supremacy hinged on this distinction: hence the taboo against "race mixing" in social contexts—from sexual relations to voluntary associations. The distinction between political and social equality, however, was a fiction and was fully revealed as such by the turn of the century with the adoption of the "white primary" and other measures of political disenfranchisement. Nonetheless, it was a fiction that the WCTU leaned on for its southern strategy.

Frances Harper expressed concerns about "the spirit of caste" in the WCTU, taking note of how "the colored question had come into [its] work." Yet she remained hopeful about its prospects. And part of that hope can be explained by her interpretation of the social equality problem. *Minnie's Sacrifice*, as with much of Harper's work, affirmed a common humanity and the cruelty of dividing this humanity by skin color. At the same time, she accepted social divisions based on education, culture, property, wealth, and other markers of "civilization." During her tours of the South, Harper wrote home of the ignorance and poverty among the former slaves, of men ill-treating their wives, squandering their votes, and living like "heathen." From this perspective, she embraced the notion of social equals based on equal conditions. "Social equality, if I rightly understand the term," Harper reasoned, "is the outgrowth of social affinities and social conditions, and may be based on talent, ability, or wealth." The mistake that the white women of the WCTU were making, however, was confusing social equality with "Christian affiliation" that must transcend social difference. In other words, Harper accepted the realities of social difference that separated middle-class white women from uneducated and poor black women, but she insisted on "the union of Christians to do Christly work" for the common good.[54]

VII.

MUCH OF THE WORK OF THE WCTU in the South focused on the votes of black men. Even after the defeat of Reconstruction, many African Americans continued to vote until the disenfranchisement laws at the end of the century. The women of the WCTU understood the importance of their ballots. "The people of African descent form no small factor in politics of this government," Sarah Early reported from Tennessee, "[a] factor whose suffrage no one can afford to turn to bad account."[55] The fate of temperance legislation, Early and the other WCTU leaders argued, hung on their efforts to uplift the black voter. Leading the efforts to recruit black voters to prohibition, Sallie Chapin spoke in African American churches and meetings across the South. She appealed to black voters by playing on the Lost Cause myth of the loyal slave: just as yesterday they remained true to their masters in the crisis of the Civil War, today they will follow their former masters in the battle against the liquor trade. Reporting on a local option campaign in a South Carolina town, Chapin declared, "Liquor is doomed in Allendale, and the liquor dealers know it." The key to victory would be the loyalty that the black majority of Allendale showed to Chapin, "a lady, and one of their own ladies, too."[56]

At the same time, the WCTU leadership believed that the black vote was unreliable and that liquor dealers could unduly influence uneducated, poor, and treacherous black men. In 1881, a prohibition referendum in North Carolina failed at the polls, and the WCTU attributed the defeat to manipulation of the black vote by Republicans and liquor dealers. In reality, black men had their reasons for voting on the temperance issues one way or the other as they navigated the racial minefields of post–Civil War politics. Nonetheless, the defeat of prohibition in North Carolina put the WCTU on guard against the potential danger of the black vote. Sallie Chapin explained this to the annual meeting of the WCTU in 1881. "We have a South, and we have a problem at the South," she said, and that was black treachery at the polls. The solution, Chapin argued, was an educational test for suffrage, and this would remove not only the "demoralized" black vote in the South but also the vote of the "beer drinking Irish and Germans."[57]

Frances Willard said similar things over the years about beer and immigrants and literacy tests for women voters. She eventually came around to Sallie Chapin's views about restricting the black vote. In an 1890 interview with the New York paper *The Voice*, Willard explained how the North had "wronged the South" by entrusting the former slaves with the ballot. The liquor seller purchased the votes of the "plantation Negro" for twenty-five cents, according to Willard. She called for restricting black votes rather than force the "Anglo Saxon race" to submit to the "dark-faced mob."

"The colored race multiplies like the locusts of Egypt," she warned, and with the "grog shop [the] center of its power," this race menaced "the safety of women, of childhood, of the home." Recognizing the error of the post–Civil War promise of black political equality, Willard believed, was the only way to "solve the problem of the South."[58]

WCTU members had debated qualified suffrage in the past, and there was dissent within the leadership over Willard's embrace of literacy tests in the South. Susan S. Fessenden of Massachusetts, for example, who supervised the WCTU's franchise work, continued to hold out for universal suffrage.[59] But resistance flagged. Significantly, Frances Harper joined the demand to restrict the vote. This was a striking turn for a woman who had spent her adult life working with the likes of Frederick Douglass and Sojourner Truth for the ideal of political equality without regard to race or sex. But she found it necessary to hedge that ideal when the Democratic Party and its allies in the press and pulpit had placed literacy tests, poll taxes, and other means of black disenfranchisement on the political agenda across the former Confederacy. So why would Harper also call for voting restrictions? Part of the answer lies with her long-held doubts about the effectiveness of universal suffrage. At least since the first days after the Civil War, she expressed that ignorance, poverty, and intemperance limited the social value of extending universal suffrage to women and to African Americans.[60]

VIII.

EVENTUALLY, FRANCES WILLARD EXPRESSED DOUBTS about whether it was worthwhile for black Americans to strive for equality in their own country. In her interview with *The Voice*, she said that if she were black, she would head for Africa, "where my color was the correct thing," and let the white people "work out their own destiny" on the American continent. She made this comment about the racial destiny of continents at a time when the imperial powers were drawing tight the global color line, a line reshaping the imagination of women's rights and egalitarian reform.

Within the ranks of the WCTU, the Native people of the American

West played an important part in their understanding of this color line. The fieldwork of the anthropologist Alice Fletcher informed much of the federal government's tribal policy, including the Dawes Act of 1887 that dispossessed Native people of tens of millions of acres of tribal lands. At the 1891 meeting of the National Council of Women, she gave a lecture titled "Our Duty to Dependent Races." Fletcher described a world in which the superior white race "held possession of the best portions of the earth's surface," and she designated the "Indian and negro" as America's two "dependent races" within this global system.[61]

Frances Harper was at that meeting and responded to Fletcher's lecture by reminding the audience that a black citizen was "a member of the body politic." To include African Americans in the category of "dependent races," she warned, would mean depriving them of their "claim on the nation for justice." African Americans, like Native Americans, Harper feared, would face marginalization and rightlessness, effectively closing the post–Civil War promise of equality. She knew of what she spoke. As a member of the WCTU leadership, she had witnessed up close the pivotal role that Native Americans had played in drawing the color line in the reform imagination.[62]

The WCTU drew two lessons from its extensive missionary work among Native Americans. On the one hand, Indians demonstrated the wretched fate of people who remained outside "civilization." In her address at the same meeting of the National Council of Women, Frances Willard retold a story of Seminole Indians working their women harder than horses and oxen. She also claimed that when she was a young girl back in Wisconsin, she had witnessed Winnebago women staggering under the weight of heavy loads while the men walked with light loads. Willard saw these unequal burdens as a "relic of barbarism" and evidence that the Indian was in need of rescue and assimilation.[63]

On the other hand, federal Indian policy showed the promise of prohibition. The members of the WCTU pushed for tighter control of liquor sales to Indian tribes, which they believed, when properly enforced, pushed Indians toward the gates of civilization. Soon after her first trip to the South, Frances Willard visited the Indian Territory as the guest of the Cherokee chief Dennis Wolf Bushyhead. She reported that an "iron clad prohibition law" had made the territory prosperous and peaceful for "87,000 red men and women . . . belonging to thirty-seven tribes." This included members of the Modoc tribe, "the synonyme of savage cruelty," as Willard called them, who had been exiled to the Indian Territory after the brutal violence unleashed by the U.S. Army in the lava beds on the California-Oregon border in 1872 and 1873. The combined impact of forced removal, missionary work, and prohibition, Willard happily reported, had turned the Modocs into perfect Christians.[64]

In 1883, Frances Willard made a "round-up" tour of the western states. The WCTU had already taken hold in California, but organizing the rest of the West was part of Willard's vision of national unification. Unlike her tour of the South, which focused on renewing white sisterhood across the Mason-Dixon Line, her trip west had a missionary purpose in regard to Indians, Mormons, Asians, and other groups perceived as outside Christian civilization. The WCTU looked to deliver the Indians "from the saloon power and the darkness of unbelief." But the aim was not to bring Indians into the polity armed with equal rights. The WCTU believed that "the poor Digger *can* be taught," but expected that even a "civilized Christian Indian" would remain on the other side of Alice Fletcher's color line.[65]

IX.

AS FOR CHINESE IMMIGRANTS, the WCTU in California rejected xenophobic efforts of expulsion and exclusion in favor of a policy similar to its approach to the Indians. Both were viewed as marginalized groups outside the body politic who were to be schooled and uplifted. The WCTU kindergartens, for example, enrolled Chinese children as part of this program of uplift. The kindergartens inspired Willard to search for means to expand the WCTU's work on both sides of the Pacific. She had a long-standing curiosity about Asia, its religions, and its people, and the sight of San Francisco's opium smokers grabbed her attention. The parallel between alcoholism and the opium habit suggested unlimited possibilities for the WCTU, because, as Willard noted, the evils of alcohol and opium "encompass the human race." The WCTU had sent missionaries to Africa and across the Pacific in the past. But with her visit to San Francisco, Willard decided to make global organizing a priority and launched the World Woman's Christian Temperance Union.[66]

The World WCTU sent delegations to Hawaii, Japan, China, Siam, India, and across the British Empire. Much of the work resembled the missionary efforts of the Protestant churches that accompanied the empire builders. But the WCTU's Christian message was more ecumenical and more focused on protecting women from the "two-fold traffic" of alcohol and opium. Amanda Smith, an African American WCTU missionary stationed in Liberia, believed that "Africa's greatest need is temperance and holiness." Saving the "poor heathen," Smith argued, meant stopping the "Christian nations" from exporting rum to the continent. With this aim, the WCTU petitioned the U.S. Congress to prohibit sales of liquor to "all uncivilized, and therefore unprotected people." As with the Native Americans, the idea was to civilize and protect those on the dark side of the global color line.[67]

At the same time, the resolutions of the World WCTU focused on women's rights. The 1893 World WCTU convention demanded "recognition of woman's equal rights" and women's "equal power in government." Here, too, the global color line was tightly drawn. The World WCTU rested on an alliance between the women temperance activists in the United States and Britain, and much of its organizing efforts focused on the white women within the British Empire: Canada, Australia, New Zealand, and South Africa. What these countries had in common, with a few exceptions such as the Maori vote in New Zealand, was that they held the nonwhite indigenous populations as "protected" or "dependent races" without political rights.[68]

When the World WCTU made its proclamations about equal political rights for women, it accepted this racial ordering of colonialism and empire. This was the context in which Frances Willard suggested that American blacks depart for Africa and let the white people of America work out their "destiny." And this was the context in which Frances Harper so strenuously protested labeling blacks a "dependent race"—a category that suggested a future not only like that of Native Americans but also like that of the marginalized and disenfranchised population of South Africa and the rest of the colonial world.

X.

MEANWHILE, FRANCES WILLARD'S political imagination turned to new possibilities of an alliance with the labor movement. Through the early 1880s, the labor work of the WCTU had focused on missionary activity to convert workers to temperance. But the recognition that the labor movement could be a potential political ally changed the equation. By the mid-1880s, the logic of what Willard called the "inherent antagonism between labor and liquor" pushed the WCTU and the Knights of Labor toward each other. The WCTU's labor work turned to building ties with the Knights and other labor organizations for common political ends. Willard understood that both the labor movement and the women's movement pursued their own egalitarian demands, and the points where they intersected created synergies of mutual reinforcement.[69]

The alliance with the Knights of Labor had its critics. Some members of the WCTU viewed it as a departure from the movement's temperance roots. Willard defended the alliance by reminding women of the role the Knights played in the cause of women's equality. They went on strike to rescue sewing women from starvation, raised the motto "Equal pay for equal work," and demanded equal political rights for women. As for the future, Willard predicted that labor was the force that would bring "an evenness between the eight-hour day of the husband and the sixteen-hour day of the wife."[70]

The labor movement, Willard believed, offered new possibilities of human equality. Influenced by the ideals of the cooperative commonwealth, she imagined a leveling of the unequal power between capital and labor, between mental and manual work, between city and country, and between men and women. Sexual equality, Willard came to understand, could only be realized by way of a radical departure from the competitive system of private enterprise. She called these ideas "Gospel socialism," and by the late 1880s they had gained a following within the WCTU's ranks.[71]

Nonetheless, the WCTU's alliances with the labor movement always rested on practical politics. Both the leadership and much of the membership came to recognize that urban and middle-class political coalitions could only do so much; a common political front with farm and labor organizations could potentially do so much more. Rather than rely on the "lily-handed men of college, court, and cloister," Willard urged, our hopes lie with "the farmers whose 'higher education' has been the Grange, and the mechanics trained by trade unions and the Knights of Labor."[72]

The WCTU looked to create a new political formation based on the voluntary associations of the day. This would eventually lead to negotiations with the Farmers' Alliance and other farm groups. But in the mid-1880s, it was the Knights—the great association of the nation's wage earners—that first captured the attention of the WCTU. Indeed, the two movements had much in common. Most important, they shared a similar road map for how to cross the tortuous grounds of post-Civil War equal rights.

PART III

LABOR'S KNIGHTS

6.

LABOR'S HOUR

O N SEPTEMBER 6, 1869, fire destroyed the Avondale mine in the anthracite coalfields of northeastern Pennsylvania. Soon after ten in the morning, while the miners worked the coal faces hundreds of feet underground, fire broke out in the structures at the top of the mine shaft and consumed the wooden linings of the shaft itself. Workers on the surface battled the flames until late in the afternoon, when the first of the rescue teams was lowered into the mine. Rubble, dead mules, and smoke clogged the gangways. Poisonous gases killed two of the rescuers. Thousands of miners and their families gathered at the mouth of the mine as the bodies of the men and boys were eventually hoisted from the smoldering depths. This slow and grisly process continued for two more days before crews pulled the last of the 108 bodies of the trapped miners to the surface. The country's worst mining disaster to that point had indiscriminately taken the lives of supervisors and laborers, veteran miners and children as young as ten years old.[1]

The disaster at Avondale provoked an outpouring of solidarity. Workers from surrounding cities and towns arrived by special train to join the vigil at the smoking ruins of the mine. John Siney, who led the efforts to bring a union to the anthracite fields, gave a speech "in behalf of the stricken people of Avondale." He indicted the mining capitalists as the responsible party and pointed out that the miners would have been alive if the operators had spent the money to dig a second shaft into the mine. He spoke a truth that matched the testimony of the surviving miners. To shave costs, the managers for the Delaware, Lackawanna & Western Railroad (DL&W), which operated the mine, skipped the construction of a second shaft that would have provided ventilation and an escape route in case of fire. Avondale was in Luzerne County, but in neighboring Schuylkill County two mine shafts were the law, and many of the miners had experience in mines in England and Wales, where Parliament mandated two shafts and where the shafts were lined with stone or brick rather than flammable wood. The state legislature would respond to the miners by eventually requiring two mine shafts in all Pennsylvania coalfields.[2]

Terence Powderly, of nearby Scranton, would make his mark as the most celebrated and reviled labor leader of his generation. In his autobiography, Powderly claimed that the vigil at Avondale inspired him to take up labor's cause. He looked into the faces of the grieving mothers, received the wisdom in John Siney's words, and returned from Avondale in search of a labor organization to join. But the problem with Powderly's account of his formation as a labor activist is that he probably invented his trip to Avondale. He had stayed home in Scranton, where, twenty years old at the time, he was happily employed in the shops of the DL&W Railroad. He showed little interest in the labor movement until 1872, when he joined the Machinists' Union. In 1876, he joined a small and obscure society called the Knights of Labor. Ten years later, the organization had risen as a colossus and did so with Powderly as its leader.

The disastrous fire was a defining moment in the tumultuous post–Civil War labor activism centered on the mills, mines, and railway shops in the anthracite fields north and west of Philadelphia. The catastrophe symbolized what Powderly described as the "ignorance, indifference, thoughtlessness, and greed" that oppressed the people. At the same time, the thousands of workers who came to the vigil and provided aid to the survivors displayed the opposite possibilities, the potential of enlightened human solidarity.[3]

I.

FOUNDED IN THE SAME YEAR as the Avondale disaster, the Knights of Labor started as a secret society of Philadelphia garment cutters. By the time Powderly had joined its ranks in the mid-1870s, it had gained a small following in the anthracite fields. But the Knights of Labor remained a small and secretive organization; even its name was kept a guarded secret from the public. In 1879, the Knights held their General Assembly in Chicago and elected Powderly as their grand master workman. With his urging, the Knights of Labor cast off the restraints of its secret society and craft origins and made rapid inroads among the burgeoning industrial working class. Railroad workers and coal miners became mainstays of the organization, and local assemblies of the Knights took hold wherever the railroads went or coalfields lay, spreading the organization from coast to coast, from the Great Lakes to the Gulf of Mexico, and from urban centers to remote railway towns and mining villages. The Knights captured the energy of the surging labor movement, gained three-quarters of a million members, and by the mid-1880s stood as the biggest and most powerful workers' organization in the country's history, and arguably any country's history, to that point.

From across the Atlantic, Friedrich Engels greeted the Knights as "the first national organization created by the American working class as a whole" and encouraged his fellow socialists to look past its inadequate leader, strange name, and odd platform. "Whatever their shortcomings and little absurdities," Engels counseled, they represented the "raw

material" from which the working-class movement and American society "ha[ve] to be shaped."[4] But even its most enthusiastic supporters
struggled to articulate exactly what the Knights of Labor was: an organization of unprecedented scope and latent power that escaped easy
definitions.

In outward structure, the Knights resembled the Grange, a secret fraternal society that was at the same time open to a broad and inclusive
membership. The Grange welcomed men and women engaged in agricultural pursuits, but the Knights of Labor was even more expansive. Any person could join except bankers, lawyers, and liquor dealers, and join they
did. Its local assemblies enrolled everyone, including shoemakers, laundry
workers, carpenters, seamstresses, musicians, clerks, domestics, machinists, and homemakers. Farmers and farm laborers joined, too, with
Granges in Texas and other rural places reorganizing as local assemblies
of the Knights. Following the Grange example, the Knights set up cooperative stores and business ventures. Also like the Grange, the Knights
adopted an initiation ritual from the Masons and kept its membership and
meetings secret from the public. However, because many of its members
were Catholics, the Knights pared down its rituals to not offend the
church. At the same time, in an era when police forces, civilian vigilantes, labor spies, and employer blacklists posed existential threats to labor
organizations, secrecy often took on a more urgent and pressing meaning for the Knights.

The rationalized and uniform structure of the Grange provided a
model for the type of order and system Powderly and other leaders of the
Knights sought to emulate. But a benevolent society embracing the nation's
wage earners proved, by the very nature of American work, an extraordinarily messy business. A comparison with the nation's farmers suggests
the fractured, multifaceted complexity of the undertaking. In the previous
decade, Granges had brought farmers together across the corn belt, the
wheat belt, and the cotton belt where neighbors for miles in every direction faced common challenges of growing, marketing, and transporting
their crops. By contrast, members of the Knights toiled in more than a

thousand different occupations, with often markedly different conditions of life and work.[5]

In the twentieth century, manufacturing industries developed systems of rationalized and machine-driven uniformity. But this was the exception to the rule in the 1880s. Although more than three million wage earners worked in manufacturing, only a relatively small number worked in places such as large-scale textile mills, where the women and men who tended the looms were bound to their machines. In most industries, skilled craftsmen continued to enjoy authority and autonomy. In iron and steel mills, for example, iron rollers and puddlers did highly skilled tasks and directed much of the work of unskilled labor. A similar pattern prevailed in coal mines and railroad shops. Moreover, many workers in manufacturing did so using hand tools, often in small workshops, to make everything from knee pants to horse collars. Wage work was similarly diverse and complex in construction, domestic service, and trade.[6]

The Knights of Labor embraced this complexity. Its twelve thousand local assemblies mapped the multifaceted landscape of wage earning. It brought together in a general organization makers of silk hats and diggers of ditches, clerks and field hands. Its so-called mixed assemblies combined workers from multiple occupations and thereby organized entire neighborhoods and communities. Women joined the Knights, both in assemblies with men and in separate women's assemblies. And in the South, the Knights organized black and white coal miners, timber workers, mill hands, and farm laborers in nominally equal but separate black and white local assemblies.

Like the Grange and other fraternal societies, the Knights of Labor attended to the "wants and peculiar interests" of its members. It provided aid for the sick, the bereaved, and the blacklisted and held labor fairs and picnics on holidays. The Knights offered an economic value to membership in the form of improved wages and conditions of work, as well as cooperative business enterprise. At the same time, the Knights of Labor underscored its moral value. The first item in its declaration of aims posited the idea that "industrial and moral worth, not wealth," was "the true standard of individual and National greatness." The second item in its declaration placed the demands of the labor movement within this moral framework. A just division of wealth and a shorter workday, the Knights argued, would allow workers "to develop their intellectual, moral, and social faculties" and thereby "share in the gains and honors of advancing civilization." This moral agenda also entailed putting labor's house in order and confronting the violence and ignorance that plagued workers' homes and communities. That meant taking on the saloon.[7]

Terence Powderly regularly lectured his fellow Knights about the harm done by intemperance. He barred membership to anyone who sold alcoholic beverages, and ordered that lemonade, not beer, be served at the Knights' social functions. Most of the membership abided Powderly's lectures and accepted the rules. In his 1886 study of the labor movement, the economist Richard Ely of Johns Hopkins University was struck by the close connections between the struggle for sobriety and the struggle for labor rights, describing labor organizations as "the chief power, in this country, making for temperance." For Ely, this was especially notable given that most members of the Knights of Labor were first- and second-generation Irish, German, and other immigrants. Frances Willard was similarly impressed. She became a friend of Powderly's and kept an image of him among the photographs above her desk. Willard's tree-lined Evanston was a long way from the soot, smoke, and cacophony of Powderly's Scranton. But the camaraderie between the two was real and reflected a coincidence of purpose between their respective organizations.[8]

The Knights of Labor, then, served as a benevolent society of wage earners committed to the moral improvement of its members. But it also had a critical function as the labor organization of specific trades and industries. Apart from the "mixed assemblies," most of its members belonged to assemblies made up of workers in a single trade, and these "trade assemblies" were often regional or national district assemblies. Shoe and boot workers, cigar makers, and window glass workers belonged to their own trade assemblies. A short-lived district assembly organized telegraph operators from coast to coast. District assemblies spread across the nation's coalfields. The railroad workers on the Union Pacific, the Wabash, and Jay Gould's southwest railroad system had their separate district assemblies. Not only did these trade assemblies provide the Knights of Labor with much of its membership and potential power; they also gave rise to sharp questions about the nature of the organization. Trade assemblies negotiated wages and working conditions with employers, organized strikes and boycotts, and performed the functions of a trade union. Although Powderly and other Knights might have insisted that trade assemblies were not the same as trade unions, what separated the two was not always evident.

Finally, the disjointed, multifaceted, and ill-defined nature of the Knights of Labor was compounded by the wide spectrum of ideological claims within its ranks. At one especially chaotic point, Powderly described the organization as a "kaleidoscopic movement" fractured by "a babel of opinion."[9] Greenback Knights looked to monetary solutions to liberate labor from the oppression of monopoly. Single-tax Knights aspired to do the same with tax and land reforms. Trade unionist Knights advocated syndicalist notions of workers' power. Cooperativist Knights hoped to end wage slavery by means of worker ownership. Socialist Knights looked to public or government ownership, while anarchist Knights desired freedom from government. These incompatible beliefs led to factional bloodletting and pushed and pulled the organization in multiple directions.

For his part, Terence Powderly argued for at least elements of all these solutions, with anarchism being the notable exception. Like most Knights, Powderly embraced a variety of solutions that enjoyed currency among labor reformers of his day. At moments, he advocated for greenbacks, for land reform, for cooperatives, for trade association, and for public ownership. Although he stood aloof from much of the ideological warfare within the organization, Powderly dismissed the notion that he lacked high ideals. He also bridled at being called a reformer. "I never was a reformer and always objected to being called one," he claimed in his autobiography, because the term was too "ill-used" and "ill-fitting" to have meaning. "If I had the right to give myself a name," Powderly wrote, "I would call it equalizer."[10]

He defined the term "equalizer" in a double sense. On the one hand, he believed in equalizing the power between capital and labor. He gave the example of a coal miner injured by a falling rock. Without work or money and at risk of eviction and blacklisting, the miner suffered unequal power in seeking redress from the company. On the other hand, Powderly believed in equalizing the relationships among wage earners and in universal solidarity without regard to occupation, skill, or position. To give "an object lesson in equality," the officers of the Knights never sat on a platform above the members but "sat on the level with all the others." "The scavenger doing his work on the street," Powderly insisted, must be admitted to the Knights "on exactly the same terms of equality as the highest priced or most skilled artisan."[11]

Looking back decades later, Powderly suggested, given the highly stratified structures of the early twentieth century, that the Knights might have placed too much faith in the egalitarian ideal. "Perhaps some lingering, belated wind from the scenes of the early days of the French Revolution," Powderly speculated, "carried to our minds the thought that equality could be won." But in the 1880s, Powderly displayed full confidence in an egalitarian ideal that was widely shared. In 1887, the veteran labor leader George McNeill explained that the burning issue of the moment—what he designated "the problem of to-day"—was "how to establish equity among men" and "equitable relations" between employers and employees.[12]

The Knights voiced their egalitarian ethos in their celebrated motto: "An injury to one is the concern of all." This expression of solidarity, the historian Norman Ware wrote, like no other idea or sentiment, "caught the popular imagination of the time."[13] This was the sentiment that had brought thousands of workers to stand vigil at the Avondale coal mine, where industrial disaster took no measure of expertise or status, with skilled miners and fire bosses suffering the same fate as unskilled laborers and boys. And it was the idea shared by hundreds of thousands of wage earners who joined the local assemblies of the Knights.

In practice, the Knights of Labor fell short of its egalitarian principles. This was true when it came to sexual equality and racial equality. Its venomous attitude toward immigrant workers from China was the most egregious example of the movement's xenophobia and intolerance. Equal rights within the organization could be nominal at best, because highly skilled workers exerted disproportionate influence despite Powderly's assertion about the equal status of the "street scavenger" and the "highest priced" artisan. Yet the ideas that the Knights professed about equality and equal rights had a profound effect. They facilitated the inclusion of black workers and white workers, men and women, the desperately poor and marginalized and the more comfortable and well positioned. Such an all-encompassing organization of wage earners tested the limits of equality on multiple fronts. Looking back at the post–Civil War labor movement that preceded the Knights of Labor is the first step in understanding the significance and limits of what it accomplished.

II.

THE CIVIL WAR WEIGHED HEAVILY and unequally on the nation's wage earners. Workers did their share of the fighting and dying, both as volunteers and as conscripts, while "class legislation" allowed men of property to avoid service in the Union army by paying a three-hundred-dollar bounty, much as in the South the twenty-slave exemption protected plantation owners from the military draft. Workers experienced the dislocations, inflation, and other demands of a wartime economy that proved so profitable for the financiers and capitalists who financed and supplied the armies. And many white workers feared that they would be the ones to suffer for the imminent destruction of slavery because freed black workers would compete for their jobs. This mix of class and racial politics exploded on July 13, 1863, ten days after the fighting at Gettysburg, in the New York City draft riot, where white workers unleashed their fury against symbols of wealth and power, even as they savagely murdered black residents of the city.[14]

A similar discontent rumbled through other working-class districts.

Opposition to the draft and the war ran strong in the anthracite coalfields north of Philadelphia, where Irish immigrants and other workers found employment and a haven from conscription. Violence flared in the coal towns. Rock-throwing women attacked draft enrollers, and groups of workers resorted to the destruction of mine property and launched attacks on mine officials and other authorities. Federal troops were deployed and rumors churned about an allegedly murderous conspiracy among Irish miners known as the "Molly Maguires." Meanwhile, miners came out in force to vote for Peace Democrats in the 1863 and 1864 elections. But even in the many other places where the workers' movement stuck with Lincoln, supported the Union effort, and sympathized with emancipation, there was a sense that the war was preparing a historical moment for workers to press their claims for equality.[15]

While the war raged on, labor activists turned their attention to this impending struggle. An opening shot was fired in December 1863, when Ira Steward of Boston and his Machinists' Union issued a call to fight for the eight-hour day. For the nation's workers—"from east to west, from north to south"—reducing the workday was "the cardinal point" to which "all else is subordinate."[16] His critics would describe Steward as an "eight hour monomaniac," but at least it can be said that he was so focused on the cause that he made this appeal in the midst of war between northern and southern armies, and only a week after the decisive clashes at Lookout Mountain and Missionary Ridge. By the close of the war, Ira Steward, along with the shoemaker George McNeill, had turned Boston into a hotbed of working-class agitation. They formed the Eight-Hour League and captured the attention of wage earners throughout the region seeking relief from long and debilitating workdays. On November 2, 1865, the abolitionist Wendell Phillips, joined by the congressman and former Union general Benjamin F. Butler, presided over a labor meeting in Faneuil Hall, where Steward read a resolution that staked out labor's postwar agenda:

> We rejoice that the rebel aristocracy of the South has been
> crushed, that . . . men of every clime, lineage, and color are

recognized as free. But . . . we want it to be known that the
workingmen of America will in future claim a more equal share
in the wealth their industry creates in peace and a more equal
participation in the privileges and blessings of those free
institutions, defended by their manhood on many a bloody
field of battle.[17]

With the arrival of peace and former slaves being "recognized as free,"
it was now labor's turn to claim an equal share and equal participation.
The Faneuil Hall meeting had taken place when the ratification of the
Thirteenth Amendment abolishing slavery was assured, but the substance
of black freedom remained an unanswered question. And it took place
only months after the meeting of the American Anti-Slavery Society where
Wendell Phillips had told advocates of women's suffrage that "this hour
belongs to the negro."[18]

The intersecting claims of equality could not have been more fraught
than they were at that historical moment. Nonetheless, Ira Steward had
no doubt about exactly whose hour it was. He overrode competing claims
with the argument that the abolition of slavery was merely the immediate precursor to the eight-hour day and the next step of freedom "yet to
come." Steward explained that the "relation between poverty and slavery"
was closer "than the average abolitionist ever recognized." Because of this
proximity, the "anti-slavery ideal" would remain but an abstract promise
until the nation made it a reality by breaking labor's chains of overwork
and unequal rewards.[19]

The historian David Montgomery explored the significance of
Steward's post–Civil War vision and its implications for the crisis of
equality. The struggle against slavery had brought wage earners, self-
employed property owners, and capitalists together under the tent of the
bourgeois Radical Republicans. In his book *Beyond Equality*, Montgomery
developed a narrative in which the workers' movement shattered this
cross-class coalition. At the close of the war, workers' demands for a
shorter workday brought into question the profits and prerogatives of the

employers, setting the working class on the path of "assault [on] the ramparts of private property, where the Radicals were among the defenders." Steward's class program, Montgomery suggested, would "carry the social debates of the day beyond Reconstruction, beyond equal rights for all citizens, beyond the limits of the Radical imagination."[20]

This move "beyond equality," however, never happened. The demands of labor fractured the Republican coalition, as a number of Radical Republicans responded to the eight-hour movement with dread and loathing. Edwin Godkin, for example, warned that labor's "passionate pursuit of equality of conditions" threatened to hurl society "down into barbarism." However, the post–Civil War issues of equal rights for all citizens did not lose their salience. Labor activists did their best to ignore or sidestep the nation's racial dilemma. But reality imposed itself. And for better and for worse—much like the farmers' movement and the women's movement—the labor movement played a critical role in the national drama of Reconstruction and the post–Civil War contest over the meanings of equality.[21]

III.

WAGE EARNERS GREETED THE CLOSE of the Civil War with a wave of organizing. In cities and towns across the country, they combined in an array of mainly local leagues, associations, unions, and assemblies. But they did so with a shared understanding that the issues they confronted required regional and national solutions. They looked to coordinate and equalize wages, hours, and conditions of employment as the welter of competition sent workers in a race to the bottom in one industry after the next. They sought a federal monetary policy to provide uniform and secure payment of wages and an equitable retirement of the war debt. They worked to create federal labor agencies to balance power between labor and capital. And they hoped for federal policies that would protect white labor from the shocks of the emancipation of black labor, ensure opportunities for settlement on western lands, and check competition from Chinese and other workers that they viewed as unfree. Labor activists turned their attention to the newly energized federal government while taking extraordinary steps to coordinate and centralize their own efforts. The first step came in August 1866, when dozens of these labor groups sent delegates to the National Labor Congress in Baltimore and formed the National Labor Union (NLU).

Illness prevented William Sylvis from taking part in the Baltimore meeting, but he had been the moving force behind the NLU and would later be elected its president. Raised in a small town near Pittsburgh, Sylvis learned the iron-molding trade before moving to Philadelphia, where he became a leader of the molders' union. A Stephen Douglas Democrat in 1860, Sylvis supported the Crittenden Compromise peace proposal and remained "anti-Lincoln, anti-Republican, and anti-war." Unemployed in the first days of the conflict, he went to Washington and took a job as a teamster. When Lee's Confederate troops threatened to invade Pennsylvania in the fall of 1862, Sylvis briefly joined a militia company as an orderly sergeant. Returning to Philadelphia, in 1863 he led a major strike of iron molders fighting for wages and equalization of prices. Molders' work involved pouring molten iron into molds to manufacture stoves and other essential appliances. But ruthless price wars between companies and regions meant unsteady work and wage cutting. Regulating prices within the industry from San Francisco to Philadelphia, Sylvis believed, could only be accomplished with a highly centralized national union. By 1865, the Iron Molders' International Union stood out as "the most powerful in number, resources, and completeness" of any labor union in the country. Its system of centralized and uniform organization would provide a model for the NLU and its efforts to bring order and equity to post–Civil War economic life.[22]

The NLU meeting in Baltimore put the question of the eight-hour workday at the top of its program. A law making eight hours "a legal day's work in every state of the American union," the NLU resolved, was "the first and grand desideratum of the hour." This emphasis on the hours of work reflected the influence of Ira Steward and his Boston group of Eight-Hour Leaguers, who popularized a theoretical system they called "the economic philosophy of the eight hour movement." Steward's theory, like that of the Marxists and other allies in the eight-hour movement, rejected the employers' contention that a shorter workday was only possible with lower wages. But in a departure from most other theories of wages and hours, Steward's theory focused on consumption and leisure. A shorter workday would give workers more leisure time, which would stimulate wants and needs, boost consumption, and promote a shared prosperity. Steward's core conclusion was that reducing the number of hours worked would increase the wages earned. In turn, that would be "the first step" toward "a more equal distribution of the fruits of industry," and following steps would approach universal emancipation, when "the producer and the capitalist will be one."[23]

It is difficult to judge how widely Steward's theory was either understood or accepted. But key arguments had practical appeal and captured the spirit of the times. Linking a shorter workday to higher wages promised relief to the overworked and the underpaid. The six-day week and the ten-hour day were the norm, but longer days were common. And low wages meant that most workers lived day to day, without savings or protection from injury, illness, and unemployment. Linking shorter hours with prosperity spoke to workers' concerns about the impact of the half a million soldiers returning to the civilian workforce and about buoying slack industries in the postwar economy. And linking the demand for the eight-hour day to "more equal distribution" addressed resentments of wartime inequities. As Jonathan Fincher of the Philadelphia labor assembly put it, "Labor is equality. Labor is dignity. Labor is power. It is able to regulate its hours."[24]

Eight hours of work with no cut in pay became a nearly universal demand of the post–Civil War labor movement. Eight-Hour Leagues, trade unions, and labor assemblies turned the issue into a political campaign with immediate results. By December 1865, Ebon Ingersoll, a Radical Republican from Illinois, and Andrew Rogers, a Democrat from New Jersey, had introduced to the U.S. Congress an eight-hour law for federal employees. William Sylvis and the NLU lobbied the issue with President Andrew Johnson, who ordered that "eight hours shall constitute a day's work." In 1868, Congress enacted an eight-hour day for workers employed in naval shipyards and by federal contractors. But the shorter hours, if they came, often brought wage cuts, and Sylvis and the NLU pressed President Grant to issue a decree in favor of no reduction in pay for eight hours of work. Congress's eight-hour law remained mainly symbolic. Several city governments adopted eight-hour laws, and where unions were strong, such as in New York and San Francisco, they were enforced at least for a time.[25]

The most promising legislative action took place at the state level. By 1868, Wisconsin, Connecticut, Missouri, New York, and Pennsylvania had adopted eight hours as the legal standard for the workday. When Illinois passed its eight-hour law, the state's attorney general, Robert Ingersoll (Ebon's brother), argued that the workday should be shortened even more to allow workers "to educate themselves until they become equals in all respects of any class." These state laws, however, were shot through with loopholes. Exemptions allowed employers to make separate contracts with their employees mandating longer hours, and when employers did cut the length of the workday, they often cut wages, too. In defiance, workers mobilized to make the standard a reality.

In the summer of 1868, months after Pennsylvania legislators passed an eight-hour law, wage workers and laborers led strikes that shut down the coal mines in the Schuylkill region to compel managers to accept the shorter workday. Teams of armed strikers marched with signs bearing the simple message "Eight Hours." Although the strike helped to spread John Siney's miners' union across the anthracite region, it ended in a compromise of a wage increase but with a ten-hour day. The eight-hour movement suffered similar setbacks across the country, yet the issue would remain high on the list of workers' most pressing demands.[26]

Federal and state measures to enforce an eight-hour day offered a direct method to bring system and order to the chaotic and destructive competition of the postwar economy. Establishing uniform standards for wages, however, proved more complicated. Thousands of enterprises spread from coast to coast used myriad pay scales and wage systems, and the postwar labor movement looked to federal and state governments to equalize these systems by providing centralized bureaus of labor statistics. Massachusetts had one of the first such bureaus, with Ira Steward serving as its first commissioner. And one of the key demands of the National Labor Union was the creation of the U.S. Bureau of Labor Statistics, which would compile data on employment, wages, prices, output, and other information to aid in the rationalization and regulation of industry. Such information gathering represented a potentially unwelcome intrusion into the business operations of private enterprises and a significant expansion of federal authority in the national economy. Yet the federal Bureau of Labor Statistics along with federal eight-hour regulations, federal currency, federal restrictions on Chinese immigration, and multiple other extensions of federal power enjoyed broad support within the labor movement. Significantly, the support extended across regions and parties, with pro-Democratic labor leaders such as William Sylvis advocating the building up of federal power on these fronts as strongly as his pro-Republican counterparts.[27]

Meanwhile, workers made use of their own organizational power to equalize and standardize pay and conditions of labor. Iron molders, for example, faced the whipsaw of midwestern and eastern employers setting workers against each other to undercut wages. William Sylvis and the Molders' Union responded with proposals for what they called "equalization." By setting a national price on iron products, Sylvis hoped, equalization would allow the union and employers to negotiate an "equal standard of wages between the East and the West." Shoe workers made similar efforts. So did coal miners, who fought to regulate and standardize how coal was weighed and measured and how payments were made. Equalization of wage structures, however, with their almost infinite complexity of skill, craft, place, and forms of payment, proved an elusive goal. Nonetheless, given the ineffectiveness of eight-hour laws, John Jarrett, an iron and steel union leader, would later argue that reducing hours of work and "making wages more uniform" went hand in hand. Making the eight-hour day a reality meant a "leveling up of the condition of the working people."[28]

IV.

JARRETT VIEWED SEXUAL EQUALITY IN WAGES—paying the same wages "to women as paid to men"—as part of the "leveling up" the workers needed. The National Labor Union and other post–Civil War workers' organizations also embraced the principle of equal pay for equal work and built alliances with women's equal rights organizations. When the NLU met in New York City in 1868, a number of delegates attended from women's groups, including Susan B. Anthony and Elizabeth Cady Stanton. William Sylvis, the new NLU president, welcomed Anthony and Stanton and supported their cause of political equality for women. But other delegates held that for the NLU to get entangled in the women's vote would hurt the labor vote, and argued against Stanton's participation because she was not a labor organizer but a women's suffrage advocate.[29]

Nonetheless, Stanton did participate, and women's rights made their mark on the meeting. Sylvis appointed Kate Mullany, the young leader of a laundry workers' union in Troy, New York, an NLU officer and national organizer. And the NLU adopted a remarkable resolution, co-authored by Anthony, on female labor. Putting the NLU on record in favor of women entering male-dominated crafts and professions, the resolution called on women "to learn trades, engage in business," "join our labor unions," and take whatever "honorable means" necessary "to do justice to women by paying them equal wages for equal work." Two years later, the NLU passed a similar resolution, asking "all working-men of our country, to do all in their power to open many of the closed avenues of industry to women, and welcome her entering into just competition with men in the industrial race of life." These NLU resolutions recognized not only the general principle of equal wages for equal work but also the lived reality that work segregated by sex was invariably treated as unequal work.[30]

Most of the NLU delegates represented male-dominated crafts and industries—printers and plasterers, carriage makers and coal miners— that would remain resolutely closed to women. These resolutions were not intended to pry them open. Their purpose might best be understood as egalitarian political gestures aimed at facilitating a political alliance between labor reform and women's rights. At the New York meeting, Anthony gave a passionate speech calling for independence from the old parties and exhorting her fellow NLU delegates to secure their rights by "break[ing] away from their party affiliations." After the meeting, Sylvis responded with an appeal to the "Workingmen and Women of the United States" to join together in a Labor Reform Party founded on "equal rights and equal privileges." But this new political alliance leaned heavily in the direction of the politics of white supremacy.[31]

Throughout that presidential election year, Stanton and Anthony had aligned themselves with the Democratic Party. Their magazine, *The Revolution*, made it clear that although the Democratic Party had failed to endorse women's suffrage, and although the party's presidential nominee, Horatio Seymour, was also a disappointment, Democrats at least shared their opposition to the Republican policy of universal male suffrage. Stanton gave a ringing front-page endorsement to a speech by the Democratic vice presidential candidate, Frank Blair, in which he spoke of the "despotism of bestial passions" unleashed by allowing black men to vote. And Stanton cited Blair's warning that women faced a dire fate "at the hands of Chinese, Indians, and Africans." Meanwhile, by background and inclination, William Sylvis was also drawn to the Democratic Party and its racial politics. *The Revolution* carried articles by and about Sylvis, including praise for his struggle against "Black Republicanism" and the party of "negro worshipers."[32]

At the same time, the leaders of the NLU were acutely aware that a policy of racial exclusion and intolerance was suicide for the labor movement. At its Baltimore meeting, Andrew Cameron, the influential labor editor, explained the postwar realities:

> Unpalatable as the truth may be to many, it is needless to disguise the fact that [black workers] are destined to occupy a different position in the future, to what they have in the past; that they must necessarily become in their new relationship an element of strength or an element of weakness, and it is for the workingmen of America to say which that shall be.

The only path forward in the new post-emancipation reality, Cameron added, was "for every union to help inculcate the grand, ennobling idea that the interests of labor are one; that there should be no distinction of race or nationality." He warned that the failure to secure "the co-operation of the African race in America" would turn black workers into strike-breakers. Moreover, given that black Americans "will soon be admitted to all the privileges and franchises of citizenship," they must be made political allies or the capitalists will "turn them as an engine against us." Delegates to the NLU meeting the following year in Chicago debated the same issues. William Sylvis cautioned that the strikes of white workers against black workers would fuel a conflict that "will kill off the trades' unions." The "negro will take possession of the shops if we have not taken possession of the negro," he predicted. "If the workingmen of the white race do not conciliate the blacks, the black vote will be cast against them."[33]

Despite such strategic declarations about the need for black and white labor solidarity, the hard truth was that the NLU represented mainly whites-only unions. Most of these found the idea of accepting black members "unpalatable" and nonnegotiable. Moreover, recognizing the need for solidarity across racial lines for the purposes of protecting labor unions usually did not extend to support for political and social equality for African Americans. The white labor movement either skirted the issue or, as in the case of Sylvis and the NLU leadership, made it clear that racial equality had no place on their agenda.

Not surprisingly, African Americans expressed deep skepticism about the intentions of the NLU and its unions. In December 1869, the National Colored Labor Convention met in Washington, D.C., to advocate for equal rights to employment, education, and access to land. Many of the delegates were Republican politicians and professional and religious leaders. Although they supported the NLU's proposal for a federal Bureau of Labor, they had bitter words for the NLU and its trade unions. The convention adopted a resolution denouncing trade unions and their policy of excluding black workers as "an insult to God, injury to us, and disgrace to humanity." A number of delegates said that the NLU was a tool of the Democratic Party and its war on racial equality. For evidence of such charges, they might have pointed to any of William Sylvis's speeches on the question, or Sylvis's tour of the South earlier that year.[34]

V.

IN FEBRUARY 1869, WILLIAM SYLVIS had set out on a tour of the South. The National Labor Union needed a southern base and political connections if it were to emerge as a national political power. Sylvis also hoped to extend the reach of his Molders' Union. Richard Trevellick of the Ship Carpenters' Union accompanied Sylvis on his tour of the former Confederacy. An emigrant from Britain and an advocate of temperance and women's rights, Trevellick eventually landed in Detroit, where he worked in the shipyards and gained prominence as a labor leader. But prior to the war, he worked for several years in New Orleans, a connection that would help open doors among southern workers.[35]

Their first stop was a visit at the Baltimore home of Duff Green. Benjamin E. Green, Duff's son, had joined the NLU, and the father and son had backed Sylvis as a potential Democratic vice presidential candidate in 1868. The elder Green had purchased fifty thousand acres of coal and iron land in Virginia and Maryland in the years prior to the Civil War. When the war came, his mills provided nearly half of the iron output of the Confederacy, and his factories supplied its armies with rifles, cannonballs, and horseshoes. The unlikely friendship between Duff Green and Sylvis was based on a common interest in boosting the iron business and a common dislike of the "military despotism" of the Radical Republicans.[36]

Sylvis and Trevellick moved on to Virginia, where political and business leaders sold them on southern charms and assured them the South would rise like a phoenix. In a letter home to Philadelphia, Sylvis wrote, "We are convinced that Norfolk will one day be the greatest commercial city on the Atlantic coast; and . . . Richmond will grow as a manufacturing city." But the prosperity of Norfolk and Richmond, they reported, was being choked by Radical Reconstruction and especially by the "huge swindle" of the Freedmen's Bureau. The problem with the Freedmen's Bureau was not that it was a federal agency extending the reach of centralized authority. After all, the NLU advocated for a labor bureau and other extensions of federal power. Rather, the problem lay in the purpose for which this federal power was being applied: relief rations for the former slaves. This type of federal intervention in the economy constituted "an outrage practiced by government, that no people should stand," Sylvis wrote. "We go for 'smashing the Bureau,' and making these lazy loafers work for a living."[37]

The NLU leaders had a similarly dismal view of the right of blacks to sit on juries. In Alabama, they were scandalized by reports of a black and white jury failing to convict "a villainous looking loafer, charged with arson." They were even more scandalized by the practice of what southerners derided as "social equality." Sylvis reported on a case where a northern white man allowed his daughters "to entertain young negro gentlemen." He explained that given the enormity of the provocation, the fact that the white citizens had not resorted to violence against this man and his daughters was evidence of white "patience" and "charity," giving the lie to Republican claims of Ku Klux Klan terror.[38]

At the same time, Sylvis and Trevellick were optimistic about uniting the "whole laboring population of the South, white and black, upon our platform." When white and black workers come together on the "great national questions" of labor reform, they predicted, "that will shake Wall Street out of its boots." During the course of their tour, they met "a number of intelligent negroes" open to this political project, potential recruits for a second "colored only" labor union. But they mainly paid attention to white workers in the foundries and railroad shops and to white farm and labor reformers such as Absolom M. West of Mississippi. West had been a cotton planter, railroad promoter, and Confederate general who was elected to Congress in 1865 but was barred from taking his seat because of his role in the war. He turned to the Grange as a political vehicle to campaign for white immigration and other interests of Mississippi's white farmers. West also joined the NLU and was recruited by Sylvis into its national leadership as the South's representative of the national labor movement.[39]

A sudden illness struck William Sylvis only months after his return from the South, taking the life of the country's most prominent labor leader at the age of forty-one. When the NLU met that September in Philadelphia, it elected Sylvis's traveling partner, Richard Trevellick, as its new president. The meeting also adopted the "Platform of the Labor Reform Party," spelling out the labor movement's position on the national issues of Reconstruction that had come to a boil in that fall of 1869. Although it addressed monetary policy, public lands, and western settlement, the platform was silent on the question of political equality and civil rights for African Americans. At the same time, the platform of the Labor Reform Party expressed outrage that the leaders of the former Confederacy had been deprived of "political equality" and demanded the full restoration of their civil rights. Since its first meeting in Baltimore, the NLU had been calling for "the speedy restoration of the agricultural interests of the Southern States." But as the Labor Reform Party platform made clear, this restoration was about not just cotton output but white political power. Southern delegates, including the former Confederate general Absolom West, thanked their NLU colleagues for their "generous, brotherly, and thoroughly patriotic position."[40]

The Labor Reform Party platform crystallized the paradox at the heart of the NLU's position on racial equality. In Philadelphia, as it had in the past, the NLU adopted a resolution saying that it knew "neither color nor sex, on the question of rights of labor," and invited black workers to join the NLU (as delegates of separate black organizations). But to join with white workers on this platform—"on the great national questions," as Sylvis had put it—meant that African Americans would have to abandon their own strivings for racial equality and submit to the restoration of white power in the former Confederate states. The partisan implications of the Labor Reform Party's policy were clear enough. In Illinois, for example, a debate over black suffrage and Reconstruction led some rural supporters of the Labor Reform Party to break ranks and return to the Republican fold. For his part, Isaac Myers, the president of the National Colored Labor Convention, called the Labor Reform Party "a grand farci-

cal claptrap, cunningly worked upon the unwary workingmen by in-
triguing [Democratic] politicians."[41]

VI.

THE POST–CIVIL WAR LABOR MOVEMENT also engaged the "great national problem" of what was to be done with the trans-Mississippi West.
The U.S. Army's unfolding wars against the Indian tribes brought into focus the dilemma of who would gain control of the newly conquered territories. Urban and rural wage earners staked their claims to ownership.
They wanted the opportunity for themselves or their children to join the
waves of new settlers who would put under the plow millions of acres of
new farmland over the next two generations. But corporate stakeholders
placed claims, too. This included railroad corporations, as well as corporate landholders, often based in Boston, New York, or London, who gob-
bled up vast tracts for speculative purposes. The platform of the Labor
Reform Party charged such land monopolies with violating the principle
that "all freemen when they form a social compact are equal in rights,"
an equality that could only be protected by dividing western lands into
parcels for "actual settlers."[42]

In the same Philadelphia meeting where it adopted this platform demanding that the West be reserved for white settlers, the NLU passed a
striking resolution in defense of Indian rights. "The Indian has the same
moral rights as any other type of people," the resolution stated, and "has
an original and inalienable right to maintain his tribal condition." Although it made no mention of the Indians' forcible alienation from the
land, it criticized as "grossly unjust" the use of government to force "an
unwilling citizenship." The inspiration for this statement might have come
from Wendell Phillips and other reformers from the abolitionist tradition
who after the war took an interest in Indian rights. The specific case of
the Cherokee Neutral Lands in Kansas also might have played a role. The
Neutral Lands had belonged to the Cherokee, but they were dispossessed
after aligning with the Confederacy. Meanwhile, white settlers staked
claims, and so did the railroad magnate James F. Joy, who held title to

what had been Cherokee land. The settlers refused to recognize Joy's title and argued that it had been granted without fair payment to the Cherokee.

When the courts and then the U.S. Army intervened on behalf of Joy's claim, the Settlers' Union of Cherokee County issued a protest demanding "equal and exact justice to all." The settlers declared their opposition to "monopolies [and] imperialism" and thanked the NLU and the workers of the country for their support. Indeed, the NLU and other anti-monopolists had taken up the cause of the Cherokee Neutral Lands (Benjamin F. Butler argued the settlers' case before the Supreme Court). For the NLU, these events reinforced its own vision of anti-monopoly equal rights and offered a way to reconcile demands for white settlement with notions that Indians had the same rights as "any other type of people."[43]

As for the place of Chinese immigrant workers, the NLU's Labor Reform Party had a blunt message of racial exclusion. It was "unalterably opposed to the importation of a servile race." Some labor activists dissented from the notion of a racial embargo, insisting that the problem with Chinese workers was not their race or origin. When a group of Chinese workers arrived to work at a Massachusetts shoe factory, for example, a workers' meeting in Boston declared that they welcomed "voluntary laborers from every clime" and assured them of "equal opportunities in every field of industry." But they wanted to block the arrival of what they considered unfree Chinese workers held under contract, or "coolie slaves." This same distinction had been made at earlier NLU meetings. The National Colored Labor Convention also welcomed "free immigration of labor of all nationalities" but opposed so-called coolie labor as a "system of slavery in a new form." Although the notion of the unfree "coolie" drew on racial stereotypes and prejudice, it allowed opponents of Chinese immigration to make a gesture of racial egalitarianism. But by the time of its 1869 meeting in Philadelphia, the NLU tabled a proposal that "voluntary Chinese emigrants ought to enjoy the protection of the laws like other citizens." The NLU leadership was no longer making even a gesture of treating Chinese workers as racial equals.[44]

VII.

THE "GREAT NATIONAL QUESTIONS" CARRIED different valence by place and region. The explosive issue of Chinese immigration on the West Coast was less so in the anthracite fields of Pennsylvania. The questions of political equality for African Americans and former Confederate generals ignited political debate in the industrial districts of the North and murderous warfare across much of the South. The eight-hour campaign waxed stronger in Boston meeting halls than on the bloody streets of New Orleans. Yet there was one set of questions that resonated with force across the entire landscape of the workers' movement: money, credit, and banking. Greenbacks and the problems of the reconstruction of the nation's monetary and financial system gained nearly universal traction from coast to coast, and that may explain why this problem eclipsed all others in the platform of the Labor Reform Party adopted at the NLU's meeting in Philadelphia in 1869. The monetary system put in place by the needs of war, as the platform explained, now served the "merciless demands of aggregated capital" and "oppress[ed] the rights of labor."[45]

Banking and currency held a special place in the political imagination of many American workers. This had been true since the days of Andrew Jackson, when "the monster bank" and similar creatures of conspiratorial politics ran amok. But there was also a practical, nuts-and-bolts side to workers' thinking: precarious money made precarious lives worse. Intense economic insecurity, living from payday to payday, gave workers a keen interest in receiving a secure form of payment. In the antebellum years, employers preferred to pay their employees with scrip or paper notes drawn from private banks rather than gold or silver coin. But such paper varied in value from bank to bank and state to state, was often worth less than advertised, and was frequently rejected as a form of payment. Too often the notes were counterfeit or the issuing bank went bankrupt, rendering the notes worthless. Workers' demands for hard money were demands for uniform, secure, and equal money.

The mix of currencies changed with the Civil War. Gold and silver coins still circulated, but they were increasingly the money of people who had money and were scarce in working-class and rural communities. State banks continued to issue notes, but now there were also the notes of the newly chartered national banks, most of which were located in the financial centers of the Northeast. Most important, greenback paper dollars were added to the mix, and for many workers greenbacks had proved their superiority. Issued to finance the war, greenbacks were patriotic and relatively plentiful money, worth the same amount in every corner of the country. Backed by the newly empowered federal government, greenbacks were "the people's money."[46]

Labor organizers had other reasons to push for a greenback policy. High on the list were the unequal burdens of the Civil War debt. During the war, financiers and other wealthy investors used greenbacks to purchase war bonds, and with the peace they demanded that the federal government redeem their bonds in gold. This unequal exchange at the expense of the people's government and the people's money drew the wrath of the labor movement. The platform of the Labor Reform Party viewed the bondholders' claims as "unjust and extortionate." Paying the war bonds in gold, William Sylvis said, was to "see our boasted *equal rights* to be the merest skeleton of liberty." Only by retiring the war debt in greenback currency would its burdens be shared equally.[47]

Then there was the question of interest rates charged by the incorporated private banks. During the Civil War, Alexander Campbell popularized a scheme to make credit cheap and plentiful. He called it the "People's Plan," and the first step was for the federal treasury to provide the people with "a currency of uniform value in all parts of the Union" that would hold the country together and form the foundation for his credit system. The people's currency would replace private banknotes and would then be convertible into government bonds yielding 3 percent interest. In this way, the "People's Plan" would serve as an industrial plan providing business enterprises with cheap credit. Campbell himself was a prosperous manager of coal mines and steel mills, and his plan was widely embraced by other entrepreneurs in the years after the war. They looked to cheap credit as the key to business success.[48]

But most wage earners were not capitalists in need of cheap credit. So why were they so attracted to a scheme to reduce interest rates? Why would the platform of the Labor Reform Party repackage Campbell's plan? The platform echoed his theories about the negative impact of high interest rates as a source of economic inequality and unequal power of bankers and financiers over productive labor. But here, too, there was a practical, nuts-and-bolts side to the labor movement's commitment to cheap credit. Workers in the postwar decades often showed keen interest in the success of their industries. Shoemakers, coal miners, and iron molders tied their own well-being to the production of shoes, coal, or iron stoves. David Montgomery suggested that the embrace of greenbackism by William Sylvis, the unions, and the NLU marked the "disintegration of radicalism" and the victory of the "labor reformers" over the "class conscious" workers. But in the postwar decades, class conflict and industrial boosterism mixed in surprising ways, as reflected in the deep and enduring influence of Greenback ideas within the labor movement.[49]

VIII.

THE NATIONAL LABOR UNION HELD its last meeting in 1872 because the trade unions that had supported it floundered in the industrial crash that began the following year. In 1874, when the Grange was still at the peak of its power, labor leaders formed two general workers' organizations based on the Grange model. The prominent labor organizer Robert Schilling led one of these. A German immigrant who grew up in St. Louis, Schilling served in the Union army before he apprenticed to a barrel maker, rose in the ranks of the Coopers' Union, and joined the NLU. When the NLU collapsed, Schilling called for a new organization built on the lines of the Grange and in "intimate cooperation with the Farmers' movement." The result was the short-lived Industrial Brotherhood. Schilling appointed Terence Powderly the Brotherhood's organizer in Pennsylvania. The other new group was the Sovereigns of Industry, which was formed by a Grange organizer in Massachusetts and described itself as "an outgrowth, or rather a complement of the Patrons of Husbandry" with the "interests of the two organizations . . . identical in many respects." What the Grange was to agriculture, the Sovereigns would be to "mechanical pursuits." William Saunders's colleague Marie Howland left the Grange for the new organization, and soon thereafter Saunders himself would launch yet another organization, the American Workers' Alliance, with similar goals. But for a moment, it was the Sovereigns of Industry that caught the attention of the reform movement. Within its first year, it recruited tens of thousands of workers across the Northeast and the Midwest, but soon thereafter it fell apart.[50]

As the economic depression of the 1870s wore on, labor organizers increasingly turned to Greenback politics. Unemployed and blacklisted union organizers campaigned as Greenback Labor Party candidates in industrial places across the country. This included Terence Powderly, who in 1878 ran on the Greenback Labor ticket for mayor of Scranton and won the first of three two-year terms. His colleague Robert Schilling served as the chair of the party in Ohio. In 1876, the Greenback Labor Party ran its first national campaign, demonstrating that, unlike most other independent labor parties of the post–Civil War decades, it had a truly national scope with ardent supporters from Texas to Maine. Its political strength derived from the fact that the Greenback movement was the product of a remarkable convergence between the wage earner and the farmer.[51]

Dating back to Shays's Rebellion of the 1780s, farmers' movements have been associated in historical memory with flexible currency and paper money. But in the years immediately after the Civil War, while the NLU and other labor organizations fought for greenbacks, the Grange stood aloof from the raging currency debates. This was because many farmers, remembering the fraud and caprice that afflicted the antebellum banknotes, favored hard money and "honest dollars." A competing school of thought, however, began to work through the ranks of the Grange. As the depression of the 1870s deepened, and as the state Granger laws proved only marginally effective, the idea took hold that flexible currency offered the nation's farmers "multiple pecuniary advantages." Expanding the currency by printing greenbacks, a growing number of Grangers and former Grangers came to believe, would reduce the cost of farmers' debts, weaken the monopoly of bankers, merchants, and other creditors, buoy the price of farm commodities, and stimulate the economy.[52]

Farmers and workers in the Midwest, the West, and the South hoped that Greenback policies would break the unequal financial and monetary power of the Northeast. Greenback currency, a graduated income tax, and other monetary and fiscal measures, however, were only the starting point of a broader farmer-labor political alliance. The Greenback movement relied on a network of political candidates and newspaper editors aligned with the Grange, farmers' associations, trade unions, and other labor groups. In Minnesota, for example, the anti-monopolist Grange leader Ignatius Donnelly emerged as the state's leading Greenbacker and potential presidential candidate. The movement embraced the familiar labor demands for the eight-hour day, a bureau of labor statistics, the prohibition of child labor, and other federal and state measures to "equalize [labor's] burdens." At the same time, it adopted the anti-monopoly positions of the Grange, including the federal regulation of interstate commerce and "moderate, fair, and uniform rates for passenger and freight traffic." The balance of power within the Greenback movement leaned toward the farmers of the Midwest and the South. Terence Powderly suspected that it leaned too far in favor of the "agrarian greenback bloc" and against the workers' interests. Yet, when it was at its strongest point in the late 1870s, the Greenback Labor Party had a footing among the wage earners of New York and Pennsylvania and among the farmers of Texas and Iowa.[53]

In the 1878 election, the Greenback Labor Party ran on a platform of equal rights for everyone everywhere. In Massachusetts, Benjamin Butler ran as the Greenback candidate for governor with the motto "EQUAL RIGHTS, EQUAL DUTIES, EQUAL POWERS, EQUAL BURDENS, EQUAL PRIVILEGES, *and* EQUAL PROTECTION, by the *laws*, TO EVERY MAN, EVERYWHERE under the Government, State or National."[54] But in its very expansiveness, the Greenback Labor Party avoided the specific issues regarding the equal rights of African Americans and the recent toppling of Reconstruction. If the Greenbackers sought deliberate ambiguity in 1878, there was perhaps greater clarity six years later, when Butler ran as the Greenback Labor Party candidate for president. He did so with the backing of leading figures from the labor movement, including Charles Lichtman, the general secretary of the Knights of Labor, and Absolom West, the southern representative of the former NLU. By adding West, with his record as a Confederate general, to their 1884 ticket, the Greenbackers hoped to draw southern voters, many of whom despised Butler for his role in the war. But the Greenback Labor Party received less than 2 percent of the vote in West's Mississippi; the Greenback movement had lost its former energy. By this time, however, a new power had appeared on the national scene with the extraordinary rise of the Knights of Labor.[55]

7.

EQUALIZERS

I N ITS EARLY YEARS IN PHILADELPHIA, the Knights of Labor was a small society of garment cutters, one of the hundreds of similar trade organizations that mainly skilled white men formed across the country. Labor organizers made valiant attempts to build a movement with a broader foundation. The National Labor Union, the Industrial Brotherhood, and the Sovereigns of Industry proved to be short-lived efforts to overcome the narrowness of the existing trade organizations. By the mid-1880s, it was the Knights of Labor that stood out as the movement that transcended parochial boundaries. It organized entire communities and industries and was national—and international—in scope. It enrolled female and male, black and white, and unskilled and skilled wage earners. And it reached deep into the ranks of poor and working people who mainly did not earn wages, from housewives to sharecroppers.

What accounts for the Knights' transformation? Part of the explanation lies with the expansive vision of Uriah Stephens, the leader of the organization for the first decade of its existence. Stephens saw his association as a means to work for equality between capital and labor. But he also saw it as the first step toward a fraternal society of "world-wide and universal scope." He defined its aim as "a compact and homogeneous amalgamation [of] all the world's workers." It would knit together a "universal brotherhood" to be "guided by the same rules, working by the same methods, practicing the same forms for accomplishing the same ends."[1]

This message of cohesion and symmetry resonated within a fractured labor movement. It attracted the likes of Robert Schilling and Terence Powderly. Blacklisted from his employment as a machinist, Powderly first joined the Knights in 1876. He would later recall that when he did so, he left behind the trade unions, which acted selfishly for their own trades. As "steam and electricity have forever broken the power of one trade" to stand alone, Powderly was looking for "one grand labor-saving invention" to combine "all the scattered battalions of labor." He believed the Knights of Labor was that invention. For the next seventeen years, even while serving as the mayor of Scranton, Powderly made its success the focus of his talents and energy.[2]

In 1878, in Reading, Pennsylvania, the Knights of Labor held its first General Assembly. Its declared purpose was to "bring order out of chaos" and to "direct the movement along well-defined, harmonized lines." Schilling and Powderly brought their copies of the platform of the Industrial Brotherhood that spelled out the now familiar "national questions" of the labor movement, including the eight-hour day, greenback currency, Chinese exclusion, equal pay for equal work "for both sexes," and "abrogation of all laws that do not bear equally upon capital and labor." At Reading, the Knights adopted this platform as their own, and its demands would remain vital to labor and farmer politics for a generation.[3]

The following year, Powderly succeeded Stephens as the grand master workman of the Knights. He worked quickly to publicize the organization in the nation's newspapers and opened the doors to new membership.

Under Stephens's leadership, the existence of the Knights of Labor was to be kept secret from the public, and the meetings of its assemblies were devoted to elaborate rituals borrowed from the Masons and other fraternal orders. On the grounds that it was a secret and ritual-bound society, the Catholic clergy barred members of the church from joining the Knights, no small matter given the number of potential members who were Catholics, Irish or otherwise. For their part, the Protestant clergy joined in with their own charges that the Knights of Labor was a secret society of "communism" and "incendiarism." Powderly, a Catholic with his own conflicts with his church, proposed making the name public and simplifying the ritual, a proposal that gained support among coal miners and other recruits. Going public had its risks, and in mining and mill towns known organizers of the Knights often faced blacklists and worse. But it proved a key step in the Knights' transformation into a national voluntary association of wage earners.[4]

With its rapid growth in the early 1880s, the Knights increasingly took on features resembling the Grange. This was due to design as well as to proximity: coal miners and railway workers often shared rural and isolated places with farmers and Grangers. In Texas and the Southwest, "a large number of Granges" had regrouped as assemblies of the labor organization. And excited rumors of a possible merger of "the two grand organizations into one" persisted well past the time when the Grange was no longer so grand.[5]

In many communities and neighborhoods, a local assembly of the Knights served a similar function as a local Grange. It also served as a federation of trade assemblies and craft associations, inheriting much of the legacy of William Sylvis and the National Labor Union. The Knights, however, proved more expansive, inclusive, and egalitarian than its predecessors. This was mainly the doing of the African Americans, the women, the unskilled, and the poor, who mobilized into assemblies of the Knights in unpredictable and forceful ways. They saw the Knights as a vehicle for their own equal rights claims and seized on the opportunities that it provided. The doors to at least some of these opportunities were left ajar by the leadership of the Knights and the perplexing Terence Powderly.

I.

POWDERLY WAS SOMETHING OF A RIDDLE. Observers noted that he did not look like a proper leader of a mighty workers' organization. A reporter for a labor newspaper noted that he was "unlike the average labor reformer in appearance." With "the looks of a man of good breeding," he was slightly built and bespectacled. "English novelists take men of Powderly's look for their poets, gondola scullers, philosophers and heroes crossed in love," the reporter explained, "but no one ever drew such a looking man as the leader of a million of the horny-fisted sons of toil." It was not just his appearance, however. His many critics accused him of lacking the grit and fire of a true labor leader. When Karl Marx's daughter Eleanor Marx and her partner, Edward Aveling, visited the United States in 1886, they observed that Powderly represented the "conservative" and "reactionary" element within the Knights. Ever since, most histories of the Knights have stressed the inadequacies of Powderly's stewardship.[6]

Whether it involved his moralistic harangues, his dislike of strikes, or his views on the class struggle—he claimed that he "hated that word 'class'"[7]—Powderly appears in the history books as a vacillating, impractical, vain, timid, ineffective, or even treacherous character, out of step with the militant labor movement that he led.[8] Notable exceptions include studies by Robert Weir and Craig Phelan that suggest Powderly was more aligned with the membership, more beloved in working-class communities, and more principled and effective as a leader than most of his critics have allowed.[9] Nonetheless, the controversies that have swirled around Powderly reflect that he was an unusual and enigmatic figure. Moreover, when the Knights fell on hard times, it was inevitable that he would take a full share of the blame.

The exact share of responsibility that Powderly carried for the successes and failures of the Knights is difficult to measure. With its top-down structure, the organization gave its grand master workman extraordinary authority over decisions large and small. In 1883, Powderly's title was changed to general master workman to better reflect the organization's democratic ethos.[10] But whatever the title, between meetings of the General Assembly, Powderly and a small group of executives had tremendous leeway to lay down the law on everything from labor conflicts and political campaigns to disputed memberships and the proper refreshments at picnics. At the same time, much of this authority was only on paper, and the local and district assemblies often could and did act on their own as they saw fit.[11]

Powderly never accumulated the political clout that Frances Willard exercised in the WCTU. He lacked Willard's political discipline and drive. Moreover, unlike the WCTU and the Grange with their relatively uniform organizational systems, the Knights of Labor was an amalgam of local, regional, and national organizations that had a variety of functions, priorities, and unique constituencies—all of which played into an intense factionalism. This did not void Powderly's authority. He was the most popular labor leader of his generation. His words carried moral weight. His scolding was often tolerated and even respected. This makes it difficult to separate Powderly's often unorthodox ideas and irascible behavior from the expansive growth of the Knights of Labor, the doors that it opened to the marginalized and ignored, and the ways in which it tested the limits and meanings of equality.

Powderly's account of his first experiences with the problems of equality began in the family home in Carbondale, a company town in the anthracite fields of Pennsylvania. Powderly was the eleventh of twelve children, and his Irish father worked for fifteen years as a mine laborer before getting a job as a mechanic. Sickly and weak as a child, Powderly would later recount that he was much closer to his Irish mother, who "ruled the part of the world that I was brought up in." She taught him to wash dishes, mend clothes, and churn butter. In the process, she provided lessons about the value of work across the sexual division of labor. During the Civil War, when two of his brothers returned home from the Battle of Antietam, his mother and the rest of the family went to the station to greet their heroes. Meanwhile, the then-thirteen-year-old Powderly stayed home to cook their dinner, only for a pot of gravy to boil over, scalding his foot. Years later, he jokingly recounted this tale of the dangers of domestic labor.[12]

Like most Irish workers in the coal towns, Powderly's father was "a pronounced Democrat." His mother, however, was "a pronounced abolitionist." In Powderly's telling, as a child he experienced the injustice of his mother not being allowed to vote for John C. Frémont and the Republican ticket in 1856. When he reached voting age, Powderly formed a local U. S. Grant club and remained a more or less loyal Republican for the rest of his life. The big exception was when he campaigned for the Greenback Labor Party and ran for mayor of Scranton on the Greenback ticket in the late 1870s. Soon thereafter, he abandoned his interest in third parties, and although he briefly probed the possibility of making alliances with the Democrats, he never did abandon his Republican leanings, nor did he overcome his dislike of the Democratic machine in the mining towns.

In 1884, when Robert Schilling, Charles Lichtman, Richard Trevellick, and other leading Knights wanted the organization to support Benjamin Butler's Greenback campaign, Powderly refused and stuck to a position of nonpartisanship. He wanted no part of independent labor tickets that played into Democratic hands, a position that set him at odds with many of his white comrades, just as it provided assurance to African American activists that the organization was not a Democratic trap.[13]

Much as he was a Republican who disliked partisanship, Powderly was a Catholic who disliked religious sectarianism. Growing up on the Protestant and Welsh side of Carbondale, he saw how divisions by faith fueled the disorder and chaos plaguing the mill towns. He stayed in the church as an adult but protested its narrowness and the inequity of its favoritism toward "the rich and the well-to-do as against the poor." His conflicts with Scranton's bishop, William O'Hara, were public and hard fought. As for the Knights and religion, he applied a humanist and inclusive standard. Because the organization only dealt with the "welfare of humanity" and not the afterlife, Powderly believed, one could be "a good Catholic, Methodist, Presbyterian, Jew, Turk, or Atheist and be a good Knight of Labor."[14]

Powderly learned similar lessons about the sectarianism of trade unions. He had the good fortune of an apprenticeship that allowed him to become a skilled and talented machinist repairing locomotives. But he was acutely aware of less skilled and unskilled labor in the shop. When he made a proposal in a meeting of the machinists' union that boilermakers be allowed into their ranks, his proposal was shot down because boilermakers were viewed as a lower class of labor with "untidy habits and lack of neatness in dress." Powderly responded with a poem lampooning "aristocrats of labor," with their "clean collars, cuffs, and shirts," and predicting that "things will change" and "men of toil will surely meet in one great combination." He later described trade unions as "factions or clans" because they divided workers by craft or trade and separated the skilled workers from the laborers whose efforts were no less essential. Prodding and preaching about the sectarian egoism of labor organizations would become a hallmark of Powderly's leadership. There was "no reason why our members should be regarded as beings of superior build or material," Powderly warned the membership in an 1886 circular. "We are no more the salt of the earth than the millions of unknown toilers who do the work of the world."[15]

Powderly's egalitarianism was inseparable from his strivings to overcome the industrial chaos and mayhem of his environment. He came of age in an insecure and dangerous world choked by coal dust and smoke. Industrial booms meant endless hours in the mine or mill, and industrial busts pushed families to the edge of starvation. During the depression of the 1870s, the railroad managers put Powderly on their blacklist, a painful lesson in the arbitrary power of the companies and the extreme insecurity of life for those who worked for them. The Avondale disaster of 1869 killed 110 miners, but in each of the ensuing years in Pennsylvania's anthracite mines, twice that number were killed by falling roofs and poisonous gases. Meanwhile, strikes and lockouts fueled recurrent bouts of lawlessness. Employers mobilized hired gunmen against striking workers and labor organizers, groups of workers beat and terrorized company men, and strikers and strikebreakers attacked each other. Powderly experienced all of this close up.[16]

The endemic violence in Powderly's world came to a head in the summer of 1877. On June 21, ten Irish workers, convicted for taking part in the alleged terrorist conspiracies of the "Molly Maguires," were hanged in Schuylkill and Carbon Counties. Ten more would be hanged in the following months. Some of their alleged crimes dated back to the labor conflicts during the Civil War. The evidence procured against the men by corrupt labor spies was thin. Nonetheless, the mass hangings sent a message as strikes and organizing drives gripped the mining towns that fateful summer. Hysteria about terrorist conspiracy was directed against any labor protest involving Irish workers. Allan Pinkerton of the labor detective agency claimed that the Knights of Labor was "an amalgamation of the Molly Maguires and the [Paris] Commune," estimating that two-thirds of the workers in "the vicinity of Scranton" were members of this dangerous order. Catholic priests warned that members of the Knights were "no better than the Moll[y] Maguires" and threatened them with excommunication. Meanwhile, the hangings of convicted "Molly Maguires" continued.[17]

On July 14, 1877, in Martinsville, West Virginia, workers went on strike against the Baltimore and Ohio Railroad in protest against wage cuts. The strike spread rapidly to Pittsburgh, Chicago, St. Louis, and dozens of railroad towns in between. Coal miners, mill hands, and unemployed laborers, driven to despair by wage cuts and slack work, joined the railway workers. In one city after the next, tens of thousands of workers rallied and marched, often leading to the destruction of locomotives and other railroad property as well as violent clashes with the private armies of the corporations and state and federal troops. The repression killed more than a hundred workers in what began as a railway strike and turned into the nation's largest and most violent labor uprising.

By the end of July, Scranton was at the center of the upheaval in the anthracite fields, with a general strike shutting down the mines, mills, and railroads of the city. On August 1, a crowd of several thousand workers descended on the shops of the Lackawanna Iron and Coal Company, destroying machinery, attacking strikebreakers, and beating unconscious Mayor Robert McKune. Lackawanna Iron and Coal's manager, William Scranton, with McKune's approval, had set up a private police force, called it the Citizens' Corps, and armed it with rifles. When Scranton gave a "shoot to kill order," the Citizens' Corps fired on the crowd, killing four strikers and wounding dozens more. Federal troops and state militias soon occupied the region, placing Scranton under martial law for the next three months until the last of the striking miners had returned defeated to work.[18]

In the days after the violence of August 1, Powderly and his fellow Knights plunged into politics, putting together a Greenback Labor Party slate. Charges that the Greenback candidates were "a mob of Molly Maguires" failed to stick, and the Greenbackers swept the Luzerne County elections that fall. In February, Powderly won the Scranton mayor's race. He campaigned as a Greenback candidate promising to end the abuses of the private police and to build "an efficient police force to protect the lives and property of our citizens." In office, he also tried to professionalize the fire department, set up a board of health, construct an adequate sewage system, and pave the city streets. The Scranton *Daily Times* described Powderly's city as "the model of order." When Powderly ran for a second term, he made the singular promise to strive for "equal rights for all men." But it was not just for men; his support for sexual equality both as a mayor and as a labor leader was one of the striking features of Powderly's career.[19]

II.

WHEN POWDERLY INSISTED THAT "there should be no sex in industry," he was referring to the principle of equal pay for equal work, a principle widely accepted by the post–Civil War labor movement. It was also widely understood that most labor organizations systematically discriminated against women and barred them from membership. In other words, it was one thing to protest an inequitable wage structure that allowed

employers to undercut wages by employing female labor; it was something else altogether to accept women as equals within the labor movement. For its first decade of existence, the Knights of Labor was no different
from other labor unions and trade associations in this regard. At its 1879
General Assembly, the Knights narrowly defeated a proposal from a socialist delegate that the constitution of the order be changed to admit
women. But change was on its way, and by 1881 the organization welcomed women into its ranks on a nominally equal footing with men.[20]

Women joining the Knights provoked significant opposition. In the
Pennsylvania mining towns, the Catholic clergy mocked female Knights
as "Biddy Maguires" and accused them of working for "immoral purposes."
Father Peter McEnroe of Mahanoy City told his female parishioners who
formed their own assemblies of the Knights that they were "helping to
drive their men to destruction." Women workers "had no right to countenance female societies," McEnroe warned, "their place being at home with
their families." Such arguments had currency within the coal towns and
other working-class communities and within the Knights as well, making
the practical organization of women slow and uneven. Nonetheless, by
1887 some sixty thousand women made up about 10 percent of the membership. Black and white women, in urban and rural places, joined more
than four hundred assemblies, two-thirds of which were so-called ladies'
locals with entirely female memberships.[21]

The Knights of Labor opened its doors to women across the spectrum
of female work. Women employed in textiles, clothing, and related industries were quick to form assemblies and made up a significant part of the
order's industrial membership. In Philadelphia, the nation's textile center,
women constituted 46 percent of the textile workforce, and the city's female carpet weavers were among the first women to join assemblies of the
Knights. And in cities across the country, women who tended laundry
presses and knitting and sewing machines, who made hats and collars and
undergarments, joined mixed assemblies with men or formed their own
female assemblies. Along with factory operatives, the Knights recruited
cooks, clothes washers, servants, and housekeepers in the domestic

service jobs where most female wage earners were employed. The Knights also organized housewives engaged in the productive labor of maintaining a household. Women employed in big factories formed separate local assemblies with a thousand or more members. But women in smaller shops often combined in assemblies with women outside their trade. In San Francisco, for example, women employed in a sewing shop formed the all-female "Woman's Labor League" as an assembly of the Knights. Despite pressure to merge into locals with men, the San Francisco local voted "to keep up the ladies assembly." At the same time, it recruited maids, housekeepers, and housewives from the community.[22]

By the mid-1880s, the Knights had gained a reputation as "practical believers in the equality of women" who "manifest their beliefs by their acts." Terence Powderly, a self-described "woman's rights man," worked to build this reputation. He forged alliances with the women's suffrage movement and the WCTU, recruiting Susan B. Anthony and Frances Willard as members of the organization. Although Powderly insisted on women's equal status within the Knights, he tiptoed around the question of an official endorsement of women's suffrage. Similarly, Powderly enforced a ban on alcoholic beverages at gatherings of the Knights but shied away from supporting prohibition. Yet he made an alliance with Frances Willard and the WCTU, just as he pushed the organization to align with the cause of women's political equality. At its May 1886 meeting in Cleveland, the General Assembly of the Knights sent a message of solidarity to the Ohio Woman's Suffrage Association in which it repeated its "guarantee of perfect equality" within its ranks and expressed that its "real mission" was "the complete emancipation and enfranchisement of all who labor." And this included women, "the more than one-half of all the most useful and deserving and industrious people."[23]

Meanwhile, Powderly gave voice to what were often idiosyncratic notions about sexual equality. Many of his contemporaries in the labor movement, both men and women, accepted Victorian ideals of separate spheres for the sexes, arguing that women's rightful place was in the home and that protections such as equal pay were necessary as long as women were compelled by misfortune into the man's world of work. Powderly, however, bent these arguments in a more egalitarian direction, insisting that women belonged in the workplace on the basis of equality. He held that women employed in "stores, shops, and factories" were not "interlopers," but faced economic pressures just as men did. "Woman is obliged to work the same as man," he told his fellow Knights. "She contracts debts and pays bills; she owns property and is swindled out of it; she has to obey laws and has to break them."[24]

Powderly admonished his fellow Knights that the role women played in home life must not be used as an excuse to deny women "every right a man enjoys." By way of example, he pointed to the right of a man to go out to the saloon in the evening and drink until midnight. If that was a husband's right, Powderly argued, a wife had the equal right "to practice at the bar for the same length of time." This was not an endorsement of late-night drinking but a repudiation of the sexual double standard. When religious leaders asked Powderly as the mayor of Scranton to take action against female prostitutes, he replied that he would do so only after they took action against the men in their congregations who patronized the women.[25]

The critique of the sexual double standard had particular significance for how the Knights recruited and organized female members. Opponents of women joining the Knights charged that it was indecent to "bring innocent, pure, delicate women in among wicked, sinful, rough men" who inhabited the male world of labor organizing. Especially in working-class communities in the South, it was often viewed as "not lady-like" for women to be members of the organization. Such views, however, were not restricted to the South. A Knight from Erie, Pennsylvania, wrote to Powderly to complain that "it was never meant that men and women should sit in each other's company from half past seven at night until eleven o'clock p.m. in an assembly of the Knights of Labor." Powderly replied, "If the Assembly is a bad place for woman to go it is a bad place for man to go."[26]

Unlike the Grange with its special rituals and levels of status for women members, Powderly insisted that women members have the same rituals, the same status, and the same rights within the organization. Moreover, unlike the Grange, whose female members joined as wives and daughters of male members, the Knights recruited women and men without regard to family status. It directly appealed to single women and widows who faced ostracism and unequal wages to "join the Knights of Labor and help remove such conditions." As for married women, the Knights appealed for them to join the organization "because it is striving for noble equality."[27]

In the context of the post–Civil War labor movement, the Knights' ideas about sexual equality, especially that women belonged in the Knights for the same reasons men did and should enjoy "every right a man enjoys," broke the prevailing mold of gender prejudice and exclusion. But such egalitarianism often mingled with more conventional and maternalist ideas of sexual difference and the special needs of mothers and children. The role of the Knights, in other words, was to pursue sexual equality but at the same time to serve as a shield protecting the female sex from the degradations of industrial life. This mix of ideas was most clearly articulated by Leonora Barry, a national officer of the Knights, whose notions of sexual equality were embedded in maternalist principles.

In 1885, as part of a "manly new departure" in the work for women's equality, Powderly set up a committee to investigate conditions and compile statistics about female labor. The General Assembly meeting in October 1886 elected Leonora Barry as the director and general investigator for "woman's work," and for the next several years she toured workplaces and communities to report on the lives of wage-earning women. This included a tour of the South. However, the former Confederacy failed to charm Barry in the way it had so many other ambassadors of reform. Her letters home described a region of jagged poverty where children were worked to death, racial hatred was palpable, and the mill owners held the textile towns as their private fiefdoms. Meanwhile, Barry's reports from northern factory towns told of the "tyranny, cruelty, and slave-driving propensities" of northern employers who often refused her access to workplaces and threatened to punish employees who aided her inspections.[28]

Among her other duties, Barry served the Knights as a national lecturer, encouraging women workers to join the organization and campaign for women's equality. Her own biography as a factory hand added to her reputation on the lecture circuit as a uniquely qualified representative of wage-earning women. Born in Ireland in 1849, Barry arrived in upstate New York as an infant, and taught school as a young woman before getting married and bearing three children. In 1881, her husband died, leaving her without means of support. With few choices, she took a job in a hosiery mill, where she tended a knitting machine and proved her skills as an organizer for the Knights. In Barry's speeches, her fate as a young widowed mother formed an important part of her argument for women's equality and for the protection of mothers and children.[29]

Realizing equal pay for equal work without regard to sex, according to Barry, was a precondition for protection of the more vulnerable sex. Barry lectured her fellow Knights for failing to fight for wage equality with the necessary urgency, making "a mockery of the principles" of the organization. Part of the urgency was because only wage equality could remove the incentive for employers to replace male workers with female workers. "I wish it were not necessary," Barry lamented, for women to work outside the home, "as I believe it was intended that man should be the bread-winner." But given the reality that widows and other women without support were compelled by need to work, low and unequal wages led women to low and immoral lives. Realizing wage equality, Barry explained, "will be a stronger incentive for women to lead purer lives."[30]

The protection of factory women, however, required more than equal wages. In this regard, Leonora Barry envisioned the Knights "building around the working-girls a wall to defend and protect them from the humiliations which they were heretofore subjected." But ultimately the wall of protection had to be built on the bedrock of governmental regulation. Barry was joined by other prominent Knights, such as Mary O'Reilly, a leader of District 1 in Philadelphia, in her campaigns for new laws proscribing child labor, enforcing sanitary and safety regulations, and requiring state inspections of work sites. For Barry, O'Reilly, and other women organizers of the Knights, as much as for Powderly and much of the rest of the membership, the collective citizenry in the form of local, state, and federal government was essential to their notions of protection, justice, and equality.[31]

III.

IN 1887, PRESIDENT GROVER CLEVELAND invited Powderly to the White House, where he offered him an appointment as the U.S. commissioner of labor. Powderly had lobbied hard for other federal offices. In 1884, when the federal Bureau of Labor Statistics was first getting started, he had strenuously but unsuccessfully campaigned to be appointed its first director. Afterward, Knights continued to petition to make Powderly the federal commissioner. This time, however, Powderly turned Cleveland down, saying that he was too busy with the Knights of Labor. He also wrote Cleveland a letter proposing to raise the Bureau of Labor to a full Department of Labor with its commissioner in the cabinet, and he sent along a memo with a twenty-five-point proposal for what the new commissioner should do. William Sylvis and other labor reformers had been demanding a department of labor with cabinet rank since the end of the Civil War, and most of the twenty-five points in Powderly's memo were long-standing demands of the labor movement. But he spelled them out in sufficient detail to provide a remarkable picture of the future role the federal government might play in the nation's economic life.[32]

Powderly's memo focused on the power of data to bring rational order to the world of the wage earner. His twenty-five-point program called for the detailed collection of information—profits, wages, prices, and output—from virtually every enterprise and industry on a national scale. Extensive studies and investigations would give the Department of Labor the "authority to step in" and peacefully settle labor conflicts "through conciliation, mediation, or arbitration." Requiring companies to provide detailed reports of job openings and new hires would allow the federal department in Washington to gain national knowledge of labor markets and to rationalize the workforce by "direct[ing] workmen from where they crowd each other idle to where they may help each other work." The new Labor Department would similarly bring order and system to workers' housing. By collecting information on the costs of rent ("securing copies of leases where obtainable"), land prices, and taxes, the federal department would "check the land speculator" and facilitate a future in which electric mass transit would make possible suburban housing development. The department would also regulate the working conditions of women and children, gathering data on education, toilet regulations, health, and pregnancy.[33]

Gathering data would require compulsion. The work of the Department of Labor was to be peaceful work in contrast, as Powderly stressed, to the Department of War, but the force of law was necessary to establish this type of peace. The "public has a right to know what a corporation earns," and "if it is for the public good that the affairs of an individual be made known," Powderly explained, "he should be compelled to state facts under oath." New laws would be needed "to make it compulsory . . . to answer every question in relation to their business that the public is at all interested in."[34] Moreover, as Powderly pointed out, the corollary to the collection of information was "the authority to step in" to labor disputes and impose arbitration.

The notion of arbitration enjoyed wide support in the labor movement. The labor publicist William Tisdale described arbitration as one of the "cardinal principles" of the Knights, a principle inscribed in the organization's program. But arbitration had its hazards. As Tisdale warned, "the word 'compulsory' has a bad sound in the ears of labor," and therefore "compulsory arbitration" was "very delicate ground on which to tread." Labor activists did, in fact, tread delicately on the subject, describing arbitration in a variety of careful ways. Most often they used the word to simply mean negotiation between capitalists and workers as two equal parties. In other cases, they suggested intervention of a third-party mediator. The General Executive Board or District Executive Boards of the Knights, for example, could and did perform that role when invited by both employer and employees.[35]

At the same time, proposals for arbitration laws involving governmental boards, labor bureaus, or similar authorities capable of "stepping in" were also widely circulated in the labor movement. Joseph Gruenhut, for example, a prominent labor activist and the statistician for the Chicago Health Department, argued that national boards of arbitration governing wages, production, and prices were needed to establish "equality . . . in our industrial relationships." But such equality required data. Only with data would the national agencies have the authority and bureaucratic capacity to adjudicate labor conflicts, rationalize labor markets, bring system to urban disorder, reform the sexual division of work, and otherwise bring peace and equality.[36]

In short, Powderly's proposals for the U.S. Department of Labor implied a significant expansion of a centralized federal authority, an authority with the capacity to intervene in the economic life of companies and citizens in unprecedented ways. There was surely something fantastical in his plans for this new data-driven national power. But there was also a logic rooted in the experience of the post–Civil War labor movement. Trade assemblies, eight-hour leagues, and other labor groups raised a nearly universal demand that state governments establish bureaus to compile data on economic conditions. Massachusetts set up its Bureau of Statistics of Labor in 1869, and twelve other states followed suit by 1883, including New York, Illinois, and California. Powderly concluded his memo to President Cleveland by noting that these state bureaus would do much of the work, "but in time these will cooperate with and work through the Federal Department of Labor." Moreover, the Knights of Labor had already demonstrated the part they would play in sustaining these bureaus. Every local assembly designated a statistician responsible for gathering information about its members and the companies for which they worked. And this information flowed upward to district assemblies and where possible to the state bureaus of labor statistics.[37]

But the flow was uneven when local statisticians failed to file their reports on time. Powderly addressed this problem in a proclamation that called on members of the Knights to fill out the statistical forms for the state labor bureaus and chastised them for their negligence in "sustaining the institutions so peculiarly of their own establishment." Powderly was not the only scold. Officers calling out delegates for delinquent statistical reports became something of a ritual in annual meetings. John Chambers served as the statistician of a coal miners' assembly in Maryland and explained that compiling data was the duty of every member of the organization. "No person, no matter how much of an expert he may be," he lectured his fellow miners, "can give a correct idea of the condition of labor from ideas or observations of his own, without the aid of the wage worker." Of course, even simple tasks of centralized reporting and record keeping could be challenging for a voluntary association, and collecting data for a local assembly of the Knights could be a time-consuming and difficult assignment, especially in the coal-mining towns.[38]

For coal miners, data was a weapon of choice in the struggle to protect their lives and livelihoods. Knowledge of ventilating systems and safety procedures was an essential tool of survival. Facts about the coal operator's investments and profitability provided leverage in the contests over pay cuts, slack work, and mine closings. Information about the price of food and rent exposed plunder by company "pluck me" stores and company housing. And data about pay scales and coal prices served the essential goal of "equalization" across the nation's coalfields. The post–Civil War extension of the railroads opened up new mining districts and unleashed disastrous price wars. By the early 1880s, miners recognized that railroads and telegraphs "had annihilated space and time until the East was no longer the market of Eastern coal-fields, nor the West of those in its section." They took up the watchword "equalization" as their only protection from price wars and wage cuts and layoffs and short hours. In effect, coal miners sought to build a rationalized and bureaucratic cartel to limit the impact of competition and overproduction. But to do so required the efficient and timely collection of data.[39]

The miners in Powderly's home district were innovators in data collection. In Scranton and its environs, thousands of miners, railroad employees, ironworkers, and laborers gathered in dozens of assemblies under the umbrella of the Knights' District 16. Allan Pinkerton and his labor spies probably only slightly exaggerated when they claimed that two-thirds of the workers in the vicinity belonged to the district. For eleven years, Powderly served as the recording secretary of the district, and from its early days he worked to improve its methods of gathering statistics. District 16 developed a system of monthly reports to "reveal the exact condition of the laboring classes of the anthracite industry," and to thereby demonstrate that their demands were "supported by justice and equity."[40]

District 16's statistical questionnaire asked about the conditions inside the mine: the quality of the coal seam, the ventilation system, the number of mules sharing the precious air with the men and boys underground. It asked about the household economy over which women bore the main responsibility in the coal towns: the cost of food and shelter, the size of garden plots, and the quality of sanitation. But its most complex questions focused on problems of equalization. How was coal weighed, measured, graded, processed, transported, and priced at points of transit? And how were the wage earners paid? Was the highly skilled miner who directed the work at the mine face paid by the ton or the carload? What was the hourly wage and hours of work for the laborer who wielded pick and shovel to break and load the coal, and for the boy who picked the slate from the coal, and for forty or fifty job categories and pay scales within each mine?[41]

Powderly proposed that other districts of the Knights adopt the same questionnaire as miners organized a network of data gathering across the anthracite fields of Pennsylvania. Meanwhile, bituminous miners from West Virginia to Missouri developed parallel systems for miners to submit monthly reports about "all kinds of labor in his locality." For this information to have power, it needed to be drawn from the local mining community, and from the mining community on the next hillside, and from the mining districts across the state and beyond. Its power came into play as much in local disputes with despotic managers as in the state, regional, and national efforts to bring order and a rational "equalization" to the chaos, violence, and disorder of the corporate-owned and -operated coal industry.[42]

Peace and equality, the Knights believed, rested on the foundation of the organized wage earners. But they could not be secured without equal treatment under the law. Collecting data was an essential part of such equal treatment and was closely integrated with a legislative agenda. Especially in the mining industry, statistics and state regulation went hand in hand. In Pennsylvania, the legislature adopted the first statewide safety standards in 1870 in the aftermath of the Avondale disaster. In the following years, Knights of Labor lobbyists, legislators, and political allies successfully pushed through the legislature a raft of new laws for arbitration boards, mine inspections, and other measures to regulate the mining industry.[43]

The 1886 elections gave the Knights a controlling bloc in the lower house of the Pennsylvania legislature, which in the following term passed more than a dozen measures regarding miners' pay, the grading and weighing of coal, health and safety, company stores, cooperatives, and the prohibition of blacklisting. In this they were led by John Byrne, a member of the Knights who drew from the organization's statistical reports for his lengthy speeches in support of his bills. The tone of the legislative session was reflected in Byrne's proposed law to "empower labor organizations" with the right to "employ police force," the same and equal right that companies had to employ Pinkertons and other private police. As with several other of Byrne's bills, the workers' police bill was approved overwhelmingly by the lower house, only to be killed in the senate.[44]

Despite setbacks, by the mid-1880s the Knights of Labor, at the height of its political power, had played its part in forging a complex regulatory regime in Pennsylvania's coalfields. Along with other miners' organizations, it accomplished much the same in Colorado, Illinois, Indiana, and Ohio. The scope of the state regulation of coal mines was comparable to the Granger laws passed a dozen years earlier regulating grain elevators and railroad rates. And just as the Granger laws often disappointed Grangers, the mining laws often disappointed the Knights. Mine owners violated regulations at will, while the same regulations imposed new layers of discipline and regimentation on miners and laborers. Inspection laws allowed coal companies to escape responsibility for accidents. And it soon became apparent that laws issued from state capitols were no match for the corporate-driven chaos and violence that continued to plague the nation's mining districts. But that did not stop the Knights from striving for stronger, more centralized, and more effective legislation. Such was the logic of data collection and centralization on which Powderly built his proposals for the U.S. Department of Labor.[45]

IV.

IN ITS ONGOING EFFORTS TO equalize industry, the Knights increasingly relied on industry-wide systems of organization. Trade assemblies dedicated to a single craft or trade had been part of the Knights since its early days among the garment cutters of Philadelphia. Carpenters and other skilled trades had their local assemblies and looked to organize them into district assemblies covering an entire city or region. But the Knights looked to a new model of industrial organization that would embrace all workers within an industry or trade and potentially place the workforce of an entire national (or international) industry under a single command.

The makers of window glass provided a model for this new type of organization. Making windowpanes required the talents of skilled glassblowers, whose livelihood and craft prerogatives were undermined by price wars among competing glass companies. The Pittsburgh-based Local 300 served as a national trade assembly of glassblowers, setting standards for hours of work, pay scales, and apprenticeships. Local 300 would also take on an international dimension in its efforts to regulate the transatlantic market in both labor and glass panes. In 1884, with the help of the General Assembly, the Pittsburgh local sent a delegation across the Atlantic. Its first order of business was setting up a Knights assembly among the glassworkers of Sunderland, England, before doing the same in Charlevoix, Belgium. Soon thereafter, the Knights organized glassmakers in Italy as well.[46]

The thoroughness and ambition of the glassblowers inspired other Knights to build national trade assemblies. In 1883, District 45 organized the nation's telegraph operators, and on July 19 they called a strike of all telegraphers in the United States and Canada. At the time, the financier Jay Gould owned Western Union, which was the largest of the telegraph companies. And Gould took a hard line to break the strike. After a month, the strike collapsed, and Gould enforced an "iron clad" oath requiring Western Union employees to swear that they would not join the Knights of Labor. Despite their defeat, the telegraphers had organized local assemblies in small towns and villages that happened to have a telegraph office, helping to extend the Knights from coast to coast, including into the eleven states of the former Confederacy.[47]

Local assemblies of coal miners similarly reached into remote communities from Appalachia to the Rocky Mountains. In May 1886, they forged a national trade assembly, District 135, with the aim of uniting coal miners under a single, centralized structure. Only such an organization, they believed, could realize their goals of industrial standardization and regulation. For years, miners had battled with operators over the size of the screens used to clean coal. Larger holes in the screens meant less coal and less pay for miners. A national district assembly allowed for miners to formalize a common front over the size of the screens and other questions of equalization.[48]

In July 1886, the carpet weavers launched District 126, a venture in the organization of the national carpet industry. In previous years, the mills had been racked by strikes. The mainly female workforce in Philadelphia's carpet mills undertook a long strike in 1884 to resist a reduction in wages and to assert their right to organize in the face of the organized power of the owners. As one striker asked, "The employers have their association, why can we not have ours?" Despite the bitterness of earlier strikes, some carpet manufacturers welcomed the efforts of District 126 to bring uniform order to the industry. One manufacturer suggested that the district would have the support of many employers, "since its ulterior object is to regulate and equalize carpet wages throughout the United States." "When wages are equalized," another employer predicted, "we will have no further strikes."[49]

The following year, boot and shoe workers took the same path to a national trade assembly. Like the glassblowers and coal miners, they looked to centralization as a way to rescue their industry from competition, overproduction, and an oversupply of labor. Their first goal was the national equalization of pay scales, with "a uniform rate of wages for the same class of work everywhere." They also looked to regulate the labor market of shoe workers by controlling the apprenticeship system, enforcing the eight-hour day, and barring child labor as well as prison labor.[50]

V.

IT WAS ON THE NATION'S railway systems that the Knights' trade assemblies demonstrated their potential force as a counterweight to corporate power. The Union Pacific had the most systematically organized workforce of any railroad in the country. In 1885, Charles Francis Adams Jr., who the year before had succeeded Jay Gould as the president of the Union Pacific, estimated that two-thirds of his fifteen thousand employees were members of the Knights' District 82. At least for a moment, District 93 had a similar impact on Jay Gould's Wabash, St. Louis & Pacific Railway, and District 101 organized across Gould's southwest system that included the Texas & Pacific, the Missouri Pacific, and other lines in Texas, Kansas, Arkansas, Missouri, southwestern Illinois, and the Indian Territory. Coal miners and shoe workers built their national trade assemblies on the foundation of hundreds of local assemblies organized over the previous decade. By comparison, the railroad trade assemblies emerged quickly in the wake of strike action and, with the notable exception of the Union Pacific, were soon broken just as quickly. But in their brief existence, the example of the railway workers led to the Knights' most explosive growth and put the organization on the map as a national political force.[51]

The railroads posed a severe test for the Knights' egalitarian ethos and inclusive model of organization. Like coal miners, railroad workers were divided between different trades and crafts, and between the skilled and the unskilled. But unlike coal miners, railroaders were spread across systems of hundreds and even thousands of miles of track. Machinists, coal

handlers, and switchmen worked in the shops and yards. Engineers, firemen, conductors, and brakemen rode the trains. Section hands and bridge
workers built and maintained the tracks across often formidable and remote terrain. Railroading, like coal mining, involved extraordinary danger. In 1885 in the state of Kansas, for example, one in twelve railroad
employees was either killed or severely injured. Unlike coal miners, however, who shared equal hazards in the same gaseous hole in the ground,
the brakemen and switchmen who applied the brakes and worked the cou-
plings outside the train faced far more danger than a conductor inside a
train or a machinist in a rail shop.[52]

Moreover, unlike coal miners, whose associations tended to organize
all the employees at a given mine, skilled railway workers organized in
separate railroad brotherhoods, which served as exclusive craft unions for
engineers, firemen, conductors, and other trades. The Knights faced the
challenge of organizing local assemblies capable of bridging the gaps between the skilled and the unskilled and knitting them together in centralized district assemblies capable of uniting thousands of widely dispersed
employees to form a common front to face some of the largest corporations
in the land.[53]

The great railroad corporations that spread across the continent in the
aftermath of the Civil War wielded highly centralized and bureaucratic
systems of authority, mobilized enormous human and material resources,
and controlled regional and national arteries of transportation and commerce. Railroad corporations, in short, represented a new type of concen-
trated economic power. But the edifice of their power was built on shaky
foundations. The railroads were controlled by investors who made their
money not from railroad operations but from buying and selling railroad
securities in New York, or in London or elsewhere in Europe. Building
and managing railway networks was only a means to that end. This left
railroad corporations vulnerable to the smash and grab of speculation,
competitive warfare, and ruinous spasms of overbuilding. The railroad
systems west of the Mississippi proved especially susceptible to these
forces of corporate mayhem. Long distances and rugged terrain meant

high costs. Lack of demand meant intense competition and rate wars over market share. Cost cutting meant shoddily built and poorly maintained tracks. And when it all led to bankruptcy, railroad corporations, too big to fail, fell into federal receivership.[54]

On May 1, 1884, the Union Pacific managers, with the corporation teetering on the edge of insolvency, slashed the wages of their unorganized and unprotected shop workers by 10 and even 15 percent. In protest, the workers closed down the roundhouses and repair shops from Omaha, Nebraska, to Ogden, Utah. The managers quickly got the message, and by May 4 they backed down on the pay cuts. Over the next month, in the towns along the Union Pacific, workers from the shops and track crews set up dozens of local assemblies of the Knights of Labor. They did so with the aid of labor organizers from Denver, including Joseph Buchanan, who was a rising star in the national leadership of the Knights. Much of the energy for the organizing campaign came from unorganized or unskilled workers, but skilled members of the brotherhoods also joined the assemblies. Despite efforts of local managers to fire organizers, the local assemblies took hold, and by February 1885 the majority of Union Pacific workers belonged to District 82. The president of the corporation, Charles Francis Adams Jr., accepted the presence of the Knights on the Union Pacific and recognized the part the organization might play in stabilizing labor relations. The corporate president and the leaders of the Knights' district assembly came to a working agreement. Vulnerable and unorganized workers of a corporate giant had gained a degree of equal protection by forging a unitary and centralized trade assembly.[55]

The Union Pacific was just the beginning, or so it seemed when the Knights of Labor took on Jay Gould's railroad empire. In the eyes of labor organizers, Gould, as much as any of the financial titans of his time, represented the tyranny of Wall Street and corporate monopoly. He made his first fortune selling watered stock from the Erie Railroad and became one of the richest people in the country gaming the price of railroad securities. His reputation was sealed by his ruthless measures to crush the Knights employed by his Western Union telegraph monopoly. Gould applied the same ruthlessness in building up his railway empire, a system of inter-locking networks at the center of the mid-continent railroad boom that controlled much of the nation's rail traffic between Ohio and New Mexico. By the mid-1880s, Gould's railroads were gripped in the cycle of overbuild-ing, low revenues, price wars, bankruptcies, and federal bailouts.[56]

The Wabash, St. Louis & Pacific was one of Gould's bankrupt roads under federal receivership. In February 1885, the Wabash managers cut the wages of its shop workers and laborers and extended their workday from nine to ten hours. The workers responded with walkouts that started in the shops and roundhouses in Illinois and Indiana but soon moved west across Gould's system, spreading to the Missouri Pacific, the Missouri, Kansas & Texas, and the Texas & Pacific Railroads. Significantly, the walk-out began with the machinists and other skilled workers, but its center of gravity shifted to the unskilled yard workers, trackmen, and other labor-ers. The strikers received an offer of thirty thousand dollars in aid from District 82 of the Knights on the Union Pacific, and the possibility of a much wider railroad strike loomed. The strike also enjoyed wide support within the railroad towns. On March 15, with the intervention of the gov-ernor of Missouri and other political leaders, a settlement was negotiated between the corporations and their employees. The managers agreed to rescind the wage cuts, pay overtime for extra hours, and allow strikers to return to work without recrimination.[57]

The March settlement of the Wabash strike marked a stunning vic-tory. But the Wabash workers were soon locked in another struggle to make the managers live up to the settlement. The sticking point was the refusal to rehire strikers and locked-out employees. By this time, the lo-cal assemblies of Wabash workers had formed District 93. But Archibald Talmadge, the railroad's general manager, rejected requests for a meet-ing with the district's arbitration board on the grounds that he would "have nothing to do with any labor organization" and that he would only "deal with his men individually." Eventually, the Wabash managers did come to the table. And on September 5, 1885, they accepted an agreement with Terence Powderly in which the corporation would rehire the strikers and

Powderly would notify the managers and talk with them before further strike action.[58]

With news of the Wabash agreement, the Knights' reputation burned bright across the region and the country. In the weeks and months afterward, thousands of wage earners formed local assemblies along Jay Gould's railroad empire, and as a national organization the Knights doubled and tripled in size, growing to more than seven hundred thousand members. This period of breakneck growth was connected to the fact that an egalitarian and inclusive mobilization of railroad workers had compelled the captains of the Gould empire to accept the Knights' principles of arbitration and equitable treatment. "Jay Gould, the railway 'king' and longtime symbol of moneyed tyranny," explains Theresa Case in her historical account of these events, "had negotiated with a national labor organization on an equal footing." Millions of Americans took note.[59]

The negotiated peace on the Wabash did not last. Less than a year later, in March 1886, Gould's railroads were engulfed in a system-wide strike that became the most destructive labor conflict since the general railroad strike of 1877. The trouble began on the bankrupt Texas & Pacific Railroad, which was under federal receivership. On February 17, a foreman fired C. A. Hall, a carpenter who worked in the shops in Marshall, Texas. Hall was a delegate to the Knights' District 101 that covered the Texas & Pacific, and two days before his firing he had received permission from the same foreman to attend a district meeting. The Knights understood the dismissal of Hall as an existential threat; if district delegates could be fired at will, there would be no viable district. Hall's firing put to the test the Knights' motto, "An injury to one is the concern of all." And on March 1, Martin Irons, the chair of the executive board of District 101, called for a strike on the Texas & Pacific and a few days later called for workers across the Gould system to refuse to handle Texas & Pacific rolling stock.[60]

The strike soon descended to industrial warfare. Railroad managers took a hard line, employing vigilantes and strikebreakers to keep the trains running. To stop the trains, strikers "killed" locomotives by sabotaging their engines. With the Texas & Pacific under federal receivership, federal and state courts issued injunctions against the strike and boycott. Law enforcement arrested hundreds of strikers, and railroad towns were filled with labor spies and vigilantes. On May 4, Powderly called for an end to the strike and boycott. None of the strikers' demands were met, and many of them were blacklisted from the shops and yards. Across Gould's railroad empire, the Knights of Labor was effectively destroyed as an organization.[61]

The defeat stood in stark contrast to the victories on the Wabash the year before. Implacable opposition from management, court injunctions, and martial law might have determined the outcome. Historians of the conflict also point to the lack of support within the community as contributing to the defeat. Unlike the earlier battles over wages and other issues that garnered wide public sympathy, it was more difficult to understand what was at stake when Martin Irons of District 101 ordered the strike, and did so over the firing of a single carpenter. In the eyes of the community, these historians note, Irons and the Knights represented a mirror image of the centralized and distant power of Gould and the railroad corporations. While this perception might have contributed to the lack of wider support in the railroad towns, however, the Knights would never have gained a following among the railroad workers without its centralized and uniform district assemblies. It was their demonstrated power that had allowed tens of thousands of widely dispersed and often marginalized railroad employees to successfully engage in equitable negotiations with some of the nation's great railroad corporations.[62]

Martin Irons received much of the blame for the strike and its failure. An immigrant from Scotland and a skilled machinist, he had been a leader of the Grange in Lexington, Missouri, where he helped the Grange establish a successful wagon factory. In 1885, he ended up working in a railroad shop in Sedalia, Missouri, a depot on Gould's Missouri Pacific Railroad. There he joined the Knights and, with his experience in the Grange, quickly rose in its ranks. In the Knights, Irons believed, he had finally found a force to "counterbalance the power of aggregated and incorporated wealth." As Irons and many other railroaders who joined the Knights understood it, corporate power could only be counterbalanced by the power of a centralized and uniform organization embracing all categories of workers along egalitarian lines. But this points to another reason for the failure of the southwest strike: the failure of egalitarian principles.[63]

A month before the strike, Irons sent out a letter polling the thirty local assemblies of his district about equal protection for unskilled workers. The underpaid and abused laborers in the yards and track crews, Irons wrote, "need more protection" than the better-paid employees in the shops. Irons wanted the local assemblies to reply by secret ballot if they were willing to take a stand on behalf of the poorly paid and vulnerable laborers. He made no mention of this in his letter, but the crews shoveling coal and working on the tracks of the Texas & Pacific included a large number of African American and in some locations Mexican American laborers, adding a racial dimension to his query. The local assemblies gave Irons a unanimous affirmation that they supported protecting the laborers. Most Knights held to this egalitarian pledge during the strike. But engineers and other skilled trainmen broke ranks to keep the trains running. This was why strikers resorted to "killing" locomotives and other drastic measures that added to sharply divided opinions about the strike in the railroad towns. As much as anything else, the 1886 defeat of the Knights on Gould's railroads was a defeat for the ideal of egalitarian organization across boundaries of trade, skill, and race.[64]

VI.

THE KNIGHTS' EFFORTS TO EQUALIZE industry led them to focus on building centralized and large-scale trade assemblies. This approach pointed the way to a new model of industrial organization. In aspiration if not always in practice, these assemblies placed many thousands of workers under a single command. They did so by embracing all workers within an industry or trade without regard to skill or status. Coal miners and others had attempted this type of organization in the past. By the mid-1880s, the Knights came close to making it a reality. The significance of this potential was widely understood by the workers with the lowest pay and least protection. The section hand working on a desolate track in eastern Texas and the mine laborer shoveling coal under a remote West Virginia mountain recognized that they were constituent parts of a rising force in national life. Even after the Knights had passed from the scene, this type of organization remained the best hope for many industrial workers seeking equity and a counterbalance to corporate power.

But the shift to large-scale trade assemblies came at a cost, working a steady transformation in the inclusive and egalitarian character of the Knights. The fate of Terence Powderly's home district assembly suggests the nature of the change. Coal miners made up the majority of the members of District 16. But the district also had locals of railroad employees, of laborers from the iron mills, and of men and women from dozens of other professions and trades throughout the Scranton area. District Assembly 16 coordinated the efforts of these diverse locals. But the formation of a coal miners' national trade assembly meant reconstituting locals to separate miners from other members and then pulling the miners' locals out of District Assembly 16. As it turned out, the officers of District 16 refused to give permission to its mining locals to join the national district. But the reorganization proceeded quickly enough in the other mining regions, which meant that most Knights who worked in coal mines belonged to the National District Assembly 135, which in turn was divided into fourteen subdivisions and organized on increasingly bureaucratic lines. Similarly, forming District Assembly 101 on the Texas & Pacific Railroad provoked protests from the mixed district assemblies when the Texas & Pacific employees were moved into their separate district.[65]

The changes in the structure of the Knights to centralized trade assemblies paralleled a similar process among trade unions. Carpenters, cigar makers, and other trade unions shifted authority to national officers as part of what the historian David Montgomery described as "a much broader process of bureaucratization." And in this process, the distinction between a Knights' trade assembly and a trade union blurred, and jurisdictional warfare raged between the two. The inclusive nature of the Knights had made it possible to be both a Knight and a member of a trade union. But jurisdictional warfare upset that arrangement.

At the Knights' 1886 General Assembly, the majority of delegates voted, in the face of vehement opposition, to expel cigar makers who refused to resign from the Cigar Makers' Union. Territorial warfare also erupted in the coalfields between the Knights of the National Trade Assembly 135 and the trade unionists of the National Federation of Miners and Mine Laborers. It turned out that the differences between the two miners' organizations were narrower than they appeared, and they would later merge to form the United Mine Workers (UMW), a model of industrial unionism into the twentieth century. But that happy result was an exception to the rule. In the southwest railroad strike, the brotherhoods broke ranks with the Knights to keep the trains running; two years later, when the brotherhoods went on strike against the Burlington system, they accused the Knights of taking their jobs. The conflicts between the Knights and the trade unions led to repeated setbacks for the Knights and destructive factional strife within the organization.[66]

VII.

MEANWHILE, THE LOGIC OF THE trade assemblies eroded the Knights' inclusive and egalitarian ethos. The coal miners formed a trade assembly with the declared purpose of the "mutual protection of our craft," but in doing so crimped their vision of solidarity. "While it is natural for us to first consider that which is good for our craft," cautioned M. F. Flannigan, a leader of a miners' subdivision, "we must not fail to remember that an injury to any branch of labor is the concern of all." Flannigan issued this warning at a convention of Pennsylvania coal miners in the summer of 1887. By this time, however, the Knights' efforts to "protect the craft" increasingly turned on preventing "Hungarians, Polanders, Italians [and] Austrians" from "overcrowding" mines and driving down wages.[67]

Terence Powderly, who did so much to popularize the Knights' egalitarian ethos, also had a hand in its anti-immigrant campaigns. In

June 1883, he penned a remarkable letter to a local Scranton newspaper about Hungarian women working with their husbands in nearby coke ovens. Forking coke was heavy, hot, noxious labor usually performed by men. That women would toil in the coke ovens might have been taken as a sign of the sexual equality that Powderly so loudly professed. But in this case, he concluded that allowing their women to do this work proved that Hungarians, like the Chinese, represented a degraded race. It was impossible, Powderly wrote, "to make good and useful citizens of these men."[68]

Such anti-immigrant views in the Pennsylvania coalfields resulted in a state law requiring state certification of coal miners. The Knights demanded the law by claiming that "ignorant" Hungarian and other non-English-speaking immigrants were responsible for mining accidents. But it was widely understood as a measure to protect "the better class of mine workers," many of whom were Welsh and Irish immigrants, from the "ignorant" class of "imported labor." The efforts of the coal miners to exclude immigrants from the mines reflected a broader syndrome afflicting the industrial strategies of the Knights: the struggle to equalize and rationalize labor markets was often contingent on exclusion and unequal treatment.[69]

In 1887, shoe workers formed a national trade assembly of the Knights, and they did so with the stated purpose of "strik[ing] a blow" at the "great national evil" of "European labor." Many of the members of this assembly were first- and second-generation immigrants themselves, mostly from Ireland. Indeed, by the 1880s, the industrial working class in the United States was overwhelmingly a class of European immigrants and their children. Yet the coal miners considered barring "cheap" and "ignorant" immigration from central and southern Europe as the key to protecting their craft and "free American labor." At the same time, shoe workers viewed Chinese labor as an existential threat. In their "struggle for protection," they organized a racial boycott to "buy only shoes that bear the White labor stamp."[70]

The centers of anti-Chinese agitation were mainly located in the West, and the Knights of Labor threw itself into the fray as it organized across the Rockies and the Pacific coast. On September 2, 1885, the Knights were implicated in the massacre of Chinese coal miners in Rock Springs, Wyoming. The mines at Rock Springs provided half of the coal used and sold by the Union Pacific, and in the 1870s Jay Gould decided to bring Chinese workers to the mine as a way to keep out labor organizations. Chinese miners constituted the majority of those who worked the mines in Rock Springs and made homes there in relative peace. But in the summer of 1885, white workers attacked Chinese section hands along the Union Pacific line, and the Knights issued demands for the expulsion of the Chinese from the railroad and the coal mines.[71]

The violence at Rock Springs began with a clash between white and Chinese miners that escalated into an armed assault by white miners on the Chinese district. They proceeded to burn the district to the ground, shooting people as they attempted to escape their flaming homes. The massacre left twenty-eight dead and nearly that many missing. The Knights as an organization might not have directed this gruesome massacre. But workers involved were members of the Knights, and they met in the Knights of Labor hall before launching their assault on the Chinese community. When sixteen workers went before a grand jury for their role in the massacre, the Knights paid for the attorney who ensured their release. Afterward, Thomas Neasham, a leader of the Denver Knights, called for a strike to complete the work begun with the massacre to expel the remaining Chinese from the region. Terence Powderly, no friend of the Chinese workers, refused to go along. "This Chinese mess in Wyoming has gone far enough," Powderly warned, "and any thought of a strike on this matter is entirely out of the question."[72]

There was no anti-Chinese strike. But local assemblies of the Knights carried the anti-Chinese violence across much of the West. Coal mines near Seattle were the next target, with the Knights calling a "Puget Sound Congress" of labor groups to demand that employers fire Chinese workers. They also formed "ouster committees" to physically intimidate and expel the Chinese from the region. Several months later, during the southwest strike, black and white members of District 101 demanded the expulsion of Chinese workers from Gould's southwest railroads. By that time, soldiers were stationed by the camps of Chinese construction workers to fend off raids from white railroaders. The Knights explained that such raids were an effort at "abatement," a euphemism for a campaign of terror and violence to drive the Chinese out of the railroad, mining, and lumber towns of the West.[73]

The massacre at Rock Springs and the ferocity of the hostility that the Knights directed at Chinese coal miners and railroad workers revealed a deep contradiction. On the one hand, as much as anyplace else, the egalitarian and inclusive vision of the Knights was realized in coal mines and railroad yards, where they organized across barriers of trade, skill, and frequently ethnicity and race. The example attracted tens of thousands of African American wage earners to look to the Knights for protection and to form their own local assemblies. On the other hand, the Knights turned the railroads and coal mines into some of the bloodiest battlefields of racial intolerance directed against the Chinese. This mainly involved white workers, but black workers also joined the anti-Chinese campaigns. As it turned out, the workers' struggle to bring equality to industry entailed extraordinary Sinophobic oppression and violence. The contradiction afflicted the movement as a whole as the Knights' efforts to organize centralized trade assemblies increasingly employed subtle and not so subtle means of racial and ethnic exclusion.

VIII.

CHINESE EXCLUSION MOCKED THE KNIGHTS' egalitarian principles. They dealt with this simple and embarrassing fact with a dodge: excluding Chinese labor was about not racial animus but unfree and therefore unequal labor. As the California Knights put it, "They are coolie slaves. Their labor is slave labor." In this way, they packaged their efforts to drive out Chinese workers as an act of emancipation. Speaking about "the Chinese evil" at the 1885 General Assembly, Powderly offered a circuitous justification for the massacre at Rock Springs and called for unity behind the efforts to expel the Chinese. "The entire Order must act as one man in this movement," he exhorted his fellow Knights. "Slave labor must die, and free labor must be its executioner." But what exactly about the Chinese workers made them "slaves"? The Knights pointed to the debts they owed for passage from China, as if immigrants from many countries did not accrue similar debts. Members of the Knights pointed to prostitution among Chinese women, as if white women did not also engage in the sex trade. And they pointed to the Chinese as "crafty," "criminal," and "depraved," as if such stereotypes were not the typical coin of racial bigotry.[74]

The racialization of the Chinese, however, came with a difference. Black Americans, as many Knights understood, were a separate (and, again for many, probably less "advanced") race. Nonetheless, the history of slavery, the Civil War, and emancipation meant that they were citizens and thereby had a claim to equal rights. Melvin Wade, a black leader who worked with the Knights in Dallas, believed in racial equality, "work[ing] a black and white horse in the same field." But as he explained to a labor meeting, he rejected the idea of allowing the Chinese into the ranks of the labor movement. His argument rested on blacks' historical claims to citizenship; "the white man brought him here and it was only right . . . that he was a citizen of this country," whereas, Wade claimed, "the Chinese never became citizens." Many Knights, black and white, had convinced themselves that Chinese immigrants were mere transients in the United States, a belief confirmed by the fact that the Chinese often lacked citizenship and therefore stood outside the egalitarian circle of the labor movement. That the Chinese were subject to racial violence, boycotts, intimidation, and legal exclusion was not part of this calculation.[75]

Significantly, black and white Knights often placed Chinese labor in the same category of enslaved labor as the prisoners in the convict labor system. The system of leasing convicts to coal mine operators and other capitalists created a pool of workers in actual chains. In the South, most of these convicts were African Americans, frequently sentenced for vagrancy and other minor offenses, and often worked to death in coal mines and other work sites. Members of the Knights vigorously protested the twin threats that convict labor and Chinese labor posed to their own freedom. The notion that Chinese workers were enchained in a comparable way to convicts in iron leggings required a leap to a racial fantasy about Chinese "bondage." Be that as it may, both Chinese and convict labor introduced inequities in the labor market. The solution was exclusion. The road to industrial equality ran through the "removal of competition" from the "coolie slave and convict labor in our midst." Meanwhile, it was a striking fact that the Knights had little or nothing to say about equal justice for African Americans caught in the maw of an inequitable legal system. And much the same was true when it came to equal rights for Chinese workers confronted by systematic discrimination.[76]

Chinese immigrants, in words and deeds, disproved the notions that they were transient slaves on American shores. Chinese litigants tenaciously fought in the courts for equal protection of the laws as mandated by the post–Civil War amendments. Perhaps the best-known Chinese American activist of his day, Wong Chin Foo spent much of his adult life working to convince his fellow citizens that people of Chinese ancestry were as deserving of equal rights as any other Americans. Born and raised in China's Shandong province, he arrived in the United States as a young man and obtained citizenship and education in American schools. In 1883, he challenged the anti-Chinese agitator Denis Kearney to a public debate, a challenge that Kearney knew enough to decline. By this time, Wong Chin Foo had gained public notice as he campaigned from coast to coast for racial equality and equal justice for Chinese immigrants. He also took part in the efforts of the Chinese residents of New York to organize into voluntary associations, including the Chinese Citizens' Union in 1888. Four years later, appealing to the "equality of manhood," Wong Chin Foo organized the Chinese Equal Rights League.[77]

Meanwhile, Chinese workers also joined the ranks of the Knights. By the spring of 1887, some five hundred cigar makers, launderers, and housekeepers had formed two local assemblies in New York City. The master workman Lee Sah led the Patrick Henry Labor Club, named for the American patriot, and the master workman Sam Wee led the Victor Hugo Labor Club, named for the French writer and humanist. These assemblies had the sanction of New York's District 49, whose socialist and radical leaders, including the African American machinist Frank Ferrell, held that the Knights' egalitarian principles applied to Chinese workers, too. And these New York radicals provided the loudest opposition to the Sinophobia that gripped the organization, especially in its western districts. The General Executive Board, however, tried to block District 49's efforts to organize Chinese workers by refusing charters to Lee Sah's and Sam Wee's assemblies.[78]

The debate within the Knights over Chinese membership came to a head when the General Assembly met in Indianapolis in the fall of 1888. The delegates by a vote of 95–42 rejected a proposal to organize Chinese workers. For Powderly and the majority, the issue was settled; organizing Chinese workers was impossible. But that forty-two delegates dissented was extraordinary given the anti-Chinese passions within the organization. The New York radicals led the dissenters. Significantly, they were joined by Leonora Barry, who deplored "Chinese immorality" but voted for organizing the Chinese presumably as a means of uplift. Powderly's old comrade Robert Schilling also dissented. With his roots among the German workers of the Midwest, Schilling understood discrimination against the Chinese as a symptom of the Knights' increasingly "narrow policy" of focusing on protection from immigrant labor. Schilling was right. And he was acutely aware that the nativist spirit afflicting the Knights had only grown bolder in the wake of a fateful explosion in Chicago's Haymarket Square.[79]

IX.

ON MAY 1, 1886, TENS OF THOUSANDS of mainly immigrant workers in Chicago staged a walkout to demand the eight-hour day. Three days later, to protest the death of two strikers felled by police bullets, workers staged a rally in Chicago's Haymarket Square. A bomb exploded as a column of police officers entered the square at the conclusion of the rally. The explosion and gunshots from police revolvers in the ensuing chaos killed seven policemen and at least four civilians and wounded dozens more. Eight labor activists were convicted for their role in the bombing, and on

November 11, 1887, four of them were hanged. The condemned men were anarchists, and along with other labor activists the anarchists had led the Central Labor Union, which had played a major role in mobilizing for the May 1 general strike.

The local Knights of Labor was also involved in the Chicago eight-hour movement and had recruited thousands of new members in preparation for May 1. This was despite instructions from Terence Powderly not to endorse a general strike that he feared would have tragic consequences. As it turned out, the Haymarket bomb was a disaster from which the Knights would never fully recover. A wave of anti-labor hysteria, repression, and blacklisting took a heavy toll. So too did the sharp internal divisions over attitudes toward the four men sentenced to death.[80]

Powderly condemned the anarchists for their role in the bloodshed, and many Knights did the same. But this did not stop political and business leaders from indicting the organization. The *Chicago Tribune* editorialized that the "dynamite knights" should be stripped of their rights as citizens, and attributed every drop of blood "to the malign influences, teachings, [and] resolutions . . . of the Knights of Labor." Down in Texas, where the repression against the Knights was in full swing after the southwest strike, *The Dallas Morning News* responded to Powderly's denunciation of the violence by calling it evidence of "hypocritical fraud," given that members of the Knights were the "instigators, movers, and expectant beneficiaries of all this communistic devilment." For proof, it needed only to point to Albert Parsons, one of the condemned anarchists, a leader of Chicago's labor movement, and a long-standing member of the Knights.[81]

A campaign for clemency for Parsons and the other anarchists spread through Knights' assemblies, trade unions, and working-class communities across the country and overseas. No matter how they felt about the anarchists' political beliefs, in the eyes of many observers the condemned men were going to be executed for those beliefs, not for a crime committed. Powderly nonetheless, urgently seeking to protect the Knights' reputation, refused to support the clemency campaign. Many Knights, even in Chicago, agreed with or at least acquiesced in Powderly's position. But he alienated other Knights, including Elizabeth Rodgers, the master of Chicago's District 24, who identified with the trade unionists and immigrant workers of Chicago's eight-hour movement.[82]

Powderly's refusal to lend aid to the accused anarchists also drew the wrath of those Knights known as revolutionary socialists or anarchists, such as Victor Drury of New York and Burnette Haskell of Denver. Haskell's collaborator Joseph Buchanan, organizer of District 82 on the Union Pacific and the Knights' most prominent leader west of the Mississippi, called himself a trade unionist, a socialist, and an anarchist. In January 1887, Buchanan moved from Denver to Chicago to work for the clemency campaign for Parsons and the other condemned men. Soon afterward, he was expelled from the Knights and formed the radical "Provisional Committee" in opposition to Powderly's leadership.[83]

The bomb at Haymarket aggravated ideological conflicts that the Knights had usually been able to keep under control. The organization's very success as a universal fraternity of wage earners was predicated on ideological flexibility and tolerance. Moreover, philosophical positions were often highly adaptive and accommodating, allowing Knights to find points of agreement on core industrial strategies. Powderly the "equalizer" believed in equality between employer and employee and between capital and labor, whereas anarchists and socialists such as Joseph Buchanan published tracts about overthrowing the tyranny of capital and abolishing classes, not equalizing them.

Yet Buchanan was something of an "equalizer" himself and organized Colorado workers under the banner of "Liberty, Justice, and Equality." The motto atop his newspaper, *The Labor Enquirer*, promised, "Not rash equality, but equal rights," and Buchanan worked tirelessly to build trade assemblies of the Knights on the western railroads on the model of equalization and fair treatment. For that matter, Albert Parsons, the most famous of the anarchists, who wrote violent editorials extolling the virtues of dynamite bombs for liberating humanity from the capitalist state, also found a place within the Knights. In 1877, Parsons helped organize Chicago's first local assembly, and despite his increasing radicalization in 1880 he took part in a delegation of Knights to lobby the U.S. Congress for the same capitalist state to enact an eight-hour law. This was not unusual within the Knights. Radicals who advocated blowing up the system often found common ground with reformers, or "equalizers," who sought equity within the system.[84]

X.

THIS DIVISION BETWEEN RADICALS AND REFORMERS blurred because of the nearly universal acceptance by all factions of the notion that the competitive or capitalist order would be replaced by human solidarity and cooperation. The cooperative commonwealth, sooner or later, would overcome the class divide. Most Knights discussed this in the peaceful and evolutionary terms of a "marriage of labor and capital" for mutual benefit. In this regard, the Knights followed the Grange, the National Labor Union, the Colored National Labor Union, the Sovereigns of Industry, and countless other reform movements that embraced the cooperative ideal. In the post–Civil War decades, cooperation was widely recognized as the antidote to the baneful results of competition. It was also a route to equality.[85]

In 1884, when John Samuel was appointed secretary of the Knights' cooperative board, he had been toiling for the cooperative cause for more than twenty years. During the Civil War, Samuel had joined with William Sylvis and other labor organizers to form the Union Cooperative Association, a society of Philadelphia skilled workers and craftsmen that promoted cooperative principles. Only cooperation, Samuel came to believe, could deliver the social equality that would be "in harmony with the principles of our form of government." He explained that "the relation of Employer & Employed" implied "Superiority & Inferiority," whereas "Co-operation supersedes this relation" and makes men "equal—& with equal rights to liberty & the pursuit of happiness." Samuel took this equal rights doctrine with him when he relocated in the early 1870s to St. Louis, where he co-edited a Grange newspaper and promoted the Grange's cooperative experiments. He later moved on to do the same with the Sovereigns of Industry.

In the early 1880s, he initiated a cooperative coal supply company and a cooperative grocery store as he emerged as a leading authority on the subject within the Knights of Labor.[86]

Samuel's views about cooperation and equality were widely accepted, with varying degrees of commitment, among his fellow Knights. Uriah Stephens, the first leader of the organization, believed that the "long term job" of the Knights was "substituting cooperation for capitalism." Powderly said much the same. "Organization once perfected," he told the General Assembly in 1880, would bring about "a system of cooperation, which will eventually make every man his own master—every man his own employer." Cooperation, Powderly noted, was "the lever of labor's emancipation" and the goal toward which "the eyes of the workingmen and women of the world are directed." Significantly, one of Powderly's harshest critics, the socialist-anarchist Victor Drury, had similar views about cooperation. A committed radical from his days fighting in the streets of Paris during the revolution of 1848, Drury used his base in New York's powerful District 49 to radicalize the Knights. But he also led efforts to set up cooperative banking and other mutual enterprises. Out west, the socialist revolutionary Burnette Haskell was similarly interested in building cooperative alternatives to the competitive system.[87]

Powderly endorsed the cooperative ideal but rarely showed passion for the subject. For other Knights, however, it was a fundamental commitment. The master workman Lemuel Biddle, for example, in his address to the 1879 annual meeting of District 7 in central Ohio, framed cooperation as a central issue in "humane freedom and the truest forms of civilization." Biddle called on his fellow Knights to "continue to fight until capitalistic production shall be utterly and forever overthrown and cooperation be the written and realized law in every land."[88] At its next annual meeting, the secretary of District 7, Thomas James, bitterly protested the lack of progress toward the cooperative future. When he joined the Knights, he had hoped that "co-operation was the prime object of the order, but alas! up to this point I have been disappointed." With eight hundred members, James calculated, his district could easily raise ten thousand dollars for cooperative businesses. An organization numbering in the tens or hundreds of thousands could surely make cooperation a reality.[89]

But the national office of the Knights never had much luck raising funds for cooperative enterprises. In 1880, the General Assembly set up a cooperative fund with compulsory contributions from the locals. But in the face of resistance, the contributions were made voluntary, and the fund dried up. Moreover, even at the district level the Knights struggled to coordinate their cooperative efforts. Knights such as Thomas James pointed to what the Grange had accomplished, including the State Cooperative Association in Texas with its wholesale agency and 150 associated stores. Similarly, a Knight from Lincoln, Kansas, wrote Powderly about the need to build flour mills and farm machine factories on the "direct trade" model of the Grange. The Knights, however, struggled to build cooperatives on a large scale.[90]

Instead, with its complex system of mixed and trade assemblies, the Knights of Labor built hundreds of mainly local and uncoordinated cooperative enterprises. Many of these were cooperative stores that provided coal miners and mill workers with an alternative to the company stores and at least gave the promise of more equitable treatment. Cooperative stores frequently occupied the first floor of Knights of Labor halls in working-class communities. The Knights also formed cooperatives that made barrels, cigars, hats, books, shirt collars, wagons, shoes, and a wide variety of other products. Workers who had been locked out or blacklisted by their employers initiated many of these enterprises. This effort included women workers who set up cooperative laundries and cooperative clothing, shoe, and cigarette factories.[91]

In Chicago, a group of women garment workers formed the Our Girls Co-operative Clothing Factory. Blacklisted by their employers for their union activity in the fall of 1886, the women formed a cooperative business that sold directly to wholesalers. "Our aim and objects are to elevate the working classes," read a cooperative circular, "especially our own sex." The company paid equitable wages and had a profit-sharing system, and the thirty or so employees elected the company president, Mary Mc-Cormick, and the other directors. A veteran seamstress by her mid-twenties, McCormick was a hard worker and a hardheaded business manager. She was also aligned with the radical factions of the Chicago Knights. She was the master of the all-women's Lizzie Rodgers assembly, named for Elizabeth Rodgers, who was the master of Chicago's District 24. In November 1887, McCormick led a women's contingent at the funeral pageant for Albert Parsons and the other executed labor leaders. She did so as the leader of the renamed Lucy Parsons assembly, so named in honor of Albert's widow, who was an influential labor activist in her own right.[92]

Meanwhile, the Knights launched a series of businesses aimed at the national market. Goods from soap to coffee to nails were produced and sold under their label. The National K. of L. Cooperative Smoking Tobacco Company was based in Raleigh, North Carolina, and sold its pipe tobacco and its shares of stock to Knights across the country. A chewing-tobacco firm, the Kentucky Railroad Tobacco Company, offered the Knights' General Executive five hundred dollars for the endorsement of a "K. of L. Plug." The company provided workers with stocks in a form of profit sharing, with "dividends [going] equally to capital and labor stock." This, the company claimed, made it a model of "equality between capital and labor." An Ohio marketing agent for cooperative goods made the same point. By purchasing products with the Knights' stamp, consumers would "promote [their] own interests" while "harmoniz[ing] Capital and Labor by creating a just and equitable division of profits."[93]

In the winter of 1883, the Buckeye Cannel Coal Company in Cannelburg, Indiana, locked out a group of coal miners who were known members of the Knights. The miners then launched a cooperative venture to mine the same vein of coal on nearby land, but to do so, they needed funds for mine machinery and for building a half-mile switch to link the mine with the Ohio and Mississippi Railroad. The General Executive Board of the Knights took up their cause and assessed the national membership to raise funds. By the summer of 1885, the Knights had invested twenty thousand dollars in the Cannelburg mine. But the railroad balked at connecting the switch to their line, the first of a series of blows that rendered the mine only marginally profitable. At the same time, Cannelburg raised questions about the nature of cooperation. The management and majority ownership were in the hands of the General Executive Board, which directed the mine much as other remote directors would. As an experiment in "the marriage of labor and capital," Cannelburg proved an unhappy and unequal relationship that soon ended in a separation, with the Knights leasing the mine to a group of local investors.[94]

For Powderly, the experiment at Cannelburg reaffirmed the unequal power exerted by the railroads. "The odds will be against co-operation," he concluded, "as long as the avenues of distribution are in the hands of monopoly." Yet the flame of the cooperative ideal burned bright. Most of the Knights' cooperatives were small-scale, undercapitalized, and lucky if they lasted a full calendar year. In substance, most of them resembled so many other small stores or artisanal shops, and the handful of larger enterprises were more like other large enterprises than not. Yet cooperation played an outsized role in the reform imagination. This quest for cooperative alternatives, as many Knights understood, was the best response to the "monstrous evils of competition" and the failure of government "to fulfill its primary functions of protecting equal rights and enforcing justice."[95]

8.

SOCIAL EQUALITY

I N JANUARY 1885, Terence Powderly took his own grand tour of the South. The Knights of Labor, in its General Assembly held the previous September, recognized that the South was the weak link in its efforts to build a national organization and decided to dispatch its general master workman to do something about it. Powderly's tour followed the same political road map as that of his predecessors. Richard Trevellick accompanied Powderly, the same Trevellick who had accompanied William Sylvis of the National Labor Union on a similar tour sixteen years earlier and who was now a leading official of the Knights of Labor.[1]

Much as Oliver Kelley, William Sylvis, and Frances Willard had done, Powderly sent home glowing reports. "The South of today," he told the Scranton newspapers, was ready to "rid[e] side by side with the North in the onward march of progress." As for the past, it was all an unfortunate misunderstanding. "The vast majority of the men who fought in the Confederate army," Powderly assured his followers, "were not battling to uphold slavery," and they "did not like the work they were engaged in." If only the "Northern man" and the "Southern man" knew each other better, all would be well. Just as Kelley, Sylvis, and Willard had done, Powderly embraced a vision of sectional reconciliation that left little room for the equal rights claims of the southerners who happened to be black.[2]

I.

AFTER POWDERLY'S RETURN FROM THE SOUTH, the General Assembly launched the Blue and Gray Association of the Knights of Labor. With Thomas Green of Arkansas as its commander, the association appealed to the "soldiers of the late war" to join together in sectional healing. Its motto was "Capital divided, labor unites us." This was unity driven by the mutual recognition that whatever might have transpired in the past could not match the evils of the present. The southern slave master had been supplanted by "the monopolist of the North," who "owns more slaves and treats them meaner than the master of any country ever did where slaves were owned as chattels." As for the slaveholders' rebellion, the association explained, "We would have all men feel that no treason is greater than the treason that monopolizes the channels of wealth." The Blue and Gray Association enjoyed only a symbolic existence. Nonetheless, just as the Grange, the National Labor Union, and the Woman's Christian Temperance Union had done, the Knights of Labor launched its campaign to organize the South with a symbolic nod to the white southern viewpoint on the questions of the war and the sectional divide.[3]

Meanwhile, African Americans in numerous southern places bore the brunt of the efforts of white members of the Knights to exclude them from their workplaces and their assemblies. In November 1885, the Knights took part in the Galveston, Texas, general strike that was initiated by demands of white longshoremen to bar black workers from jobs on the city's waterfront. The Galveston Knights called on white labor to struggle against "Colored Rat and Scab labor from other countries." In Savannah, Georgia, white members of the Knights protested the hiring of black laborers by a local railroad. In the spring of 1886, a contributor to Timothy Thomas Fortune's influential black newspaper, *The New York Freeman*, took note that the Knights, "not as an organization but as individuals, have, at the workshops, manufactories and in all the trades, proscribed the black worker." Meanwhile, where white members did accept the organization of black members, they usually insisted on separate assemblies. The result was an organizational pattern that resembled that of the WCTU, with racially segregated local assemblies that sent white and black delegates to integrated district and state assemblies.[4]

The Knights of Labor was in familiar waters. With its views about race and reunion and in its segregated organizational practice, the Knights followed the mainstream of white post–Civil War reform movements. That was the case through the immediate aftermath of Powderly's southern tour. But the Knights, or at least its southern wing, would soon drift out of the mainstream as its racial makeup changed. By 1887, African Americans formed the majority of the membership in much of the South. The Knights became an organization of cotton pickers, sugarcane cutters, domestic servants, lumbermen, washerwomen, and fish cannery workers, an organization of black men and women engaged in the most strenuous labor, for the longest hours, at the lowest pay. The organizer J. A. Bodenhamer wrote to Powderly from Jacksonville, Florida, explaining that the Knights "must of necessity be composed largely of the Negro race," because in the South the "great bulwark of the labor . . . is performed by colored hands." The enemies of the Knights, Bodenhamer added, accused him of inciting "insurrectionary movements among the Negroes," an accusation that he considered "the best indorsement he could get, in the estimation of working people."[5]

The defenders of the southern hierarchies of power did indeed view the organization of the men and women at the bottom of these hierarchies as an insurrectionary act. In that sense, as the vehicle of the black field hand and the domestic servant, the Knights came to occupy a special place in the fevered nightmares of white southerners. This was surely not what the leaders of the Knights had in mind when they launched their efforts to organize in the South. Nonetheless, self-organization allowed African Americans to claim the Knights as their own. By 1887, the Knights had ninety thousand black members. Richmond, New Orleans, and other cities had strong assemblies of black workers. But most black Knights toiled in the coal mines, plantations, lumber camps, and railroad yards of the smaller towns and remote corners of the rural South.[6]

The sociologist Richard Ely observed that southern blacks "are now everywhere joining the Knights of Labor." And he explained this enthusiasm for the Knights by the fact that black people were "so much inclined to societies of various kinds," estimating that "ninety-five out of a hundred belonged to a mutual aid society of one description or another." How Ely came up with this percentage is unclear and underscores that for many white observers such as Ely the black working class remained shrouded in mystery. But he had a point. African Americans sustained a "multiplicity of societies"—Union Leagues, WCTU chapters, Equal Rights Leagues, Prince Hall Masonic lodges, Zion Lyceums, and countless other self-help and voluntary associations—with the church often tying them together into a dense network of collaborative effort. By the late 1880s, this organizational network came to embrace the Knights of Labor.[7]

How did it come to pass that African Americans would take their chances with the Knights? Part of the answer lies with the relative success of the Knights in organizing across the color line among coal miners and railroad employees. In Mississippi, the Knights recruited among the black workers in the railroad towns of Meridian and Vicksburg.[8] In the context of a southern racial order of suffocating exclusion and closed doors, such efforts sent an effective message of possibility that African Americans who dug coal or laid railroad tracks spread to black neighborhoods and communities across the South and beyond. African Americans also took careful note of the prominent role racial egalitarians, especially the radicals of New York's District 49, played in the organization.

Then there was Terence Powderly, who at moments could sound like a racial egalitarian and, perhaps more important, who was known for his commitment to black membership rights. Powderly's hostility to Chinese and other immigrant workers revealed the narrow and patchy nature of his views on equal rights; he advocated a color-blind policy that had gaping exceptions. Nevertheless, with a remarkable doggedness over the course of more than a decade of leadership, Powderly lectured, scolded, and sanctioned white members of the Knights who resisted the rules of equal treatment for black members. African Americans knew this about Powderly. And for black workers concerned about labor alliances with Democrats, they would also have noticed Powderly's resistance to such alliances and his partisan Republican leanings. Given the alternatives, many African Americans saw in Powderly's Knights a vehicle for navigating the post-Reconstruction terrain of racial caste and violent inequality.

Significantly, not only black men but also black women recognized the possibilities that the Knights offered. Since the close of the Civil War, African American washerwomen, cooks, and domestic servants had been forming associations and demanding fair and uniform wages and just treatment in their employment. In 1866, domestic workers in Jackson, Mississippi, went on strike. In 1877, washerwomen in Galveston, Texas, struck for wages of $1.50 a day or $9.00 a week and demanded that the city put Chinese commercial laundries out of business, threatening to close the shops of their Chinese competitors with axes and nails. In 1881, hundreds of Atlanta washerwomen formed the Washing Society and undertook a work stoppage to enforce their fixed wage rates. When the city council attempted to break this effort at self-regulation by imposing a $25 business license on the washerwomen, they responded that they would be willing to pay for the licenses, "and then we will have full control of the city's washing at our own prices."[9]

By the mid-1880s, the organizing efforts of black women workers turned toward the Knights of Labor as applications for membership by washerwomen, cooks, and domestic servants poured in from across much of the South. This posed a double challenge to assumptions of white and male prerogatives within an organization dedicated to the principle of equality. More often than not, the white male leaders and members of the Knights failed to live up to this challenge. In Savannah, Georgia, several of the city's assemblies issued a formal protest against black women organizing an assembly of their own. Similar opposition confronted the African American washerwomen and domestic servants who in the spring of 1885 looked to form an assembly in Raleigh, North Carolina. Raleigh's Pioneer Assembly "advised against giving the work into the hands of the Colored Women, knowing that it will be the death of the White Assembly."[10]

The Knights' organizer in Raleigh, John R. Ray, rejected this advice and looked for ways to organize the black women. As he put it, the Knights' egalitarian principles meant that "the poor ignorant underpaid and overworked cook" was equally as deserving of protection as the skilled worker. Yet Ray thought it necessary to ask Powderly "if it would be advisable to organize" Raleigh's washerwomen and domestic servants. Expressing his typical caution, Powderly advised that if need be, postpone the organization of the black women until more black and white men were organized in the city. Meanwhile, the opposition of the city's white members stiffened John Ray's resolve to enroll the overworked and underpaid black women who were in such need of organization and, as Ray put it, "some way to protect them from the avariciousness of some of the brethren."[11]

Over the next several years, in the face of stubborn internal opposition, African American cooks and cotton pickers, domestics and washerwomen, made use of the Knights to exploit cracks in the barriers of race, class, and sex. In so doing, they turned the labor organization into an imperfect vehicle for pressing their equal rights claims. This transformation was the work of black workers and activists. But Terence Powderly's own stubborn insistence on certain egalitarian claims attracted these workers and activists to the Knights in the first place and facilitated this transformation. So too did the support of these claims from key organizers such as John Ray and from enough of the white membership in enough places to give them organizational life. By the mid-1880s, the Knights of Labor appeared as a potential alternative to the dismal realities of the post-Reconstruction racial order.

For good reason, scholars exploring race and class in U.S. history have fixed their attention on the Knights of Labor. They have studied the late nineteenth-century labor movement in search of models of interracial cooperation and to explore the relationship between race consciousness and class consciousness. This has led to debates between those scholars who have seen the promise of class solidarity in interracial organizing and those who have emphasized the power of white supremacy and racist ideology. The intractable nature of these debates reflects the reality that even within the context of the most oppressive relationships it is possible to find examples of human empathy and solidarity that nevertheless fail to transcend those relationships. And in that regard, the American system of racial caste involved an extraordinarily pervasive and brutal set of hierarchical relationships that the Knights could not and did not transcend. Examining the Knights through the lens of equal rights raises a different set of questions. It sheds light on how wage earners—black and white, women and men—engaged political ideas about equality within the prevailing systems of hierarchical power and privilege. In doing so, it helps explain how in the former Confederacy the Knights evolved into an organization of some of the most exploited and impoverished sections of African American workers.[12]

II.

THE KNIGHTS OF LABOR MADE the nation's coalfields its first target of large-scale industrial organizing. After that it was the railroads. In both of these industries, black workers were a force to be reckoned with. From antebellum times, African Americans dug coal and built railroads across much of the South. And after the war, and the breaking of the chains of slavery, they migrated in large numbers to work in West Virginia coal mines and on Texas railroads. The majority of black miners and railroad workers were wage earners, paid for their labor even if it was in company scrip at the company store. In mines near Birmingham, Alabama, and in southern West Virginia, African Americans often made up more than half of the workforce. The most famous such miner was Booker T. Washington, who as a young man labored deep under a West Virginia mountainside.

Similarly, African Americans toiled in railroad yards and on track and construction crews from New Mexico to Virginia.[13]

Some of these workers were unpaid and unfree. They were convicts on lease to mine operators and railroad companies for whom they labored under murderous conditions of mistreatment and overwork. John Henry, the legendary "steel driving man," was a convict laborer who dug tunnels under Virginia hillsides for the Chesapeake and Ohio Railway. The Knights of Labor demanded the abolition of the brutal convict labor system, and this demand was often placed next to its demands to ban Chinese labor, charging that both represented unfree labor and therefore unequal competition. African American wage earners in the coal mines and on the railroads supported the demands against convict labor, and often Chinese labor, too, as they vigorously asserted their equal rights as free laborers. This made an impression on the white organizers of the Knights. The presence of black wage earners meant that the Knights' egalitarian strategy of organizing across divisions of skill and craft mandated cooperation across divisions of race as well.[14]

Few black miners worked the anthracite fields of northeastern Pennsylvania, where the Knights set up their first miners' assemblies. But by the end of the 1870s, when they sent organizers to the bituminous fields to the west and south, the Knights were confronted by the dilemma of racial competition for mine work. Failed efforts to drive black workers from the mines proved that exclusion was not a viable strategy. Black miners replacing white miners during strikes meant that this issue cried out for a solution. Only by bringing black miners into the fold could the Knights sustain their organization. Powderly and his organizers developed a two-pronged strategy to persuade white workers to admit African Americans into the Knights, and to persuade African Americans to join the Knights. The Knights of Labor employed this strategy across the midwestern and Appalachian mining districts, and it played a key role in its organizing in the South.[15]

The first part of the strategy was to overcome white resistance to opening the doors of the Knights to black members. In August 1880, after a series of unsuccessful strikes in the midwestern coal districts, Powderly directed the following question to "any white miner who objects to the admission of colored men into our Order." "If you are forced to strike against a reduction of wages," Powderly asked, "will your employer stop to inquire the color or nationality of any man who will take your place at the reduction offered?" A month later, when white miners in Alabama objected to black men joining their assembly, Powderly admonished them to "remember that when capital strikes at us it does not strike at the white working man, or the black working man, but it strikes at *Labor*," adding, "Can the wisest of us tell what color *labor* is? I doubt it." Such arguments were based on a simple calculus: adopt a color-blind policy or capital will crush labor. The message carried across the coalfields. West Virginia District 5 passed a resolution to make a color-blind policy the law among its fellow miners. Any person "who shall attempt to raise any question of color or nationality," the assembly resolved, "shall, upon proof of the same, be deprived of work in any mines of this valley."[16]

Powderly received a steady flow of inquiries testing how serious he was about enforcing the organization's stated rules about the membership rights of African Americans. In one such inquiry, Gilbert Rockwood, an organizer from Pittsburgh, suggested that the best solution would be to "quietly" reject black applications for membership while publicly adhering to "the *letter* of the law." Surely, Rockwood was not the only Knight who favored such "quiet" methods of exclusion, methods that had allowed the Grange, among others, to remain a whites-only organization. But Powderly rejected any such subterfuge. In his correspondence, he often gave a terse reminder that the rules were explicit and that he had no choice but to insist they be obeyed.[17]

In a letter to W. H. Lynch of Maysville, Kentucky, Powderly delivered one of his stinging reprimands about a color-blind policy. Lynch had reported that the master workman of his local assembly had barred black members from visiting its meetings. Powderly replied that the master workman had violated his vows to the organization and it was Lynch's duty to demand his resignation. Human solidarity demanded no less. "There can be no trifling in our Assemblies," Powderly wrote to Lynch. "I tell you . . . capital makes no difference in oppressing labor whether it is white or black and we *must* know no differences if we would win as a unit on the question of HUMAN RIGHTS."[18]

Persuading white workers to accept black members was only part of the equation; it was no less essential to convince black workers that the Knights would protect their rights. The rules about admitting candidates without regard to race surely helped. Black coal miners paid close attention to Powderly's edicts enforcing those rules. A local assembly of African American miners in Wheeling, West Virginia, hung the Emancipation Proclamation on the wall of its meeting room, and next to Lincoln's words it mounted an artistic rendering of one of Powderly's "Decisions" ordering that the "color of a candidate shall not bar him from admission; rather let the coloring of his mind and heart be the test."[19]

At the same time, African Americans looked for assurance that once they were admitted, the Knights would provide some measure of equal treatment. The miners of West Virginia's District 5 offered such assurance to their black members, passing a resolution "that the Colored Brothers [will] be protected by the Order in their just rights while they are in the minority." Commitments to racial equality were also essential to the success of the Knights' organizing in Texas. The Knights in Austin emphasized that they accepted members "without reference to race or creed, section, condition, or occupation," and that workers "no matter what race" were "equally welcome, equally respected."[20]

III.

JUST WHAT DID THE KNIGHTS mean by "equally welcome, equally respected"? Frank Ferrell forced this question on the national stage in October 1886 when the Knights of Labor held its General Assembly in Richmond, Virginia. The city was a stronghold of the Knights, with some seven thousand members organized in separate black and white district assemblies. It was also reportedly the city where Ferrell was born forty years earlier. It is unclear whether he was born a slave or free, because little is known of his early life before he emerged as a prominent figure in the New York labor movement. An engineer who worked in an apartment house near Union Square, Ferrell was elected to the city's Central Labor Union, and he found an intellectual home among the radicals and egalitarians of District 49, where he served as secretary-treasurer. When the manager of Murphy's Hotel in Richmond learned that the delegates from New York would include Ferrell, he informed them that the hotel would not be able to provide equal service to a black man. In response, the New York delegation boycotted the hotel and found rooms in a boardinghouse run by African Americans. The members of the New York Knights had passed this test of their commitment to racial equality with flying colors. But the Richmond convention would present more tests, with strikingly mixed results for the Knights as a whole.[21]

The opening ceremonies were held in Armory Hall, where political dignitaries welcomed more than eight hundred delegates from across the country along with twice that many guests. As a gesture of solidarity across the color line, District 49 proposed that Frank Ferrell introduce Virginia's governor, Fitzhugh Lee. But Powderly was concerned about how this would be received by white Virginians and arranged for Ferrell to introduce Powderly rather than the governor. Ferrell obliged and used his introductory remarks to explain that the goal of the Knights was the abolition of racial distinctions, concluding with the words "Here we stand as brethren and as equals." Ferrell made these remarks standing on the platform with Governor Lee and the other political dignitaries. Powderly did his best to soothe any hurt feelings, and he spoke in Ferrell's defense. He praised the New York delegates for standing by their "colored brother" when he was denied lodgings in the hotel. And he explained that he had asked Ferrell to introduce him to make the same point about equal treatment, and "so that it might go to the entire world that we practice what we preach."[22]

The hotel incident and the convention's opening set telegraph wires humming as the word spread to newspaper offices around the country that the nation's mightiest labor organization had arrived in Richmond to preach and practice "social equality" between the races. If anyone had doubts about the Knights' intentions, two days later Frank Ferrell and the delegates from District 49 attended a performance of *Hamlet* at the Mozart Academy. Ferrell's presence with his white colleagues in the "choicest" orchestra seats provoked cries of outrage from the white citizens of the former Confederate capital. The next day, in preparation for Ferrell's possible return, the Law and Order League armed and marched, while thirty-five police officers guarded the theater's entrance. Ferrell did not return, but the news reports from Richmond were no less alarming. "The social equality question," reported the Philadelphia *Times*, "has set the colored people here wild and correspondingly incensed the native whites." This included a white delegate who told the *Times* "that '49' and other champions of social equality are pressing this matter too far." Banquets and other social functions planned for the convention by local black and white assemblies were canceled to avoid perceived breaches of the color line, especially involving the wives and daughters of white members of the Knights.[23]

Outside the convention, meanwhile, thousands of African Americans took part in a celebratory labor parade on the streets of Richmond. Black residents also put on a festive banquet in honor of District 49, with Victor Drury treating his hosts to his trademark revolutionary oratory. African American journalists and equal rights advocates greeted the events in Richmond with similar enthusiasm. Harry Smith's *Cleveland Gazette* told readers that the black race had "secured a needed ally in the Knights of Labor" and described the Richmond convention as "the most remarkable thing since emancipation." *The New York Freeman* praised the members of District 49 for their "most unusual courage" in a "simple matter of justice and fair play." The Ohio Equal Rights League adopted a resolution applauding Powderly and District 49 for their defense of Frank Ferrell's equal rights, a position deserving of "the unstinted praises of the colored Americans of the United States."[24]

African Americans, however, often expressed skepticism about the white membership of the Knights. "Mr. Powderly and District 49 have immortalized themselves, as far as the Negro is concerned," observed Christopher Perry's *Philadelphia Tribune*, but "it is doubtful that the rank and file of the order are ready to preach and practice industrial equality." Indeed, many white Knights saw the events in Richmond as an outrage against the white race. James Hirst from Galveston wrote to Powderly to renounce his membership: "Since you have changed from a Knight of Labor advocate to a nigger social equality man I hereby denounce you as a low, vulgar buffoon. . . . [I]f you have a daughter she should be taken from you else you may marry her to a nigger. . . . Yr's in contempt [signed] James Hirst—now and henceforth an ex–Knight of Labor." Meanwhile, District 49 received a postcard from Philadelphia that suggested that it was not only southern members of the Knights who were incensed by its breach of the color line. "Ain't you fellows ashamed of yourselves for insulting the people of Richmond, whose guests you are?" queried a Knight from the City of Brotherly Love, adding, "You are doing injury to the order and heaping disgrace upon yourself."[25]

Powderly had a crisis on his hands. Five months before, the bomb in Chicago's Haymarket had embroiled the Knights in the national hysteria about anarchy and terror. Now it was racial hysteria about "social equality." Hoping to calm the storm, the General Assembly passed a resolution clarifying the Knights' position on "social equality." The resolution recognized "civil and political equality," rejected racial distinctions "in the broad field of labor," and pledged to not "interfere or disrupt the social relations which may exist between different races in any part of the country."[26]

On October 11, Powderly sent a long letter to the newspapers making the same points. The letter repeated his axiom that black and white workers deserve "an equal share of protection" because "no human eye can detect a difference between the article manufactured by the black mechanic and that manufactured by the white mechanic." At the same time, Powderly swore that he had no interest in "social equality" and "no wish to interfere with the social relations which exist between the races of the South." He reassured the citizens of Richmond that "the time-honored laws of social equality will be allowed to slumber on undisturbed." Powderly concluded his letter by drawing a distinction between rules against "social equality," which the South was free to live by if it so desired, and the universal political equality of American citizenship. "The equality of American citizenship is all that we insist on," Powderly wrote, "and that equality *must not, will not*, be trampled upon."[27]

The New York Freeman criticized Powderly's letter for having "pandered his honest convictions." Worse, he had done so in vain because his efforts to disclaim "social equality" would fail to "appease the implacable indignation of the Southern dog in the manger and its degraded ally the Southern press." This prediction proved true. *The South Alabamian*, adopting a tone of sympathy for the Knights, warned that Powderly's failure to "keep questions of social equality out of politics" could cost him the "influence and power he wields." *The Montgomery Advertiser* explained that "Mr. Powderly's letter is full of evil," because, although it was necessary to accept "the presence of negroes in conventions in which they are interested," the reports of interracial social events including white wives and daughters pass "beyond the bounds of propriety." Meanwhile, the editor of *The Norfolk Virginian* lectured Powderly for his "imprudent position on social equality" and his attempts to "override recognized social distinctions at the South." In the state of Virginia, the editor claimed, white citizens accepted that "the colored man has equal rights with the whites in courts of law and at the ballot-box and equality of citizenship." But when it came to "social equality," that was something "the whites refuse to tolerate in any form."[28]

Both Powderly and his detractors seemed to concur on this one point: equality of citizenship, defined as legal and political equality, could and must be kept separate from "social equality." They agreed that the Fourteenth and Fifteenth Amendments to the Constitution were the settled law of the land. At the same time, however, they recognized an unwritten law of "social relations" between the races with incontrovertible rules regarding "social equality." But what was the nature of these laws and rules? An answer to this question was provided by a group of delegates at Richmond who circulated a statement about social equality. The *Richmond Dispatch* published the text under the title "What We of the South and the Knights of Labor of the South Believe." And although there is no record of its authorship, the statement itself was boilerplate white supremacist rhetoric of the day. Its starting point was the so-called laws of social relations, "that the negro is inferior to the white man" and "that when a white man puts himself on a level with the negro he is 'meaner than a negro.'" From this, the statement emphasized that the white race had "the sacred duty" to maintain racial "integrity" and "to resist to the death any attempt to be reduced to a lower level" by way of "natural degradation." The Charleston *News and Courier* spelled out the meaning of such degradation in clear terms. Commenting on the Frank Ferrell events, the newspaper warned that "social equality means miscegenation," intermixing that would "leave the Southern country in the possession of a nation of mongrels and hybrids."[29]

IV.

AFRICAN AMERICANS RESPONDED TO THIS talk of racial integrity with mockery and ridicule. They were fully aware of just how perverse this talk was given the history and realities of sex between the races, having only recently emerged from enslavement built on the systematic rape and sexual exploitation of black women by white men. When the black citizens of Richmond held their banquet to honor District 49, they discussed the "social equality" question in the context of that history. "The only social equality that had ever existed," the speakers pointed out, "was thrust on them by the whites." In his welcoming address, Colonel Wilson, a light-skinned African American, observed that slavery replaced the black race by "a people of all colors and complexions." Such arguments were not lost on Powderly. In the chapter titled "Social Equality" in his 1889 autobiography, Powderly took note of the many "half-white faces" in the South to indict "the insincerity and hypocrisy of the southern aristocrat[s]," whose public strictures about "social equality" did not match their secret practice. Yet Powderly concluded the chapter with the pledge that "no labor advocate seeks to interfere with the social relations of the races in the South, for it is the industrial, not the race, question we endeavor to solve."[30]

Despite Powderly's assurances, however, "the social relations of the races" were inextricably bound to fundamental questions of equal rights in politics, law, and industry. The rules on "social equality" governed virtually every sphere of social interaction, fastening a system of racial caste and subjugation across the former slave states and beyond. Most of these rules remained unwritten, some of them were unevenly enforced, but they governed virtually every sphere of social interaction. The rules on "social equality" systematically denied African Americans equal access to education, to employment, and to the law. They denied them the most basic protections of their own bodies. Violations—or the mere suspicion of violations—of a carefully choreographed social etiquette of racial submission could and often did result in extrajudicial punishment: beatings, whippings, rape, torture, and execution. Lynch mobs, like the armed vigilantes prepared to meet Frank Ferrell at the Mozart Academy, made a mockery of constitutional and legal rights. In the 1880s, the Jim Crow laws segregating public accommodations were still mainly in the future. Yet Frank Ferrell could only stay in the Richmond hotel if he took his meals in the back kitchen, separate from the dining tables of the white delegates. Segregated accommodations meant unequal participation in organizational and political life.[31]

Nor could the rules on "social equality" be separated from the industrial question. The system of racial caste relegated most black workers to agricultural labor and domestic service at desperately low pay. Their opportunities in industry were increasingly confined to backbreaking toil digging coal, tending coke ovens, milling lumber, and laying railroad tracks. Since the days of slavery, African Americans had been employed as carpenters, as masons, and in other skilled work. But in the postwar years, they faced mounting obstacles to entering the building trades or similar professions. Meanwhile, the rules against "social equality" restricted the access of black workers to textile mills, smoking-tobacco factories, and other key new industries.

The Knights of Labor recognized the inequity of these restrictions on black labor. The 1886 General Assembly in Richmond passed a resolution for the admission of black apprentices to the country's workshops and factories. The Negro Press Committee sent a telegram to Powderly to "hail with joy" the Knights' efforts to put black apprentices "on Equal footing with white apprentices." However, it was easier to pass a resolution than to pry open the factory doors. In Georgia, black members of the Knights asked the organization to back their demand for a share of the work in the cotton mills. But white women were employed in those mills, and for the Knights to press the issue of opening the mills to African Americans would have kicked the hornet's nest of "social equality." The mills remained closed to black workers.[32]

Powderly's dilemma was to find a way to skirt the "social equality" question while still engaging African American demands for equal rights. This led to an extraordinary meeting during the Richmond convention, where Powderly met at Ford's Hotel with fifteen delegates of black assemblies from across the South. The aim of the meeting was to set up the "Bureau of Colored Knights," which would have as its purpose the gathering of "accurate statistics relative to the condition of the colored people and their relation to white laborers." It would collect information on wages and conditions of work and life. It was also "purposed to learn whether [black workers] receive the full liberty and rights to which they are legally entitled."[33]

Much like the Knights' Women's Bureau, the Bureau of Colored Knights reflected Powderly's enduring ideals of equalization through data. The Women's Bureau, however, was provided with a salaried director and other resources, while the Bureau of Colored Knights amounted to nothing more than the meeting at the hotel between the African American delegates and Powderly. The seeds of this failure were planted in its stated purpose, which placed "the question of social equality" off-limits as a topic of investigation and would not be "one of the objects of the bureau." The bureau was to be charged with gathering comprehensive data about black work and life, and to measure the "full liberty and rights" of African

Americans, but it was to do so without taking into account the mainly unwritten rules regarding "social equality." This proved an untenable assignment.[34]

The Knights' leadership and organizers accepted that the "social equality" question required concessions and maneuvers. Separating the local assemblies by race was one such compromise with far-reaching impact. Powderly made it clear that forming separate locals was the best way to balance the objections of white workers to black membership with black workers' desire to join the Knights on equal terms. His advice to an organizer in the Alabama coalfields was typical of his approach. Powderly told him to bring the black miners into the white assembly, "until they are strong enough to form a new colored assembly." But the main thing was to encourage membership. "Whichever is most convenient for the brothers to do," Powderly suggested, "should be done to keep them in the order." His instructions to an organizer in Chattanooga were more direct: "The best plan is to organize a colored assembly in your city and turn all applicants of that kind over to them."[35]

African Americans had their own views about this plan. Some black members of the Knights in Kansas and other northern states objected to separate assemblies as incompatible with the principle of equality. Joe Kewley, writing from an industrial town in central Indiana, reported to Powderly that the black members of his local assembly were resisting the pressures to form their own local. "'Tis the only organization in which we stand on an equal footing with the whites," explained a black member of the local, "and it is a big thing, and unless we can work here we will work nowhere." As Kewley noted, "This equality is what seems to be sticking in their craw."[36]

The process of separating the assemblies by race was uneven but widely practiced, especially south of the Mason-Dixon Line. Nonetheless, even in separate assemblies, membership in the Knights offered an arena to address racial inequities. "A Knight of Labor is a Knight of Labor, be he black or white," wrote *The New York Freeman*. "If the inequality in the relative wages paid black and white laborers is to be rectified," the newspaper added, it would be accomplished by way of a "union of forces" within the Knights "to compel equalization." On the southwestern railroads, black and white laborers worked in separate labor gangs, but belonging to the Knights offered what the historian Theresa Case describes as a type of "stomach equality" on basic issues of equitable treatment.[37]

Moreover, separate black and white assemblies corresponded to prevailing practices among other voluntary associations, practices that provided African Americans with a degree of autonomy. Black local assemblies sent delegates to the periodic meetings of the racially mixed district assemblies. Some black assemblies received visits from state and national organizers. And in some cities they held public events jointly with their white colleagues. The African American journalist Ida B. Wells attended such a meeting of the Knights in Memphis, reporting that "everyone who came was welcomed and every woman from black to white was seated with courtesy." This made an impression on Wells as "the first assembly of the sort in this town where color was not the criterion to recognition as ladies and gentlemen."[38]

The New York Freeman reported with similar enthusiasm about a Knights of Labor parade in Baltimore, proudly noting the banner of the "T. V. Powderly Assembly 2397 of Colored Knights" and the success of the parade as an interracial display of labor solidarity. "The procession was a very orderly one," the *Freeman* noted, "the colored and white fraternizing as if it had been a common thing all their lives." However, the very wording of the report suggested that this type of fraternizing was not common at all. What's more, a labor parade as a type of political event did not have the same implications for the rules of "social equality" that a social event with women present would have had.[39]

In many southern places such as Birmingham, white assemblies of the Knights held picnics and other social events for white members only. On July 4, 1887, in Pensacola, Florida, more than twelve hundred lumber workers, organized into separate black and white assemblies, marched jointly in an Independence Day celebration. But the picnics that were held afterward were carefully separated by race. "The colored Knights of

Labor will go to the park and the whites to Magnolia Bluff," *The New York Freeman* reported. "They could not possibly all go to the same place and whoop off the 'glorious 4th' together. That would be too much like social equality for our Southern brethren."[40]

V.

THE MAINTENANCE OF RACIAL DISTANCE, however, proved an unreliable shield from the destruction wrought by the "social equality" question. The limits of this protection were revealed when the Knights turned to politics in the summer and fall of 1886. In what the historian Leon Fink describes as possibly "the American workers' single greatest push for political power," the Knights launched labor and independent campaigns in some two hundred cities, towns, and hamlets across the country, putting Knights on city councils, in mayors' offices, and in state legislatures. The Knights also claimed that it had sent a dozen members to the U.S. Congress. In the South, the success of these independent campaigns at times rested on the Knights' ability to mobilize interracial political alliances of disaffected white Democrats and black Republicans behind labor candidates. Such alliances ran up a string of victories from Fort Worth, Texas, to Oxford, North Carolina. Their platforms included federal regulation of railroads, greenback currency, protection of labor organizations, shorter workdays, and abolition of convict and child labor. They also called for federal funds for public schools, equitable bankruptcy laws, and other demands of particular interest to African American voters. The Richmond General Assembly of the Knights took place in the midst of these independent political campaigns, which came under extraordinary pressure as the Democratic Party hurled the charge of "social equality" against the Knights and their candidates.[41]

In the fall of 1886, John Nichols, a printer and the master workman of the North Carolina Knights, won a seat in the U.S. Congress. He did so with a base of support among the fifteen hundred black and white members of the Knights in the Raleigh-Durham area. Nichols was a Radical Republican in the years after the Civil War and maintained links to the

Republican Party and the black community. The Democrats accused Nichols, who was white, of "negrophilism" and "the vile propaganda of social equality." Citing the recent events at the Knights' convention in Richmond, the editors of the Durham *Tobacco Plant* called on the workers of the city to support the Democratic candidate and "show Mr. Powderly and Mr. Nichols that you are opposed to social equality." Durham voters responded to such appeals by helping to send Nichols to Washington. But Nichols's victory did nothing to slow the attacks on the North Carolina Knights as a threat to the racial order. The master workman of an African American assembly wrote to the *Journal of United Labor* to explain the "unenviable position of the Knights of Labor" in his district. Chicago's "anarchist riot," the "disregard of the 'color-line' by the Richmond General Assembly," and Republican Party gains in the recent elections "were all used against us." The enemies of the Knights, he wrote, "kept crying 'Nigger! Nigger!' until the two words 'nigger' and 'Knight' became almost synonymous."[42]

Where Nichols succeeded in his run for Congress, the campaign of William Mullen in Richmond, Virginia, fell victim to a deepening political rift separating black and white members of the Knights. Like Nichols, Mullen was a printer and labor activist and was elected the master workman of the Knights of his state. Mullen also had a base of support among the workers in his state's capital. Unlike Nichols, however, Mullen had been a Democrat, and white workers were his main constituency. The pull of race and party on members who were white Democrats and black Republicans bedeviled the Knights across the South and beyond. And in Richmond these tensions played out in a deeply segregated city where not only the local assemblies but also the two district assemblies were separated by race. For black residents of Richmond, District 92 was at the center of their community life. Within District 92, Mullen's independent campaign had the backing of a number of members who saw in Mullen a supporter of Powderly's equal rights policies. But the all-white District 84 provided Mullen with his political connections and strongest following.[43]

The Knights of Labor held its General Assembly in Richmond in the

midst of Mullen's congressional campaign. Mullen hoped that the enthusiasm that it would generate for the Knights would translate to victory at
the polls. Instead, Frank Ferrell's challenge to the color line and the ensuing fury over "social equality" caused many members of District 84 to rethink their allegiance to Mullen and to the Knights. The great labor
parade that Mullen hoped would buoy his campaign turned into a black
celebration of equal rights, a parade mainly shunned by white workers.
Mullen was faced with a choice. He could stay in the race and try to explain to his white supporters that he was not acting as a spoiler on behalf
of African Americans and Republicans. Or he could withdraw from the
race and thereby ensure the victory of the Democratic candidate, a choice
that would confirm the suspicions within the black community that Mullen and other white members of the Knights were beholden to the Democrats and their system of white supremacy. Mullen chose to withdraw from
the race.[44]

VI.

BY THE TIME THAT MULLEN bowed out of the congressional race in the
fall of 1886, both white and black members of the Richmond Knights were
withdrawing from the organization. This was part of a general pattern.
The Knights suffered one blow after another from court injunctions, corporate blacklists, competition from trade unions, and racial and partisan
division. There was, however, one striking exception to this pattern. In the
South, the Knights lost urban and rural white members, as well as urban
black members in Richmond, Raleigh, and other cities. But in mainly
rural places, where the great majority of African Americans lived, there
was a steady surge in black membership. Powderly and the other officers
of the Knights paid scant attention to this rising membership and turned
down their requests for assistance in times of trial. But this neglect accompanied the process that allowed African American cotton pickers, mill
hands, and domestic workers to make the Knights their own.[45]

The Knights of Labor suited the needs of the black rural poor at multiple levels. It allowed their existing neighborhood and community

networks to coalesce under the name of a national movement, a movement whose leaders had earned a reputation as advocates of racial equality—a reputation enhanced by the virulence of the white supremacist attacks on Powderly and his colleagues. And the Knights' model of inclusive organization offered unique advantages to mainly unskilled, overworked, and underpaid rural workers. In the pine forests of the Gulf Coast lumber industry, thousands of black workers organized into the Knights to fight for a shorter workweek, cash wages, and other urgent needs. Mississippi lumber workers joined the Knights and went on strike to gain the twelve-hour day at a time when the fourteen-hour day was the rule in the sawmills and the lumber and turpentine camps of the region.[46]

In the cotton districts of the South, African American farmers and tenants looked to the Knights' model of cooperation to escape inequitable treatment at the hands of middlemen and merchants. South of Little Rock, black members of the Arkansas Knights pooled resources for a cooperative cotton gin. Near Calera, Alabama, a village called Knightsville was "composed of nothing but colored people." The residents, who were "solid for the Knights," looked to start a cooperative store. Meanwhile, landless cotton pickers and field hands joined the Knights in collective efforts to raise wages and improve their lives.[47]

The center of gravity of the Knights of Labor in much of the South was shifting to not only an African American membership but also a membership of the landless rural poor. In terms of their aims and methods, these Knights were very much like their whiter, more economically diverse, and more urban counterparts. They held meetings, agitated, networked, cooperated, and occasionally went on strike to achieve equitable treatment. Yet many white observers viewed the demographic shift within the Knights as uniquely menacing, even insurrectionary. In April 1886, during the strike on the southwest railroad system, frightening reports circulated in the Texarkana area of "secret societies among colored men," and the *Texarkana Independent* warned that black assemblies of the Knights were "far more dangerous" than "the white brotherhood of the Knights" and might "become the blind instruments of some bold Communist."[48]

Later that summer, the black men and women working on the Tate plantation in Pulaski County, Arkansas, formed assemblies of the Knights and went on strike demanding a dollar a day in cash wages. The county sheriff responded by mobilizing a posse to arrest and intimidate the strikers. In turn, several hundred strikers mobilized in self-defense, igniting rumors of race war. The white authorities and planters mobilized to crush what they saw as the first step in a revolt of black laborers in the surrounding cotton districts. No such revolt occurred, but these events in Pulaski County pointed to the fact that within the white community the black assemblies of the Knights in the rural South were viewed as an extraordinary danger to be met, as necessary, with extraordinary violence.[49]

On the evening of May 19, 1887, Hiram Hover, a white organizer of black field hands, was at the receiving end of that violence. Hover was speaking to an audience of several hundred people in the black Methodist church in Warrenton, Georgia, when a group of men in masks and robes rode up to the windows of the church and fired on him with shotguns. The buckshot took out one of Hover's eyes and left him near death. A message had been sent. *The Atlanta Constitution* praised the assassination attempt for providing a "salutary lesson" to "the enemies of law and order." "Buckshot should not be resorted to except in an emergency," the newspaper warned, but it was needed "under some circumstances." The circumstance in this case was the organization of black farm laborers. "It is difficult enough to keep white laborers within proper bounds," warned the Charleston *News and Courier*, but "colored people . . . when acting in a body are proportionately more dangerous." *The New York Times* chimed in to agree. When white Knights went on strike for higher wages, it was "the mildest form of intimidation"; when the black field hands of Georgia threatened to do so, it promised a bloodbath: "Pay us more wages, they say, or we will kill you."[50]

As for Hiram Hover, he disapproved of strikes and labor conflict and preached a peaceful message of cooperative self-help. A native of Texas, he moved to North Carolina, where he lectured for the Knights before he began an organizing tour of the cotton districts of South Carolina and

Georgia in the winter of 1886–87. By this time, he had separated from the Knights, criticizing its involvement in strikes and other policies. Instead of Knights assemblies, Hover organized lodges of what he called the Co-operative Workers of America (CWA). But the goals and methods of the two organizations resembled each other, and observers described the CWA as being part of the Knights.[51]

The CWA spread rapidly across several counties, organized by local black leaders and attracting mainly farm laborers on white-owned cotton farms. This self-organization of black field hands ignited a "Hoover Scare" of a murderous black insurrection. Under the heading "A Threatened Race War," the *St. Louis Globe-Democrat* warned that black field hands in South Carolina were organizing into the Knights of Labor to demand a dollar a day for their labor, and to get what they want, "they will kill the old white men and women and make the young women their wives and enslave the white boys." Hiram Hover survived his wounds and was able to escape to New York. But in a display of force, white vigilance committees and militia units murdered several CWA organizers, broke up their lodges, and let it be known that the white community was not about to tolerate the organization of the black poor.[52]

In November 1887, the violence directed against African American members of the Knights of Labor came to a head on the sugar estates in Louisiana. The plantations in the "sugar bowl" parishes southwest of New Orleans had experienced sharp and violent conflicts over questions of black rights and white power since the arrival of Union troops a quarter century before. The conflict often focused on the question of wages. The former slaves and their offspring who worked the sugar estates viewed a living wage and payment in "United States money" as essential to receiving equitable treatment and to making freedom a reality. The planters viewed such demands as a challenge to their authority that threatened to deprive them of their right to compensate their employees as they saw fit.

This conflict took a turn in 1886 with the organization of the sugar workers into assemblies of the Knights. What had been an intractable conflict now took a more organized and systematic form. The following year, in the lead-up to the fall harvest or "rolling season," the Knights District 194 requested a wage increase from seventy-five cents to a dollar a day plus rations, to be paid in cash, not "commissary paste-board." When the Sugar Planters' Association refused to negotiate, the district called for a work stoppage to begin on November 1. On the appointed day, ten thousand sugar workers, 90 percent of them African Americans, went on strike. The sugar estates faced a "rolling season" without workers.[53]

The planters responded with a violent campaign of racial hysteria. They warned that the strikers—"fiendish negroes"—if left to their own devices would kill all the white women and children. Divisions of the state militia, paramilitary groups, and vigilantes mobilized to break the strike. A number of white members of the Knights joined the militia as several white assemblies took the side of the planters, while white workers arrived from other parts of the state to take the jobs of black strikers. An editorial in the New Orleans *Times-Democrat* argued that race war, not a labor conflict, gripped the sugar districts. "There was no question of labor in this matter," the editorial noted, but the threat of violence "by bad and dangerous negroes left behind as a relic of Radical days." Meanwhile, the strikers, including veterans of the Union army and of the Republican Club militias that in the previous decade faced the Ku Klux Klan and other paramilitary forces, vowed to defend themselves. Casualties mounted in exchanges of gunfire.[54]

Strikers and their families, expelled from their homes, sought shelter in the town of Thibodaux. But there would be no shelter. In the early morning of November 23, the militias and posses entered the town and unleashed a bloodbath, killing at least thirty strikers and possibly many more. Among the dead were strike leaders "taken from the jail and shot openly." The retributive violence against the strikes continued in the following days. Mary Pugh, the widow of a prominent planter, witnessed the cold-blooded murder on the streets of Thibodaux. "I am sick with the horror of it," she wrote, but at the same time she believed it needed to be done. "I think this will settle the question of who is to rule the nigger or the white man? For the next 50 years."[55]

As Mary Pugh understood it, the massacre at Thibodaux was about fundamental questions. For Pugh and other supporters of white supremacy, it was about defending the hierarchies of racial caste. For the ten thousand sugar workers, it was about fair and equal treatment. That the sugar workers chose to organize for this struggle within the ranks of the Knights of Labor suggested profound egalitarian possibilities. But Thibodaux also showed the limits of those possibilities. The state authorities and planters mobilized extraordinary violence and did so with broad support within the white community. White and black members of the Knights in New Orleans protested this violence, while Powderly and the national leadership remained aloof.[56]

The owners of the Louisiana sugar estates responded to the demands for equitable wages by their employees as capitalists were wont to do in post–Civil War America. Significantly, however, the owners embraced an alternative identity, not as capitalist bosses but as oppressed "farmers and planters" engaged in the struggle for equal and fair treatment. Months prior to the bloodbath at Thibodaux, a mass meeting convened by the Sugar Planters' Association in Ascension Parish made an "emphatic protest" against unequal treatment, discrimination, and oppression. What stirred the planters to action was a ruling by the federal Railway Commission granting San Francisco's American Sugar Refining Company a low rate to transport Hawaiian sugar from the Pacific coast to midwestern markets. An editorial in the New Orleans *Daily Picayune* called for the state's planters to stand tall. The owner of the *Picayune*, Eliza Jane Nicholson, had a keen interest in shipping Louisiana sugar to Pacific ports, having served as the secretary of the Ladies' New Orleans Pacific Railroad Aid Association. For sugar shipments to be moving in the opposite direction was clearly an affront to the sugar planters of Louisiana.[57]

The planters' protest was couched in the anti-monopoly language of equal rights. It appealed to "fairness and equity toward all men and all localities" and condemned the Pacific Railroad "monopolists" for their long- and short-haul freight rates that discriminated against New Orleans and the rest of the country in favor of New York. But the railroad "monopolists" were responsible for only half of the injustice. The other half lay at the feet of the Hawaiian sugar planters who employed Chinese labor. The *Picayune* editorial attacked the "shameless greed" of the Hawaiian planters, "American plutocrats," who trafficked in a "semi-slave product." Or, as the Planters' Association protest put it, Hawaiian sugar, "grown by coolie labor," represented unfair competition.[58]

The planters made this protest without any sense of their own "shameless greed." In the first days after emancipation, Louisiana planters had themselves been clamoring for Chinese labor. They saw an opportunity to "drive the niggers out and import coolies that will work better, at less expense." But that was before experience taught them that Chinese workers would stake their own claims to fair treatment, including equal treatment to that of black workers. At the same time, the African American field hands on the sugar estates toiled under the heavy burdens of racial caste. And when they combined in an effort to gain equitable wages, the planters mobilized the white community to greet their demands with bullets and brutality.[59]

PART IV

CRISIS OF INEQUALITY

9.

PROPERTY
AND POVERTY

S TEPHEN J. FIELD arrived in San Francisco in December 1849 to join the stream of new arrivals searching to prosper from California gold. The son of a prominent Congregationalist minister, Field stood out for his Williams College education, his experience as a New York City lawyer, and his relentless ambition. Within months of his arrival, he was elected alcalde of the gold-rush town of Marysville and soon thereafter won a seat in the state assembly. In 1857, he was appointed to the California Supreme Court, a position he held until 1863, when President Lincoln placed him on the U.S. Supreme Court. By choosing Field for the Court, a Democrat and a unionist from the West, Lincoln hoped to expand the base of the Union war effort. His elevation to the highest court in the land, however, only fed Field's hunger for political influence, and he made an unsuccessful bid for the Democratic nomination for president in 1880. Nonetheless, as it turned out, Field would have an outsized impact on the post–Civil War contest over the meanings of equality.

I.

HIS EARLY YEARS IN CALIFORNIA shaped Stephen Field's ideas about law and society. He arrived in the state as a scion of a powerful family, and from the beginning he cultivated links with the people of wealth who were consolidating power in the new state. His close friendship with Leland Stanford was only one such relationship. Field devoted some of his first legal efforts to protecting the property rights of his powerful friends. As Anglo settlers dispossessed the Mexican and Indian populations, Field championed the interests of the wealthiest of the new landowners in the face of the squatters' movements of prospectors and homesteaders. Among his contributions to the new social order in the Golden State was his defense of the infallibility of vast land patents, often forged through the manipulation of Mexican land grants, in the face of legal and political challenges from propertyless miners and small farmers. Field took these commitments to wealth and property with him to the U.S. Supreme Court.[1]

Prior to the Civil War, Field had advocated for excluding African Americans from California, and after emancipation he made no secret of his indifference to the plight of the former slaves. He believed that only the Thirteenth Amendment was needed to address the status of African Americans, dismissing the postwar measures taken to protect the equal rights of black citizens as "vindictive and prescriptive measures" imposed on the white South by the "violent partisans of the North." As a Democrat with presidential aspirations, Field opposed federal measures to protect African Americans from violence, discrimination, and unequal justice.[2]

Yet Field would soon find a use for the Fourteenth Amendment. He was among the first to recognize the potential of refashioning the federal promise of equality into a legal weapon to protect property rights and corporate power. He tested this new weapon in his dissent in the *Slaughter-House Cases* of 1873. The Louisiana legislature had passed a regulation requiring that the butchering of hogs and cattle in New Orleans be done in a central location to protect the city's water supply from contamination from the offal. The Court upheld the regulation, but Field wrote a dissent claiming that by targeting butchers for state action, the legislature had violated the equal rights protections of the butchering companies.

Similarly, in 1877, when the Supreme Court majority in *Munn v. Illinois* sustained the Granger law that regulated Chicago grain elevators, Field wrote a scathing dissent. Regulating the giant elevator monopolies, he wrote, was "subversive of the rights of private property" and was a discriminatory and unequal law under the Fourteenth Amendment. He further developed this argument in a series of cases in the 1870s and early 1880s. The majority of the Supreme Court justices stuck to the notion that the intention of the amendment was to protect the equal rights of the former slaves, not to protect slaughterhouses, grain elevator monopolists, or other businesses from public regulation. Nonetheless, change was on the way as political and legal elites increasingly looked for ways to make use of the Fourteenth Amendment to protect corporate power.[3]

Change came with the Supreme Court's decision in the railroad tax cases involving the Southern Pacific Railroad. The California legislature had passed a law allowing taxpayers to deduct their outstanding mortgages from the value of their taxed property. However, it made an exception for railroads, which were not allowed the mortgage deduction. The logic of the law was that because the railroads carried so much debt, and because this debt originated in New York or London and was therefore beyond the reach of state tax collectors, without this exception railroads would escape paying any taxes at all. Leland Stanford's Southern Pacific, the state's biggest employer and one of its largest landowners, refused to pay the tax, and the railroad's lawyers forced individual counties into court if they wanted to try to collect it.

Justice Field took a personal interest in defeating the railroad tax. He argued that it was unequal taxation. Moreover, Field hoped to turn the railway tax cases into an affirmation of corporate equal rights; that is, he hoped to make the Fourteenth Amendment's promise of equal protection and due process apply to legal persons (corporations) just as it did to natural persons (living and breathing human beings). If corporations were the legal equals of humans, then state laws regulating corporations ran afoul of the federal promise of equality. Field did not invent corporate equal rights—it was an idea that had been gaining supporters among prominent corporate attorneys—but he used the railroad tax cases to press hard on the issue.

In 1886, the Supreme Court ruled against the railroad taxes in *Santa Clara County v. Southern Pacific.* In making their ruling, the majority said nothing about corporate equal rights. Nonetheless, Bancroft Davis, a former railroad president himself, served as the Court recorder and inserted into the official record a note stating that the justices were "all of the opinion" that the equal protection of the law applied to corporations. Davis had recorded his own views on corporate equal rights into the legal record, views that were soon understood as the established law of the land. Stephen Field and his allies had successfully stood the Fourteenth Amendment on its head. Originally adopted as a means to protect the men and women emerging from slavery and the most vulnerable and impoverished section of the population, the amendment would now serve as a legal device to protect the wealthiest and most powerful.[4]

The new legal framework meant that the window for Granger laws and state regulation of railroad corporations was closing. In the fall of 1886, in *Wabash, St. Louis & Pacific Railway v. Illinois,* the Supreme Court ruled in favor of the railroad and rolled back the power of legislatures to regulate commerce that the Court had affirmed in *Munn v. Illinois* nine years earlier. After a similar ruling in a Minnesota case, Ignatius Donnelly, who was now the leader of the Minnesota Farmers' Alliance, charged that the repeated use of the Fourteenth Amendment to break state railroad regulations showed the need for railroads to be owned by the public. The Court's blows to railroad regulation, however, were only signs of what was to come, because corporate equal rights soon stood in the way of every type of equity and protection, from safety and health regulations to child labor laws. In the years after *Santa Clara,* the Fourteenth Amendment would serve as a bulwark of corporate power, part of the legal framework that elevated the corporation to what the political theorist Jeff Lustig aptly called the "master institution of American life." With the corporate engagement in the contest over the meaning of equality, the rules had decidedly changed.[5]

The assertion of corporate equality was one front of a counteroffensive against the egalitarian social movements of the time. The defeat of the Knights of Labor on the southwestern railroads on May 1, 1886, and the Haymarket bombing three days later, left the labor movement reeling. Court injunctions and the corporate blacklist took a heavy toll. The Knights of Labor, trade unionists, and other labor organizations responded to the new political environment with their nationwide political campaigns of that summer and fall. These labor campaigns represented complex coalitions and drew from the earlier experience of the Grangers, Greenbackers, and other anti-monopolists. They also brought new ideas and new personalities into the political mix. Most significantly, many of these campaigns rallied under the banner of the freshly minted United Labor Party (ULP) and Henry George, the new party's candidate for mayor of New York City.[6]

II.

IN THE SPRING OF 1886, New York City experienced its own labor upheavals centered on the city's mass transit system. Streetcar drivers and conductors fought to limit work shifts to twelve hours and to raise wages to two dollars a day. Many of them joined the Knights of Labor, and in the first week of March they organized a citywide strike across the transit system. This was at the moment when their fellow Knights were battling Jay Gould on his southwest railroad system, the same Jay Gould who was heavily invested in the city's elevated trains. And in New York City, too, the courts sided with employers against the Knights, putting organizers in prison under conspiracy laws.[7]

Meanwhile, New York's political establishment was mired in scandal. Jacob Sharp, the owner of the city's biggest streetcar line, seeking to win a franchise to extend his line on Broadway Avenue, gave twenty-thousand-dollar payoffs to twenty-two city aldermen. The bribes went to seven Republicans, seven Tammany Hall Democrats, seven anti-Tammany Democrats, and one independent. The door was open for a good-government labor campaign.[8]

That summer, New York's labor organizations came together to form the United Labor Party and nominated Henry George as their mayoral candidate. The new party quickly became a national party as workers across the country looked to its example of political solidarity and to Henry George. "Your success is ours," the Central Labor Union of St. Louis cabled the New York ULP. "Henry George and Labor will be the battle cry for all enslaved toilers from the Atlantic to the Pacific."[9]

Exactly how Henry George emerged as labor's champion requires an explanation. Only Terence Powderly enjoyed the type of respect and admiration within the labor movement that George did. Yet he was not a labor organizer, nor was he a veteran of labor politics. Rather, Henry George was a political economist whose books were widely read and even more widely cited in gatherings of working people. His writings challenged the prevailing economic theories that justified the status quo, and, most important, they exposed the growth of poverty amid plenty and the sharp division of society between those who had wealth and those who did not. As much as anything else, the labor movement's elevation of Henry George and his theories marked a growing recognition that economic inequality itself posed a dangerous social and political crisis.

Henry George had an unlikely background for one of the world's most influential political economists of his day. George was born in Philadelphia in 1839, the second of ten children. His family home had good furniture and middle-class comforts. His father, a devout Episcopalian, ran a business publishing religious texts for his church. Henry attended fine schools but chafed at his instruction at a church academy and quit his formal education at the age of thirteen. Two years later, serving as a foremast boy on a ship captained by a family friend, he sailed to Melbourne and Calcutta. When he returned home, he took a job setting type in a print shop, but two years later he was back at sea, working his way on a steamer through the Strait of Magellan and up to California.[10]

Henry George arrived on the San Francisco docks in May 1858. He made several attempts at mining, but he mainly worked in print shops setting type, an unstable profession in an unstable economy. He moved from job to job and back and forth from Sacramento to Oakland to San Francisco again. His speculative purchases in mining company stocks went nowhere. He started his own print shop, but now he was married and had a second child on the way, and lack of business landed his family in poverty. He turned to writing for the newspapers as a way to help keep the household afloat. This led to a collaboration with James McClatchy, the editor of *The Sacramento Bee*, who hired George first as a reporter and then as an editor for the newly launched San Francisco *Times*.[11]

In the months before the rails of the Southern Pacific and the Union Pacific met at Promontory, Utah, Henry George warned of the social impact of the transcontinental railroad. Under the title "What the Railroad Will Bring Us," he published an article in *The Overland Monthly* concurring with the general expectation that the rail connection would usher in prosperity. He even suggested that it would make San Francisco the second city of the continent. But he also warned that the railroad would come with costs, including soaring real estate values in San Francisco and its environs. "As a general rule," he wrote, the new prosperity would be divided unequally, for "those who *have*, it will make wealthier; for those who *have not*, it will make it more difficult to get." Yes, California was about to become "populous and rich," yet George cautioned, "Let us not forget that the distribution of wealth is even more important than its production."[12]

The social cost of land speculation, the relationship between progress and poverty, and the inequities of wealth would be the themes running through Henry George's writings for the rest of his life. He would later claim that these ideas came to him in a transcendent revelation while horseback riding in the Oakland hills above the San Francisco Bay. Resting his horse, he asked a passing teamster about the price of land in the area. The teamster pointed to some cows grazing on a distant hill and said,

"I don't know exactly, but there is a man over there who will sell some land for a thousand dollars an acre." At that point, it struck George that the mere anticipation of development had sent the price of unworked grazing land sky-high. This "moment of clairvoyance" would enter into the folklore of George's celebrity.[13]

Henry George, however, was also an intellectual creature of the anti-monopolist milieu in which he was formed as a journalist. His mentor and friend James McClatchy had taken part in earlier squatters' protests and had long been an advocate for miners and homesteaders in their struggles against land monopoly. George's intellectual debts to this tradition were reflected in his 1871 pamphlet, *Our Land and Land Policy*, which provided a biting critique of the depredations of the big property owners—land-grant holders and railroad corporations—and the courts that shielded them. He added to this critique an urban dimension, lamenting San Francisco's loss of its public land (the municipal pueblo inherited from Mexico), seized by "a few hundred land grabbers" at the expense of its citizens who needed homes.[14]

III.

JAMES McCLATCHY URGED HENRY GEORGE to follow his pamphlet on land policy with a book-length treatment. It took several years of reading and writing, and in 1879 George finally published *Progress and Poverty*. This was his masterwork. George's stated purpose was to solve what he considered the Sphinx's riddle of modern civilization: How to explain "the connection of poverty with material progress"? Using California as a test case, he explored the usual lines of inquiry suggested by the political economists: population, productivity, capital, wages, and interest. Each path of George's investigation led the reader "to the same truth—that the unequal ownership of land necessitates the unequal distribution of wealth."[15]

All human beings were equal, Henry George believed, and therefore they all had equal claim to the use of the land. The private ownership of land distorted this natural equality, compelling the propertyless to pay tribute to the propertied. Only abolishing private property in land, he explained, could free humanity from paying this unearned rent and thereby solve the crisis of inequality. He reassured his readers that this would not require seizing holdings, voiding titles, or taking any type of drastic measure. *"It is not necessary to confiscate land,"* George reassured his readers, *"it is only necessary to confiscate rent."* To do so, he proposed replacing all sources of government revenue with a single tax on land values, "the most just and equal of all taxes."[16]

Under George's proposal, a person who owned an empty lot or an acre of unimproved land would pay the same tax as a person who owned a similar lot or acre with a home, a factory, or a farm on it. This, he predicted, would accomplish three goals. First, it would take the profits out of land speculation, break up land monopolies, and make land available for those who needed it. Second, it would provide incentive to build more homes, factories, and farms and make other improvements because such improvements would no longer be taxed. And third, it would raise revenue for the common benefit, paying for museums, libraries, gardens, lecture rooms, music halls, theaters, universities, technical schools, playgrounds, and gymnasiums—not to mention public power, light, and transportation, as well as scientific research for the public good. In these ways, George predicted that his tax on land values would reverse the engines of inequality, allow government to become "a great co-operative society," and realize the "ideals of the socialist" but without confiscations or repression.[17]

Henry George's "socialism" contained a good dose of free market capitalism. In writing *Progress and Poverty*, he claimed to have united the liberal economic school of Adam Smith and Thomas Malthus with the socialism of Pierre-Joseph Proudhon and Ferdinand Lassalle. Or, as George put it, he had shown that *"laissez faire* (in its full true meaning) opens the way to a realization of the noble dreams of socialism." A number of socialists pointed out that the result was less than advertised. After reading *Progress and Poverty*, Karl Marx penned a letter to a friend in the United States in which he praised George for his attempt to break with economic orthodoxy. Nonetheless, he also noted that George had failed to address the exploitation of labor in capitalist production and had proposed a tax remedy, "tricked out with socialism," that would put capitalist rule *"on an even broader basis."*[18]

Marx had a point. Henry George did indeed believe that his tax plan would develop capitalist enterprise on a more egalitarian and therefore broader foundation. At the same time, he believed that "man is social in nature" and rejected the competitive individualism of the orthodox economists. Like so many other Americans in the post–Civil War years, he understood that cooperation and association were essential to a society based on equality and justice. Hence the formula in *Progress and Poverty*: "Association in equality is the law of progress."[19]

While association was his theory, in practice George was skeptical of existing associational life. He described labor organizations as "destructive of the very things which workmen seek to gain"; economic cooperation was similarly futile. California's Democratic Party was the one organization that sustained George's attention. Although his father and mother were Democrats, as a young man during the Civil War he cast his first votes for Lincoln and the Union. However, by the late 1860s, rejecting "carpet-bag reconstruction," he had returned to the Democratic Party of his parents. He ran unsuccessfully as the party's candidate for a seat in the California assembly, served as a delegate to the 1872 Democratic National Convention, formed alliances with the Democratic governor and other party leaders, and landed himself a patronage job as the state inspector of gas meters, a sinecure that kept him afloat during the years of writing *Progress and Poverty*.[20]

California's Democratic Party made for a good fit with George's politics, including his hostility to Chinese immigration. In 1869, he published an essay in the *New-York Tribune* comparing the virtues and vices of the Chinese in California with those of African Americans in the South. The essay had the appearance of a careful study and balanced assessment rather than a racial screed. But his conclusions were bigoted enough, warning that the soon-to-be-completed transcontinental railroad was about to bring the scourge of Chinese immigration to the villages of the Midwest. His essay led to an exchange of public letters with John Stuart

Mill, with the famous English liberal urging tolerance if not equality and George advocating for exclusion. The latter position would soon be Democratic Party dogma on the West Coast, dogma that George clung to for the rest of his life.[21]

The Democratic Party also drew advocates of land reform, railroad regulation, and labor rights. It was this anti-monopolist wing of the party that pushed for the railroad tax that led to the fateful legal battle between Santa Clara County and the Southern Pacific Railroad. During the 1870s, it was here that Henry George found a comfortable political home for his ideas about land monopoly and the unequal distribution of wealth. But with the publication of his big book, that home soon proved too small as Henry George negotiated his way to international celebrity.

IV.

IN 1880, HENRY GEORGE MOVED to New York in search of new opportunities. His *Progress and Poverty* had been widely reviewed on both sides of the Atlantic, was the talk of radical circles in London and New York, and would soon be published in multiple editions as well as in several German translations. But despite its reception, the book failed to provide the income George expected. Nor did it build the constituency for his ideas that he hoped for. As it turned out, though, he soon found success by the unexpected route of the transatlantic Irish community.[22]

George's closest Irish connections were with his wife's parents and his longtime collaborator, James McClatchy. In December 1879, at McClatchy's urging, George published "The Irish Land Question" in *The Sacramento Bee*, applying his critique of land monopoly to the problems of the Irish rural crisis. When he arrived in New York, George met Patrick Ford, the leader of the Irish Land League and the editor of *The Irish World*, an influential newspaper on both sides of the Atlantic. Ford helped George turn his essay "The Irish Land Question" into a book by the same name, and then he offered George a chance to travel to London and Dublin as an *Irish World* correspondent.[23]

In what was to be the first of several extended visits to the British Isles,

Henry George was welcomed as a celebrated guest of English and Irish radicals, socialists, labor organizers, and land reformers. After his return to New York, he took to the lecture circuit of the Irish Land League. With more than fifteen hundred branches, the league provided George with the organized connection to working people that he had aspired to but had never before attained. It also brought him into contact with Terence Powderly and the Knights of Labor.[24]

For Powderly, the Irish cause and labor's cause were closely linked. In the late 1870s, Powderly served as the finance secretary of the Irish republican organization Clan na Gael, and in 1881 he was elected vice president of the Irish Land League. The league was especially strong in Powderly's stomping grounds in northeastern Pennsylvania, where its meetings attracted Irish as well as Welsh, German, English, and other miners and railway employees. These meetings also provided cover for organizing workers into the Knights of Labor; when a public Land League meeting was over, a secret meeting of the Knights would begin. *The Irish World* noted that Powderly represented "the joining of the Land League and American forces of labor."[25]

Meanwhile, Powderly studied Henry George's writing and embraced much of it. He was soon urging his fellow Knights to put the land question at the top of the agenda. As Scranton's mayor, Powderly promoted a tax on land values as a way to secure homes for workers, break the fear of the blacklist, and prevent the coal companies from speculating in farmland. Moreover, compared with other taxes, the land tax was "the very essence of equity." In broader egalitarian terms, Powderly held that "every person has an equal right with every other person to use the earth," and therefore should pay an equal share for its use.[26]

Powderly and Henry George first met at a Knights of Labor picnic in Baltimore in the summer of 1883. By that time, George was enrolled as a member of the Knights, and his ideas were gaining currency within the organization. He would soon take to the Knights' lecture circuit. Knights' reading rooms carried *Progress and Poverty*, and in at least one district, Elizabeth Rodgers's District 24 in Chicago, members read from the book at the opening of its meetings. It was also read by Knights in New York, and when that city's labor organizations wrote the platform for the United Labor Party in 1886, they endorsed George's tax remedy. Notably, Frank Ferrell, the African American Knight of District 49, announced their land tax platform at a mass meeting on September 23, less than two weeks before he crashed the color line during the Knights' convention in Richmond.[27]

New York City's 1886 mayoral contest turned into a three-way race. The Democratic factions united behind Abram Hewitt, the Republicans ran the political novice Theodore Roosevelt, and the labor movement filled the streets with parades and rallies for Henry George. The George campaign cast a wide political net and drew support from surprising quarters such as the Republican stalwart Robert Ingersoll. But mainly it was a working-class campaign with the Knights of Labor in the thick of it. Powderly traveled to New York and gave dozens of speeches, often joining George on the platform. When the votes were counted, George came in second with 68,110 votes compared with 90,552 for Hewitt. Labor voters suspected that the Democrats had cheated George of victory. Perhaps they had, but whether or not there was that level of ballot theft, this was a surprising showing for a labor candidate, who had received nearly eight thousand more votes than the Republican Roosevelt. People took note.[28]

V.

ALTHOUGH HENRY GEORGE WOULD NEVER match the political success he had in his run for New York's mayor, in the following months and years his influence grew wider and deeper. Single Tax Clubs formed in cities and towns across the country. Led mainly by people like George himself—the urban, professional, entrepreneurial, and highly skilled—the clubs met to discuss egalitarian paths to prosperity and development. A young dynamic lawyer by the name of Clarence Darrow, who was later known for his courtroom orations, arrived in Chicago a "pronounced disciple" of Henry George and honed his speaking skills in the meetings of the Chicago

Single Tax Club. The soap manufacturer Joseph Fels, who gained fame for the Fels-Naptha brand, was an early convert and key patron of the single-tax cause.[29]

The single tax also drew surprising levels of rural support, even though many farmers suspected that it might raise the taxes on their land. Because it would remove taxes on farm buildings, cotton gins, tile drainage, and other improvements, rural people saw the single tax as a means to encourage development just as urban people did. That was true in southern Illinois and in central Texas. Members of the Texas Farmers' Alliance looked to the single tax to break up land monopoly and "to put a stop to the alienation of the land." In Alabama, the leader of the farmers' Agricultural Wheel, R. G. Malone, was a single taxer. Eleanor Marx and Edward Aveling found that even the cowboys of the western plains believed in Henry George.[30]

In Kansas, the stock raiser Jerry "Sockless" Simpson lectured across the state and much of the country for the Farmers' Alliance, spreading the message that the single tax was the best means to combat the railroad monopolists. Another lecturer for the Kansas Farmers' Alliance, Mary Elizabeth Lease, looked to the single tax as part of her broader egalitarian agenda. Lease was a part-time farmer and schoolteacher and a lifelong Republican and Irish nationalist. She first lectured for the WCTU before joining the Knights of Labor and campaigning for the Union Labor Party. For Lease, the single tax was one piece of the strategy for toppling class and sexual inequality.[31]

African American support for Henry George and his principles was also something of a surprise. Critics within the black community argued that taxing land values would make it that much more difficult for the freed people to realize their aspirations to own their homes and farmsteads. Moreover, George himself, from his perch on the West Coast, had shown little interest in the fate of the former slaves. Yet by the mid-1880s, Georgism gained a significant following within the African American community. Part of this was due to the efforts of Timothy Thomas Fortune—editor of black newspapers and author of *Black and White: Land,*

Labor, and Politics in the South, a searing indictment of land monopoly, racial oppression, and the nation's betrayal of human equality.[32]

Fortune's life experience had provided stark lessons about blacks and whites, land and freedom. Four years before the outbreak of the Civil War, he was born a slave in rural Jackson County in Florida's panhandle. After emancipation, his family farmed, his father took part in Republican politics, and he began his education, which included a term at a Freedmen's Bureau school. But then came the Ku Klux Klan, the threats, the beatings, and the murders. Night riders assassinated more than 150 politically active members of Jackson County's black community. The Fortune family fled to the relative safety of Jacksonville, giving up their livestock and their hopes of making a life on the land. Like many families who experienced the post-emancipation white terror, the Fortune family never fully recovered, and Timothy's mother apparently died of the trauma.[33]

As a teenager, Fortune served as a page in the state legislature in Tallahassee, where he witnessed the disintegration of the Republican coalition. For the rest of his life, he harbored bitterness at the treachery of the Republican Party for leaving the African American people "alone and single handed" in the face of their armed and self-confident white oppressors. When Fortune returned to Jacksonville, he found a job setting type for a local newspaper. He considered a career in law and studied at Howard University until a lack of funds sent him back to Florida. Much as they had for the young Henry George, useful skills in a print shop kept the young T. Thomas Fortune afloat during hard times and opened the way for a career in the newspaper business.[34]

In 1881, Fortune received a job offer from a New York City print shop. Within months of his arrival, he was editing *The New York Globe* (later renamed *The New York Freeman*), which quickly gained national prominence as a sharp-edged voice for racial justice. Fortune recognized that New York's small black community needed allies, and his closest ally was John Swinton, a prominent labor editor and disciple of Georgism. The *Globe* promoted George's "great book," and soon Fortune was sharing the stage in mass meetings with Henry George himself. In Fortune's speeches, he adapted the Georgist philosophy to "the needs of the colored masses," and especially to the problem of land hunger in the South. In 1884, Fortune published *Black and White*, a book that attacked the two-headed monster of white supremacy and land monopoly. It was the latter, he concluded, that was "at bottom the prime cause of the inequalities." As for solutions, he pointed to "Mr. George," who "not only sees the gross social wrongs," suffered by both whites and blacks, "but boldly applies the remedy."[35]

Given his partisan leanings, Fortune supported George's Democratic opponent in the New York mayor's race. Yet the pages of his *Freeman* continued to point to the Georgist remedy for inequality. When Henry George spoke at a Knights of Labor rally held in Boston's Faneuil Hall, a correspondent for the *Freeman* reported that "colored men do not hesitate to say that Henry George's party is the party of the colored man." It similarly reported that when African American women employed as cooks and domestic servants organized a local of the Knights in New York City, they called themselves the Henry George Assembly.[36]

George welcomed this support from the black community. He had his eye on a run for national office and was aware of the potential value of the black vote. In his speech at Faneuil Hall, he called for "equal and exact justice" without regard to race. He also made specific appeals to the landless black poor of the South. At the time of the "Hoover conspiracy" in South Carolina, George issued a statement in support of the black victims of the white terror. Reprinted in the *Freeman*, the statement called for racial peace based on the egalitarian principle that "the land belongs to all the people . . . to the black as well as to the white."[37]

This message resonated within the Colored Farmers' Alliance. Formed in 1886, the Colored Alliance lacked the resources of the all-white Farmers' Alliance and relied on an extensive network of African American churches, a network that claimed a membership of a million black farmers and farmworkers across the former Confederacy. Most of its members suffered acute land hunger, mainly toiling on the land of white owners as sharecroppers and day laborers. When African Americans did gain title to the land, it tended to be of marginal value. In Texas, where the Colored

Alliance had its greatest strength, black-owned farms averaged a quarter of the value of white-owned farms. The Colored Alliance looked to Henry George's taxing system as a way to break the white land monopoly, much as Fortune had done in his book *Black and White*. Its leaders saw the system as a way to "place homes within reach of all the people."[38]

VI.

IN ALABAMA, THE REVEREND I. N. FITZPATRICK of the AME church explained that the members of the Colored Alliance in his district saw the single tax as "the consummation of freedom" and "the only means of political salvation of our race." At the same time, as a landowner he suspected that the single tax would add to his own tax burden. Fitzpatrick was not alone in this suspicion; Henry George and his land tax had plenty of supporters who had little at stake in the tax itself. So why did they find Georgism compelling? Why did so many people in the United States and around the world embrace a man and his tax remedy that might not have done them much good, at least directly and in the short term? The answer lies in the dual nature of George's appeal. On the one hand, George the political economist wrote in the language of hardheaded class interest: taxing land values would remedy specific economic inequities and thereby serve the particular interests of the worker, the farmer, and the entrepreneur. On the other hand, George the ethical philosopher wrote in the moral language of human solidarity and universal equality. "The equality of men is not a dream of latter-day visionaries," he assured his readers. "It is the order of nature."[39]

In 1883, George published his second big book, *Social Problems*, which focused on the post–Civil War social transformations. These were years "when thought [was] being quickened," he explained, and science, education, travel, and a "critical spirit" were "widening sympathies" and "extending the idea of human equality and brotherhood." It was the Henry George of widening sympathies and human brotherhood that caught the attention of the Russian novelist Leo Tolstoy. After reading *Social Problems*, Tolstoy wrote that in the works of George he had found "a genuine humanitarian [in] thought and heart." It would take several more years for Tolstoy to fully embrace George's land tax, but his message of human solidarity made an immediate impact.[40]

Clarence Darrow was known for his admiration of Tolstoy, but before he was a Tolstoyan, he looked to Georgism as the path to human fellowship. Francis George Shaw was another humanist who arrived at the single tax in the same way. George dedicated *Social Problems* to the memory of Shaw, the father of Robert Gould Shaw who had commanded the African American troops of the famous 54th Massachusetts Infantry. Francis George Shaw had been a benefactor to abolitionism, feminism, cooperative socialism, and other egalitarian and humanitarian causes. By the end of his life, Shaw looked to Georgism as the best hope to realize human solidarity. And across the country, people with similar hopes— stock raisers and cowboys, domestic servants and cooks, lawyers and manufacturers, ditch diggers and cotton pickers—embraced George and his tax scheme.[41]

Henry George warned his followers against taking egalitarianism too far. A "false and impossible equality," he explained in *Social Problems*, would "reduc[e] everyone to the same dead level." He had in his sights the socialists and anarchists and their circles of mainly immigrant radicals. By the late 1880s, however, the type of "impossible equality" that he had warned about had gained wider popularity. Laurence Gronlund's *Cooperative Commonwealth* played a part in this by translating European evolutionary socialism into the American vernacular of equal rights. The promises of America's founding, Gronlund wrote, could only be realized in a collectivist "State of EQUALITY"; equal rights were mere words without the social changes that would bring "*substantial*, perhaps absolute, *equality*." This meant eradicating the unequal power of employer over employee by means of cooperative and public ownership. And it meant "economic equality of woman" as the precondition to make man and woman, husband and wife, "equals of each other."[42]

Gronlund's ideas about equality were brought to life in 1888 with Edward Bellamy's futuristic novel *Looking Backward*. This was a future rooted in the egalitarian, rationalist, and centralizing ethos of the post–Civil War era. In this future, competitive capitalist enterprise evolved into the single "Great Trust," a uniform and planned national capitalist. Warring classes dissolved into an egalitarian citizenship, with each citizen taking part in the work of the industrial army on exactly equal terms. Women cast off their unequal burdens in the household and marriage by means of public kitchens and laundries and economic independence in the "feminine army of industry" (providing women with careers suitable to their maternal role). If there was a future of "absolute equality," in which everyone was reduced to what George derided as "the same dead level," *Looking Backward* revealed that future.[43]

Bellamy's book was a sensation. Over the next decade, it sold four hundred thousand copies, making it the nation's most popular book apart from the Bible. In 1897, Bellamy published a sequel under the title *Equality*, expanding on the egalitarian themes of *Looking Backward*, but it was the earlier book that made a mark. Much like the Single Tax Clubs, Nationalist Clubs inspired by *Looking Backward* spread to cities and towns across the country. However, whereas Single Tax Clubs tended to attract male voters, the Nationalist Clubs appealed to women who found Bellamy's treatment of the "woman question" especially convincing. Charlotte Perkins Gilman, the feminist author, said that he had put "the truth of the ages" in popular form.[44]

Frances Willard did as much as anyone to promote Bellamy's truth. She and her allies in the WCTU had already been moving toward a Christian or "Gospel socialism." They realized that sexual equality and the other reforms they sought would require a collectivist social transformation. Searching for what that would entail, Willard met with Laurence Gronlund, who recommended that she read *Looking Backward*, a book he said that put his collectivist ideas "into a story." After reading the book, Willard wrote to her secretary asking her to find out the true identity of the author, suspecting that "a great hearted, big-brained *woman* wrote this book." She soon became Bellamy's disciple. Willard worked to convince the WCTU and the wider women's movement of the need to transform society along the egalitarian lines indicated by Bellamy's story. Her efforts brought her into contact with the British Fabian Society, and by the early 1890s Willard spent much of her time in England among her fellow socialists.[45]

A wide ideological gap separated Bellamy's utopia from George's proposal to tax land values. For his part, George warned his supporters of the dangers of socialist schemes "to nationalize capital." Nonetheless, the egalitarian collectivism of Gronlund, Bellamy, *and* George mixed freely within the social movements of the day. A striking product of this mixing was the Fairhope Single Tax Colony on Alabama's Mobile Bay. The colony attracted cooperativists, Bellamyists, and socialists. It organized a Woman's Suffrage Society and a WCTU chapter. And it was all done in the name of Henry George and "the law of equal freedom." Significantly, Marie Howland—William Saunders's old friend and early Granger—ended up at Fairhope, where she pursued her lifelong commitments to sexual equality and cooperative experiments. Here it should be noted that Fairhope's egalitarianism stopped at the color line, as the Alabama colony adopted a whites-only policy.[46]

A similar ideological mixing took place within the Farmers' Alliance, the Knights of Labor, the WCTU, and other associations that provided the foundation of the Populist coalition of the 1890s. In Illinois, California, and elsewhere, single taxers, Nationalists, and socialists played an outsized role in organizing the Populist movement. In Kansas, the cooperative socialists Henry and Cuthbert Vincent serialized *Looking Backward* on the front page of their *Nonconformist* newspaper, which would soon become the voice of much of midwestern Populism. At the same time, Kansas Populists sent the single taxer Jerry "Sockless" Simpson to the U.S. Congress. And no Kansas Populist was better known than Mary Elizabeth Lease, who continued her lectures for the single tax while at the same time pursuing her growing interest in socialism.[47]

These bits and parts did not always make for a neat fit. Like any movement of such scope and ambition, the Populist coalition was racked by inconsistency and at times incoherence. Henry George rejected Populism as a mishmash that failed to put his tax plan front and center. The business of politics alienated Edward Bellamy, who also kept his distance from the Populist coalition. Yet by the beginning of the 1890s, the Populists had successfully cobbled together an intellectual arsenal for an unprecedented political assault on corporate power and economic inequality.

10.

SEPARATE
AND UNEQUAL

IN 1881, authorities arrested Tony Pace, a black man, and Mary J. Cox, a white woman, for violating Alabama's law against "adultery or fornication." The court found them guilty and sentenced each of them to two years in the state penitentiary. Pace appealed on the grounds that the law was racially discriminatory and infringed on the Fourteenth Amendment protections against unequal treatment. This was because in Alabama the crime of adultery for an interracial couple carried a two- to seven-year sentence at hard labor, whereas for a white couple or a black couple the charge carried a maximum six-month sentence. In 1883, a unanimous Supreme Court rejected Pace's appeal.[1]

For Justice Stephen J. Field, *Pace v. Alabama* presented yet another opportunity to twist the Fourteenth Amendment against its original purposes. Field argued that the law against interracial sex complied with the equal protection clause because "the punishment of each offending person, whether black or white, is the same." This, of course, was a mere sleight of hand. The post–Civil War system of white power required fierce vigilance to guard the border of racial caste. Interracial sex was a dangerous and violent point on this border. And the Alabama legislators, citing the danger of "mongrelization," clearly looked to reinforce it by imposing an extraordinary penalty for sexual transgressions. Yet this discriminatory act of white power passed Fourteenth Amendment muster, according to Field, because the punishment for violating it had the appearance of racial neutrality.[2]

Ten months after the Supreme Court handed down its decision in *Pace v. Alabama*, it issued its decision in the *Civil Rights Cases*, which overturned parts of the Civil Rights Act of 1875. In the *Civil Rights Cases*, the Court overturned federal laws requiring equal access to public accommodations on the grounds that the Fourteenth Amendment only applied to state action and had no bearing on the transportation companies, hotels, and other businesses that chose to deny African Americans equal access. The decision in *Pace v. Alabama*, however, pointed to new possibilities for state action: legislatures could enact brutally discriminatory laws just so long as they maintained the fiction of racial symmetry.

Some years later, Stephen Field voted with the Supreme Court majority in the *Plessy v. Ferguson* decision sustaining Louisiana's law segregating railroad cars. The Louisiana legislature had passed its Separate Car Act in 1890. It was one of dozens of so-called Jim Crow laws enacted across the former Confederacy and beyond to mandate segregated trains, streetcars, hospitals, schools, parks, hotels, libraries, and virtually every other public place. The avowed purpose of such laws was to protect the interests of the state from the dangers of interracial mixing. Given the state's interest, the Court ruled, requiring separate public facilities did not violate the Fourteenth Amendment as long as whites and blacks had equal facilities. No matter that in reality the railroad cars, schools, libraries, parks, and other facilities reserved for African Americans were inferior, underfunded, inaccessible, or nonexistent.[3]

Decided in 1896, the *Plessy* ruling was one of Stephen Field's last cases on the Supreme Court. Decades earlier, he had argued that a Louisiana law to protect the drinking water of New Orleans from the pollution of slaughterhouses violated the equal rights of the owners of the slaughter-houses. He had fought Granger laws and railroad taxes as violations of private property and corporate equal rights. When it came to the danger of racial mixing, however, Field had no qualms about state action. In *Pace v. Alabama*, he upheld draconian state laws to regulate private sexual relations. And in *Plessy*, he supported the Louisiana law requiring railroads and other private companies to take extraordinary measures—separate train cars, separate entrances, separate washrooms, separate most everything—to ensure that white people would be kept separate from black people. Field's logic may be taken as inconsistent or cynical. But it might best be understood as the crowning achievement of years of effort to convert the post–Civil War promise of equality into a legal shield for economic and racial hierarchies of power.

The *Plessy* doctrine of "separate but equal" served as the constitutional foundation of an American system of apartheid, a system sustained with brutal and unconstitutional violence. White lynch mobs beat, dismembered, shot, hanged, and burned to death African American men, and sometimes women, in elaborate and public rituals of racial sadism. The regime of white supremacy, as W.E.B. Du Bois put it, had undertaken its "descent to Hell." This descent placed intense pressure on social movements that organized across the color line. Most of them cracked or buckled.[4]

I.

FRANCES WILLARD HOPED TO STEER the WCTU clear of the danger of racial controversy. Despite her best efforts, however, the lynching question embroiled Willard and her movement in a bruising transatlantic polemic. In the early 1890s, Willard had gained a popular following among English audiences with her lectures about temperance, women's equality, and Gospel socialism. During these same years, the African American journalist Ida B. Wells also spent time in England, where she gained her own popular following. Wells gave lectures on the extraordinary sadism and inhumanity of the American practice of lynching. She shared her investigative work demonstrating that most victims of lynch mobs were punished not for the crime of rape, as the apologists of lynch mobs claimed, but often for petty infractions against the order of social caste. Moreover, Wells's investigations showed, when lynching did involve punishing a black man for having sex with a white woman, it was likely not rape but consensual sex based on mutual attraction. Confronting the false premises of lynch law had forced Wells into exile from her home state of Tennessee, and she at times faced a tough reception in the North, too.

Her English audiences gave Wells a good hearing. But her lectures provoked a question: If the practice of lynching was the great American barbarity that she said it was, then why did the great American reformer Frances Willard not mention it? Wells had little choice but to respond. And respond she did, criticizing Willard for avoiding the subject and for giving legitimacy to the false claim that lynch mobs were taking defensive action against black sexual predators attacking white womanhood. Wells published her criticism in the English journal *Fraternity*, which also reprinted Willard's 1890 interview in which she described African Americans as "locusts" and black men as a menace to white women and children. And thus began a bitter transatlantic polemic.[5]

The storm over the lynching issue swirled around the WCTU's annual meeting in November 1894. Frances Willard confronted the issue head-on. She reassured the delegates that the WCTU took "no cognizance of color," that the separate black and white state unions were on "the plane of equality," and that while "the nameless outrages perpetrated upon white women and little girls were a cause of constant anxiety," it was "inconceivable that the W.C.T.U. will ever condone lynching." Willard then proceeded with a direct attack on Ida B. Wells, and in so doing got to the crux of the problem. "It is my firm belief that in the statements made by Miss Wells concerning white women having taken the initiative in nameless acts between the races," she told the delegates, "she has put an imputation upon half the white race that is unjust."[6]

It would be difficult to overstate the danger that this "imputation" posed to Willard's political ambitions. Any concession to the lived reality of mutual desire between white women and black men threatened to blow up her political project. Willard's vision of political power rested on the alliance she had crafted with prominent women of the former Confederacy. She had built this alliance in the name of "home protection," and for Sallie Chapin, Belle Kearney, Rebecca Felton, Lide Meriwether, and the other white southern WCTU leaders, the politics of "home protection" were rooted in the mythic purity of white womanhood and the menace of the whiskey-drenched black rape fiend. Chapin and her southern colleagues were willing to abide words from Willard and the WCTU leaders in Chicago about equal rights between the races. But to question the myths of purity and menace would shatter the WCTU as a national political force. Willard's response was swift and implacable. She mocked Wells and impugned her character even as she mobilized allies to support her own position.[7]

On February 6, 1895, two weeks before his death, Frederick Douglass signed a statement vouching for the WCTU's commitment to racial equality. The statement was co-signed by Julia Ward Howe, Lyman Abbott, William Lloyd Garrison Jr., and other veterans of the struggles for abolition and women's rights. The signatories undoubtedly recognized in Frances Willard a person of national influence who had been known to express humanistic and egalitarian views about race. But their statement failed to reflect the conflicted nature of Willard's commitments to racial equality. The statement noted that Willard had threatened to resign from a Chicago woman's club if it failed to admit black women on equal terms, while failing to mention the extent to which the WCTU tolerated the color line in its own ranks and not only in the South. And it praised Willard for the WCTU's public statements against lynching, without mention of just how muted the WCTU's response to lynching had been. Nor did it mention that Willard and the WCTU continued to issue apologies for lynch mobs, with the resolution of the WCTU's 1894 annual meeting attributing the "lawlessness" of the lynchers to the "unspeakable outrages" of black rapists.

British supporters of Wells, claiming to have the backing of Frederick Douglass's widow, Helen Douglass, suggested that the statement would never have been written if the signatories had been better informed about this resolution. But the signatories also overlooked the racial contradictions underlying the long trajectory of the WCTU's politics of national reconciliation.[8]

The Wells-Willard controversy brought the contradictions to a boil. A reckoning had been in the works for some time. In 1890, Frances Harper was eased out of the national leadership, just as she pressed the WCTU to take a more forceful position against lynching and racial violence. Three years later, at the World's Congress of Representative Women, Harper called for action against the "brutal cowardly men who torture, burn, and lynch their fellow-men." The specific measure she proposed was to restrict the right to vote, arguing that "moral and educational tests" would keep the ballot from the hands of "lynchers too red with blood." Harper believed that no right was more precious than "the claim for protection to human life." The right to vote or hold property or other claims could not be compared to the right to not be tortured and burned to death. Such were the narrow and perilous choices offered by the regime of white supremacy, choices that would push Harper away from the WCTU.[9]

In 1893, Lucy Thurman protested "a color line" in the WCTU's work in the northern cities. Organizing among black women was increasingly separate and slighted. Meanwhile, across the South, the white members of the WCTU switched their focus from mobilizing the black vote against the liquor trade to calling for literacy tests to disenfranchise black voters. When disenfranchisement became a reality, white WCTU members abandoned organizing among African Americans; African American women completed their migration from the WCTU to the Colored Women's Clubs and other associations; and the WCTU further disengaged from the post–Civil War question of racial equality.[10]

From its earliest days, the WCTU's promise of racial inclusion and equality had been a limited, conditional half of a promise. That was enough, however, to bring the likes of Harper, Thurman, and other African

American women to its ranks. Most of that half promise was withdrawn as Willard and the WCTU leadership accommodated the advent of Jim Crow and lynch law. The element of betrayal was what made the Wells-Willard controversy so fraught.

II.

A SIMILAR SURRENDER BY THE leadership of the Knights of Labor might have stirred less public acrimony, but if anything it went further and left more destruction in its wake. By the late 1880s, the center of gravity of the Knights had moved toward rural places, with African American farm laborers providing a vital base of support. In Texas, North Carolina, and elsewhere, white farmers, unhappy with the Knights' indiscretions regarding Republican politics and social equality, looked for a new organizational home. They found it in the Farmers' Alliance and Industrial Union, otherwise known as the Southern Farmers' Alliance. With its roots in the cotton districts of central Texas, it had spread its network of organization across the South and rapidly expanded to the Great Plains and the Pacific coast. By 1890, the Farmers' Alliance claimed 1.2 million members, making it the largest voluntary association of them all.[11]

In many ways, the Farmers' Alliance was a new Grange. It shared the same functions of a fraternal society and business organization. It adopted much of the Grange organizational model. Grange newspaper editors, cooperativists, and lapsed members found a place in the Farmers' Alliance. Like the Grange, many of its members were farm owners, although especially in the South they tended to be poorer owners of smaller farms. They shared with the Grange a similar faith in large-scale cooperative enterprise and in the federal government's role in the national economy. One of the Farmers' Alliance's most innovative proposals was the "subtreasury," a system to be directed from the Treasury Department in Washington that would set up thousands of warehouses in agricultural communities, providing the nation's farmers with low-interest federal credit on their stored crops and equal access to markets.[12]

The Farmers' Alliance pursued a nationalist vision of sectional reconciliation, much as the Grange had done. And like its predecessor, it demanded an equality between the North and the South that subordinated the equal rights claims of African Americans. The Farmers' Alliance, however, introduced something new: a strict "whites only" rule for membership. It recognized a "common citizenship" and a "commercial equality" between the races but drew an organizational color line in the name of averting the danger of "social equality." As the Farmers' Alliance expanded from its southern base, it extended the whites-only rule across the Midwest and the West. At the same time, the white Farmers' Alliance facilitated and at least for a while tolerated the Colored Farmers' Alliance. One condition of this toleration was that white officers hold key positions in the Colored Alliance. This included Richard Humphrey, a white minister, who served as the general superintendent of the Colored Alliance. In short, the white and black alliances were separate and decidedly unequal.[13]

Here it should be noted that the Farmers' Alliance was not a passive bystander at the advent of the new Jim Crow regime. Rather, the all-white membership supported and, in some cases, initiated the new segregation laws. Most of these laws governed urban spaces such as streetcars, libraries, theaters, hospitals, and public parks. But they involved rural spaces, too, and most important the railroad cars that served rural communities. Local Alliances from Texas to North Carolina endorsed new railroad laws "with separate cars for white and colored." Public control of the railroads, white farmers believed, would mean segregated railroads. In 1890, Farmers' Alliance–backed candidates formed "farmers' legislatures" in Alabama, Georgia, Louisiana, and elsewhere, and one of their first orders of business was "separate accommodation" laws on the railroads.[14]

The rapid rise of the Farmers' Alliance caught the attention of the labor movement. Joining with this powerful and dynamic organization of farmers made a lot of sense to many within the Knights of Labor and other labor activists struggling to keep their organizations intact in the face of court injunctions and employer blacklists. The Knights of Labor and the Farmers' Alliance entered into negotiations toward unification. In Alabama, Texas, and elsewhere across the South, the two organizations held joint meetings, and talk of unity was in the air. With this aim, in December 1889, Terence Powderly traveled to St. Louis, where he addressed the national convention of the Farmers' Alliance. He reassured those farmers in the audience who employed hired hands that the Knights had no intention of supporting an eight-hour day for laborers working on farms. But his biggest peace offering had to do with white supremacy. He repeated his old phrases about the Knights having no interest in the social relations of the races. He also added something new. To the applause of the gathered white farmers, Powderly pledged that the Knights "believe that the Southern people are capable of managing the negro."[15]

The white supremacist logic of the southern "management" of African Americans was always the implicit message of Powderly's earlier statements about nonintervention in southern social relations. This logic, however, remained in tension with Powderly's insistence on a color-blind policy and with the Knights' official racial egalitarianism. But here Powderly spelled it out, endorsing the prerogative of white southerners to "manag[e] the negro." And he made this endorsement of the white management of black people before a convention of a whites-only organization whose ranks included planters and farmers who "managed" black labor.

In the late summer of 1891, Richard Humphrey, the white superintendent of the Colored Farmers' Alliance, called for a strike of cotton pickers across the cotton South. Planters and farm owners were committed to slashing wages to below fifty cents for a hundred pounds of picked cotton. Black field hands responded by agitating to raise wages to as high as a dollar for a hundred pounds. Humphrey set a September strike date if their demands were not met. The white Farmers' Alliance threatened dire consequences in the event that members of the Colored Alliance withheld their labor. As it turned out, the strike was mainly broken before it began, but it unleashed the furies of white vengeance. In Arkansas, a white posse lynched the strike organizer Ben Patterson and fourteen of his comrades. The failed strike and ensuing violence ruptured what was left of the tenuous cooperation between the black and the white alliances. It also put in stark relief the evolution of the Knights' leadership, which by this time had placed their fate in a coalition with white planters and farmers and had turned their backs on the black poor.[16]

III.

POWDERLY'S ADDRESS TO THE 1889 meeting of the Farmers' Alliance was part of a complex negotiation. The leaders of the Farmers' Alliance, the Knights of Labor, the WCTU, and several other farm, labor, and reform groups convened a series of "industrial conferences" to form a new political force. By the summer of 1891, it had a name, the People's Party, and a nickname, the Populist Party. In February 1892, delegates from a wide spectrum of "industrial organizations" met in St. Louis to give the new party organizational strength. The Farmers' Alliance set much of the agenda, with representatives of the Knights of Labor and other associations dedicated to farm and labor reform, the single tax, Bellamy Nationalism, greenbacks, silver currency, prohibition, and women's rights all taking part. Frances Willard of the WCTU was elected vice-chair of the conference. The St. Louis meeting made it clear that the People's Party was not an ordinary party but a political unification of voluntary associations "representing all divisions of urban and rural organized industry."[17]

On July 4, 1892, the new party held its national convention in Omaha, Nebraska. The convention adopted the Omaha Platform, the most celebrated declaration of Populist principles. The preamble was written by none other than Ignatius Donnelly, who in his florid language indicted the inequality of wealth and the division of society into "tramps and millionaires." The platform demanded specific federal action to overcome this inequality and redistribute wealth: the subtreasury system of farm credits, greenback currency, and a progressive income tax. It also called for "expanding the powers of government" to counter corporate power, including public ownership of railroads and postal savings banks and restrictions on corporate landownership.[18]

The People's Party realized mixed results in the polls. Many of its supporters had hoped to break the two-party monopoly, but especially at the presidential level the logic of the two-party system weighed heavily against the Populist presidential candidate, James Weaver. Nonetheless, Populism was the most successful third party since the Republicans in the 1850s. Weaver, a veteran Greenback candidate from Iowa, received over a million votes, far more votes than any previous farmer-labor candidate. Meanwhile, over the course of its short career, the People's Party won the governor's offices in Colorado, Kansas, and Nebraska. Six Populists served in the U.S. Senate, and more than forty of its candidates from California to North Carolina gained seats in the U.S. Congress. Many of these electoral victories were scored in the Great Plains and the West, where Populists formed fusion agreements with Democrats to overturn the dominant power of Republicans. In North Carolina, however, white Populists fused with black Republicans in a historic victory over Democratic Party rule.[19]

IV.

POPULISM MARKED THE CRESTING of the post–Civil War egalitarian wave. The slogan "equal rights to all and special privileges to none" never had such resonance. Anti-monopoly and anti-corporate politics never had such traction. Collectivist and democratic socialist ideas never had such wide and diverse audiences. The self-mobilization of farmers and workers never had such promise. The organization of women never had such extent. And, at least for a brief moment, the Populist upheaval opened fissures that allowed African Americans to press their own demands for economic and racial equality.

Yet the Populist movement could not and did not escape the conflicting claims to equality. Hundreds of thousands of women took part in the Farmers' Alliance, the Knights of Labor, the WCTU, and other associations that sustained the Populist movement. For these women, Populism held the promise of economic independence and sexual equality. And in Colorado, Kansas, and elsewhere, Populist women realized historic victories in terms of women's suffrage. For Frances Willard, the social democratic framing of the Populist coalition matched her own political commitments of the time. When she was elected vice-chair of the St. Louis conference, she held great hopes for the Populist enterprise.[20]

But it was not to be. The St. Louis conference decided to defer women's suffrage to the states and avoided the liquor question. At the Omaha convention, a majority of delegates decided that women's voting rights and prohibition were "secondary to the great issues" of economic inequality and corporate power. Willard decamped for her socialist and other ventures, and many of the women who had sustained the Populist movement also turned elsewhere.[21]

The Omaha Platform announced "the union of the labor forces" of the country, and by multiple measures the breadth of the Populist coalition of working people was extraordinary. At least on paper, this was so. Much of it was fiction. The Knights of Labor and its egalitarian ethos played a special role in the Populist coalition, although this egalitarianism was muted by the demand in the Omaha Platform to restrict immigrant labor. Moreover, Knights and former Knights could be found among coal miners and railway employees, two major Populist constituencies. But the major presence that the Knights of Labor had at the Populist conferences could not disguise that it was a shell of what it had been. Its biggest assemblies had melted away in the face of corporate and legal repression. By the 1890s, the craft unions of the American Federation of Labor (AFL) proved more durable, and while Populism had its supporters among the Mine Workers and other AFL unions, most craft unions restricted their memberships to a set of skilled white men.

The biggest fiction, however, involved the Colored Farmers' Alliance. As the Knights' leadership neglected what was left of their base among the African American rural poor, the Colored Farmers' Alliance rapidly expanded its network across the cotton belt. Several white and black leaders of the Colored Alliance were early supporters of the new People's Party, and the presence of Colored Alliance delegates in the first Populist conferences made it possible for the Populists to claim the support of organized black labor across the South. But as the People's Party took shape, the Colored Alliance fell apart. The cotton pickers' strike had proved to the white Farmers' Alliance that even a segregated and subordinated Colored Alliance could not be trusted. White intolerance for the self-organization of black labor grew, and black distrust for the white Populists hardened. Most white Populists viewed their party as a white man's party for white's man's rule. The black poor, with some notable exceptions, mainly kept their distance.[22]

V.

THE EXCEPTIONS WERE REAL ENOUGH. In the midst of the depression of 1894, Populist "Industrial Armies" or "tramp armies" of the unemployed marched on Washington to demand jobs and equal treatment. The marchers deliberately broke the color line as white marchers shared meals and tenting grounds with black marchers. And when the tramp armies arrived in the nation's capital, they found a warm welcome and solidarity among black Washingtonians, who opened their churches and homes to the mainly white marchers. These events were closely covered in the nation's newspapers, even more closely watched by the black community, and suggested the egalitarian possibilities of Populist protest.[23]

Especially in the South, however, there was little daylight between white Populists and white Democrats when it came to their support of white supremacy. Nevertheless, as long as African American men had access to the ballot, the competition between the two parties opened breaches in the wall of the white political monopoly. At times, both Populists and Democrats recruited black party delegates, stump speakers, and poll workers. At times, both parties made promises to black voters regarding funding schools and placing blacks on juries. At times, both parties swore that they recognized racial equality in the fields of political rights and economic opportunity and only objected to "social equality." As the insurgent party, the Populists took more chances when it came to attracting black voters, and now and then in the ensuing political wars white and black Populists undertook daring collaborations.[24]

Yet even at their most daring, white Populists recoiled from challenging the regime of Jim Crow and lynch law. This was as true of the North

Carolina Populists as any others. But the Tar Heel Populists made a clear-eyed political calculation and realized that the only way to cobble together an electoral majority was by forming a voting bloc with black Republicans. African Americans made a similar calculation. They had been more successful than elsewhere in the former Confederacy in sustaining a viable Republican Party, and they understood that a voting bloc or fusion with the Populists was their best chance of removing from office the increasingly corrupt and abusive Democrats.

On the ground in North Carolina, the Knights of Labor played its part in facilitating cooperation between African American and white constituencies. In Edgecombe County, for example, Ellen Williams, a black farmworker and gifted organizer for the Knights, recruited both white and black farmers to the Populist cause. But she did so at a moment when the leadership of the Knights had decidedly abandoned the black worker.[25]

In the fall of 1893, James Sovereign succeeded Powderly as the master workman of the Knights. That following spring, Sovereign took the obligatory southern tour, but he did so delivering a new message. The black population, he told his hosts, was "a clog in the wheels of progress in the South." Therefore "the only solution to the race question" was the mass deportation of African Americans to Liberia or the Congo. With the aid of the U.S. Navy, Sovereign calculated, "20,000 people could be landed each week at the foot of the Congo railway," where King Leopold would gladly welcome his new subjects. White audiences from Pensacola to Memphis reportedly greeted Sovereign and his scheme with enthusiasm. But Sovereign's proposal for mass deportations of black Americans also provoked an outcry from those Knights who saw it as a betrayal of their egalitarian vision. It drew fierce opposition from within the black community.[26]

The deportation scheme of the master workmen of the Knights of Labor was testimony to the depths of the racial crisis afflicting the farm and labor movements of the 1890s. Nonetheless, through the efforts of organizers such as Ellen Williams, Populist-Republican fusionists in North Carolina won a series of dramatic victories. Promising "a free ballot and a fair count," the fusionists swept every contested statewide office, gained control of the legislature, and in 1895 sent the Populist Marion Butler to the U.S. Senate. They took measures to protect local self-government, to fund public schools, and to provide debt relief and other needs of the black and white poor. In terms of democratic governance and political equality, Populist-Republican fusion was a remarkable success.[27]

White Democrats met this success with a white supremacy campaign of violence and intimidation. They charged that no white woman was safe under the "Negro rule" of fusion government, and only force could rescue the white women of North Carolina. In the summer of 1898, White Supremacy Clubs made the port city of Wilmington a special target. This was a majority-black city, a stronghold of Populist-Republican fusion, and the home of Alexander Manly's *Daily Record*, the only daily black newspaper in the state. With the aim of whipping up racial passions, *The Wilmington Messenger*, a white newspaper, republished a speech that Rebecca Felton had delivered to the Georgia Agricultural Society a year earlier. In her speech, Felton, a prominent lecturer for the WCTU, had made a fiery defense of lynching, arguing that if lynching was necessary to protect white women from black beasts, "then I say lynch, a thousand times a week if necessary."[28]

Alexander Manly responded to the reprinting of Felton's speech in an editorial in the August 18 issue of *The Daily Record*. He turned the charge of rape around, pointing to white men who raped black women and, much as Ida B. Wells had done, took note of the reality of consensual sex between white women and black men. White women, Manly wrote, "are not any more particular in the matter of clandestine meetings with colored men than are the white men with colored women." Felton would respond that Manly deserved to be lynched for so impugning the character of white womanhood. The White Supremacy Clubs drew the same conclusion, and plans were laid to shut down Manly's newspaper and drive out Wilmington's Populist-Republican government. On November 10, armed white men descended on the black neighborhoods of the city, burned the offices of *The Daily Record*, murdered more than thirty black citizens, and drove out of town the surviving leaders of Wilmington's fusion administration.[29]

North Carolina Democrats rode their white supremacy campaign back to power. But a lesson had been learned about the need to prevent black voters from exploiting the cracks between competing white factions. In North Carolina and across the former Confederacy, white Democrats adopted poll taxes and literacy tests to strip African Americans of the franchise. And for good measure, in most southern states they added the white primary, freezing any remaining black voters out of the electoral process.

By this time, however, Populism as a national political force had succumbed to a thousand blows: the two-party system cornered the People's Party and left it without options; the combination of corporate money and corporate newspapers unleashed a potent political counterattack; white supremacy tormented the movement with particular menace and violence; and conflicting claims on equality buffeted the Populist coalition from within. It was more than a political setback. Under the same pressures, the great voluntary associations that had given Populism life fell into disrepair or collapsed altogether. Equality remained an unresolved and multipronged dilemma. The egalitarian and collectivist movements unleashed by the Civil War faced an impasse, and new types of movements with new types of commitments would soon make their mark.

EPILOGUE

MOST OF THE OLD GRANGE HALLS that can still be found in rural communities were built during the Grange revival at the close of the nineteenth century. In the early twentieth century, farm families gathered in these halls in much the same way that Grangers had met during the movement's heyday in the 1870s. They kept parts of the egalitarian structure and ethos. The women's rights campaigner Susan B. Anthony gave her last public speech at the 1903 annual meeting of the National Grange. During these years, the Grange also kept its faith in government action and built up its headquarters in Washington, D.C., to put its stamp on federal farm policy.[1]

Generations and geography, however, separated the post–Civil War Grange from its later twentieth-century iteration. In 1875, over three-quarters of the members of the Grange lived in the Midwest or the South. By 1910, 74 percent of the Grange's membership was in the Northeast, and it nearly disappeared in the South. Moreover, the new Grange shared the field with several other farm associations, some of them larger, more dynamic, or better placed in the federal bureaucracy. In the aftermath of World War I, the farm population began its sharp decline, and decade by decade the Grange declined with it.[2]

The twenty-first-century Grange defines its purpose as serving local communities in rural places. Its halls host bingo games, baked-bean suppers, and educational functions. The focus on community, however, has not allowed the contemporary Grange to escape from the broader ideological winds. While much of the old guard sees corporate agribusiness as an integral part of the rural community, environmentalist Grangers look to the future of a sustainable, local, and anti-corporate agriculture. At the same time, libertarian activists have joined the Grange in search of a new type of anti-statist and libertarian politics.[3]

The Woman's Christian Temperance Union has also had a long life. When Frances Willard died at the age of fifty-eight in 1898, the WCTU had been struggling to find its footing. The wide umbrella of its "Do Everything" policy had narrowed as many women looked to women's clubs, the settlement movement, suffrage associations, labor societies, and other avenues for women's politics and activism. Equality and sisterhood remained part of the WCTU's language, but it focused more narrowly on legal measures against the liquor trade and drew away from egalitarian and feminist movements.

During Prohibition, the WCTU's dry politics took a sharper Protestant edge of religious intolerance, and temperance education shifted toward enforcement and support of the expanding police power of the federal authorities. In both regards, the WCTU found an ally in the second Ku Klux Klan, and the two movements made practical alliances against their common non-Protestant, nonwhite, and wet enemies. Years later, the WCTU tied itself to the so-called war on drugs and lent what was its now much weakened voice to the "Just Say No" campaign of the Reagan administration. At the same time, chapters added homosexuality and abortion to their list of proscriptions. The WCTU maintains a nominal existence, serving as a reminder of the absence on a national scale of the expansive, dynamic, and egalitarian voluntary association of women that the WCTU once was, or at least promised to be.[4]

Although the Knights of Labor did not survive, its legacy of inclusive and egalitarian industrial organization would shape America's twentieth century. By the early 1890s, the organization was on the edge of collapse. Internecine conflicts led to Terence Powderly's removal from the leadership in 1893, after which he attended law school and was appointed general commissioner of immigration by President William McKinley. This was the beginning of his long second career as an official in the federal bureaucracy enforcing the Chinese exclusion laws and other restrictive policies. At the same time, Powderly kept ties with colleagues in the labor movement. Perhaps his closest colleague was Mary Harris "Mother" Jones, who lived with Powderly and his wife in Washington for several years and was a friend and collaborator until his death in 1924.[5]

During her years of friendship with Powderly, Mother Jones was known for her fearless organizing in the coalfields and her regular stints in prison for her efforts. She campaigned for the United Mine Workers, the Industrial Workers of the World, and other movements that kept alive the principles of egalitarian industrial organizing. In the depths of the Great Depression, coal miners from the UMW provided the catalyst for the formation of the Congress of Industrial Organizations (CIO), a coalition of industrial unions that organized the country's steel, automobile, electronics, and other mass industries.

∎

BY MID-CENTURY, INDUSTRIAL UNIONISM SERVED as a powerful counterforce to corporate power. It also served as a proactive force sustaining the federal New Deal policies that brought a historic level of economic well-being and security to millions of working-class families. As shown in the now famous charts of Thomas Piketty—the French economist whose critique of wealth inequality has striking similarities to that of Henry George—the postwar years witnessed economic "convergence" and the "compression of inequalities." That is, the wealth gap between the haves and the have-nots markedly narrowed. By such economic measures, the postwar years were not just prosperous years but also relatively egalitarian years.[6]

That is only half the story. New Deal institutions proved stubbornly indifferent or even hostile to women's efforts to gain sexual equality: social policy was built on the notion of the male breadwinner; most unions reinforced the sexual segmentation of employment; and the unrealized demand for equal pay for equal work ran up against the reality of closed access to jobs, skills, and career paths. The power and breadth of the late twentieth-century women's movement had roots in the stark inequities of the postwar years.[7]

The postwar years were also years of deep racial inequality. In 1944, the Swedish sociologist Gunnar Myrdal published *An American Dilemma*, a widely influential study of the American system of racial caste. Myrdal made a comprehensive survey of the causes and consequences of social, political, and economic racial inequality. And he concluded his over one thousand pages of text with the observation that America's treatment of its black citizens was its "greatest and most conspicuous scandal." Yet as an optimistic social scientist, Myrdal predicted that careful policy could see America through its dilemma. The New Deal coalition, however, much like virtually every reform coalition since the founding of the Grange, rested on an alliance with the white supremacists of the South. After the war, this meant that white supremacists continued to bend New Deal policy to favor white people, deny black people, and deepen the racial divide in education, employment, housing, and wealth.[8]

The labor movement played a complex role in these postwar developments. Too often, unions defended white male prerogatives and exclusion. At the same time, they provided a vast and in many ways favorable arena for the contest over the meaning of equal rights. From the steel mills of Alabama in the 1930s to the 1963 March on Washington for Jobs and

Freedom, where Martin Luther King Jr. spoke of his dream, unions served as an institutional base for the civil rights movement. On April 4, 1968, King was shot in Memphis, where he had gone to support a union drive among the city's sanitation workers. Similar union drives among public sector workers and in health-care and other service industries went hand in hand with movements for equality and social justice, especially among women and people of color.

In the 1980s, corporate managers adopted new strategies to dismantle the union movement. They gave their employees a clear choice: either abandon unions and the pensions, health care, job security, and other protections they provide, or face the full arsenal of corporate power: lockouts, mass firings, intimidation, blacklists, court injunctions, and police action. The singular achievement of the Reagan administration was overseeing the cascading effect of these strategies and the ensuing collapse of much of the labor movement. For their part, public sector workers avoided some of the direct blows but perhaps only temporarily.

■

IN THE FIRST DECADES of the twenty-first century, a multisided crisis of inequality has taken on proportions unseen since the 1920s. Not only have multibillionaires accrued fantastic wealth, but they have strategically invested in political and institutional power. Members of Congress and the Supreme Court have again learned how to show special deference to Wall Street and to the equal rights claims of corporate money. Meanwhile, low wages, high levels of debt, and job insecurity have taken a rising toll on working-class lives. At the same time, the criminal justice system has expanded its gulag of racial oppression and unequal justice, and the forces of white supremacy have searched out new means of racial disenfranchisement and marginalization.

The lines of inequality have been sharply drawn. Movements against the depredations of Wall Street and for living wages, labor rights, and affordable health care have reflected a popular recognition of the deepening economic divide. Movements for reproductive and LGBTQ rights and against sexual assault have pointed to an increasing awareness of sexual inequities. Movements in defense of black lives in the face of police violence, in defense of immigrant lives, and in defense of voting rights for people of color have suggested a growing recognition of profound racial injustice. And movements against carbon pollution and for environmental justice have placed inequality in a global context. At the same time, "fusion" movements have pointed to the need for new paths to unification, linking and mutually reinforcing egalitarian movements that pursue a range of interwoven yet at times divergent claims. Nonetheless, the problem of association—the ways and means to establish living forms of solidarity and the design of twenty-first-century counterinstitutions to corporate power—remains unresolved. The solution to this problem may only be found in collective efforts, the multiple struggles of women and men to realize their visions of a just and equal society.

NOTES

ABBREVIATIONS USED IN THE NOTES

AAW: African Americans in the Woman's Christian Temperance Union, Frances Willard Memorial Library and Archives, Evanston, Ill.

DWAP: David Wyatt Aiken Papers, South Caroliniana Library, Digital Collections

FEWL: Frances Elizabeth Willard Letters, Schlesinger Library, Radcliffe Institute for Advanced Study

FWMLA: Frances Willard Memorial Library and Archives, Evanston, Ill.

GAMD: Greenback Anti-Monopoly Documents, Wisconsin State Historical Society

IDP: Ignatius Donnelly Pamphlets, Minnesota Historical Society

KLR: Knights of Labor Records, Bancroft Library, University of California, Berkeley

LPM: Lide Parker Smith Meriwether Papers, Schlesinger Library, Radcliffe Institute for Advanced Study

MNHS: Minnesota Historical Society

MPIS: McCaull Papers, Iowa State Historical Society

NGPH: National Grange of Patrons of Husbandry, Kroch Library, Cornell University

NGWSHS: National Grange, Wisconsin State Historical Society

OHKP: O. H. Kelley Papers, Wisconsin State Historical Society
PP: Terence Vincent Powderly Papers, 1864–1937, Catholic University of America (microform)
WASM: Women and Social Movements in the United States, Digital Collection
WCPG: Winnebago County Pomona Grange, Abraham Lincoln Presidential Library, Springfield, Ill.

INTRODUCTION: EQUALITY

1. Allen C. Cuelzo, *Gettysburg: The Last Invasion* (New York: Knopf, 2013), 471–73; Jim Weeks, *Gettysburg: Memory, Market, and an American Shrine* (Princeton, N.J.: Princeton University Press, 2003), 13–18; Garry Wills, *Lincoln at Gettysburg: The Words That Remade America* (New York: Simon & Schuster, 1992), 19–22.
2. William Saunders's handwritten notes on the design of the cemetery at Gettysburg in "The Journal of William Saunders, 1898–1899," William Saunders Papers, box 4, NGPH.
3. Ibid.
4. Ibid.; Drew Gilpin Faust, *This Republic of Suffering: Death and the American Civil War* (New York: Knopf, 2008), 99–101, 250–65.
5. "Journal of William Saunders"; Weeks, *Gettysburg*, 60.
6. "Journal of William Saunders."
7. Ibid.; "The Gettysburg Cemetery," clipping, William Saunders Papers, box 8, NGPH.
8. Margaret S. Creighton, *The Colors of Courage: Gettysburg's Forgotten History: Immigrants, Women, and African Americans in the Civil War's Defining Battle* (New York: Basic Books, 2005), 125–34.
9. "The Gettysburg Solemnities: Dedication of the National Cemetery at Gettysburg, Pennsylvania, November 19, 1863," *Washington Chronicle* (supplement), box 8, NGPH.
10. Wills, *Lincoln at Gettysburg*, 30.
11. Ibid., 145.
12. Sean Wilentz, *The Politicians and the Egalitarians: The Hidden History of American Politics* (New York: W. W. Norton, 2016); Matthew Rainbow Hale, "Regenerating the World: The French Revolution, Civic Festivals, and the Forging of American Democracy," *Journal of American History* 103 (March 2017), 891–920; James L. Huston, *The American and British Debate over Equality: 1776–1920* (Baton Rouge: Louisiana State University Press, 2017); Manisha Sinha, *The Slave's Cause: A History of Abolition* (New Haven, Conn.: Yale University Press, 2016); Ellen Carol DuBois, *Feminism and Suffrage: The Emergence of an Independent Women's Movement in America, 1848–1869* (Ithaca, N.Y.: Cornell University Press, 1978); Richard D. Brown, *Self-Evident Truths: Contesting Equal Rights from the Revolution to the Civil War* (New Haven, Conn.: Yale University Press, 2017).
13. James M. McPherson, *The Struggle for Equality: Abolitionists and the Negro in the Civil War and Reconstruction* (Princeton, N.J.: Princeton University Press, 1964); Ira Berlin, *The Long Emancipation: The Demise of Slavery in the United*

States (Cambridge, Mass.: Harvard University Press, 2015), 159; Eric Foner, *Reconstruction: America's Unfinished Revolution, 1863–1877* (New York: Harper & Row, 1988), 64–67, 113–15; Kate Masur, *An Example for All the Land: Emancipation and the Struggle for Equality in Washington, D.C.* (Chapel Hill: University of North Carolina Press, 2010), 2–7.

14. Foner, *Reconstruction*, 230.
15. William Graham Sumner, *What Social Classes Owe to Each Other* (New York: Harper & Brothers, 1883); Abraham Lincoln, "An Open Field and a Fair Chance," from a speech to the 166th Ohio Regiment, Aug. 22, 1864, in *The Political Thought of Abraham Lincoln*, ed. Richard N. Current (New York: Macmillan, 1967), 330.
16. Jeremy Waldron, *One Another's Equals: The Basis of Human Equality* (Cambridge, Mass.: Harvard University Press, 2017); James T. Kloppenberg, *Uncertain Victory: Social Democracy and Progressivism in European and American Thought, 1870–1920* (New York: Oxford University Press, 1986), 6, 7, 184.
17. Alexis de Tocqueville, *Democracy in America*, vol. 2, chap. 5; Arthur M. Schlesinger, "Biography of a Nation of Joiners," *American Historical Review* 50 (1944): 1–25.
18. Charles A. Beard and Mary R. Beard, *The Rise of American Civilization* (New York: Macmillan, 1927), II, 2:761; Anne Firor Scott, *Natural Allies: Women's Associations in American History* (Urbana: University of Illinois Press, 1991), 2; Mary Ann Clawson, *Constructing Brotherhood: Class, Gender, and Fraternalism* (Princeton, N.J.: Princeton University Press, 1985); Elisabeth S. Clemens, *The People's Lobby: Organizational Innovation and the Rise of Interest Group Politics in the United States, 1890–1925* (Chicago: University of Chicago Press, 1997).
19. Émile Durkheim, *The Division of Labor in Society* (New York: Macmillan, 1933), 228.
20. Elisabeth S. Clemens, "Organizational Repertoires and Institutional Change: Women's Groups and the Transformation of U.S. Politics, 1890–1920," *American Journal of Sociology* 98 (1993): 755–98.

1. FEDERAL ORIGINS

1. Aaron B. Grosh, *Mentor in the Granges and Homes of Patrons of Husbandry* (New York: Clark & Maynard, 1876), 3; D. Wyatt Aiken, "The Grange: Its Origin, Progress, and Educational Purposes" (speech delivered in Washington, D.C., Jan. 23, 1883), National Grange, 1927, NGPH; *Popular Science Monthly*, Dec. 1887, in Solon Justus Buck, *The Granger Movement: A Study of Agricultural Organization and Its Political, Economic, and Social Manifestations, 1870–1880* (Cambridge, Mass.: Harvard University Press, 1913), 42; "National Grange Treasurer's Book & State Grange Dues, 1868–1875," NGPH.
2. Grant McConnell, *The Decline of Agrarian Democracy* (Berkeley: University of California Press, 1953); Clemens, *People's Lobby*, 145–83.
3. Oliver Kelley to Saunders, Aug. 5, 1867, NGPH; Kelley to Anson Bartlett, Oct. 15, 1867, in Oliver H. Kelley, *Origin and Progress of the Patrons of Husbandry: A History from 1866 to 1873* (Philadelphia: J. A. Wagenseller, 1875), 41.

4. Constance Smith and Anne Freedman, *Voluntary Associations: Perspectives on the Literature* (Cambridge, Mass.: Harvard University Press, 1972), 5–6.

5. FDR to L. J. Taber, Oct. 22, 1941, NGPH (italics added).

6. Lida Skilton Ives, "O. H. Kelly Biography and List of Belongings," National Grange, MNHS; "Declaration of Purposes of the National Grange," Feb. 1874, NGPH.

7. "Declaration of Purposes."

8. Hugh Davis, *"We Will Be Satisfied with Nothing Less": The African American Struggle for Equal Rights in the North During Reconstruction* (Ithaca, N.Y.: Cornell University Press, 2011), 59; *Christian Recorder*, Feb. 2, 1867; Masur, *Example for All the Land*, 1–9, 28, 49.

9. Jessica Ziparo, *This Grand Experiment: When Women Entered the Federal Workforce in Civil War–Era Washington, D.C.* (Chapel Hill: University of North Carolina Press, 2017), 1–14, 193–220; Masur, *Example for All the Land*, 179.

10. *Cincinnati Enquirer*, Oct. 15, 1874.

11. Buck, *Granger Movement*, chap. 7.

12. Ibid., chaps. 4–6.

13. Thomas A. Woods, *Knights of the Plow: Oliver H. Kelley and the Origins of the Grange in Republican Ideology* (Ames: Iowa State University Press, 1991), 22–23, 52–58.

14. Ibid., 52–58.

15. Kelley, *Origin and Progress*, 11; Charles M. Gardner, *The Grange: Friend of the Farmer* (Washington, D.C.: National Grange, 1947).

16. Woods, *Knights of the Plow*, 82–83.

17. Scott W. Berg, *38 Nooses: Lincoln, Little Crow, and the Beginning of the Frontier's End* (New York: Pantheon Books, 2012), 46; Gardner, *Friend of the Farmer*; Woods, *Knights of the Plow*, 83.

18. Mark Wahlgren Summers, *The Ordeal of the Reunion: A New History of Reconstruction* (Chapel Hill: University of North Carolina Press, 2014), 180; Ari Kelman, *A Misplaced Massacre: Struggling over the Memory of Sand Creek* (Cambridge, Mass.: Harvard University Press, 2013), 31–35.

19. Berg, *38 Nooses*.

20. James McPherson, *Battle Cry of Freedom: The Civil War Era* (New York: Oxford University Press, 1988), 538–44, 557–58.

21. Ibid., 756–57.

22. Kelley, *Origin and Progress*, 12–15.

23. Aiken, "Grange"; Grosh, *Mentor in the Granges*, 28–43; William D. Barnes, "Oliver Hudson Kelley and the Genesis of the Grange: A Reappraisal," *Agricultural History* 14 (1967): 229–42.

24. "Industrial Men: William Saunders," *Rural New Yorker* (1874), clipping, NGPH; *Washington Sunday Chronicle*, Sept. 24, 1865; *New York Times*, Sept. 14, 1900.

25. "Journal of William Saunders"; David S. Reynolds, *Walt Whitman's America: A Cultural Biography* (New York: Knopf, 1995), 412; William S. McFeely, *Frederick Douglass* (New York: W. W. Norton, 1991), 310–20; David W. Blight, *Frederick Douglass: Prophet of Freedom* (New York: Simon & Schuster, 2018), 649–54.

26. "Industrial Men."

27. Donald A. Rowland, "The Eleusinian Mysteries and the Patrons of Husbandry," *Crooked Lake Review*, April 1991, www.crookedlakereview.com/articles/34 _66/37apr1991/37rowland.html.

28. Grosh, *Mentor in the Granges*, 31.

29. Connie L. Lester, "'Let Us Be Up and Doing': Women in the Tennessee Movements for Agrarian Reform," *Tennessee Historical Quarterly* 54 (1995): 80–97; *Cincinnati Star*, July 5, 1875.

30. "Constitution," in James D. McCabe [Edward Winslow Martin], *History of the Grange Movement, or, The Farmer's War Against Monopolies* (Philadelphia: National, 1873; reprint 1967), 431–39; Aiken, "Grange"; Louis Bernhard Schmidt, "Farm Organization in Iowa," *Palimpsest* 31 (1950): 117–64.

31. Kelley, *Origin and Progress*, 19, 41, 63–65; Grosh, *Mentor in the Granges*, 31.

32. Grosh, *Mentor in the Granges*, 57–62.

33. Kelley to Saunders, Aug. 5, 1867, NGPH.

34. Kelley, *Origin and Progress*, 40.

35. Ibid., 92.

36. Ibid., 21.

37. Ibid., 25.

38. Ibid., 110, 130.

39. Ibid., 227.

40. Ibid., 35, 265.

41. Ibid., 54.

42. Ibid., 111.

43. Lynn Dumenil, *Freemasonry and American Culture, 1880–1930* (Princeton, N.J.: Princeton University Press, 1984), 10; Michael A. Halleran, *The Better Angels of Our Nature: Freemasonry in the American Civil War* (Tuscaloosa: University of Alabama Press, 2010), 52, 154–56.

44. Halleran, *Better Angels of Our Nature*, 8–30.

45. Kelley, *Origin and Progress*, 13.

46. "Proceedings of the Grand Lodge of Ancient Free and Accepted Masons of Minnesota, at Its Ninth Grand Annual Communication in the City of Saint Paul," Oct. 23, 1860, IDP.

47. D. Sven Nordin, *Rich Harvest: A History of the Grange, 1867–1900* (Jackson: University Press of Mississippi, 1974), 10.

48. Kelley, *Origin and Progress*, 16, 31, 47, 76–77.

49. "Personal Reminiscences of Father O. H. Kelley," clipping from *American Grange Bulletin and Scientific Farmer*, Aug. 24, 1905, OHKP.

50. Kelley, *Origin and Progress*, 23, 31, 54.

51. T. J. Jackson Lears, *No Place of Grace: Antimodernism and the Transformation of American Culture* (New York: Pantheon, 1981; reprint 1994), 189.

52. Anson Bartlett, "Educated Labor," *Jeffersonian Democrat* (Chardon, Ohio), March 6, 1863.

53. Kelley, *Origin and Progress*, 72–75.

54. Ibid., 75.

55. *Dr. Webster's Unabridged Dictionary* (London: Bell & Duldy, 1864), 585; Kelley, *Origin and Progress*, 30, 45.

56. Kelley, *Origin and Progress*, 118, 167, 237, 247, 270–92; Woods, *Knights of the Plow*, 107–10, 137–38.

57. Grosh, *Mentor in the Granges*, 42.

58. March 6, 1869, Feb. 2, 1882, North Star Grange No. 1, "Minutes, 1868–1884," MNHS.

59. Sept. 25, 1868, Oct. 17, 1868, North Star Grange No. 1, "Minutes, 1868–1884," MNHS.

60. Sept. 2, 1868, Nov. 2, 1872, Feb. 2, 1882, North Star Grange No. 1, "Minutes, 1868–1884," MNHS.

61. Woods, *Knights of the Plow*, 130; Kelley, *Origin and Progress*, 95.

62. Eva S. McDowell, "One of the Grange Pioneers, Miss Caroline Hall, the 'First Woman of the Grange,' a Tribute by Mrs. McDowell," *National Grange Monthly* 9 (1912), 11; Caroline A. Hall, *Songs for the Grange: Set to Music and Dedicated to the Order of Patrons of Husbandry in the United States* (Philadelphia: J. A. Wagenseller, 1874).

63. Kelley, *Origin and Progress*, 157, 202, 208.

64. Robert L. Tontz, "Memberships of General Farmers' Organizations, United States, 1874–1960," *Agricultural History* 38 (1964): 147.

65. "Statistics of the Patrons of Husbandry," in Buck, *Granger Movement*, 52–69 (note that the text on page 67 mistakenly refers to Kansas, where the Grange was strong, rather than Nebraska, where it was stronger yet); *Columbia (S.C.) Daily Phoenix*, Aug. 6, 1874.

66. Huston, *American and British Debate over Equality*, 125.

67. *Ninth Census*, vol. 3, table 13 (Washington, D.C.: Government Printing Office, 1872), 812; Huston, *American and British Debate over Equality*, 79; Fred A. Shannon, *The Farmers' Last Frontier: Agriculture, 1860–1897* (New York: Holt, Rinehart and Winston, 1945), 360–61.

68. *Compendium of the Ninth Census* (Washington, D.C.: Government Printing Office, 1872), 594.

69. Kelley, *Origin and Progress*, 277.

70. *Charleston Daily News*, March 7, 1870; McCabe, *History of the Grange Movement*, 428.

71. Paul M. Gaston, *Women of Fair Hope* (Athens: University of Georgia Press, 1984), 21–43.

72. Howland to Saunders, Jan. 19, 1876, NGPH.

73. Ibid.; Jonathan Periam, *The Groundswell: A History of the Origin, Aims, and Progress of the Farmers' Movement* (Cincinnati: E. Hannaford, 1874), 575.

2. ANTI-MONOPOLY

1. "Speech of the Hon. James M. Scovel Before the Anti-Monopoly Convention, at Trenton, N.J., February 1, 1865," GAMD.

2. Robert Franklin Bensel, *The Political Economy of American Industrialization, 1877–1900* (Cambridge, U.K.: Cambridge University Press, 2000), 289–354; William W. Cochrane, *The Development of American Agriculture: A Historical Analysis*, 2nd ed. (Minneapolis: University of Minnesota Press, 1993), 78–98; Richard White, *The Republic for Which It Stands: The United States During Re-*

construction and the Gilded Age, 1865–1896 (New York: Oxford University Press, 2017), 216–24.

3. Buck, *Granger Movement*, 80–238.
4. Alfred D. Chandler, *The Visible Hand: The Managerial Revolution in American Business* (Cambridge, Mass.: Belknap Press, 1977); Richard White, *Railroaded: The Transcontinentals and the Making of Modern America* (New York: W. W. Norton, 2011).
5. Philip N. Backstrom, "The Mississippi Valley Trading Company: A Venture in International Cooperation, 1875–1877," *Agricultural History* 46 (1972): 425–37.
6. Kelley, *Origin and Progress*, 242.
7. "Speech of the Hon. James M. Scovel Before the Anti-Monopoly Convention, at Trenton, N.J., February 1, 1865."
8. Periam, *Groundswell*, 242–56; John Cochrane, Master of State Grange of Wisconsin, Circular, Oct. 3, 1874, NGWSHS.
9. McCabe, *History of the Grange Movement; Monthly Circular of the National Anti-Monopoly Cheap-Freight Railway League, Document IV* (New York: National Anti-Monopoly Cheap-Freight Railway League, Aug. 1867), IDP.
10. "Grand Rally in Behalf of the Producing Interests, Call for a National Convention," Cincinnati, May 19, 1868, National Cheap-Freight Railway League, IDP; Chester McArthur Destler, *American Radicalism, 1865–1901* (New London: Connecticut College, 1946; reprint 1966), 4–6; David Montgomery, *Beyond Equality: Labor and the Radical Republicans, 1862–1872* (Urbana: University of Illinois Press), 433.
11. *Monthly Circular of the National Anti-Monopoly Cheap-Freight Railway League.*
12. White, *Railroaded*; Scott Reynolds Nelson, *Iron Confederacies: Southern Railways, Klan Violence, and Reconstruction* (Chapel Hill: University of North Carolina Press, 1999).
13. *Monthly Circular of the National Anti-Monopoly Cheap-Freight Railway League.*
14. Chandler, *Visible Hand*; White, *Railroaded*, xxx–xxxi.
15. "Proposed National System of Cheap Freight Railways," Nov. 21, 1867, IDP; "Supplement," National Anti-Monopoly Cheap-Freight Railway League, New York, Aug. 1867.
16. *Journal of Proceedings of the Tenth Session of the National Grange, Held in the Palmer House, Chicago, Ill., Nov. 13 to 15, 1876* (Louisville: John P. Morton, 1876), 6; Periam, *Groundswell*, 575; Grosh, *Mentor in the Granges*, 7; *Rochester (Minn.) Federal Union*, May 10, 1873.
17. *Anderson Intelligencer* (Anderson Court House, S.C.), Aug. 20, 1874.
18. Kelley, *Origin and Progress*, 265.
19. "Declaration of Purposes."
20. Kelley to McDowell, Feb. 14, 1868, in Kelley, *Origin and Progress*, 79, 180; Feb. 21, 1874, North Star Grange No. 1, "Minutes, 1868–1884," MNHS.
21. Jan. 28, Aug. 1, Sept. 12, Oct. 31, Dec. 12, 1874, March 20, 1875, Minute Book, Kendaia Grange no. 64, box 32, NGPH.
22. May 2, July 6, 1874, Minute Book, Kendaia Grange no. 64, box 32, NGPH.
23. "Confidential Circular, No. 7," Iowa State Grange Business Agency, MPIS; *The*

History of the Iowa State Grange Patrons of Husbandry from 1868 to 1946 (Manchester: Iowa State Grange, 1946), 15–20, NGPH; Schmidt, "Farm Organizations in Iowa."

24. June 2, Sept. 1, Dec. 1, 1874, March 2, Sept. 5, 1875, Sept. 4, 1874, Minutes of Meetings, WCPG.

25. *Minutes of the First Annual Meeting of the State Grange of Virginia, Patrons of Husbandry* (Richmond: Patrons of Husbandry, 1874), 35, NGWSHS.

26. William Free Hill, *A Brief History of the Grange Movement in Pennsylvania* (Chambersburg: Pennsylvania Grange News, 1923), NGPH.

27. *Proceedings of the State Grange of the Patrons of Husbandry of Alabama, Second Session* (Montgomery, Ala.: Southern Plantation Print., 1875), 7, 17, NGWSHS; Dec. 6, 1876, Jan. 20, Sept. 4, 1877, Minutes of Meetings, WCPG.

28. Shankland to Robert McCaull, June 28, 1876, MPIS.

29. *Tenth Session of the National Grange*, 25–31, 56.

30. Corbett to Kelley, May 20, 1870, in Kelley, *Origin and Progress*, 256–59.

31. *State Grange of Alabama, Second Session*, 26; Theodore Saloutos, "The Grange in the South, 1870–1877," *Journal of Southern History* 19 (1953): 473–87; *Columbia (S.C.) Daily Phoenix*, July 16, 1874; Ezra S. Carr, *The Patrons of Husbandry on the Pacific Coast* (San Francisco: Bancroft and Co., 1875), 129–30.

32. Backstrom, "Mississippi Valley Trading Company."

33. *Tenth Session of the National Grange*, 49–61, 146–48.

34. Periam, *Groundswell*, 564.

35. Buck, *Granger Movement*, 80–123.

36. *Tenth Session of the National Grange*, 76; Hill, *Grange Movement in Pennsylvania*; *History of the Iowa State Grange*, 4; Kelley, *Origin and Progress*, 95.

37. *New York Herald*, Sept. 3, 1873.

38. Buck, *Granger Movement*, 134–238.

39. Joseph Hinckley Cordon, "Illinois Railway Legislation and Commission Control Since 1870," *University Studies* (University of Illinois), 1 (1904): 213–89.

40. Corbett to Kelley, May 20, 1870, in Kelley, *Origin and Progress*, 256–59.

41. Buck, *Granger Movement*, 121–237; John Cochrane, "Patrons of Wisconsin," Oct. 3, 1874, NGWSHS.

42. Martin Ridge, *Ignatius Donnelly: Portrait of a Politician* (Chicago: University of Chicago Press, 1962; reprint 1991), 96–101.

43. Greeley's speech quoted in "Address to the People," National Anti-Monopoly League, New York, GAMD.

44. Greeley to Donnelly, Aug. 19, 1872, Donnelly Papers, MNHS.

45. Martin Ridge, "Ignatius Donnelly and the Granger Movement in Minnesota," *Mississippi Valley Historical Review* 42 (1956): 693–709.

46. "Munn v. Illinois," in *The Supreme Court and the Constitution: Readings in American Constitutional History*, ed. Stanley I. Kutler (New York: Norton, 1984), 243.

47. Bensel, *Political Economy of American Industrialization*, 307–14; Cordon, "Illinois Railway Legislation," 18.

48. *Munn v. Illinois*, 94 U.S. 113 (1877); Ronald M. Labbé and Jonathan Lurie, *The*

Slaughterhouse Cases: Regulation, Reconstruction, and the Fourteenth Amendment (Lawrence: University Press of Kansas, 2003), 248–50.

3. RACE AND REUNION

1. Kelley, *Origin and Progress*, 12; David Warren Bowen, *Andrew Johnson and the Negro* (Knoxville: University of Tennessee Press, 1989), 122–56.
2. Foner, *Reconstruction*, 180–81; Bowen, *Andrew Johnson and the Negro*.
3. "Interview with a Colored Delegation Respecting Suffrage," Feb. 7, 1866, in Edward McPherson, *The Political History of the United States: From April 15, 1865 to July 15, 1870* (Washington, D.C.: Philip & Solomons, 1871), 52–55; Blight, *Frederick Douglass*, 473–76.
4. Kelley, *Origin and Progress*, 15.
5. Ibid.
6. Ibid.
7. Foner, *Reconstruction*, 281–307; Steven Hahn, *A Nation Under Our Feet: Black Political Struggles in the Rural South from Slavery to the Great Migration* (Cambridge, Mass.: Harvard University Press, 2003), 180–91.
8. David W. Blight, *Race and Reunion: The Civil War in American Memory* (Cambridge, Mass.: Harvard University Press, 2001); Edward J. Blum, *Reforging the White Republic: Race, Religion, and American Nationalism, 1865–1898* (Baton Rouge: Louisiana State University Press, 2005); Caroline E. Janney, *Remembering the Civil War: Reunion and the Limits of Reconciliation* (Chapel Hill: University of North Carolina Press, 2013); Nina Silber, *The Romance of Reunion: Northerners and the South, 1865–1900* (Chapel Hill: University of North Carolina Press, 1993); Barbara Gannon, *The Won Cause: Black and White Comradeship in the Grand Army of the Republic* (Chapel Hill: University of North Carolina Press, 2011).
9. Foner, *Reconstruction*, 460–563; C. Vann Woodward, *Origins of the New South, 1877–1913* (Baton Rouge: Louisiana State University Press, 1951), 23–141; Nancy Cohen, *The Reconstruction of American Liberalism: 1865–1914* (Chapel Hill: University of North Carolina Press, 2002), 61–85; Heather Cox Richardson, *The Death of Reconstruction: Race, Labor, and Politics in the Post–Civil War North, 1865–1901* (Cambridge, Mass.: Harvard University Press, 2001).
10. Charles Dudley Warner, "Equality," *Atlantic Monthly*, January 1880, 19–32; Mark Twain and Charles Dudley Warner, *The Gilded Age: A Tale of To-Day* (Hartford, Conn.: F. G. Gilman, 1873); Thomas R. Lounsbury, "Biographical Sketch," in *The Complete Writings of Charles Dudley Warner* (Hartford, Conn.: American Publishing Co., 1904), i–xxxviii.
11. "Declaration of Principles."
12. Kelley, *Origin and Progress*, 96.
13. Jacques, Athens, Ga., to Boston Union of Associationists, Sept. 24, 1849, midd archive.middlebury.edu/cdm/compoundobject/collection/abercoll/id/1696 /rec/16.
14. Kelley, *Origin and Progress*, 180, 291, 320; William Warren Rogers, *The One-Gallused Rebellion: Agrarianism in Alabama, 1865–1896* (Baton Rouge:

Louisiana State University Press, 1970), 64; *Hartford (Ky.) Herald*, May 10, 1876; *Gallipolis (Ohio) Journal*, Dec. 23, 1875.

15. McCabe, *History of the Grange Movement*, 425–27.

16. Kelley, *Origin and Progress*, 354–55; David Wyatt Aiken, "Autobiography," DWAP; Biography of David Wyatt Aiken, DWAP.

17. Claudius Hornby Pritchard Jr., *Colonel D. Wyatt Aiken, 1828–1887: South Carolina's Militant Agrarian* (Hampden-Sidney, Va.: self-published, 1870), 50; *Abbeville (S.C.) Press*, April 24, 1868; *Anderson Intelligencer* (Anderson Court House, S.C.), Aug. 26, 1868.

18. Douglas R. Egerton, *Wars of Reconstruction: The Brief, Violent History of America's Most Progressive Era* (New York: Bloomsbury Press, 2014), 158–59, 237–39; Matthew Hild, *Greenbackers, Knights of Labor, and Populists: Farmer-Labor Insurgency in the Late-Nineteenth-Century South* (Athens: University of Georgia Press, 2007), 20; "A Brace of Carpetbaggers," *Orangeburg (S.C.) News*, Aug. 8, 1886.

19. "Murder of B. F. Randolph," *Orangeburg (S.C.) News*, Oct. 24, 1869; "The Murder in the Up-Country," *Charleston (S.C.) Daily News*, Oct. 28, 1868.

20. Summers, *Ordeal of the Reunion*, 148; *Abbeville (S.C.) Press*, Sept. 18, 1868; *Columbia (S.C.) Daily Phoenix*, Feb. 23, 1869; *Fairfield Herald* (Winnsboro, S.C.), Dec. 9, 1868, March 3, 1869; *Columbia (S.C.) Daily Phoenix*, Nov. 18, 1868.

21. David Wyatt Aiken to Ella Gaillard Aiken, Nov. 11, 1868, DWAP.

22. *Abbeville (S.C.) Press*, Feb. 26 and March 19, 1869.

23. "The Patrons of Husbandry," *Southern Planter and Farmer* (Richmond), July 1872.

24. William Saunders, interview in *New York Herald*, Aug. 11, 1873.

25. Periam, *Groundswell*, 159–61.

26. Hild, *Greenbackers, Knights of Labor, and Populists*, 17–18; Rogers, *One-Gallused Rebellion*, 77; Kenneth Stampp, *The Era of Reconstruction, 1865–1877* (New York: Knopf, 1966), 205; Saloutos, "Grange in the South," 477; W.E.B. Du Bois, *Black Reconstruction in America, 1860–1880* (New York: Harcourt Brace, 1935; reprint 1995), 359; "The Colored Element and the Grangers," *New York Herald*, Aug. 30, 1873.

27. "The Grange," *Southern Planter and Farmer* (Richmond), Aug. 1875, 454; David Wyatt Aiken, "The Order of the Patrons of Husbandry," pamphlet, 1872, DWAP; Robert Partin, "Black's Bend Grange, 1873–77: A Case Study of a Subordinate Grange of the Deep South," *Agricultural History* 31 (1957): 54.

28. James S. Ferguson, "The Grange and Farmer Education in Mississippi," *Journal of Southern History* 8 (1942): 497–512; Partin, "Black's Bend Grange," 55; "Dog Tax," *Southern Planter and Farmer* (Richmond), Oct. 1875, 551.

29. "Many Drops a River," *Newberry (S.C.) Herald*, June 3, 1874; "The Georgia Grangers," *Fairfield Herald* (Winnsboro, S.C.), July 22, 1874; *State Grange of Alabama, Second Session*, 7, 17; Saloutos, "Grange in the South," 481.

30. Saloutos, "Grange in the South," 487.

31. "The Labor Question," *Anderson Intelligencer* (Anderson Court House, S.C.), Oct. 22, 1874; *Abbeville (S.C.) Press*, Feb. 19, 1869; *Abbeville (S.C.) Press*, July 17, 1869.

32. "Virginia State Grange," *Southern Planter and Farmer* (Richmond), March 1877, 190.

33. *State Grange of Alabama, Second Session*, 6–7, 17; Michael W. Fitzgerald, *Reconstruction in Alabama: From Civil War to Redemption in the Cotton South* (Baton Rouge: Louisiana State University Press, 2017), 289.

34. "Virginia State Grange," 190.

35. Michael Perman, *The Road to Redemption: Southern Politics, 1869–1879* (Chapel Hill: University of North Carolina Press, 1984), 242–44; Foner, *Reconstruction*, 593–94.

36. Foner, *Reconstruction*, 85–87, 171–75; Rogers, *One-Gallused Rebellion*, 69.

37. Egerton, *Wars of Reconstruction*, 132.

38. Saloutos, "Grange in the South," 478; Partin, "Black's Bend Grange," 57.

39. Kelley, *Origin and Progress*, 12.

40. Saloutos, "Grange in the South," 484; "The Grangers," *Orangeburg (S.C.) Times*, July 16, 1874; *Gallipolis (Ohio) Journal*, Jan. 8, 1874.

41. Minutes of the First Annual Meeting of the State Grange of Virginia, Patrons of Husbandry, Held at Richmond, Dec. 29–31, 1873, NGWSHS.

42. *State Grange of Alabama, Second Session*, 6–7, 17; "Agricultural and Mechanical Society of South Carolina," *Charleston (S.C.) Daily News*, April 29, 1869.

43. Pritchard, *Colonel D. Wyatt Aiken*, 71; *Charleston (S.C.) Daily News*, May 19, 1870; "White Labor in the South," *New York Times*, Feb. 20, 1882.

44. *Columbia (S.C.) Daily Phoenix*, July 16, 1869; *Charleston Daily News*, May 19, 1870; Rogers, *One-Gallused Rebellion*, 88.

45. Foner, *Reconstruction*, 425–44, 454–59; Egerton, *Wars of Reconstruction*, 284–320.

46. Foner, *Reconstruction*, 548–49; Rogers, *One-Gallused Rebellion*, 65–67; Saloutos, "Grange in the South," 478; "Grangers Becoming KuKlux," *Cleveland Daily Herald*, May 24, 1874; *Orangeburg (S.C.) Times*, Aug. 6 and Sept. 17, 1874.

47. *State Grange of Alabama, Second Session*, 18.

48. Thomas C. Atkeson, "History of the Declaration of Purposes of the Grange," 1924, NGPH.

49. Grosh, *Mentor in the Granges*, 49.

50. Bensel, *Political Economy of American Industrialization*, 124–30; Buck, *Granger Movement*, 115–16.

51. *Columbia (S.C.) Daily Phoenix*, Oct. 16, 1873; *Anderson Intelligencer* (Anderson Court House, S.C.), April 18, 1872, and Dec. 24, 1874; *State Grange of Alabama, Second Session*, 21; "Adjournment of Congress," *New York Herald*, in *Abbeville (S.C.) Press and Banner*, July 1, 1874.

52. Atkeson, "History of the Declaration of Purposes"; *Birmingham Age-Herald*, Sept. 11, 1894; "James W. Abert Wright," *Northern Alabama Historical and Biographical Illustrated* (Birmingham: Smith & De Land, 1888), 221–22.

53. James W. A. Wright, *Lecture on Cotton in California and Our Educational Interests* (San Francisco: Pacific Rural Press, 1875).

54. James W. A. Wright, *Addresses on Rochdale and Grange Co-operation and Other Grange Topics* (San Francisco: Pacific Rural Press, ca. 1877).

55. Carr, *Patrons of Husbandry on the Pacific Coast*, 51–52.

56. Kelley, *Origin and Progress*, 12, 211.

57. Frank L. Klement, "Middle Western Copperheadism and the Genesis of the Granger Movement," *Mississippi Valley Historical Review* 8 (1952): 679–94.

58. "The Farmers in Politics," *New York World*, reprinted in *Anderson Intelligencer* (Anderson Court House, S.C.), Oct. 16, 1873.

59. *New-York Tribune*, April 15 and 24, May 6, Aug. 11, 1873.

60. *Anderson Intelligencer* (Anderson Court House, S.C.), Oct. 16, 1873; *Daily Record of the Times* (Wilkes-Barre, Pa.), Oct. 31, 1873.

61. Ridge, *Ignatius Donnelly*, 17–27, 57, 66–68.

62. Ibid., 69.

63. Speech of Hon. Ignatius Donnelly, of Minnesota, on the Reconstruction of the Union, Delivered in the House of Representatives, May 2, 1864, IDP.

64. Speech of Hon. Ignatius Donnelly, of Minnesota, on Reconstruction, Delivered in the House of Representatives, Jan. 18, 1867, IDP.

65. McPherson, *Political History of the United States*, 353–54; Davis, *"We Will Be Satisfied with Nothing Less,"* 50–51.

66. Woods, *Knights of the Plow*, 148.

67. Ridge, *Ignatius Donnelly*, 141–45.

68. Charles W. Calhoun, *Conceiving a New Republic: The Republican Party and the Southern Question, 1869–1900* (Lawrence: University of Kansas Press, 2006), 37–44.

69. Ibid., 1–5.

70. Heather Cox Richardson, *To Make Men Free: A History of the Republican Party* (New York: Basic Books, 2014), 105; Waldo E. Martin Jr., *The Mind of Frederick Douglass* (Chapel Hill: University of North Carolina Press, 1984), 81.

71. Ridge, *Ignatius Donnelly*, 150; Woods, *Knights of the Plow*, 152.

72. Donnelly's most famous books include *Atlantis: The Antediluvian World* (1882), *The Great Cryptogram: Francis Bacon's Cipher in the So-Called Shakespeare's Plays* (1888), and *Caesar's Column* (1890).

73. *Federal Union* (Rochester, Minn.), March 29, May 10, June 13, 1873; *American Farmer* (Baltimore), March 1875, 115.

74. Woods, *Knights of the Plow*, 153–54.

75. *Federal Union* (Rochester, Minn.), Aug. 8, 1873.

76. *Grange Advance* (Red Wing, Minn.), Dec. 24 and 31, 1873.

77. *Grange Advance* (Red Wing, Minn.), Dec. 31, 1873; Woods, *Knights of the Plow*, 152–53.

78. Ridge, "Ignatius Donnelly and the Granger Movement in Minnesota."

79. *Federal Union* (Rochester, Minn.), Oct. 3, 1873; *Grange Advance* (Red Wing, Minn.), Sept. 30, 1874.

80. McCabe, *History of the Grange Movement*; James D. McCabe Jr., *The Guerrillas: An Original Domestic Drama, in Three Acts* (Richmond, Va.: West & Johnston,

1863); Michael T. Bernath, *Confederate Minds: The Struggle for Intellectual Independence in the Civil War South* (Chapel Hill: University of North Carolina Press, 2010), 208.

81. *Columbia (S.C.) Daily Phoenix*, June 5, 1874; *Columbia (S.C.) Daily Phoenix*, May 28, 1874; *Edgefield (S.C.) Advertiser*, Sept. 25, 1873.

82. "The Farmers in Politics," *New York World*, reprinted in *Anderson Intelligencer* (Anderson Court House, S.C.), Oct. 16, 1873.

83. "Adjournment of Congress," *New York Herald*, reprinted in *Abbeville (S.C.) Press and Banner*, July 1, 1874.

84. Nicolas Barreyre, "The Politics of Economic Crises: The Panic of 1873, the End of Reconstruction, and the Realignment of American Politics," *Journal of the Gilded Age and Progressive Era* 10 (2011): 403–23.

85. Schmidt, "Farm Organizations in Iowa," 129.

86. Ralph Hazeltine, "Victor E. Piollet: Portrait of a Country Politician," *Pennsylvania History* 40 (1973): 1–18; *Reading (Pa.) Times*, April 2, 1870.

87. *Pittsburgh Commercial*, June 13, 1874; *Harrisburg Telegraph*, Sept. 13, 1875; *Lucerne Union* (Wilkes-Barre, Pa.), Sept. 15, 1875; *Pittsburgh Weekly Gazette*, Sept. 29, 1875; *Indiana (Pa.) Progress*, Sept. 23, 1875.

88. Hill, *Grange Movement in Pennsylvania*.

89. R. Douglas Hurt, "The Ohio Grange, 1870–1900," *Northwest Ohio Quarterly* 53 (1981): 19–33; "Diamond Jubilee History Ohio State Grange," State Grange Ohio, 1947, NGPH.

90. *Cincinnati Enquirer*, Sept. 9, 1874.

91. *Lima (Ohio) Times-Democrat*, Oct. 8, 1874.

92. *Clarksville Weekly Chronicle*, Jan. 24, 1874; *New York Herald*, Jan. 13, 1874.

93. Robert W. Winston, *Andrew Johnson: Plebeian and Patriot* (New York: Henry Holt, 1928), 498; Bowen, *Andrew Johnson and the Negro*.

94. Connie L. Lester, *Up from the Mudsills of Hell: The Farmers' Alliance, Populism, and Progressive Agriculture in Tennessee, 1870–1915* (Athens: University of Georgia Press, 2006), 53–57; *Nashville Union and American*, Jan. 15, 1874.

95. Hans L. Trefousse, *Andrew Johnson: A Biography* (New York: W. W. Norton, 1989), 367–77; Robert B. Jones, "The Press and the Legislature: Andrew Johnson's Election to the U.S. Senate in 1875," *Tennessee Historical Quarterly* 62 (2003): 238–57.

96. "The Grangers Take a Hand," *Cincinnati Star*, Feb. 1, 1875.

97. Ibid.

98. Calhoun, *Conceiving a New Republic*, 84–89; Richard H. Abbott, *The Republican Party and the South, 1855–1877: The First Southern Strategy* (Chapel Hill: University of North Carolina Press, 1986), 231–32; Foner, *Reconstruction*, 559–63.

99. Calhoun, *Conceiving a New Republic*, 87.

100. Rutherford B. Hayes, diary entries March 28 and April 28, 1875, and letter to Guy M. Bryan, July 27, 1875, in *Diary and Letters of Rutherford Birchard Hayes, Nineteenth President of the United States*, ed. Charles Richard Williams (Columbus: Ohio State Archeological and Historical Society, 1924), 269, 271, 286.

101. C. Vann Woodward, *Reunion and Reaction: The Compromise of 1877 and the End of Reconstruction* (Boston: Little, Brown, 1951), 11; Vincent DeSantis, "Rutherford B. Hayes and the Removal of the Troops and the End of Reconstruction," in *Region, Race, and Reconstruction: Essays in Honor of C. Vann Woodward*, ed. J. Morgan Kousser and James M. McPherson (New York: Oxford University Press, 1982), 417–50; Perman, *Road to Redemption*, 135–77.

102. Gregory P. Downs, *After Appomattox: Military Occupation and the Ends of War* (Cambridge, Mass.: Harvard University Press, 2015); Summers, *Ordeal of the Reunion*, 347–71; Calhoun, *Conceiving a New Republic*, 137–68; Foner, *Reconstruction*, 512–87; Michael Les Benedict, "Reform Republicans and the Retreat from Reconstruction," in *The Facts of Reconstruction: Essays in Honor of John Hope Franklin*, ed. Eric Anderson and Alfred E. Moss Jr. (Baton Rouge: Louisiana State University Press, 1991), 53–77; Stampp, *Era of Reconstruction*, 186–215; Richardson, *Death of Reconstruction*.

103. Michael E. McGerr, "The Meaning of Liberal Republicanism: The Case of Ohio," *Civil War History* 28 (Dec. 1982): 307–23.

104. Du Bois, *Black Reconstruction in America*, 388–89; Foner, *Reconstruction*, 570–75; Summers, *Ordeal of the Reunion*, 366–67.

105. W. Scott Poole, "Religion, Gender, and the Lost Cause in South Carolina's 1876 Governor's Race: 'Hampton or Hell!,'" *Journal of Southern History* 68 (Aug. 2002): 573–92.

106. Wright, *Rochdale and Grange Co-operation and Other Grange Topics*.

107. "Appendix," *Journal of the Proceedings of the Twelfth Session of the National Grange of the Patrons of Husbandry, Held in the Hall of the House of Delegates, Richmond, Va., November 20th to 30th, Inclusive, 1878* (Philadelphia: J. A. Wagenseller, 1878), 121–22.

108. *New York Times*, Dec. 23, 1879, and Jan. 2, 1880.

109. *Southern Cultivator* (Augusta, Ga.), March 1885, 127; *Massachusetts Plowman and New England Journal of Agriculture*, May 28, 1887.

110. *Twelfth Session of the National Grange*, 12–14.

111. Ibid.

112. Ibid.

113. Woods, *Knights of the Plow*, 198–203.

4. SEX EQUALITY

1. *Congressional Record*, Feb. 1, 1875, 870.

2. Ibid., 866.

3. The number of those killed at Colfax is uncertain. Eric Foner's account gives half this number of dead while describing it as the "bloodiest single instance of racial carnage in the Reconstruction era" (*Reconstruction*, 437); see also Downs, *After Appomattox*, 239; LeeAnna Keith, *The Colfax Massacre: The Untold Story of Black Power, White Terror, and the Death of Reconstruction* (New York: Oxford University Press, 2008).

4. *Congressional Record*, Feb. 1, 1875, 870–77.

5. Ruth Bordin, *Woman and Temperance: The Quest for Power and Liberty,*

1873–1900 (Philadelphia: Temple University Press, 1981), 49; *Congressional Record*, Feb. 1, 1875, 870.

6. Bordin, *Woman and Temperance*, 15–16; Scott, *Natural Allies*, 93–94.
7. Bordin, *Woman and Temperance*, 18–23.
8. *Ohio Farmer* (Cleveland), March 24, 1874; Frances E. Willard, "Everybody's War," Oct. 1874, in *Let Something Good Be Said: Speeches and Writings of Frances E. Willard*, ed. Carolyn De Swarte Gifford and Amy R. Slagell (Urbana: University of Illinois Press, 2007), 4–5.
9. Bordin, *Woman and Temperance*, 34–38.
10. *Signal*, Jan. 15, 1880.
11. Ian R. Tyrrell, *Sobering Up: From Temperance to Prohibition in Antebellum America, 1800–1860* (Westport, Conn.: Praeger, 1979), 87, 159–95, 269–93.
12. David M. Fahey, *Temperance and Racism: John Bull, Johnny Reb, and the Good Templars* (Lexington: University Press of Kentucky, 1996), 13.
13. Tyrell, *Sobering Up*; Glenda Elizabeth Gilmore, *Gender and Jim Crow: Women and the Politics of White Supremacy in North Carolina, 1896–1920* (Chapel Hill: University of North Carolina Press, 1996), 46; Fahey, *Temperance and Racism*, 24–29; *Constitutions of the Order of the Sons of Temperance of North America* (Boston: Wright & Potter, 1866); Bordin, *Woman and Temperance*, xviii, 4–5.
14. Patricia Hill, *The World Their Household: The American Woman's Foreign Mission Movement and Cultural Transformation, 1870–1920* (Ann Arbor: University of Michigan Press, 1985); Louise Michele Newman, *White Women's Rights: The Racial Origins of Feminism in the United States* (New York: Oxford University Press, 1999), 53; Leslie Kathrin Dunlap, "In the Name of the Home: Temperance Women and Southern Grass-Roots Politics, 1873–1933," PhD diss., Northwestern University, 2001, 2.
15. Londonderry, Pa., WCTU, Minute Books (1887–92), Jan. 15, 1887, FWMLA.
16. "Constitution," Warren Central, Pa., WCTU no. 3, Minute Book, 1888, FWMLA; "Constitution for a Local W.C.T.U.," in Willard, *Woman and Temperance*, 639.
17. *Signal*, Oct. 14, 1880.
18. *Signal*, Feb. 5, 1880.
19. Upton Sinclair, *The Cup of Fury* (Great Neck, N.Y.: Channel Press, 1956).
20. Joseph R. Gusfield, *Symbolic Crusade: Status Politics and the American Temperance Movement* (Champaign: University of Illinois Press, 1963); Lisa McGirr, *The War on Alcohol: Prohibition and the Rise of the American State* (New York: W. W. Norton, 2016); Bordin, *Woman and Temperance*, 23; Alison M. Parker, *Purifying America: Women, Cultural Reform, and Pro-Censorship Activism, 1873–1933* (Urbana: University of Illinois Press, 1997).
21. Frances E. Willard, *Glimpses of Fifty Years: The Autobiography of an American Woman* (Chicago: Woman's Temperance Publication Association, ca. 1889), 368; *Daily Saratogian*, June 23, 1881, Scrapbook no. 5, FWMLA; Emma Adroit to Willard, May 24, 1880, FWMLA.
22. Annie Wittenmyer, preface to *Under the Guns: A Woman's Reminiscences of the Civil War* (Boston: E. B. Stillings & Co., 1895); George M. Frederickson, *The Inner Civil War: Northern Intellectuals and the Crisis of the Union* (New York: Harper & Row, 1965), 98; Frank Moore, *Women of the War: Their Heroism and*

Self-Sacrifice (Chicago: R. C. Treat, 1868), 576–80; Linus P. Brockett and Mary C. Vaughan, *Woman's Work in the Civil War: A Record of Heroism, Patriotism, and Patience* (Philadelphia: Zeigler, McCurdy, 1867), 375–77.

23. Wittenmyer, *Under the Guns*, 259–67; Willard, *Woman and Temperance*, 160–67.

24. Frederickson, *Inner Civil War*, 112; Dunlap, "In the Name of the Home," 26.

25. K. Austin Kerr, *Organized for Prohibition: A New History of the Anti-Saloon League* (New Haven, Conn.: Yale University Press, 1985); Kenneth Lipartito, "The Utopian Corporation," in *Constructing Corporate America: History, Politics, Culture*, ed. Kenneth Lipartito and David B. Sicilia (New York: Oxford University Press, 2004), 94–119.

26. *Inter Ocean* (Chicago), Aug. 24, 1881, Scrapbook no. 5, FWMLA; Joshua Paddison, "Woman Is Everywhere the Purifier," in *California Women and Politics: From the Gold Rush to the Great Depression*, ed. Robert W. Cherny, Mary Ann Irwin, and Ann Marie Wilson (Lincoln: University of Nebraska Press, 2011), 59–76; "Address of the President," *Minutes of the National Woman's Christian Temperance Union at the Tenth Annual Meeting in Detroit, Michigan, October 31 to November 3, 1883* (Cleveland: Home Publishing Co., 1883), 55–56, WASM; Bordin, *Woman and Temperance*, 90–91.

27. Toyoji Sasaki to Willard, Oct. 16, 1890, FWMLA.

28. Bordin, *Woman and Temperance*, 67.

29. Frances Willard to Mary Willard, June 19, 1881, FWMLA; "Home Protection," *Association for the Advancement of Women: Papers Read at the Fourth Congress of Women in Philadelphia* (Washington, D.C.: Todd Brothers, 1877), 81–87; Gifford and Slagell, *Let Something Good Be Said*, 24.

30. Ray Strachey, *Frances Willard: Her Life and Work* (London: T. Fisher Unwin, 1912), 87, 109.

31. Mary Earhart, *Frances Willard: From Prayer to Politics* (Chicago: University of Chicago Press, 1944), 48–96; Willard, *Glimpses of Fifty Years*, 133.

32. Strachey, *Frances Willard*, 160–61; Frances Willard, "Address Before the Illinois Senate," *Citizen's League*, June 14, 1879, Scrapbook no. 32, FWMLA; Eglise Reforme de Paris to Willard, Feb. 7, 1878, FWMLA.

33. Bordin, *Frances Willard*, 3–73; Willard, *Glimpses of Fifty Years*, 198–244.

34. *Minutes of the Tenth WCTU Annual Meeting, 1883*.

35. Bordin, *Woman and Temperance*, 130.

36. Willard, *Glimpses of Fifty Years*, 368–69.

37. *Minutes of the National Woman's Christian Temperance Union, at the Eleventh Annual Meeting in St. Louis, Missouri, October 22 to 25, 1884* (Chicago: Woman's Temperance Publication Association, 1884), 67, WASM; Kathryn Kish Sklar, *Florence Kelley and the Nation's Work: The Rise of Women's Political Culture, 1830–1900* (New Haven, Conn.: Yale University Press, 1995), 74; Strachey, *Frances Willard*, 228–29.

38. W. J. Rorabaugh, *The Alcoholic Republic: An American Tradition* (New York: Oxford University Press, 1979).

39. Tyrrell, *Sobering Up*, 28, 316; Bordin, *Woman and Temperance*, 6.

40. "Address of State Pres. Mrs. S. H. Barteau, St. Paul, Sept. 28, 1880," in *A Brief*

History of the Minnesota Woman's Christian Temperance Union, ed. Bessie Lathe Scovell (St. Paul: Bruce, 1939), 64.

41. *Signal*, Jan. 15, 1880; John McDonald, *Secrets of the Whiskey Ring* (Chicago: Belford, Clarke, 1880), FWMLA.

42. *Signal*, March 9, 1882; *Minutes of the Woman's National Christian Temperance Union at the Eighth Annual Meeting, in Washington, D.C., October 26–29, 1881* (Brooklyn: Union-Angus Steam Publishing, 1881), cxxii, WASM; *Minutes of the National Woman's Christian Temperance Union, at the Ninth Annual Meeting, in Louisville, Ky.* (Brooklyn: Martin, Carpenter, 1882), lx–lxi, lxxvii, WASM.

43. World WCTU, 1893; *Signal*, May 4, 1882; Terence Powderly to Willard, Dec. 12, 1886, Sept. 20, 1889, FWMLA; *Report of the Sixth Annual Meeting of the WCTU of Tennessee, Held in Chattanooga, Sept. 14, 15 & 16, 1887* (Memphis: Press of S. C. Touf, 1887), 35–36.

44. Frances Willard, "Home Protection [II]," July 4, 1879, in Gifford and Slagell, *Let Something Good Be Said*, 42; Frances Willard, "Reflex Influence of This Work upon the Workers," in *The Minutes of the Woman's National Christian Temperance Union* (New York: National Temperance Society and Publication House, 1880), 9–25; *Daily Saratogian*, June 23, 1881, Scrapbook no. 5, FWMLA; Frances Willard, "The Dawn of Woman's Day," Oct. 4, 1888, in Gifford and Slagell, *Let Something Good Be Said*, 136; Frances E. Willard, *A Wheel Within a Wheel: How I Learned to Ride the Bicycle* (Chicago: Fleming H. Revell, 1895), 39.

45. *Signal*, April 20, 1882; Willard to John H. Vincent, Sept. 29, 1877, FEWL.

46. *Methodist*, Jan. 28, 1882, Scrapbook no. 19, FWMLA.

47. *Daily Saratogian*, June 23, 1881, Scrapbook no. 5, FWMLA; *A Brief History of the Minnesota Woman's Christian Temperance Union*, ed. Bessie Lathe Scovell (St. Paul: Bruce, 1939), 34–43; Dorcas James Spencer, *A History of the Woman's Christian Temperance Union of Northern and Central California* (Oakland: West Coast Printing Co., 1911), 38; Paddison, "Woman Is Everywhere the Purifier," 70.

48. Bordin, *Woman and Temperance*, 58; Willard, "Home Protection."

49. *Signal*, April 6 and 13, 1882; Frances Willard, "Address Before the Illinois Senate," *Citizen's League*, June 14, 1879, in Gifford and Slagell, *Let Something Good Be Said*, 26–32.

50. *Signal*, April 27, 1882.

51. *Union Signal*, Oct. 21, 1886.

52. Frances Willard, *A White Life for Two* (Chicago: Woman's Temperance Publishing Association, 1890); Newman, *White Women's Rights*, 128.

53. Sue Davis, *The Political Thought of Elizabeth Cady Stanton* (New York: New York University Press, 2008), 85–92; *Boston Woman's Journal*, April 18, 1874, in Jack S. Blocker Jr., "Separate Paths: Suffragists and the Women's Temperance Crusade," *Signs* 10 (1985): 460–76.

54. Lucy Stone to Frances Willard, Dec. 1, 1881, FWMLA; Elisabeth S. Clemens, "Securing Political Returns to Social Capital: Women's Associations in the United States, 1880s–1920s," *Journal of Interdisciplinary History* 29 (1999): 613–38.

55. Lide Meriwether, lecture notes before Memphis Equal Suffrage Club, ca. 1890, LPM.
56. Willard, "Dawn of Woman's Day," 133–36; Willard, "Home Protection," 136; Bordin, *Woman and Temperance*, 111; Anastatia Sims, "'The Sword of the Spirit': The WCTU and Moral Reform in North Carolina, 1883–1933," *North Carolina Historical Review* 64 (1987): 409–10; *Minutes of the Woman's Christian Temperance Union at the Annual Meeting Held in Methodist Church at High Point, North Carolina, September 10 and 11, 1885* (Greensboro, N.C.: Thomas, Reese, & Co., 1885), 22; Crystal N. Feimster, *Southern Horrors: Women and the Politics of Rape and Lynching* (Cambridge, Mass.: Harvard University Press, 2009), 68–74.
57. Mary Ellen Curtin, *Black Prisoners and Their World: Alabama, 1865–1900* (Charlottesville: University Press of Virginia, 2000), 112–29; Feimster, *Southern Horrors*, 62–71; Sarah Haley, *No Mercy Here: Gender, Punishment, and the Making of Jim Crow Modernity* (Chapel Hill: University of North Carolina Press, 2016), 119–55.
58. *Signal*, Feb. 16 and March 9, 1882; Silena Moore Holman, "Mrs. Lide Meriwether," LPM; "Address of the President," *Minutes of the Tenth WCTU Annual Meeting, 1883*, 63–64; Sarah B. Cooper to Frances Willard, Aug. 15, 1887, FWMLA; *Minutes of the Thirteenth Annual Convention of the Woman's Christian Temperance Union of California at San Jose, October 18 to 21, 1892* (Woodland, Calif.: Lee & Warren, 1892), 59, 130–31; Spencer, *Woman's Christian Temperance Union of Northern and Central California*, 28.
59. *Signal*, March 9 and 30, April 20, 1882; Spencer, *Woman's Christian Temperance Union of Northern and Central California*, 24, 28.
60. Dio Lewis to Frances Willard, Aug. 24, 1885, FWMLA; Bordin, *Woman and Temperance*, 109; "Hygiene," *Minutes of the Eighth WCTU Annual Meeting, 1881*, lxxiv–lxxv; "Report on the Department of Hygiene," *Minutes of the Tenth WCTU Annual Meeting, 1883*, lvii.
61. *Signal*, June 8, 1882; Warren Central, Pa., WCTU no. 3, Minute Book, Dec. 6, 1888, Feb. 5, 1889, FWMLA; Bordin, *Woman and Temperance*, 111.
62. Willard, *Wheel Within a Wheel*; *Minutes of the Tenth WCTU Annual Meeting, 1883*, 63–64; Willard, "Dawn of Woman's Day," 131.

5. WOMEN'S PARTY

1. *Rock Islander*, July 16, 1881, Scrapbook no. 5, FWMLA; *National Liberator*, Aug. 28, 1881, Scrapbook no. 5, FWMLA; Willard, *Glimpses of Fifty Years*, 371–74; Bordin, *Woman and Temperance*, 77.
2. Willard, *Glimpses of Fifty Years*, 372; Gordon to Mary Willard, March 18, 1881, FWMLA.
3. *Rock Islander*, July 16, 1871, Scrapbook no. 5, FWMLA; *Our Union*, Aug. 1881, Scrapbook no. 5, FWMLA; *National Liberator*, Aug. 28, 1881, Scrapbook no. 5, FWMLA; Ellen E. Hebron to Mrs. J. F. Willard, April 25, 1889, FWMLA.
4. Dunlap, "In the Name of the Home," 29–35; Willard, *Glimpses of Fifty Years*, 33; "Annual Address," *Minutes of the Eighth WCTU Annual Meeting, 1881*, lxxv.
5. Willard, *Glimpses of Fifty Years*, 372.
6. Ruth Bordin, *Frances Willard: A Biography* (Chapel Hill: University of North Carolina Press, 1986), 15, 22; Strachey, *Frances Willard*, 87.

7. Barton to Willard, Aug. 26, Oct. 1, 1881, FWMLA; Barton to Saunders, Jan. 15, April 7, 1885, NGPH.

8. The WCTU in Grass Valley, California, had claimed to be the first union, but Frances Willard decided that the honor belonged to Fredonia. See Spencer, *Woman's Christian Temperance Union of Northern and Central California*, 15; Bordin, *Woman and Temperance*, 34.

9. Donald B. Marti, *Women of the Grange: Mutuality and Sisterhood in Rural America, 1866–1920* (New York: Greenwood Press, 1991), 8–10, 113; Thomas Summerhill, *Harvest of Dissent: Agrarianism in Nineteenth-Century New York* (Urbana: University of Illinois Press, 2005), 195, 210–11.

10. Blum, *Reforging the White Republic*.

11. Willard, *Glimpses of Fifty Years*, 373; *Central Christian Advocate* (St. Louis), June 15, 1881, Scrapbook no. 5, FWMLA; *Minutes of the Eighth WCTU Annual Meeting, 1881*, lxxv; *Rock Islander*, July 16, 1881, Scrapbook no. 5, FWMLA; *National Liberator*, Aug. 28, 1881, Scrapbook no. 5, FWMLA.

12. Willard, *Glimpses of Fifty Years*, 162–63; "The Race Problem: Miss Willard on the Political Puzzle of the South," *Voice*, Oct. 23, 1890, WASM.

13. *Rock Islander*, July 16, 1881, Scrapbook no. 5, FWMLA.

14. H. A. Scomp, *King Alcohol in the Realm of King Cotton* (Chicago: Blakely, 1888), 719.

15. *National Liberator*, Aug. 28, 1881, Scrapbook no. 5, FWMLA.

16. *Minutes of the Eighth WCTU Annual Meeting, 1881*, 26–27; Joan Marie Johnson, "Sallie Chapin: The Woman's Christian Temperance Union and Reconciliation After the Civil War," in *South Carolina Women: Their Lives and Times*, ed. Marjorie Julian Spruill, Valinda W. Littlefield, and Joan Marie Johnson (Athens: University of Georgia Press, 2010), 2:87–104.

17. *Minutes of the Eighth WCTU Annual Meeting, 1881*, lxxviii, 32; Frances Willard, "Address to the Committee on Resolutions of the Republican National Convention, June 4, 1884," in Gifford and Slagell, *Let Something Good Be Said*, 88.

18. Varina Davis to Willard, March 24, 1882, and Jan. 22, 1888, FWMLA.

19. Bradley T. Johnson, *Address Delivered by Gen. Bradley T. Johnson Before the Society of the Army and Navy of the Confederate States in the State of Maryland, and the Association of the Maryland Line, at Maryland Hall, Baltimore, Md., on Tuesday, November 16, 1886* (Baltimore: Andrew J. Conlon, 1886); Mrs. Gen. Bradley T. Johnson to Willard, Oct. 25, 1883, FWMLA.

20. Lucian Lamar Knight, *A Standard History of Georgia and Georgians* (Chicago: Lewis, 1917), 6:3226; Willard, *Woman and Temperance*, 557.

21. Willard, "Address to the Committee on Resolutions," 88.

22. Clara C. Chapin, *Thumb Nail Sketches of White Ribbon Women* (Chicago: Woman's Temperance Publishing, 1895), 28–29; Caroline E. Janney, *Burying the Dead but Not the Past: Ladies' Memorial Associations and the Lost Cause* (Chapel Hill: University of North Carolina Press, 2008); Willard, *Woman and Temperance*, 543–46; Johnson, "Sallie Chapin."

23. Sallie F. Chapin, *Fitz-Hugh St. Clair, the South Carolina Rebel Boy; or, It Is No Crime to Be Born a Gentleman* (Philadelphia: Claxton, Remsen & Haffelfinger, 1873), 247–52.

24. Willard, "Address to the Committee on Resolutions," 88.

25. Rebecca Edwards, *Angels in the Machinery: Gender in American Party Politics from the Civil War to the Progressive Era* (New York: Oxford University Press, 1997), 43.

26. *Signal*, Sept. 7, 1882.

27. *Minutes of the Eighth WCTU Annual Meeting, 1881*, lxxx; *Signal*, Feb. 16, June 15, and Sept. 7, 1882.

28. Willard, *Woman and Temperance*, 546; Belle Kearney, *A Shareholder's Daughter* (St. Louis: St. Louis Christian Advocate Co., 1900), 118.

29. Kearney, *A Slaveholder's Daughter*, 34, 108–109; Feimster, *Southern Horrors*, 199.

30. Sarah Wilkerson Freeman, "The Pursuit of Gender Equality," in *Tennessee Women: Their Lives and Times*, ed. Beverly Greene Bond and Sarah Wilkerson Freeman (Athens: University of Georgia Press, 2015), 2:182–214.

31. Ebenezer Lafayette Dohoney, *Man: His Origin, Nature and Destiny* (St. Louis: J. Burns Publishing Co., 1885), 22, 52–53, 331–35.

32. *Signal*, Feb. 23, 1882; Strachey, *Frances Willard*, 87; James D. Ivy, "'The Lone Star State Surrenders to a Lone Woman': Frances Willard's Forgotten 1882 Texas Temperance Tour," *Southwestern Historical Quarterly* 102 (1988): 44–61; "Ebenezer Lafayette Dohoney," *The Handbook of Texas*, tshaonline.org/handbook/online/articles/fdo07; *Minutes of the Eighth WCTU Annual Meeting*, 1881, lxxx.

33. Richard Jensen, *The Winning of the Midwest: Social and Political Conflict, 1888–1896* (Chicago: University of Chicago Press, 1971), 93; Edwards, *Angels in the Machinery*, 46–47; Strachey, *Frances Willard*, 265; Bordin, *Woman and Temperance*, 131.

34. Willard, *Glimpses of Fifty Years*, 447–52.

35. *Union Signal*, Jan. 24, 1889, in Dunlap, "In the Name of the Home," 39.

36. Kearney, *Slaveholder's Daughter*, 187–88; *Union Signal*, June 21, 1888, in Edwards, *Angels in the Machinery*, 47.

37. Howard to Willard, Dec. 3, 1891, FWMLA.

38. Strachey, *Frances Willard*, 258; Wittenmyer, *Under the Guns*, 134–37; Frances Willard, "The Greatest Party," *Our Day*, June 1, 1888, in Gifford and Slagell, *Let Something Good Be Said*, 117–22.

39. Bordin, *Woman and Temperance*, 129; Edwards, *Angels in the Machinery*, 49–50; Ian Tyrrell, *Woman's World/Woman's Empire: The Woman's Christian Temperance Union in International Perspective, 1880–1930* (Chapel Hill: University of North Carolina Press, 1991), 44.

40. Strachey, *Frances Willard*, 271–72; *History and Minutes of the National Council of Women of the United States*, ed. Louise Barnum Robbins (Boston: E. B. Stilling, 1898), 1–23.

41. Elizabeth Cady Stanton, "Address to Anniversary of American Equal Rights Association, May 12, 1869, New York City," in *Elizabeth Cady Stanton, Feminist as Thinker: A Reader in Documents and Essays*, ed. Ellen Carol DuBois and Richard Cándida Smith (New York: New York University Press, 2007), 189–91; Faye E. Dudden, *Fighting Chance: The Struggle over Woman Suffrage and Black Suffrage in Reconstruction America* (New York: Oxford University Press, 2011), 158–69.

42. Rachel Foster Avery, *Transactions of the National Council of Women of the United*

States, Assembled in Washington, D.C., February 22 to 24, 1891 (Philadelphia: J. B. Lippincott, 1891), 86–91.

43. Monroe A. Majors, *Noted Negro Women, Their Triumphs and Activities* (Chicago: Donohue & Henneberry, 1893), 23–26; Chapin, *Thumb Nail Sketches of White Ribbon Women*, 60; Frances Smith Foster, *A Brighter Coming Day: A Frances Ellen Watkins Harper Reader* (New York: Feminist Press at the City University of New York, 1990), 13.

44. William Still, *The Underground Railroad* (Chicago: Johnson Publishing Co., 1872), 784–91; Bettye Collier-Thomas, "Frances Ellen Watkins Harper: Abolitionist and Feminist," in *African American Women and the Vote, 1837–1965*, ed. Ann D. Gordon (Amherst: University of Massachusetts Press, 1997), 41–65; Nell Irvin Painter, *Sojourner Truth: A Life, a Symbol* (New York: W. W. Norton, 1996), 223–25; Margaret Washington, *Sojourner Truth's America* (Urbana: University of Illinois Press, 2009), 286, 316; "Frances Ellen Watkins Harper," in *Black Women in America*, 2nd ed., ed. Darlene Clark Hine (New York: Oxford University Press, 2005), 22–25.

45. Dudden, *Fighting Chance*, 54–55; Foster, *Brighter Coming Day*, 217.

46. Still, *Underground Railroad*, 791; Davis, *"We Will Be Satisfied with Nothing Less,"* 67–69.

47. Dudden, *Fighting Chance*, 57–62, 79–88, 154–58; Laura E. Free, *Suffrage Reconstructed: Gender, Race, and Voting Rights in the Civil War Era* (Ithaca, N.Y.: Cornell University Press, 2015), 159–60.

48. Frances E. W. Harper, *Minnie's Sacrifice*, in *Minnie's Sacrifice; Sowing and Reaping; Trail and Triumph: Three Rediscovered Novels by Frances E. W. Harper*, ed. Frances Smith Foster (Boston: Beacon Press, 1994), 78–79.

49. Still, *Underground Railroad*, 797–804.

50. Frances Harper, "The Great Problem to Be Solved" (lecture at centennial of the Pennsylvania Society for Promoting the Abolition of Slavery, Philadelphia, April 14, 1875), in Foster, *Brighter Coming Day*, 219–20.

51. Harper, *Minnie's Sacrifice*, 78–79; Frances Harper, "The Woman's Christian Temperance Union," in Foster, *Brighter Coming Day*, 281; Lisa G. Materson, *For the Freedom of Her Race: Black Women and the Electoral Politics in Illinois, 1877–1932* (Chapel Hill: University of North Carolina Press, 2009), 52–53.

52. Hellen M. Barker to Frances Willard, Feb. 15, 1896, and National WCTU Convention Minutes, 1895, clipping, and handwritten biography, in "Lucy Thurman Correspondence and Articles, 1895," AAW.

53. Harper, "Woman's Christian Temperance Union," 282; Gilmore, *Gender and Jim Crow*, 48–52; Bordin, *Woman and Temperance*, 82–84.

54. Harper, "Woman's Christian Temperance Union," 281–83; Still, *Underground Railroad*, 801–808; Alison M. Parker, "Frances Watkins Harper and the Search for Women's Interracial Alliances," in *Susan B. Anthony and the Struggle for Equal Rights*, ed. Mary M. Huth and Christine L. Ridarsky (Rochester, N.Y.: University of Rochester Press, 2012), 159.

55. *Union Signal*, Feb. 16, 1888, WASM.

56. *Union Signal*, April 26, 1883.

57. Gilmore, *Gender and Jim Crow*, 46; *Minutes of the Eighth WCTU Annual Meeting, 1881*, xiii, 26–27.

58. Willard, "Race Problem."

59. Dunlap, "In the Name of the Home," 37n48.

60. Foster, *Brighter Day Coming*, 217; Still, *Underground Railroad*, 801.

61. Avery, *Transactions of the National Council of Women*, 81–86.

62. Ibid., 86–91.

63. "Address of Frances E. Willard, President of the Woman's National Council of the United States, at Its First Triennial Meeting, Albaugh's Opera House, Washington, D.C., February 22–25, 1891," in Gifford and Slagell, *Let Something Good Be Said*, 156–57; Strachey, *Frances Willard*, 102; Newman, *White Women's Rights*, 117.

64. Bushyhead to Mrs. L. H. Staples, May 18, 1881, FWMLA; Frances Willard, "A Quaker Conquest," *Boston Daily Advertiser*, Aug. 19, 1881.

65. Bordin, *Woman and Temperance*, 85; Spencer, *WCTU of Northern and Central California*, 48–49; *Minutes of the Thirteenth Annual Convention of the WCTU of California*, 128.

66. Paddison, "Woman Is Everywhere the Purifier," 64; Elizabeth Wheeler Andrew, "The Origin, History, and Development of the World's Woman's Christian Temperance Union," in *The World's Congress of Representative Women*, ed. May Wright Sewall (Chicago: Rand, McNally, 1891), 399–412.

67. *Union Signal*, Sept. 20, 1888, Feb. 5, 1891, WASM.

68. *Minutes of the Second Biennial Convention and Executive Committee Meetings of the World's Christian Temperance Union* (Chicago: Woman's Temperance Publishing Assoc., 1893), 25; Tyrrell, *Woman's World/Woman's Empire*, 85, 223.

69. Willard, "Address to the Woman's National Council."

70. Ibid.

71. Bordin, *Woman and Temperance*, 92, 108; *Minutes of the Second Biennial WCTU Convention, 1893*, 90.

72. Willard, "Address to the Woman's National Council."

6. LABOR'S HOUR

1. Donald L. Miller and Richard E. Sharpless, *The Kingdom of Coal: Work, Enterprise, and Ethnic Communities in the Mine Fields* (Philadelphia: University of Pennsylvania Press, 1985), 110; Thomas W. Knox, *Underground; or, Life Below the Surface* (Hartford: J. B. Burr, 1874), 578–89; James J. Corrigay, "The Great Disaster at Avondale Colliery, September 6, 1869," Mine Safety and Health Administration, U.S. Department of Labor, n.d., arlweb.msha.gov/District/Dist_01/Reports/Avondale/letter.htm.

2. Mark Aldrich, "The Perils of Mining Anthracite: Regulation, Technology, and Safety, 1870–1945," *Pennsylvania History* 64 (1997): 361–83; Anthony F. C. Wallace, "The Perception of Risk in Nineteenth Century Anthracite Mining Operations," *Proceedings of the American Philosophical Society* 127 (1983): 99–106; Terence V. Powderly, *The Path I Trod: The Autobiography of Terence Powderly*, ed. Harry J. Carman, Henry David, and Paul N. Guthrie (New York: Columbia University Press, 1940), 24; *Labor World* (Duluth, Minn.), Dec. 11, 1915.

3. Powderly, *Path I Trod*, 24, 35; Craig Phelan, *Grand Master Workman: Terence Powderly and the Knights of Labor* (Westport, Conn.: Greenwood Press, 2000), 40n20; Richard Oestreicher, "Terence V. Powderly, the Knights of Labor, and Artisanal Republicanism," in *Labor Leaders in America*, ed. Melvyn Dubofsky and Warren Van Tine (Urbana: University of Illinois Press, 1987), 30–61.

4. Engels to Kelley-Wischnewetzky, Dec. 28, 1886, and preface to the American edition of *The Condition of the Working Class in England*, Jan. 26, 1887, in *Marx and Engels on the Trade Unions*, ed. Kenneth Lapides (New York: Praeger, 1987), 130–40, 142.

5. *Historical Statistics of the United States, Colonial Times to 1970* (Washington, D.C.: U.S. Government Printing Office, 1975), 138–39; Jonathan Garlock, *Guide to the Local Assemblies of the Knights of Labor* (Westport, Conn.: Greenwood Press, 1982), xv.

6. Powderly, *Path I Trod*, 48; David Montgomery, *The Fall of the House of Labor: The Workplace, the State, and American Labor Activism, 1865–1925* (Cambridge, U.K.: Cambridge University Press, 1987), 9–57.

7. Calvin Ewing, "Address on the Organization of a State [California] Assembly," 1886, KLR; "Knights of Labor Platform," in *Labor: Its Rights and Wrongs, Statements and Comments by the Leading Men of Our Nation on the Labor Question of To-Day* (Washington, D.C.: Labor Publishing Co., 1886), 29–33.

8. Powderly, *Thirty Years of Labor*, 76, 121, 151, 301–25; Richard T. Ely, *The Labor Movement in America* (New York: Thomas Y. Crowell & Co., 1886), 130, 375–89; Earhart, *Frances Willard*, 75.

9. Powderly, *Path I Trod*, 48.

10. Ibid., 36.

11. Ibid., 49, 51.

12. Ibid., 55; George McNeill, "The Problem of To-Day," in McNeill, *Labor Movement, the Problem of To-Day*, ed. George McNeil (New York: M. W. Hazen Co., 1887), 454–69.

13. Norman J. Ware, *The Labor Movement in the United States, 1860–1895* (New York: D. Appleton, 1929), xiv.

14. Foner, *Reconstruction*, 32–33; Grace Palladino, *Another Civil War: Labor, Capital, and the State in the Anthracite Regions of Pennsylvania, 1840–68* (Urbana: University of Illinois Press, 1990), 95–120; Kevin Kenny, *Making Sense of the Molly Maguires* (New York: Oxford University Press, 1998), 82–83; Montgomery, *Beyond Equality*, 107, 158.

15. Kenny, *Making Sense of the Molly Maguires*, 83–85.

16. *Fincher's Trades' Review*, Dec. 2, 1863, in *A Documentary History of Industrial Society, IX*, ed. John R. Commons et al. (Cleveland: Arthur H. Clark, 1910), 279–83.

17. "Plan of Action," in *Documentary History of Industrial Society*, ed. Commons et al., 302–305; Hyman Kuritz, "Ira Steward and the Eight Hour Day," *Science and Society* 20 (1956): 118–34.

18. Dudden, *Fighting Chance*, 62.

19. Stuart Ewen, "Poverty, Middle-Class Poverty, and the Tyranny of Debt: Excerpt of 'Poverty' by Ira Steward, 1873," *Women's Studies Quarterly* 42 (2014): 131–36.

20. Montgomery, *Beyond Equality*, 260.

21. *Nation*, Sept. 5, 1872.

22. Jonathan Grossman, *William Sylvis: Pioneer of American Labor* (New York: Columbia University Press, 1945), 27, 64–65, 80; Montgomery, *Beyond Equality*, 224; *The Life, Speeches, Labors & Essays of William H. Sylvis*, ed. James C. Sylvis (Philadelphia: Claxton, Remsen & Haffelfinger, 1872), 45–47.

23. *Fincher's Trades' Review*, Oct. 14, 1865, in *Documentary History of Industrial Society, IX*, ed. Commons et al., 287; George Gunton, *Wealth and Progress: A Critical Examination of the Labor Problem* (New York: D. Appleton, 1887; reprint 1970).

24. David R. Roediger and Philip S. Foner, *Our Own Time: A History of American Labor and the Working Day* (London: Verso Press, 1989), x, 81–121.

25. Grossman, *William Sylvis*, 426; Powderly, *Thirty Years of Labor*, 43, 242; Montgomery, *Beyond Equality*, 307, 313.

26. Montgomery, *Beyond Equality*, 307; Roediger and Foner, *Our Own Time*, 101–21; Harold W. Aurand, *From the Molly Maguires to the United Mine Workers: The Social Ecology of an Industrial Union, 1869–1897* (Philadelphia: Temple University Press, 1971), 68.

27. Ely, *Labor Movement in America*, 70.

28. William Sylvis, "Equalization," in Sylvis, *Life*, 264; John J. Jarrett in *Labor: Its Rights and Wrongs*, 60.

29. John B. Andrews, "Nationalisation (1860–1877)," in John R. Commons, *History of Labor in the United States*, vol. 2 (New York: Macmillan, 1918), 127–28.

30. Proceedings of the Second Session of the National Labor Union, New York, Sept. 21, 1868, and Cincinnati Congress, Aug. 1870, in *Documentary History of Industrial Society, IX*, ed. Commons et al., 195–207, 267; DuBois, *Feminism and Suffrage*, 105–25; Grossman, *William Sylvis*, 229.

31. Davis, *Political Thought of Elizabeth Cady Stanton*, 161–62; Second Session of the National Labor Union, 1868, 207; *Revolution*, Oct. 22, 1868, 241.

32. Dudden, *Fighting Chance*, 154–55; *Revolution*, July 2 and Oct. 1, 1868.

33. Baltimore Congress, Aug. 1866, in *Documentary History of Industrial Society, IX*, ed. Commons et al., 159, 187.

34. The National Colored Labor Convention, 1869, in *Documentary History of Industrial Society, IX*, ed. Commons et al., 244–53; Sylvis, *Life*, 231–49.

35. Powderly, *Thirty Years of Labor*, 52–53; Montgomery, *Beyond Equality*, 223; Obadiah Hicks, *Life of Richard F. Trevellick, the Labor Orator, or the Harbinger of the Eight-Hour System* (Joliet, Ill.: J. E. Williams, 1896), 52–60.

36. Montgomery, *Beyond Equality*, 224–25; W. Stephen Belko, *The Invincible Duff Green: Whig of the West* (Columbia: University of Missouri Press, 2006), 318, 443.

37. Sylvis, *Life*, 333–36.

38. Ibid., 83–84, 333–44.

39. Ibid., 333, 341; Montgomery, *Beyond Equality*, 404; Stephen Cresswell, *Multiparty Politics in Mississippi, 1877–1902* (Jackson: University Press of Mississippi, 1995), 24.

40. Baltimore Congress, Aug. 1866, and Philadelphia Congress, Aug. 1869, 139, 233–39.

41. Philadelphia Congress, 1869, and National Colored Labor Convention, 1869, 233–39, 254; Montgomery, *Beyond Equality*, 439.

42. Philadelphia Congress, 1869, 236.

43. Powderly, *Thirty Years of Labor*, 57; Cincinnati Congress, Aug. 15–22, 1870, in *Documentary History of Industrial Society, IX*, ed. Commons et al., 268; "Report of the House Committee Appointed to Visit the Cherokee Neutral Lands, 1870" (Topeka, Kans.: S. S. Prouty, 1870), 77–78.

44. *Boston Investigator*, July 6, 1870; Philadelphia Congress, 1869, National Colored Labor Convention, 1869, and Cincinnati Congress, 84, 87, 237, 250, 267.

45. New York Congress, 1868, in *Documentary History of Industrial Society, IX*, ed. Commons et al., 233–42.

46. Walter T. K. Nugent, *The Money Question During Reconstruction* (New York: W. W. Norton, 1967).

47. New York Congress, 1868, 235; Sylvis, *Life*, 239.

48. Destler, *American Radicalism*, 50–77.

49. Montgomery, *Beyond Equality*, 334, 425–47.

50. McNeill, *Labor Movement*, 150; Powderly, *Thirty Years of Labor*, 62; Leon Fink, *Workingmen's Democracy: The Knights of Labor and American Politics* (Urbana: University of Illinois Press, 1983), 185–86; Ware, *Labor Movement in the United States*, 15–17; *Ohio Farmer* (Cleveland), March 21 and Nov. 7, 1874; Ely, *Labor Movement in America*, 175; Steven B. Leikin, *The Practical Utopians: American Workers and the Cooperative Movement in the Gilded Age* (Detroit: Wayne State University Press, 2005), 19–20; Timothy Messer-Kruse, *The Yankee International: Marxism and the American Reform Tradition, 1848–1876* (Chapel Hill: University of North Carolina Press, 1998), 232–42.

51. Hild, *Greenbackers, Knights of Labor, and Populists*, 20–44.

52. Woods, *Knights of the Plow*, 129–30, 207.

53. Hild, *Greenbackers, Knights of Labor, and Populists*, 20–44; Ridge, *Ignatius Donnelly*, 170–71; Nicolas Barreyre, *Gold and Freedom: The Political Economy of Reconstruction* (Charlottesville: University of Virginia Press, 2015), 222–27; "National Greenback Platform of 1880," in Ellis B. Usher, *The Greenback Movement of 1875–1884 and Wisconsin's Part in It* (Milwaukee: Meisenheimer, 2011), 79–80; Mark A. Lause, *The Civil War's Last Campaign: James B. Weaver, the Greenback Labor Party, and the Politics of Race and Section* (Lanham, Md.: University Press of America, 2001); Phelan, *Grand Master Workman*, 65.

54. *Journal of United Labor*, June 15, 1880.

55. Cresswell, *Multiparty Politics in Mississippi*, 88.

7. EQUALIZERS

1. Powderly, *Thirty Years of Labor*, 81–91; McNeill, *Labor Movement*, 408.
2. *Labor: Its Rights and Wrongs*, 73.
3. Hild, *Greenbackers, Knights of Labor, and Populists*, 45–46; Powderly, *Thirty Years of Labor*, 64–65, 128.
4. Ware, *Labor Movement in the United States*, 35; Phelan, *Grand Master Workman*, 70–71; Ely, *Labor Movement in America*, 78; Record of the Proceedings of D.A. No. 7, of Ohio, Dec. 3–4, 1879, reel 65, PP; "Name of the Order," *Journal of United Labor*, June 15, 1880.
5. Cleveland Convention of the Knights of Labor, May 26, 1886, in *Labor: Its Rights and Wrongs*, 186; Ely, *Labor Movement in America*, 73, 177–78; William J. Tisdale, *The Knights Book* (New York, 1886), reel 91, 35, PP.
6. *John Swinton Paper*, Oct. 17, 1886, in Ware, *Labor Movement in the United States*, 83; Eleanor Marx and Edward Aveling, *The Working Class Movement in America* (London: Swan Sonnenschein and Co., 1891; reprint 2000), 144.
7. *Journal of United Labor*, June 15, 1880.
8. Selig Perlman, "Upheaval and Reorganization," in Commons, *History of Labor in the United States*, 2:347, 420; Ware, *Labor Movement in the United States*, 85–87; Charles A. Madison, *American Labor Leaders: Personalities and Forces in the Labor Movement* (New York: Harper & Brothers, 1950), 49–69; Gerald Grob, *Workers and Utopia: A Study of Ideological Conflict in the American Labor Movement, 1865–1900* (Evanston, Ill.: Northwestern University Press, 1961), 135–36; Oestreicher, "Terence V. Powderly, the Knights of Labor, and Artisanal Republicanism," in *Labor Leaders in America*, ed. Melvyn Dubofsky and Warren Van Tine, 57–59; Bruce Laurie, *Artisans into Workers: Labor in Nineteenth-Century America* (New York: Hill and Wang, 1989), 141–74; Kim Voss, *The Making of American Exceptionalism: The Knights of Labor and Class Formation in the Nineteenth Century* (Ithaca, N.Y.: Cornell University Press, 1993), 239.
9. Robert E. Weir, *Beyond Labor's Veil: The Culture of the Knights of Labor* (University Park: Pennsylvania State University Press, 1996); Phelan, *Grand Master Workman*.
10. Phelan, *Grand Master Workman*, 122.
11. Ware, *Labor Movement in the United States*, 61.
12. Powderly, *Path I Trod*, 14–17; Phelan, *Grand Master Workman*, 11–12.
13. Powderly, *Path I Trod*, 11–12; Edward T. James, "T. V. Powderly, a Political Profile," *The Pennsylvania Magazine of History and Biography* (Oct. 1975): 443–59; Phelan, *Grand Master Workman*, 15, 136; *Labor: Its Rights and Wrongs*, 28–29; Powderly, *Thirty Years of Labor*, 143–48.
14. Powderly, *Path I Trod*, 36, 317–82, 407–408.
15. Ibid., 42; *Journal of United Labor*, June 15, 1880; *Labor: Its Rights and Wrongs*, 67.
16. Peter Roberts, *The Anthracite Coal Industry: A Study of the Economic Conditions and Relations of the Cooperative Forces in the Development of the Anthracite Coal Industry of Pennsylvania* (New York: Macmillan, 1901), 159, 172–83;

Samuel Walker, "The Police and the Community: Scranton, Pennsylvania, 1866–1884, a Test Case," *American Studies* 19 (1978): 79–90; Powderly, *Path I Trod*, 30.

17. Kenny, *Making Sense of the Molly Maguires*, 281–84; Allan Pinkerton, *Strikers, Communists, Tramps, and Detectives* (New York: G. W. Carleton, 1878), 88; James, "Powderly, a Political Profile," 446; *Boston Congregationalist*, Feb. 27, 1878.

18. Roberts, *Anthracite Coal Industry*, 181–82; Robert V. Bruce, *1877: Year of Violence* (Indianapolis: Bobbs-Merrill, 1959), 296–99; Philip S. Foner, *The Great Labor Uprising of 1877* (New York: Monad Press, 1977), 77; Phelan, *Grand Master Workman*, 24–27.

19. *Journal of United Labor*, May 15, 1880; Vincent J. Falzone, "Terence V. Powderly: Politician and Progressive Mayor of Scranton, 1878–1884," *Pennsylvania History: A Journal of Mid-Atlantic Studies* 41 (1974): 288–309; Walker, "Police and the Community"; Phelan, *Grand Master Workman*, 27–30.

20. Powderly, *Thirty Years of Labor*, 57, 327–29; Powderly, *Path I Trod*, 381–89; Robert E. Weir, *Knights Unhorsed: Internal Conflict in a Gilded Age Social Movement* (Detroit: Wayne State University Press, 2000), 143.

21. *Saint Paul Globe*, Oct. 4, 1887, Feb. 13, 1888; Weir, *Knights Unhorsed*, 151; Powderly, *Thirty Years of Labor*, 303; Susan Levine, "Labor's True Woman: Domesticity and Equal Rights in the Knights of Labor," *Journal of American History* 70 (1983): 323–39.

22. Susan Levine, *Labor's True Woman: Carpet Weavers, Industrialization, and Labor Reform in the Gilded Age* (Philadelphia: Temple University Press, 1984), 7–21; Minutes of the Woman's Labor League Knights of Labor L.A. 5855 San Francisco, Feb. 24, 1886, Feb. 16 and March 2, 1887, KLR.

23. *Saint Paul Globe*, May 30, 1886; *Labor: Its Rights and Wrongs*, 176–77, 194, 201–206.

24. Powderly, *Path I Trod*, 381–89.

25. Ibid., 78, 388.

26. Ibid., 384; Hild, *Greenbackers, Knights of Labor, and Populists*, 83; George Bennie to Powderly, Jan. 24, 1887, and Powderly to Bennie, Jan. 28, 1887, in Levine, *Labor's True Woman*, 111–12.

27. Phelan, *Grand Master Workman*, 155; Levine, *Labor's True Woman*, 109.

28. *Saint Paul Globe*, May 30, 1886; Ware, *Labor Movement in the United States*, 347–49; Weir, *Knights Unhorsed*, 152; *Saint Paul Globe*, Oct. 8 and 9, 1887; *Minneapolis Star Tribune*, Oct. 5, 1887.

29. *Philadelphia Times*, Nov. 24, 1886; *Wilkes-Barre (Pa.) Sunday News*, Dec. 2, 1888; *Harrisburg Telegraph*, April 12, 1888; *San Francisco Chronicle*, Sept. 4, 1889.

30. Sklar, *Doing the Nation's Work*, 140–41; Weir, *Knights Unhorsed*, 147, 154; *Philadelphia Times*, Nov. 24, 1886.

31. *Los Angeles Herald*, March 29, 1888; *Inter Ocean* (Chicago), March 29, 1888; *Pittsburgh Dispatch*, Sept. 8, 1891.

32. *San Francisco Daily Evening Bulletin*, April 4, 1885; Powderly, *Path I Trod*, 230–33; Phelan, *Grand Master Workman*, 134; Sylvis, *Life*, 316–17.

33. Powderly, *Path I Trod*, 230–33.

34. Powderly, *Thirty Years of Labor*, 153–163.

35. William J. Tisdale, *The Knights Book: Matters Concerning Capital and Labor* (New York: Concord Cooperative, ca. 1886), 8–10, 20–22, reel 91, PP; Report of the Executive Board, Knights of Labor, Jan. 26, June 30, 1885, reel 91, PP; Proceedings of Division 31, N.D.A., 135, Knights of Labor, June 9, 1888, reel 91, PP.

36. *Labor: Its Rights and Wrongs*, 55.

37. Powderly, *Path I Trod*, 234; Powderly, *Thirty Years of Labor*, 84.

38. *Journal of United Labor*, July 15, 1880; Proceedings of the Second Semi-annual Convention of Sub-division No. 2 of N.D.A. 135, Knights of Labor, Held at Altoona, Pa., July 27–30, 1887, reel 91, PP.

39. *Journal of United Labor*, Oct. 15, 1880; Harold W. Aurand, *Coalcracker Culture: Work and Values in Pennsylvania Anthracite, 1835–1935* (Selinsgrove, Pa.: Susquehanna University Press, 2003), 17–22; John McBride, "Coal Miners," in McNeill, *Labor Movement*, 242–67; Proceedings of District Assembly No. 5, of West Virginia, April 6, 1881, reel 65, PP.

40. Proceedings of District Assembly No. 16, Nov. 28, 1882, Jan. 13, 1883, July 10, 1886, reel 65, PP; Aurand, *Coalcracker Culture*, 125; Thomas Dublin and Walter Licht, *Face of Decline: The Pennsylvania Anthracite Region in the Twentieth Century* (Ithaca, N.Y.: Cornell University Press, 2005), 21.

41. Statistician's Report Delivered Before District Assembly 16, Knights of Labor, at Its Session Held at Wilkes-Barre, Pa., July 30–31 and Aug. 1–2, 1888, reel 65, PP.

42. Proceedings of District Assembly No. 5, of West Virginia, April 6, 1881, reel 65, PP; Statistician's Report District Assembly 16, 1888; David Brody, *In Labor's Cause: Main Themes on the History of the American Worker* (New York: Oxford University Press, 1993), 131–74.

43. Roberts, *Anthracite Coal Industry*, 96.

44. Report of the Pennsylvania Knights of Labor Legislative Committee, Session of 1887, reel 91, PP.

45. Aurand, *From the Molly Maguires to the United Mine Workers*, 152–53; Aurand, *Coalcracker Culture*, 65–67; Pennsylvania Department of Internal Affairs, *Reports of the Inspectors of Mines, 1881* (Harrisburg, Pa.: State Printer, 1882), 118.

46. Report of the Executive Board, Oct. 2, 1884, reel 91, PP; Frank Gessner to Powderly, Apr. 21, 1884, reel 8, PP; Léon Watillon, *The Knights of Labor in Belgium* (Los Angeles: University of California, Institute of Industrial Relations, 1959), 6–13; Steven Parfitt, *Knights Across the Atlantic: The Knights of Labor in Britain and Ireland* (Liverpool: Liverpool University Press, 2016), 10–11.

47. Phelan, *Grand Master Workman*, 90, 118–19; Ware, *Labor Movement in the United States*, 129; Hild, *Greenbackers, Knights of Labor, and Populists*, 51.

48. Proceedings of the Miners' and Mine Laborers' K. of L. National Convention Held at St. Louis, Mo., May 20 to 22, 1886, and Report of Committee on Scale Basis, Cleveland, Ohio, Aug. 13, 1888, reel 91, PP.

49. Levine, *Labor's True Woman*, 74, 95–96.

50. First Annual Session of the Boot and Shoe Workers of the United States and Canada, Brockton, Mass., June 7 to 10, 1887, reel 91, PP.

51. White, *Railroaded*, 289; Shelton Stromquist, *Generation of Boomers: The Pattern of Railroad Conflict in Nineteenth-Century America* (Urbana: University of Illinois Press, 1987), 66–69; David Brundage, *Making of Western Labor Radicalism: Denver's Organized Workers, 1878–1905* (Urbana: University of Illinois Press, 1994), 54–57.

52. Mark Aldrich, *Death Rode the Rails: American Railroad Accidents and Safety, 1828–1965* (Baltimore: Johns Hopkins University Press, 2009), 103–105; Theresa A. Case, *The Great Southwest Railroad Strike and Free Labor* (College Station: Texas A&M University Press, 2010), 51.

53. Stromquist, *Generation of Boomers*, 48–69.

54. White, *Railroaded*.

55. Brundage, *Making of Western Labor Radicalism*, 54–60; Case, *Great Southwest Railroad Strike and Free Labor*, 107–108; John P. Enyeart, *The Quest for "Just and Pure Law": Rocky Mountain Workers and American Social Democracy, 1870–1924* (Stanford, Calif.: Stanford University Press, 2009), 41.

56. White, *Railroaded*, 186–223.

57. Case, *Great Southwest Railroad Strike and Free Labor*, 108–26; Stromquist, *Generation of Boomers*, 32.

58. Report of the Executive Board, June 30, July 27, Aug. 1, 1885, reel 91, PP.

59. Case, *Great Southwest Railroad Strike and Free Labor*, 129, 147.

60. Ruth A. Allen, *The Great Southwest Strike* (Austin: University of Texas Press, 1941), 71–91.

61. Powderly, *Path I Trod*, 134–39.

62. Michael J. Cassity, "Modernization and Social Crisis: The Knights of Labor and a Midwest Community, 1885–1886," *Journal of American History* 66 (1979): 41–61; Case, *Great Southwest Railroad Strike and Free Labor*, 152.

63. Martin Irons, "My Experience in the Labor Movement," *Lippincott's Magazine* 37 (1886): 618–27; Allen, *Great Southwest Strike*, 43; Charles Postel, *The Populist Vision* (New York: Oxford University Press, 2007), 215–18.

64. Case, *Great Southwest Railroad Strike and Free Labor*, 154, 161–77; Eric Arnesen, "'Like Banquo's Ghost, It Will Not Down': The Race Question and the American Railroad Brotherhoods, 1880–1920," *American Historical Review* 99 (1994): 1601–33.

65. Proceedings of District Assembly No. 16, July 10, 1886, reel 65, PP; Proceedings of Division 13, N.D.A. 135, June–July 1888, reel 91, PP; Weir, *Knights Unhorsed*, 61; Phelan, *Grand Master Workman*, 191.

66. Montgomery, *Beyond Equality*, 151–56; Proceedings of the Miners' and Mine Laborers' K. of L. National Convention Held at St. Louis, Mo., May 20 to 22, 1886, reel 91, PP; C. H. Salmons, *The Burlington Strike* (Aurora, Ill.: Bunnell and Ward, 1889), 255–60; Weir, *Knights Unhorsed*, 52, 61, 82.

67. Proceedings of the Second Semi-annual Convention of Sub-division No. 2 of N.D.A. 135, Knights of Labor, Held at Altoona, Pa., July 27–30, 1887, reel 91, PP; Proceedings of Division 13, N.D.A. 135, Knights of Labor, Wilkes-Barre, Pa., June–July, 1888, reel 91, PP; Proceedings of the Second Annual Session of the Miners' and Mine Laborers' Nat. Dist. Assembly, No. 135, Held at Cincinnati, Ohio, June 1–8, 1887, reel 91, PP.

68. McNeill, *Labor Movement*, 420–21.

69. Aurand, *From the Molly Maguires to the United Mine Workers*, 153–54.

70. First Annual Session of the Boot and Shoe Workers of the United States and Canada, Brockton, Mass., June 7 to 10, 1887, reel 91, PP; Herbert Gutman, *Power and Culture: Essays on the American Working Class* (New York: Pantheon Books, 1987), 385; Minutes of the Woman's Labor League Knights of Labor L.A. 5855 San Francisco, Dec. 15, 2016, KLR.

71. Craig Storti, *Incident at Bitter Creek: The Story of the Rock Springs Chinese Massacre* (Ames: Iowa State University Press, 1991), 65, 100–162.

72. Alexander Saxton, *The Indispensable Enemy: Labor and the Anti-Chinese Movement in California* (Berkeley: University of California Press, 1971; reprint 1995), 202–11; Brundage, *Making of Western Labor Radicalism*, 65; Storti, *Incident at Bitter Creek*, 131–62.

73. Carlos A. Schwantes, "Anti-Chinese Agitation to Reform Politics: The Legacy of the Knights of Labor in Washington and the Pacific Northwest," *Pacific Northwest Quarterly* 88 (1997): 174–84; Storti, *Incident at Bitter Creek*, 161–62; Case, *Great Southwest Railroad Strike and Free Labor*, 90–92.

74. *Journal of United Labor*, Aug. 15, 1880; Proceedings of the Ninth General Assembly [Knights of Labor], Held at Hamilton, Ont., Oct. 5–13, 1885, 160; Gunther Peck, *Reinventing Free Labor: Padrones and Immigrant Workers in the North American West, 1880–1930* (New York: Cambridge University Press, 2000); Stacey L. Smith, *Freedom's Frontier: California and the Struggle over Unfree Labor, Emancipation, and Reconstruction* (Chapel Hill: University of North Carolina Press, 2013).

75. Lawrence Goodwyn, *Democratic Promise: The Populist Moment in America* (New York: Oxford University Press, 1976), 288; Case, *Great Southwest Railroad Strike and Free Labor*, 179–80; *Journal of United Labor*, Aug. 15, 1880; Edlie L. Wong, *Racial Reconstruction: Black Inclusion, Chinese Exclusion, and the Fictions of Citizenship* (New York: New York University Press, 2015).

76. Melton Alonza McLaurin, *The Knights of Labor in the South* (Westport, Conn.: Greenwood Press, 1978),16; Daniel Letwin, *The Challenge of Interracial Unionism: Alabama Coal Miners, 1878–1921* (Chapel Hill: University of North Carolina Press, 1998), 77; Case, *Great Southwest Railroad Strike and Free Labor*, 14; Leon Fink, *The Long Gilded Age: American Capitalism and the Lessons of a New World Order* (Philadelphia: University of Pennsylvania Press, 2015), 25; Calvin Ewing, "Address on the Organization of a State [California] Assembly," 1886, KLR.

77. Charles J. McClain, *In Search of Equality: The Chinese Struggle Against Discrimination in Nineteenth-Century America* (Berkeley: University of California Press, 1994); Scott D. Seligman, *The First Chinese American: The Remarkable Life of Wong Chin Foo* (Hong Kong: Hong Kong University Press, 2013), 111–17, 199–202.

78. *Der Deutsche Correspondent* (Baltimore), May 12, 1887; *Saint Paul Globe*, May 29, 1887; James Winston, "Being Red and Black in Jim Crow America: On the Ideology and Travails of Afro-America's Socialist Pioneers," in *Time*

Longer than Rope: A Century of African American Activism, 1850–1950, ed. Charles M. Payne and Adam Green (New York: New York University Press, 2003), 361.

79. Proceedings of the Twelfth Regular Session of the General Assembly [Knights of Labor], Indianapolis, Nov. 13–27, 1888.

80. Jacqueline Jones, *Goddess of Anarchy: The Life and Times of Lucy Parsons, American Radical* (New York: Basic Books, 2017), 117–38; James Green, *Death in the Haymarket: A History of Chicago, the First Labor Movement and the Bombing That Divided Gilded Age America* (New York: Pantheon Books, 2006); Paul Avrich, *The Haymarket Tragedy* (Princeton, N.J.: Princeton University Press, 1984); Timothy Messer-Kruse, *The Haymarket Conspiracy: Transatlantic Networks* (Urbana: University of Illinois Press, 2012).

81. Green, *Death in the Haymarket*, 203; Phelan, *Grand Master Workman*, 169.

82. *Chicago Tribune*, Oct. 18, 1887; *Pittston (Pa.) Evening Gazette*, Dec. 29, 1886; Weir, *Knights Unhorsed*, 73–96.

83. Phelan, *Grand Master Workman*, 203; Green, *Death in the Haymarket*, 240, 251–52.

84. Enyeart, *"Just and Pure Law,"* 25–26; *Denver Labor Enquirer*, Dec. 16, 1882, in Brundage, *Making of Western Labor Radicalism*, 34; Weir, *Knights Unhorsed*, 73–96; Green, *Death in the Haymarket*, 97; *Journal of United Labor*, May 15, 1880.

85. Leikin, *Practical Utopians*; Ware, *Labor Movement in the United States*, 320–33; Brundage, *Making of Western Labor Radicalism*, 109–11; Alex Gorevitch, *From Slavery to the Cooperative Commonwealth: Labor and Republican Liberty in the Nineteenth Century* (Cambridge, U.K.: Cambridge University Press, 2015), 97–137.

86. Leikin, *Practical Utopians*, 12–13, 32.

87. Ware, *Labor Movement in the United States*, 322–23; Powderly, *Thirty Years of Labor*, 235; Leikin, *Practical Utopians*, 34; Messer-Kruse, *Haymarket Conspiracy*, 144; Messer-Kruse, *Yankee International*, 63, 74.

88. Proceedings of D.A. No. 7, of Ohio, Dec. 3–4, 1879, reel 65, PP.

89. Proceedings of D.A. No. 7, of Ohio, Oct. 6, 1880, reel 65, PP.

90. Franklin Henry Giddings, "Co-operation," in McNeill, *Labor Movement*, 508–31; M. Robertson, Lincoln, Kans., Apr. 17, 1884, reel 8, PP.

91. Ware, *Labor Movement in the United States*, 322; Fink, *Workingmen's Democracy*, 155; Levine, *Labor's True Woman*, 114–15.

92. *Inter Ocean* (Chicago), Dec. 18 and 29, 1886; *Chicago Tribune*, April 12, 1887; *Manhattan (Kans.) Mercury*, Oct. 10, 1887; *Philadelphia Times*, Nov. 14, 1887.

93. Report of the Directors and Officers to the Stockholders of the National K. of L. Cooperative Tobacco Co., Raleigh, N.C., 1886, reel 91, PP; Report of the Executive Board, March 23, 1885, reel 91, PP; Ely, *Labor Movement in America*, 187; Leikin, *Practical Utopians*, 81.

94. Report of the Executive Board, Sept. 23, Nov. 9, 1884, March 25, Aug. 1, 1885, reel 91, PP; Ware, *Labor Movement in the United States*, 329–32.

95. Powderly, *Thirty Years of Labor*, 234–39; McNeill, *Labor Movement*, 531.

8. SOCIAL EQUALITY

1. *Journal of United Labor*, Jan. 25, 1885; Proceedings of the General Assembly of the Knights of Labor, Sept. 1–10, 1884, 698; Phelan, *Grand Master Workman*, 151; Claudia Miner, "The 1886 Convention of the Knights of Labor," *Phylon* 44 (1983): 147–59; Hild, *Greenbackers, Knights of Labor, and Populists*, 52.

2. Powderly, "The South of Today," *Scranton Truth*, March 17, 1885, in Foner and Lewis, *Black Worker*, 250.

3. *Labor: Its Rights and Wrongs*, 212–14; Ely, *Labor Movement in America*, 139.

4. *Galveston Daily News*, Nov. 4 and 5, 1885; *Vicksburg (Miss.) Herald*, Nov. 14, 1885; *New York Times*, Nov. 4, 10, and 29, 1885; Case, *Great Southwest Railroad Strike and Free Labor*, 134–35; *New York Freeman*, April 10, 1886; Matthew Hild, "Organizing Across the Color Line: The Knights of Labor and Black Recruitment Efforts in Small-Town Georgia," *Georgia Historical Quarterly* 18 (1997): 287–310.

5. Bodenhamer to Powderly, April 10, 1889, in Foner and Lewis, *Black Worker*, 263.

6. Hild, *Greenbackers, Knights of Labor, and Populists*, 290; *Washington Bee*, July 2, 1887.

7. Ely, *Labor Movement in America*, 83, 89; Robin D. G. Kelley, "'We Are Not What We Seem': Rethinking Black Working-Class Opposition in the Jim Crow South," *Journal of American History* 80 (1993): 75–112; *New York Freeman*, Nov. 7, 1885.

8. Ross Carlin, Meridian, to Powderly, June 22, 1885, reel 10, PP.

9. Tera W. Hunter, *To 'Joy My Freedom: Southern Black Women's Lives and Labors After the Civil War* (Cambridge, Mass.: Harvard University Press, 1997), 74–97.

10. Hild, *Greenbackers, Knights of Labor, and Populists*, 83; V. E. St. Cloud to Powderly, Jan. 23, 1887, in Foner and Lewis, *Black Worker*, 257; J. M. Broughton to Powderly, June 10, 1885, reel 47, PP.

11. Ray to Powderly, May 19 and June 22, 1885, in Foner and Lewis, *Black Worker*, 251–52; Powderly to J. M. Broughton, June 12, 1885, reel 47, PP.

12. Herbert Gutman, "The Negro and the United Mine Workers of America: The Career and Letters of Richard L. Davis and Something of Their Meaning, 1890–1900," in *The Negro and the American Labor Movement*, ed. Julius Jacobson (Garden City, N.Y.: Anchor Books, 1968), 48–127; Ronald L. Lewis, *Black Coal Miners in America: Race, Class, and Community Conflict, 1780–1980* (Lexington: University Press of Kentucky, 1987), 39; Stephen Brier, "Interracial Organizing in the West Virginia Coal Industry: The Participation of Black Mine Workers in the Knights of Labor and the United Mine Workers, 1880–1894," in *Essays in Southern Labor History*, ed. Gary M. Fink and Merl E. Reed (Westport, Conn.: Greenwood Press, 1976); Herbert Hill, "Myth-Making as Labor History: Herbert Gutman and the United Mine Workers of America," *International Journal of Politics, Culture, and Society* 2 (1988): 132–200; Stephen Brier, "In Defense of Gutman: The Union's Case," *International Journal of Politics, Culture, and Society* 2 (1989): 382–95; Peter J. Rachleff, *Black Labor in the South: Richmond, Virginia, 1865–1890* (Philadelphia: Temple

University Press, 1984); Letwin, *Challenge of Interracial Unionism*; Joseph Gerteis, *Class and the Color Line: Interracial Class Coalition in the Knights of Labor and the Populist Movement* (Durham, N.C.: Duke University Press, 2007).

13. Ronald L. Lewis, *Black Coal Miners in America: Race, Class, and Community Conflict, 1780–1980* (Lexington: University Press of Kentucky, 1987), 39; Joe William Trotter Jr., *Coal, Class, and Color: Blacks in Southern West Virginia, 1915–32* (Urbana: University of Illinois Press, 1990), 117–18; Stephen Brier, "Interracial Organizing in the West Virginia Coal Industry: The Participation of Black Mine Workers in the Knights of Labor and the United Mine Workers, 1880–1894," in *Essays in Southern Labor History*, ed. Gary M. Fink and Merl E. Reed, 18–43; Booker T. Washington, *Up from Slavery: An Autobiography* (New York: Doubleday, Page, 1919), 38–39.

14. Douglas A. Blackmon, *Slavery by Another Name: The Re-enslavement of Black Americans from the Civil War to World War II* (New York: Random House, 2008), 54, 70–78, 94–99, 343; Edward L. Ayers, *Vengeance and Justice: Crime and Punishment in the 19th-Century American South* (New York: Oxford University Press, 1984), 185–222; Scott Reynolds Nelson, *Steel Drivin' Man: John Henry, the Untold Story of an American Legend* (New York: Oxford University Press, 2008); Letwin, *Challenge of Interracial Unionism*, 77.

15. Hild, *Greenbackers, Knights of Labor, and Populists*, 49–50; Trotter, *Coal, Class, and Color*, 53.

16. *Journal of United Labor*, Aug. 15, 1880; Powderly to Brother Wright, Sept. 19, 1880, reel 44, PP; Proceedings of District Assembly No. 5 of West Virginia, Oct. 7–10, 1880, reel 65, PP.

17. Powderly to M. W. Pattell of Chattanooga, Tenn., May 15, 1883, and Rockwood to Powderly, May 17, 1883, in Foner and Lewis, *Black Worker*, 245.

18. Powderly to Lynch, April 13, 1886, in Foner and Lewis, *Black Worker*, 253.

19. Phelan, *Grand Master Workman*, 94.

20. Proceedings of District Assembly No. 5 of West Virginia, Oct. 7–10, 1880, reel 65, PP; *Irish World and American Industrial Liberator*, July 12, 1884, in Foner and Lewis, *Black Worker*, 73.

21. *Harrisburg Telegraph*, Oct. 1, 1886; *Washington Bee*, July 2, 1887; Miner, "1886 Convention"; Fink, *Workingmen's Democracy*, 148–77; Rachleff, *Black Labor in the South*, 171–78.

22. *Baltimore Sun*, Oct. 5, 1886; Gerteis, *Class and the Color Line*, 96–97; Powderly, *Thirty Years of Labor*, 347–50.

23. Miner, "1886 Convention"; Fink, *Workingmen's Democracy*, 163; *Inter Ocean* (Chicago), Oct. 7, 1886; *Philadelphia Times*, Oct. 6, 1886; *Atlanta Constitution*, Oct. 6, 1886.

24. Fink, *Workingmen's Democracy*, 164; Winston, "Being Red and Black in Jim Crow America," 362; *New York Freeman*, Oct. 2, 1886; "Resolutions of the Equal Rights League, Columbus, Ohio," in Foner and Lewis, *Black Worker*, 125.

25. *New York Freeman*, Oct. 16, 1886; Hirst to Powderly, Oct. 13, 1886, in Foner and Lewis, *Black Worker*, 114; *Richmond Dispatch*, Oct. 9, 1886.

26. *Raleigh (N.C.) News and Observer*, Oct. 12, 1886.

27. *Raleigh (N.C.) News and Observer*, Oct. 17, 1886.

28. *New York Freeman*, Oct. 30, 1886; *South Alabamian* (Geneva, Ala.), Nov. 3, 1886; *Montgomery Advertiser*, Oct. 14, 1886; *Norfolk Virginian*, Oct. 30, 1886, in Foner and Lewis, *Black Worker*, 133.

29. *Richmond Dispatch*, Oct. 14, 1886; McLaurin, *Knights of Labor in the South*, 143–44.

30. *Pittsburgh Dispatch*, Oct. 15, 1886; Powderly, *Thirty Years of Labor*, 352.

31. Leon F. Litwack, *Trouble in Mind: Black Southerners in the Age of Jim Crow* (New York: Knopf, 1998); Ayers, *Vengeance and Justice*, 223–55; Feimster, *Southern Horrors*, 37–86.

32. McLaurin, *Knights of Labor in the South*, 12–21; Negro Press Committee to Powderly, Little Rock, Ark., Oct. 19, 1886, in Foner and Lewis, *Black Worker*, 115; *Indianapolis News*, Oct. 21, 1886.

33. *New York Times*, Oct. 15, 1886; Miner, "1886 Convention."

34. *Pittsburgh Dispatch*, Oct. 15, 1886.

35. Powderly to Brother Wright, Sept. 19, 1880, and Powderly to M. W. Pattell of Chattanooga, Tenn., May 15, 1883, in Foner and Lewis, *Black Worker*, 243, 245.

36. Kewley to Powderly, Richmond, Ind., May 14, 1883, in Foner and Lewis, *Black Worker*, 244–45.

37. *New York Freeman*, Oct. 2, 1886; Case, *Great Southwestern Railroad Strike and Free Labor*, 83, 139.

38. *New York Freeman*, Jan. 15, 1887.

39. *New York Freeman*, Sept. 11, 1886.

40. McLaurin, *Knights of Labor in the South*, 60–61, 145; *New York Freeman*, July 9, 1887.

41. Hild, *Greenbackers, Knights of Labor, and Populists*, 79–121; Fink, *Workingmen's Democracy*, 26–27; Postel, *Populist Vision*, 218; Laura F. Edwards, *Gendered Strife and Confusion: The Political Culture of Reconstruction* (Urbana: University of Illinois Press, 1997), 218–54.

42. Hild, *Greenbackers, Knights of Labor, and Populists*, 96–97; *Durham Tobacco Plant*, Oct. 20, 1886; "John Nichols," *Dictionary of North Carolina Biography*, www.ncpedia.org/biography/nichols-john; Edwards, *Gendered Strife and Confusion*, 242; *Journal of United Labor*, June 11, 1887.

43. *Richmond Dispatch*, Sept. 11, 25, and Oct. 9, 1886; *Staunton (Va.) Spectator*, Oct. 6, 1886; Fink, *Workingmen's Democracy*, 159–62; Gerteis, *Class and the Color Line*, 73, 78, 85.

44. *Richmond Dispatch*, Oct. 31, 1886; Rachleff, *Black Labor in the South*, 157–92.

45. McLaurin, *Knights of Labor in the South*, 138, 148; Rachleff, *Black Labor in the South*, 191.

46. *Journal of United Labor*, June 9, 1888.

47. *Journal of United Labor*, Sept. 25, 1886, and July 2, 1887.

48. *Texarkana Independent*, April 19 and 21, 1886, in Case, *Great Southwest Railroad Strike and Free Labor*, 214.

49. *Journal of United Labor*, Sept. 25, 1886; Hahn, *Nation Under Our Feet*, 418.

50. *Atlanta Constitution*, May 22, 1887; Bruce E. Baker, "The 'Hoover Scare' in

South Carolina, 1887: An Attempt to Organize Black Farm Labor," *Labor History* 40 (1999): 261–82; *New York Times*, June 19, 1887.

51. Hild, "Organizing Across the Color Line."

52. Baker, "'Hoover Scare' in South Carolina"; *St. Louis Globe-Democrat*, June 18, 1887; *New York Freeman*, July 9, 1887. The press often misspelled Hover's name as "Hoover."

53. *New Orleans Daily Picayune*, Oct. 27 and 30, 1887; *Journal of United Labor*, Nov. 26, 1887; John C. Rodrigue, *Reconstruction in the Cane Fields: From Slavery to Free Labor in Louisiana's Sugar Parishes, 1862–1880* (Baton Rouge: Louisiana State University Press, 2001), 183–92.

54. *New Orleans Daily Picayune*, Oct. 31, Nov. 1 and 2, 1887; *New Orleans Times-Democrat*, Nov. 3, 1877; Rebecca J. Scott, "'Stubborn and Disposed to Stand Their Ground': Black Militia, Sugar Workers, and the Dynamics of Collective Action in the Louisiana Sugar Bowl, 1863–87," *Slavery and Abolition* 20 (1999): 103–26.

55. *New Orleans Daily Picayune*, Nov. 6, 1887; *New Orleans Times-Democrat*, Nov. 24, 1887; Scott, "Stubborn and Disposed to Stand Their Ground"; Rodrigue, "Epilogue: The Sugar War of 1887," in *Reconstruction in the Cane Fields*.

56. *Journal of United Labor*, Dec. 3, 1887; W. R. Ramsay to Powderly, Dec. 11, 1887, in Foner and Lewis, *Black Workers*, 210–11.

57. *New Orleans Daily Picayune*, April 22, 1887; *New York Times*, April 22, 1887; Lamar W. Bridges, "Eliza Jane Nicholson and the *Daily Picayune*, 1876–1896," *Louisiana History: The Journal of the Louisiana Historical Association* 30 (1989): 263–78.

58. *New Orleans Daily Picayune*, April 22, 1887.

59. Moon-Ho Jung, *Coolies and Cane: Race, Labor, and Sugar in the Age of Emancipation* (Baltimore: Johns Hopkins University Press, 2006), 79, 186–87.

9. PROPERTY AND POVERTY

1. Paul Kens, *Justice Stephen Field: Shaping Liberty from the Gold Rush to the Gilded Age* (Lawrence: University Press of Kansas, 1997), 55, 88–89, 226.

2. Williamjames Hull Hoffer, *Plessy v. Ferguson: Race and Inequality in Jim Crow America* (Lawrence: University of Kansas, 2012), 110; Stephen J. Field, "Hostility to the Supreme Court After the Civil War," in *Personal Reminiscences of Early Days in California, with Other Sketches* (Stephen J. Field, 1893).

3. Kens, *Justice Stephen Field*, 148; Foner, *Reconstruction*, 529–31; Ronald M. Labbé and Jonathan Lurie, *The Slaughterhouse Cases: Regulation, Reconstruction, and the Fourteenth Amendment* (Lawrence: University Press of Kansas, 2003), 183–206; Melvin I. Urofsky, *Supreme Decisions: Great Constitutional Cases and Their Impact* (Boulder, Colo.: Westview Press, 2012), 107–126; Hoffer, *Plessy v. Ferguson*, 72; Martin J. Sklar, *The Corporate Reconstruction of American Capitalism, 1890–1916* (Cambridge, U.K.: Cambridge University Press, 1988), 49.

4. Adam Winkler, *We the Corporations: How American Businesses Won Their Civil Rights* (New York: Liveright Publishing, 2018), 113–160; Paul Kens, *The Supreme Court Under Morrison R. Waite, 1874–1888* (Columbia: University of

South Carolina Press, 2010), 120–25; David H. Gans and Douglas T. Kendall, "A Capitalist Joker: The Strange Origins, Disturbing Past, and Uncertain Future of Corporate Personhood in American Law," *John Marshall Law Review* 44 (2011): 643–99.

5. Jenny Bourne, *In Essentials Unity: An Economic History of the Grange Movement* (Athens: Ohio University Press, 2017), 43–44; Ridge, *Ignatius Donnelly*, 295–96; R. Jeffrey Lustig, *Corporate Liberalism: The Origins of Modern American Political Theory, 1890–1920* (Berkeley: University of California Press, 1982), 90–97.

6. Voss, *Making of American Exceptionalism*, 185–228; Fink, *Workingmen's Democracy*, 19, 26; Robert E. Weir, "A Fragile Alliance: Henry George and the Knights of Labor," *American Journal of Economics and Sociology* 56 (1997): 421–39.

7. Edward O'Donnell, *Henry George and the Crisis of Inequality: Progress and Poverty in the Gilded Age* (New York: Columbia University Press, 2015), 175–94.

8. Ibid., 183–86.

9. Ibid., 206.

10. Henry George Jr., *The Life of Henry George* (New York: Doubleday, 1900), 8, 18, 42, 93; Charles Albro Barker, *Henry George* (New York: Oxford University Press, 1955), 3–33.

11. George, *Life of Henry George*, 141, 176–79; Barker, *Henry George*, 34–71.

12. Henry George, "What the Railroad Will Bring Us," *Overland Monthly*, Oct. 1868, 297–306.

13. George, *Life of Henry George*, 210; Barker, *Henry George*, 135, 274.

14. George, *Life of Henry George*, 210; Mark A. Lause, "Progress Impoverished: Origin of Henry George's Single Tax," *Historian* 52 (1990): 394–410; Barker, *Henry George*, 61–62; Henry George, *Our Land and Land Policy, National and State* (San Francisco: White and Bauer, 1871); Carr, *Patrons of Husbandry on the Pacific Coast*, 6, 290–303.

15. Barker, *Henry George*, 255; Henry George, *Progress and Poverty: An Inquiry into the Cause of Industrial Depressions, and the Increase of Want with Increase of Wealth* (New York: D. Appleton, 1881), ix–x, 9, 295–96, 346–52.

16. George, *Progress and Poverty*, 364, 377.

17. Ibid., 410.

18. Ibid., xi; Marx to Friedrich Adolph Sorge in Hoboken, June 20, 1881, in *Marx & Engels Collected Works, Volume 46, Letters, 1880–83* (London: Lawrence & Wishart Electric Book, 2010), 98–101.

19. Lustig, *Corporate Liberalism*, 72; George, *Progress and Poverty*, 457.

20. George, *Progress and Poverty*, 284–87; George, *Life of Henry George*, 206–62; Barker, *Henry George*, 50; O'Donnell, *Henry George and the Crisis of Inequality*, 28.

21. "The Chinese in California," *New-York Tribune*, May 1, 1869; George, *Life of Henry George*, 202; Barker, *Henry George*, 133–34.

22. Kenneth C. Wenzer, ed., *Henry George, the Transatlantic Irish, and Their Times* (Bingley, U.K.: Emerald Group, 2009), xxx; David Brundage, *Irish National-*

ists in America: The Politics of Exile, 1798–1998 (New York: Oxford University Press, 2016), 116.

23. Barker, Henry George, 319–20, 335–39.

24. George, Life of Henry George, 335; Weir, "Fragile Alliance."

25. Powderly, Path I Trod, 179; Eric Foner, "Class, Ethnicity, and Radicalism in the Gilded Age: The Land League and Irish America," Marxist Perspectives 1 (1978): 6–55.

26. Powderly, Thirty Years of Labor, 173, 180, 191, 193; Ware, Labor Movement in the United States, 101.

27. Barker, Henry George, 435, 462; Weir, "Fragile Alliance," 423; Ware, Labor Movement in the United States, 101.

28. George, Life of Henry George, 475, 481; Weir, "Fragile Alliance"; Baker, Henry George, 478.

29. Clarence Darrow, The Story of My Life (New York: Scribner's Sons: 1932; reprint 1966), 41–43; Mary Fels, Joseph Fels: His Life-Work (London: George Allen & Unwin, Ltd.: 1920), 128–48.

30. Destler, American Radicalism, 168–70; Chicago Searchlight, July 19, Aug. 2 and 9, 1894; Southern Mercury (Dallas), Dec. 6, 1888; Rogers, One Gallused Rebellion, 125; Marx and Aveling, Working Class Movement in America, 156.

31. John D. Hicks, The Populist Revolt: A History of the Farmers' Alliance and the People's Party (Minneapolis: University of Minnesota, 1931), 161.

32. T. Thomas Fortune, Black and White: Land, Labor, and Politics in the South (New York: Fords, Howard, & Hulbert, 1884).

33. Emma Lou Thornbrough, T. Thomas Fortune: Militant Journalist (Chicago: University of Chicago Press, 1972), 3–34; Foner, Reconstruction, 426, 431; Kidada E. Williams, They Left Great Marks on Me: African American Testimonies of Racial Violence from Emancipation to World War I (New York: New York University Press, 2012), 17–22.

34. Thornbrough, T. Thomas Fortune, 19–33; Fortune, Black and White, 99.

35. Thornbrough, T. Thomas Fortune, 35–43; New York Globe, Feb. 24, Sept. 22 and 29, 1883, Sept. 13, 1884; Fortune, Black and White, iv, 155.

36. New York Freeman, Dec. 11 and 18, 1886.

37. New York Freeman, Dec. 11, 1886, July 9, 1887.

38. Postel, Populist Vision, 41–42; Woodward, Origins of the New South, 220; Southern Mercury (Dallas), Dec. 6, 1888; National Economist (Washington, D.C.), Dec. 14, 1889, and Dec. 20, 1890; Lawrence D. Rice, The Negro in Texas, 1874–1900 (Baton Rouge: Louisiana State University Press, 1971), 178.

39. Omar H. Ali, In the Lion's Mouth: Black Populism in the New South, 1886–1900 (Jackson: University Press of Mississippi, 2010), 76; Henry George, "The Land Question," in McNeill, Labor Movement, 565.

40. Henry George, Social Problems (Chicago: Belford, Clark & Co., 1883), 53, 59; Kenneth C. Wenzer, "The Influence of Henry George's Philosophy on Lev Nikolaevich Tolstoy: The Period of Developing Economic Thought (1881–1897)," Pennsylvania History: A Journal of Mid-Atlantic Studies 62 (1996): 232–52.

41. Lorien Foote, Seeking the One Great Remedy: Francis George Shaw and

Nineteenth-Century Reform (Athens: Ohio University Press, 2003), 5–6, 177; Fels, *Joseph Fels*, 16.

42. George, *Social Problems*, 102, 121; George, *Life of Henry George*, 487; Laurence Gronlund, *Cooperative Commonwealth in Its Outlines: An Exposition of Collectivism* (New York: John W. Lovell Co., 1887), 94, 205, 210, 250.

43. Edward Bellamy, *Looking Backward: 2000–1887* (Boston: Ticknor and Co., 1888); Gillis Harp, *Positivist Republic: Auguste Comte and the Reconstruction of American Liberalism, 1865–1920* (University Park: Pennsylvania State University Press, 1995), 96–106; Postel, *Populist Vision*, 233–36.

44. Sylvia E. Bowman, *The Year 2000: A Critical Biography of Edward Bellamy* (New York: Bookman, 1958), 112–52; Edward Bellamy, *Equality* (New York: D. Appleton, 1897); Edward K. Spann, *Brotherly Tomorrows: Movements for a Cooperative Society in America, 1820–1920* (New York: Columbia University Press, 1989), 188–90; Mary A. Hill, *Charlotte Perkins Gilman: The Making of a Radical Feminist, 1860–1896* (Philadelphia: Temple University Press, 1980), 171.

45. Bordin, *Woman and Temperance*, 92, 108, 138–39; Mari Jo Buhle, *Women and American Socialism, 1870–1920* (Urbana: University of Illinois Press, 1983), 75, 80; Willard to Lillian Wald, May 15 and June 4, 1888, in Bellamy Papers, Houghton Library, Harvard.

46. George, *Life of Henry George*, 497; Paul E. Alyea and Blanch R. Alyea, *Fairhope, 1894–1954* (Birmingham: University of Alabama Press, 1956), 1–38; Paul Gaston, *Women of Fair Hope* (Athens: University of Georgia Press, 1984), 48–61.

47. Destler, *American Radicalism*, 162–211; John T. McGreevy, "Farmers, Nationalists, and the Origins of California Populism," *Pacific Historical Review* 58 (1989): 417–95; Postel, *Populist Vision*, 205–42; *Nonconformist* (Winfield, Kans.), starting June 6, 1888; Brooke Speer Orr, *The "People's Joan of Arc": Mary Elizabeth Lease, Gendered Politics, and Populist Party Politics in Gilded-Age America* (New York: Peter Lang, 2014), 178–81.

10. SEPARATE AND UNEQUAL

1. Julie Lavonne Novkov, *Racial Union: Law, Intimacy, and the White State in Alabama, 1865–1954* (Ann Arbor: University of Michigan Press, 2008), 58–65.

2. *Interracialism: Black-White Intermarriage in American History, Literature, and Law*, ed. Werner Sollors (New York: Oxford University Press, 2000), 26.

3. Hoffer, *Plessy v. Ferguson*.

4. Litwack, *Trouble in Mind*, 280–325; Williams, *They Left Great Marks on Me*, 101–44; W.E.B. Du Bois, *Darkwater: Voices from Within the Veil* (New York: Harcourt Brace, 1920; reprint 2007), 16.

5. Ida B. Wells, *Southern Horrors: Lynch Law in All Its Phases* (New York: New York Age Print, 1892); Gail Bederman, *Manliness and Civilization: A Cultural History of Gender and Race in the United States, 1880–1917* (Chicago: University of Chicago Press, 1995), 45–76; Mia Bay, *To Tell the Truth Freely: The Life of Ida B. Wells* (New York: Hill and Wang, 2009), 185–90, 206–11.

6. Frances Willard, "Fifteenth Presidential Address, November 16, 1894," in Gifford and Slagell, *Let Something Good Be Said*, 203–5.

7. Litwack, *Trouble in Mind*, 213.

8. Frederick Douglass et al., "The Position of the National Woman's Christian Temperance Union of the United States in Relation to the Colored People, Boston, Mass., February 6th, 1895," AAW; Patricia Schechter, *Ida B. Wells-Barnett and American Reform, 1880–1930* (Chapel Hill: University of North Carolina Press, 2001), 110–12, 282n200; Vron Ware, *Beyond the Pale: White Women, Racism, and History* (London: Verso Press, 1992), 198–224.

9. *World's Congress of Representative Women* (Chicago: Rand, McNally, 1894), 433–37; Avery, *Transactions of the National Council of Women*, 86–91.

10. Collier-Thomas, "Frances Ellen Watkins Harper," 58; *Sunday Tribune*, Oct. 22, 1893, in Scrapbook no. 66, FWMLA; Gilmore, *Gender and Jim Crow*, 59.

11. Robert C. McMath Jr., *Populist Vanguard: A History of the Southern Farmers' Alliance* (Chapel Hill: University of North Carolina Press, 1975), 106.

12. Ibid., 90–91.

13. Robert C. McMath Jr., "Southern White Farmers and the Organization of Black Farm Workers: A North Carolina Document," *Labor History* 18 (1977): 115–19; Postel, *Populist Vision*, 3–103, 173–84, 205–20.

14. *Caucasian* (Clinton, N.C.), Feb. 20, 1890; *Southern Mercury* (Dallas), July 5, 1888, in *Women in the Texas Populist Movement: Letters to the* "Southern Mercury," ed. Marion K. Barthelme (College Station: Texas A&M University Press, 1997), 46–47; McMath, *Populist Vanguard*, 126; Woodward, *Origins of the New South*, 211–12; Bruce Palmer, *"Man over Money": The Southern Populist Critique of American Capitalism* (Chapel Hill: University of North Carolina Press, 1980), 56; Charles Crowe, "'Tom Watson, Blacks, and Populists Reconsidered," *Journal of Negro History* 55 (1970): 99–119; Robert Saunders, "Southern Populists and the Negro," *Journal of Negro History* 54 (1969): 240–61; Robert Allen, *Reluctant Reformers: Racism and Social Reform Movements in the United States* (Washington, D.C.: Howard University Press, 1974), 62; Gaither, *Blacks and the Populist Revolt*, 70–72; Sheldon Hackney, *Populism to Progressivism in Alabama* (Princeton, N.J.: Princeton University Press, 1969), 45–46.

15. Hild, *Greenbackers, Knights of Labor, and Populists*, 130–31; *Journal of the Knights of Labor*, Jan. 16, 1890.

16. *Caucasian* (Clinton, N.C.), Sept. 17, 1891; William F. Holmes, "The Arkansas Cotton Pickers' Strike and the Demise of the Colored Farmers' Alliance," *Arkansas Quarterly* 32 (1973): 107–19.

17. Hild, *Greenbackers, Knights of Labor, and Populists*, 122–33; Robert C. McMath Jr., *American Populism: A Social History, 1877–1898* (New York: Hill and Wang, 1993), 160; "St. Louis Platform, February, 1892," in Hicks, *Populist Revolt*, 435–39.

18. "Omaha Platform, July, 1892," in Hicks, *Populist Revolt*, 439–44.

19. McMath, *American Populism*, 143–79; Hicks, *Populist Revolt*, 238–73, 321–39.

20. Edwards, *Angels in the Machinery*, 91–110; Michael Lewis Goldberg, *An Army*

of Women: Gender and Politics in Gilded Age Kansas (Baltimore: Johns Hopkins University Press, 1997), 127–83; Postel, *Populist Vision*, 69–102; McMath, *American Populism*, 160; Bordin, *Woman and Temperance*, 132–33.

21. "St. Louis Platform, February, 1892," and "Omaha Platform, July, 1892," in Hicks, *Populist Revolt*, 435–44.

22. Ali, *In the Lion's Mouth*, 78–112; Hild, *Greenbacks, Knights of Labor, and Populists*, 147; Gaither, *Blacks and the Populist Revolt*.

23. "Omaha Platform, July, 1892"; Donald L. McMurry, *Coxey's Army: A Study of the Industrial Army Movement of 1894* (Boston: Little, Brown, 1929); Postel, *Populist Vision*, 257–58, 264.

24. Postel, *Populist Vision*, 173–203.

25. Deborah Beckel, "Southern Labor and the Lure of Populism: Workers and Power in North Carolina," in *Reconsidering Southern Labor History: Race, Class, and Power*, ed. Matthew Hild and Keri Leigh Merritt (Gainesville: University Press of Florida, 2018), 126–41.

26. *Journal of the Knights of Labor*, March 8 and 22, 1894; *St. Louis Post-Dispatch*, March 3, 1894; *Fisherman and Farmer* (Edenton, N.C.), March 2, 1894; *Cincinnati Inquirer*, March 5, 1894; *Inter Ocean* (Chicago), March 6 and 10, 1894; Philip S. Foner, *Organized Labor and the Black Worker, 1619–1973* (New York: Praeger, 1974), 62–63.

27. Deborah Beckel, *Radical Reform: Interracial Politics in Post-Emancipation North Carolina* (Charlottesville: University of Virginia Press, 2011), 155–77; James M. Beeby, *Revolt of the Tar Heels: The North Carolina Populist Movement, 1890–1901* (Jackson: University Press of Mississippi, 2008).

28. Feimster, *Southern Horrors*, 126–35.

29. Gilmore, *Gender and Jim Crow*, 105–13; *Democracy Betrayed: The Wilmington Race Riot of 1898 and Its Legacy*, ed. David S. Cecelski and Timothy B. Tyson (Chapel Hill: University of North Carolina Press, 1998).

EPILOGUE

1. *Cincinnati Enquirer*, Oct. 15, 1874; "Address of Aaron Jones, Master, National Grange, P. of H., Thirty-Seventh Annual Session, Rochester, N.Y.," 1903, National Grange, MNHS.

2. Tontz, "Memberships of General Farmers' Organizations," 143–56; Marylyn Watkins, *Rural Democracy: Family Farmers and Politics in Western Washington, 1890–1925* (Ithaca, N.Y.: Cornell University Press, 1995).

3. Nick Gillespie, "Krist Novoselic's Alternative Politics," *Reason*, Aug.–Sept. 2014.

4. McGirr, *War on Alcohol*, 121–56.

5. Phelan, *Grand Master Workman*, 255–61; Delber L. McKee, "'The Chinese Must Go!': Commissioner General Powderly and Chinese Immigration, 1897–1902," *Pennsylvania History: A Journal of Mid-Atlantic Studies* 44 (1977): 37–51; Elliot J. Gorn, *Mother Jones: The Most Dangerous Woman in America* (New York: Hill and Wang, 2001).

6. Thomas Piketty, *Capital in the Twenty-First Century* (Cambridge, Mass.: Harvard University Press, 2014).

7. Alice Kessler-Harris, *In Pursuit of Equity: Women, Men, and the Quest for Economic Citizenship in 20th-Century America* (New York: Oxford University Press, 2001), 203–38.

8. Gunnar Myrdal, *An American Dilemma: The Negro Problem and Modern Democracy* (New York: Harper & Row, 1944), 1020; Ira Katznelson, *When Affirmative Action Was White: An Untold History of Racial Inequality in Twentieth-Century America* (New York: W. W. Norton, 2005).

SELECTED BIBLIOGRAPHY

Ali, Omar H. *In the Lion's Mouth: Black Populism in the New South, 1886–1900*. Jackson: University Press of Mississippi, 2010.

Allen, Ruth A. *The Great Southwest Strike*. Austin: University of Texas Press, 1941.

Aurand, Harold W. *From the Molly Maguires to the United Mine Workers: The Social Ecology of an Industrial Union, 1869–1897*. Philadelphia: Temple University Press, 1971.

Avery, Rachel Foster. *Transactions of the National Council of Women of the United States, Assembled in Washington, D.C., February 22 to 24, 1891*. Philadelphia: J. B. Lippincott, 1891.

Barker, Charles Albro. *Henry George*. New York: Oxford University Press, 1955.

Barreyre, Nicolas. *Gold and Freedom: The Political Economy of Reconstruction*. Charlottesville: University of Virginia Press, 2015.

Beckel, Deborah. *Radical Reform: Interracial Politics in Post-Emancipation North Carolina*. Charlottesville: University of Virginia Press, 2011.

Bellamy, Edward. *Looking Backward: 2000–1887*. Boston: Ticknor, 1888.

Bensel, Robert Franklin. *The Political Economy of American Industrialization, 1877–1900*. Cambridge, U.K.: Cambridge University Press, 2000.

Berg, Scott W. *38 Nooses: Lincoln, Little Crow, and the Beginning of the Frontier's End*. New York: Pantheon Books, 2012.

Blight, David W. *Frederick Douglass: Prophet of Freedom*. New York: Simon & Schuster, 2018.

———. *Race and Reunion: The Civil War in American Memory*. Cambridge, Mass.: Harvard University Press, 2001.

Blum, Edward J. *Reforging the White Republic: Race, Religion, and American Nationalism, 1865–1898*. Baton Rouge: Louisiana State University Press, 2005.

Bordin, Ruth. *Woman and Temperance: The Quest for Power and Liberty, 1873–1900*. Philadelphia: Temple University Press, 1981.

Bourne, Jenny. *In Essentials Unity: An Economic History of the Grange Movement*. Athens: Ohio University Press, 2017.

Bowen, David Warren. *Andrew Johnson and the Negro*. Knoxville: University of Tennessee Press, 1989.

Brundage, David. *The Making of Western Labor Radicalism: Denver's Organized Workers, 1878–1905*. Urbana: University of Illinois Press, 1994.

Buck, Solon Justus. *The Granger Movement: A Study of Agricultural Organization and Its Political, Economic, and Social Manifestations, 1870–1880*. Cambridge, Mass.: Harvard University Press, 1913.

Calhoun, Charles W. *Conceiving a New Republic: The Republican Party and the Southern Question, 1869–1900*. Lawrence: University Press of Kansas, 2006.

Carr, Ezra S. *The Patrons of Husbandry on the Pacific Coast*. San Francisco: Bancroft, 1875.

Case, Theresa A. *The Great Southwest Railroad Strike and Free Labor*. College Station: Texas A&M University Press, 2010.

Chandler, Alfred D. *The Visible Hand: The Managerial Revolution in American Business*. Cambridge, Mass.: Belknap Press, 1977.

Chapin, Sallie F. *Fitz-Hugh St. Clair, the South Carolina Rebel Boy; or, It Is No Crime to Be Born a Gentleman*. Philadelphia: Claxton, Remsen & Haffelfinger, 1873.

Clemens, Elisabeth S. *The People's Lobby: Organizational Innovation and the Rise of Interest Group Politics in the United States, 1890–1925*. Chicago: University of Chicago Press, 1997.

Cohen, Nancy. *The Reconstruction of American Liberalism, 1865–1914*. Chapel Hill: University of North Carolina Press, 2002.

Collier-Thomas, Bettye. "Frances Ellen Watkins Harper: Abolitionist and Feminist." In *African American Women and the Vote, 1837–1965*, edited by Ann D. Gordon. Amherst: University of Massachusetts Press, 1997.

Commons, John R. *History of Labor in the United States*. Vol. 2. New York: Macmillan, 1918.

Commons, John R., et al., eds. *A Documentary History of Industrial Society, IX*. Cleveland: Arthur H. Clark, 1910.

Cresswell, Stephen. *Multiparty Politics in Mississippi, 1877–1902*. Jackson: University Press of Mississippi, 1995.

Davis, Hugh. *"We Will Be Satisfied with Nothing Less": The African American Struggle for Equal Rights in the North During Reconstruction*. Ithaca, N.Y.: Cornell University Press, 2011.

Davis, Sue. *The Political Thought of Elizabeth Cady Stanton*. New York: New York University Press, 2008.

Destler, Chester McArthur. *American Radicalism, 1865–1901*. New London: Connecticut College, 1946. Reprint, Chicago: Quadrangle Books, 1966.

Dohoney, Ebenezer Lafayette. *Man: His Origin, Nature and Destiny*. St. Louis: J. Burns, 1885.

Downs, Gregory P. *After Appomattox: Military Occupation and the Ends of War*. Cambridge, Mass.: Harvard University Press, 2015.

Du Bois, W.E.B. *Black Reconstruction in America, 1860–1880*. New York: Harcourt Brace, 1935. Reprint, New York: Simon & Schuster, 1995.

Dudden, Faye E. *Fighting Chance: The Struggle over Woman Suffrage and Black Suffrage in Reconstruction America*. New York: Oxford University Press, 2011.

Dunlap, Leslie Kathrin. "In the Name of the Home: Temperance Women and Southern Grass-Roots Politics, 1873–1933." PhD diss., Northwestern University, 2001.

Earhart, Mary. *Frances Willard: From Prayer to Politics*. Chicago: University of Chicago Press, 1944.

Edwards, Laura F. *Gendered Strife and Confusion: The Political Culture of Reconstruction*. Urbana: University of Illinois Press, 1997.

Edwards, Rebecca. *Angels in the Machinery: Gender in American Party Politics from the Civil War to the Progressive Era*. New York: Oxford University Press, 1997.

Egerton, Douglas R. *Wars of Reconstruction: The Brief, Violent History of America's Most Progressive Era*. New York: Bloomsbury Press, 2014.

Ely, Richard T. *The Labor Movement in America*. New York: Thomas Y. Crowell, 1886.

Feimster, Crystal N. *Southern Horrors: Women and the Politics of Rape and Lynching*. Cambridge, Mass.: Harvard University Press, 2009.

Fink, Leon. *Workingmen's Democracy: The Knights of Labor and American Politics*. Urbana: University of Illinois Press, 1983.

Foner, Eric. *Reconstruction: America's Unfinished Revolution, 1863–1877*. New York: Harper & Row, 1988.

Foner, Philip S., and Ronald L. Lewis. *The Black Worker: A Documentary History from Colonial Times to the Present*. Vol. 3. Philadelphia: Temple University Press, 1978.

Fortune, T. Thomas. *Black and White: Land, Labor, and Politics in the South*. New York: Fords, Howard & Hulbert, 1884.

Foster, Frances Smith. *A Brighter Coming Day: A Frances Ellen Watkins Harper Reader*. New York: Feminist Press at the City University of New York, 1990.

Free, Laura E. *Suffrage Reconstructed: Gender, Race, and Voting Rights in the Civil War Era*. Ithaca, N.Y.: Cornell University Press, 2015.

Gaither, Gerald H. *Blacks and the Populist Revolt: Ballots and Bigotry in the "New South."* Tuscaloosa: University of Alabama Press, 1977.

Garlock, Jonathan. *Guide to the Local Assemblies of the Knights of Labor*. Westport, Conn.: Greenwood Press, 1982.

Gaston, Paul M. *Women of Fair Hope*. Athens: University of Georgia Press, 1984.

George, Henry. *Our Land and Land Policy, National and State*. San Francisco: White and Bauer, 1871.

———. *Progress and Poverty: An Inquiry into the Cause of Industrial Depressions, and the Increase of Want with Increase of Wealth*. New York: D. Appleton, 1881.

———. *Social Problems*. Chicago: Belford, Clark, 1883.

George, Henry, Jr. *The Life of Henry George*. New York: Doubleday, 1900.

Gerteis, Joseph. *Class and the Color Line: Interracial Class Coalition in the Knights of Labor and the Populist Movement*. Durham, N.C.: Duke University Press, 2007.

Gifford, Carolyn De Swarte, and Amy R. Slagell, eds. *Let Something Good Be Said: Speeches and Writings of Frances E. Willard*. Urbana: University of Illinois Press, 2007.

Gilmore, Glenda Elizabeth. *Gender and Jim Crow: Women and the Politics of White Supremacy in North Carolina, 1896–1920*. Chapel Hill: University of North Carolina Press, 1996.

Green, James. *Death in the Haymarket: A History of Chicago, the First Labor Movement, and the Bombing That Divided Gilded Age America*. New York: Pantheon Books, 2006.

Gronlund, Laurence. *The Cooperative Commonwealth in Its Outlines: An Exposition of Collectivism*. New York: John W. Lovell, 1887.

Grosh, Aaron B. *Mentor in the Granges and Homes of Patrons of Husbandry*. New York: Clark & Maynard, 1876.

Grossman, Jonathan. *William Sylvis: Pioneer of American Labor*. New York: Columbia University Press, 1945.

Hahn, Steven. *A Nation Under Our Feet: Black Political Struggles in the Rural South from Slavery to the Great Migration*. Cambridge, Mass.: Harvard University Press, 2003.

Haley, Sarah. *No Mercy Here: Gender, Punishment, and the Making of Jim Crow Modernity*. Chapel Hill: University of North Carolina Press, 2016.

Harper, Frances E. W. *Minnie's Sacrifice*. In *Minnie's Sacrifice; Sowing and Reaping; Trail and Triumph: Three Rediscovered Novels by Frances E. W. Harper*. Edited by Frances Smith Foster. Boston: Beacon Press, 1994.

Hicks, John D. *The Populist Revolt: A History of the Farmers' Alliance and the People's Party*. Minneapolis: University of Minnesota Press, 1931.

Hild, Matthew. *Greenbackers, Knights of Labor, and Populists: Farmer-Labor Insurgency in the Late-Nineteenth-Century South*. Athens: University of Georgia Press, 2007.

Hoffer, Williamjames Hull. *Plessy v. Ferguson: Race and Inequality in Jim Crow America*. Lawrence: University Press of Kansas, 2012.

Hunter, Tera W. *To 'Joy My Freedom: Southern Black Women's Lives and Labors After the Civil War*. Cambridge, Mass.: Harvard University Press, 1997.

Huston, James L. *The American and British Debate over Equality, 1776–1920*. Baton Rouge: Louisiana State University Press, 2017.

Jung, Moon-Ho. *Coolies and Cane: Race, Labor, and Sugar in the Age of Emancipation*. Baltimore: Johns Hopkins University Press, 2006.

Kearney, Belle. *A Slaveholder's Daughter*. St. Louis: St. Louis Christian Advocate, 1900.

Kelley, Oliver H. *Origin and Progress of the Patrons of Husbandry: A History from 1866 to 1873*. Philadelphia: J. A. Wagenseller, 1875.

Kenny, Kevin. *Making Sense of the Molly Maguires*. New York: Oxford University Press, 1998.

Kens, Paul. *Justice Stephen Field: Shaping Liberty from the Gold Rush to the Gilded Age*. Lawrence: University Press of Kansas, 1997.

Kloppenberg, James T. *Uncertain Victory: Social Democracy and Progressivism in European and American Thought, 1870–1920*. New York: Oxford University Press, 1986.

Labor: Its Rights and Wrongs, Statements and Comments by the Leading Men of Our Nation on the Labor Question of To-Day. Washington, D.C.: Labor Publishing Co., 1886.

Leikin, Steven B. *The Practical Utopians: American Workers and the Cooperative Movement in the Gilded Age*. Detroit: Wayne State University Press, 2005.

Letwin, Daniel. *The Challenge of Interracial Unionism: Alabama Coal Miners, 1878–1921*. Chapel Hill: University of North Carolina Press, 1998.

Levine, Susan. *Labor's True Woman: Carpet Weavers, Industrialization, and Labor Reform in the Gilded Age*. Philadelphia: Temple University Press, 1984.

———. "Labor's True Woman: Domesticity and Equal Rights in the Knights of Labor." *Journal of American History* 70 (1983): 323–39.

Litwack, Leon F. *Trouble in Mind: Black Southerners in the Age of Jim Crow*. New York: Knopf, 1998.

Lustig, Jeffrey. *Corporate Liberalism: The Origins of Modern American Political Theory, 1890–1920*. Berkeley: University of California Press, 1982.

Marti, Donald B. *Women of the Grange: Mutuality and Sisterhood in Rural America, 1866–1920*. New York: Greenwood Press, 1991.

Marx, Eleanor, and Edward Aveling. *The Working Class Movement in America*. London: Swan Sonnenschein, 1891. Reprint, Amherst, N.Y.: Humanity Books, 2000.

Masur, Kate. *An Example for All the Land: Emancipation and the Struggle for Equality in Washington, D.C.* Chapel Hill: University of North Carolina Press, 2010.

McCabe, James D. [Edward Winslow Martin]. *History of the Grange Movement; or, The Farmer's War Against Monopolies*. Philadelphia: National, 1873. Reprint, New York: B. Franklin, 1967.

McClain, Charles J. *In Search of Equality: The Chinese Struggle Against Discrimination in Nineteenth-Century America*. Berkeley: University of California Press, 1994.

McGirr, Lisa. *The War on Alcohol: Prohibition and the Rise of the American State*. New York: W. W. Norton, 2016.

McLaurin, Melton Alonza. *The Knights of Labor in the South*. Westport, Conn.: Greenwood Press, 1978.

McMath, Robert C., Jr. *Populist Vanguard: A History of the Southern Farmers' Alliance*. Chapel Hill: University of North Carolina Press, 1975.

McNeill, George, ed. *The Labor Movement: The Problem of To-Day*. New York: M. W. Hazen, 1887.

McPherson, Edward. *The Political History of the United States: From April 15, 1865, to July 15, 1870*. Washington, D.C.: Philip & Solomons, 1871.

Montgomery, David. *Beyond Equality: Labor and the Radical Republicans, 1862–1872*. Urbana: University of Illinois Press.

Myrdal, Gunnar. *An American Dilemma: The Negro Problem and Modern Democracy.* New York: Harper & Row, 1944.

Newman, Louise Michele. *White Women's Rights: The Racial Origins of Feminism in the United States.* New York: Oxford University Press, 1999.

Nordin, D. Sven. *Rich Harvest: A History of the Grange, 1867–1900.* Jackson: University Press of Mississippi, 1974.

Nugent, Walter T. K. *The Money Question During Reconstruction.* New York: W. W. Norton, 1967.

O'Donnell, Edward T. *Henry George and the Crisis of Inequality: Progress and Poverty in the Gilded Age.* New York: Columbia University Press, 2015.

Paddison, Joshua. "Woman Is Everywhere the Purifier." In *California Women and Politics: From the Gold Rush to the Great Depression,* edited by Robert W. Cherny, Mary Ann Irwin, and Ann Marie Wilson. Lincoln: University of Nebraska Press, 2011.

Periam, Jonathan. *The Groundswell: A History of the Origin, Aims, and Progress of the Farmers' Movement.* Cincinnati: E. Hannaford, 1874.

Phelan, Craig. *Grand Master Workman: Terence Powderly and the Knights of Labor.* Westport, Conn.: Greenwood Press, 2000.

Powderly, Terence V. *The Path I Trod: The Autobiography of Terence Powderly.* Edited by Harry J. Carman, Henry David, and Paul N. Guthrie. New York: Columbia University Press, 1940.

———. *Thirty Years of Labor.* Columbus, Ohio: Excelsior, 1890.

Pritchard, Claudius Hornby, Jr. *Colonel D. Wyatt Aiken, 1828–1887: South Carolina's Militant Agrarian.* Hampden-Sidney, Va.: self-published, 1870.

Rachleff, Peter J. *Black Labor in the South: Richmond, Virginia, 1865–1890.* Philadelphia: Temple University Press, 1984.

Richardson, Heather Cox. *The Death of Reconstruction: Race, Labor, and Politics in the Post–Civil War North, 1865–1901.* Cambridge, Mass.: Harvard University Press, 2001.

Ridge, Martin. *Ignatius Donnelly: The Portrait of a Politician.* Chicago: University of Chicago Press, 1962. Reprint, St. Paul: Minnesota Historical Society Press, 1991.

Robbins, Louise Barnum, ed. *History and Minutes of the National Council of Women of the United States.* Boston: E. B. Stilling, 1898.

Rogers, William Warren. *The One-Gallused Rebellion: Agrarianism in Alabama, 1865–1896.* Baton Rouge: Louisiana State University Press, 1970.

Saunders, William. "The Journal of William Saunders, 1898–1899" (handwritten notes). William Saunders Papers, box 4, National Grange of Patrons of Husbandry, Kroch Library, Cornell University.

Scott, Anne Firor. *Natural Allies: Women's Associations in American History.* Urbana: University of Illinois Press, 1991.

Sklar, Kathryn Kish. *Florence Kelley and the Nation's Work: The Rise of Women's Political Culture, 1830–1900.* New Haven, Conn.: Yale University Press, 1995.

Spencer, Dorcas James. *A History of the Woman's Christian Temperance Union of Northern and Central California.* Oakland: West Coast Printing Co., 1911.

Stampp, Kenneth. *The Era of Reconstruction, 1865–1877.* New York: Knopf, 1966.

Still, William. *The Underground Railroad.* Chicago: Johnson, 1872.

Storti, Craig. *Incident at Bitter Creek: The Story of the Rock Springs Chinese Massacre*. Ames: Iowa State University Press, 1991.

Strachey, Ray. *Frances Willard: Her Life and Work*. London: T. Fisher Unwin, 1912.

Stromquist, Shelton. *A Generation of Boomers: The Pattern of Railroad Conflict in Nineteenth-Century America*. Urbana: University of Illinois Press, 1987.

Summers, Mark Wahlgren. *The Ordeal of the Reunion: A New History of Reconstruction*. Chapel Hill: University of North Carolina Press, 2014.

Sylvis, James C., ed. *The Life, Speeches, Labors, and Essays of William H. Sylvis*. Philadelphia: Claxton, Remsen & Haffelfinger, 1872.

Thornbrough, Emma Lou. *T. Thomas Fortune: Militant Journalist*. Chicago: University of Chicago Press, 1972.

Tontz, Robert L. "Memberships of General Farmers' Organizations, United States, 1874–1960." *Agricultural History* 38 (1964), 143–56.

Trotter, Joe William, Jr. *Coal, Class, and Color: Blacks in Southern West Virginia, 1915–32*. Urbana: University of Illinois Press, 1990.

Tyrrell, Ian R. *Sobering Up: From Temperance to Prohibition in Antebellum America, 1800–1860*. Westport, Conn.: Praeger, 1979.

———. *Woman's World/Woman's Empire: The Woman's Christian Temperance Union in International Perspective, 1880–1930*. Chapel Hill: University of North Carolina Press, 1991.

Voss, Kim. *The Making of American Exceptionalism: The Knights of Labor and Class Formation in the Nineteenth Century*. Ithaca, N.Y.: Cornell University Press, 1993.

Ware, Norman J. *The Labor Movement in the United States, 1860–1895*. New York: D. Appleton, 1929.

Warner, Charles Dudley. "Equality." *Atlantic Monthly*, Jan. 1880.

Weir, Robert E. *Beyond Labor's Veil: The Culture of the Knights of Labor*. University Park: Pennsylvania State University Press, 1996.

———. *Knights Unhorsed: Internal Conflict in a Gilded Age Social Movement*. Detroit: Wayne State University Press, 2000.

Wells, Ida B. *Southern Horrors: Lynch Law in All Its Phases*. New York: New York Age Print, 1892.

White, Richard. *Railroaded: The Transcontinentals and the Making of Modern America*. New York: W. W. Norton, 2011.

Willard, Frances E. *Glimpses of Fifty Years: The Autobiography of an American Woman*. Chicago: Woman's Temperance Publication Association, ca. 1889.

———. *A Wheel Within a Wheel: How I Learned to Ride the Bicycle*. Chicago: Fleming H. Revell, 1895.

———. *A White Life for Two*. Chicago: Woman's Temperance Publishing Association, 1890.

———. *Woman and Temperance; or, The Work and Workers of the Woman's Christian Temperance Union*. Hartford, Conn.: Park, 1883.

Williams, Kidada E. *They Left Great Marks on Me: African American Testimonies of Racial Violence from Emancipation to World War I*. New York: New York University Press, 2012.

Wills, Garry. *Lincoln at Gettysburg: The Words That Remade America*. New York: Simon & Schuster, 1992.

Winkler, Adam. *We the Corporations: How American Businesses Won Their Civil Rights*. New York: Liveright, 2018.

Winston, James. "Being Red and Black in Jim Crow America: On the Ideology and Travails of Afro-America's Socialist Pioneers." In *Time Longer than Rope: A Century of African American Activism, 1850–1950*, edited by Charles M. Payne and Adam Green. New York: New York University Press, 2003.

Wittenmyer, Annie. *Under the Guns: A Woman's Reminiscences of the Civil War*. Boston: E. B. Stillings, 1895.

Wong, Edlie L. *Racial Reconstruction: Black Inclusion, Chinese Exclusion, and the Fictions of Citizenship*. New York: New York University Press, 2015.

Woods, Thomas A. *Knights of the Plow: Oliver H. Kelley and the Origins of the Grange in Republican Ideology*. Ames: Iowa State University Press, 1991.

Woodward, C. Vann. *Origins of the New South, 1877–1913*. Baton Rouge: Louisiana State University Press, 1951.

ACKNOWLEDGMENTS

As Henry George put it, "Association in equality is the law of progress." I never would have made progress on this book without the help of generous and thoughtful people in a number of societies and institutions. In the first place, I am indebted to the archivists and librarians at the Iowa State Historical Society, the Minnesota Historical Society, and the Wisconsin State Historical Society, as well as at the Abraham Lincoln Presidential Library, the Bancroft and Doe Libraries at Berkeley, and the Green Library at Stanford. I am especially thankful for the assistance provided by Heather Furnas at the Cornell University Library and by the intrepid Janet Olson, archivist at the Frances E. Willard Memorial Library and Archives. I also had the valuable research help of excellent graduate and undergraduate assistants, including Sarah Gold-McBride, Brian Banker, and Molly Culhane. I owe a special debt to my students at San Francisco State, whose humanity makes my job meaningful and who inspired my work on this project.

Several institutions provided essential support to launch and then complete this book. The College of Liberal and Creative Arts at SF State generously made it possible to take time to research and write. The Heidelberg Center for American Studies hosted me as a Ghaemian scholar-in-residence, and a Fulbright fellowship allowed me to study at the Roosevelt Institute for American Studies in the Netherlands. I also had the good fortune of a fellowship at the Stanford Humanities Center. I am thankful to my wonderful colleagues in each of these places, as well as to the encouragement and advice provided by participants in seminars at SF State, Heidelberg, Stanford, the School for Advanced Studies in Social Research (Paris), and the University of Nottingham. The same goes for participants in conference panels at Agricultural History, Policy History, and the Organization of American Historians.

I am grateful to numerous colleagues and friends who encouraged me along the way, showed me possibilities, and saved me from missteps. This includes valuable exchanges with Boyd Cothran, Leslie Dunlap, Robin Einhorn, Estelle Friedman, Kirsten Fischer, Eric Foner, Robert Johnston, Detlef Junker, Louise Knight, Leon Litwack, Waldo Martin, Kate Masur, Elizabeth Sanders, Anja Schüler, Richard White, and Nicolas Barreyre. Fred Block, Carl Guarneri, Sherry Katz, and Caitlin Rosenthal read the manuscript and provided sage advice. Close readings of drafts by Thomas Dublin, Matthew Hild, and Kathryn Kish Sklar proved extraordinarily helpful and made this book better. My agent, Sandy Dijkstra, ushered this book along its way with grace and skill. And Ileene Smith, my editor at FSG, did a masterful job in helping turn a final draft into the book in your hands.

I owe special thanks to the fascinating and multitalented Michael Strange, who read drafts and lent aid, encouragement, and advice at every step. She provided the love and intellectual camaraderie that made it worthwhile. I am also grateful to our children and their partners, Sam

Postel, Julian Prentice, Rafael Postel, and Tony and Line Fader, who generously tolerated this project from the outset. But much more, their goodness made all the difference when the family faced the ordeal of the death of their sister, Sableu Cabildo. In her beloved Oakland, Sableu touched the lives of so many people from every corner of the city and in doing so taught us all something about the substance of human equality. This book is dedicated to her memory. Finally, I would be remiss to fail to mention Sa'Niyah Jones-Hampton and Shohei and Yuji Postel, who were too small to be helpful with this book but brought joy to the task.

CHARLES POSTEL
Oakland, California
2019

INDEX